THE DIALOGICAL SPIRIT

THE DIALOGICAL SPIRIT

*Christian Reason
and Theological Method
in the Third Millennium*

Amos Yong

CASCADE *Books* · Eugene, Oregon

THE DIALOGICAL SPIRIT
Christian Reason and Theological Method in the Third Millennium

Cascade Books
An Imprint of Wipf and Stock Publishers
199 W. 8th Ave., Suite 3
Eugene, OR 97401

www.wipfandstock.com

ISBN 13: 978-1-62564-564-7

Cataloging-in-Publication data:

Yong, Amos.

    The dialogical spirit : Christian reason and theological method in the third millennium / Amos Yong.

    xvi + 336 p.; 23 cm—Includes bibliographical references and index.

    ISBN 13: 978-1-62564-564-7

    1. Theology—Methodology. 2. Holy Spirit. 3. Religions. 4. Religion and science. I. Title.

BR 118 Y38 2014

Manufactured in the USA.

Dedicated to
F. LeRon Shults
&
Terry Muck,
exemplary dialogicians along the way

Table of Contents

Preface

Is THERE ANY NEED for another (long!) book on theological method, potential readers might query? Yet Christian theologians in our post-Enlightenment context realize we need more than ever to be self-reflective about how to think Christianly and to make our claims, especially to the non-Christian world. In conversation with more or less recent developments in Third Article theology—which begins consciously with the person and work of the Holy Spirit, the Third Article of the Nicene confession—the thesis of this volume is that such a pneumatological starting point provides the needed theological platform to enable both retrieval and renewal of historic Christian faith on the one hand and authentic engagement with the many voices across the contemporary global landscape on the other hand. While the four parts and twelve chapters to follow will elaborate variously on this claim, the book's introductory chapter will delineate more precisely the present ferment of Christian theology, even as the concluding chapter will carefully demonstrate how such a dialogical reappropriation allows for a more faithful expression of Christian commitment in the twenty-first-century context. The latter goal is also defended at substantial length in a companion to this book, *The Missiological Spirit: Christian Mission Theology for the Third Millennium Global Context* (Cascade, 2014), to which those interested are referred.

The chapters to come demonstrate the book's thesis through a series of theological conversations. These chapters have been written over the course of more than fifteen years (from about 1997 through 2012) and all except one have been previously published. Those previously published are being reproduced almost verbatim here, with minimal emendations that are signaled by brackets in the notes (used to indicate changes of mind, rarely, but more often to point to other developments). I have chosen to reprint without revision for three reasons. First, these articles and essays exemplify the dialogical nature of theological thinking needed for the present time, precisely the argument sustained herein. Second, their ordering, which is more or less chronological according to initial writing and publication, re-flects the dynamic nature of theological reflection; while I continue to stand by what I have written, the careful reader will note revisions in how some earlier themes are enunciated in later work, both to clear up misunderstand-ings and to reassert fundamental commitments. Thirdly, collecting these essays spanning one and a half decades gives me the opportunity to reflect methodologically on my own theological journey, an exercise unfolded in the introduction and conclusion, which have been written expressly for this book.

Each chapter includes acknowledgments (usually in the initial or fi-nal footnote) that document my gratitude at the time of writing. Thinking back over the last fifteen-plus years, however, I have to thank again my wife, Alma, for providing me with the space, encouragement, and love to work as a theologian. She has always been my faithful dialogue partner in the most important task of all: living faithfully in the Christian way.

Enoch Charles, my former graduate assistant at Regent University, helped immeasurably in formatting the text according to Cascade guide-lines and creating the bibliography, among so many other tasks. Ryan Seow, my current graduate assistant at Fuller Seminary, helped with the indexing. I eagerly anticipate the emergence of their dialogical voices in the theologi-cal academy.

Robin Parry and especially Rodney Clapp, my editors at Wipf and Stock and both significant theologians in their own right, saw the value of pulling together this collection of previously published essays and including the new material to indicate my thinking at the present time. I am grateful for their support of this project. The staff at Wipf and Stock has also been professional at every turn, and their contribution to turning these disparate pieces into a unified, perhaps even coherent, whole is to be acknowledged.

This book is dedicated to F. LeRon Shults and Terry Muck. I got to know LeRon back in the fall of 1999 when I ended up at Bethel University in St. Paul, Minnesota, fairly fresh out of graduate school. I was in the under-graduate theology department at the college and he was working graduate students at the seminary, and we hit it off right away. He had just published his book *The Postfoundationalist Task of Theology: Wolfhart Pannenberg and the New Theological Rationality* (Eerdmans, 1999), and I had just finished my dissertation and was already thinking about my second book, which turned out to be on theological method. We met regularly for lunch for the next six years, talked a lot of theology, and spurred each other on before we parted ways (me to Regent University in Virginia, and LeRon to University of Agder in Norway—literally an ocean apart).

Terry Muck has been a model evangelical scholar, missiologist, and theologian who I have worked with over the years, the last five of which have been primarily in the context of the Society for Buddhist-Christian Studies. Terry has expertly navigated the terrain where evangelicalism and Buddhist studies have converged, exemplifying on the one hand how an evangelical can be a respected Buddhologist and on the other hand how Buddhological expertise can deepen evangelical faith. His life and work reflect the kind of Christian commitment, intellectual humility, academic inquiry, and relational hospitality so needed in the twenty-first century. Surely neither scholar will agree with everything to come. But those who appreciate the *oeuvre* of LeRon and Terry will be in a better position to understand why *The Dialogical Spirit* is dedicated to them and perhaps also see a need for a book such as this, even if LeRon's and Terry's versions would still differ from mine.

Pasadena, California

Acknowledgments

ALMOST ALL OF THE chapters in this book have been previously published; I am grateful to the editors and publishers (listed first if not clearly identifiable in the citation) for permission to reuse the material within for this volume, and have in some specific cases appended their own requested acknowledgments:

1. "The Demise of Foundationalism and the Retention of Truth: What Evangelicals Can Learn from C. S. Peirce," *Christian Scholar's Review* 29, no. 3 (Spring 2000): 563–88.

2. "Pragmati(ci)sm and Evangelical Theology in a (Post)Modern World." Paper presented to Postmodernism and Evangelical Theology Study Group of the Evangelical Theological Society, Toronto, Canada, November 20–22, 2002 (previously unpublished).

3. Brill, "In Search of Foundations: The *Oeuvre* of Donald L. Gelpi, S.J., and Its Significance for Pentecostal Theology and Philosophy," *Journal of Pentecostal Theology* 11, no. 1 (2002): 3–26.

4. "The 'Baptist Vision' of James William McClendon, Jr.: A Wesleyan-Pentecostal Response," *Wesleyan Theological Journal* 37, no. 2 (Fall 2002): 32–57.

5. "Whither Evangelical Theology? The Work of Veli-Matti Kärkkäinen as a Case Study of Contemporary Trajectories," *Evangelical Review of Theology* 30, no. 1 (2006): 60–85.

6. Brill, "Radical, Reformed, and Pentecostal: Rethinking the Intersection of Post/Modernity and the Religions in Conversation with James K. A. Smith," *Journal of Pentecostal Theology* 15, no. 2 (2007): 233–50.

7. Metanexus. "From Quantum Mechanics to the Eucharistic Meal: John Polkinghorne's Vision of Science and Theology," *Metanexus.net*, originally published 2005, last modified September 1, 2011, http://www.

metanexus.net/book-review/quantum-mechanics-eucharistic-meal-john-polkinghornes-bottom-vision-science-and-theology.

8. University of Hawai'i Press, "Mind and Life, Religion and Science: The Dalai Lama and the Buddhist-Christian-Science Trilogue," *Buddhist-Christian Studies* 28 (2008): 43–63.

9. "Tibetan Buddhism Going Global? A Case Study of a Contemporary Buddhist Encounter with Science," *Journal of Global Buddhism* 9 (2008), http://www.globalbuddhism.org/9/yong08.htm.

10. "Francis X Clooney's 'Dual Religious Belonging' and the Comparative Theological Enterprise: Engaging Hindu Traditions," *Dharma Deepika: A South Asian Journal of Missiological Research* 16, no. 1 (2012): 6–26.

11. Equinox Publishing Ltd., "Observation-Participation-Subjunctivation: Methodological Play and Meaning-Making in the Study of Religion and Theological Studies," *Religious Studies and Theology* 31, no. 1 (2012): 17–40.

12. "Toward a Relational Apologetics in Global Context: A Review Essay on Benno Van Den Toren's *Christian Apologetics as Cross-Cultural Dialogue*," *Philosophia Christi* 14, no. 2 (2012): 437–45. Permission has been granted by the editor of *Philosophia Christi* to use this material; more information about the journal can be found at www.epsociety.org/philchristi.

Introduction

Soon after completing my PhD thesis I wrote a book on theological method, *Spirit-Word-Community: Theological Hermeneutics in Trinitarian Perspective.*[1] I was motivated in this direction in part because the theological academy was caught up, around the turn of the millennium, on questions related to method,[2] and in part because my own graduate training under a philosophical theologian alerted me to the importance of providing methodological argumentation in a time when theological claims were no longer being received merely because they were asserted. Both trends were reactions to the post-Enlightenment world that had been emerging with increasing clarity across the last century. Yet even in *Spirit-Word-Community*, I realized that questions regarding theological method were bound up with theological content, and vice versa. One could not write about the former apart from the latter. Hence this earlier book urged a pneumatological imagination driven by reflection on the person and work of the Holy Spirit, even as it presented itself as a pneumatological and therefore Trinitarian theology.

This volume does not depart from the major thrusts of *Spirit-Word-Community*. Rather, it provides exemplifications of the methodology proffered there in order to refine the pneumatological imagination and its Trinitarian and methodological payoff (the latter will be articulated most clearly in the conclusion of this book). Along the way, however, we shall see why starting with the Spirit theologically and methodologically opens up the kind of dialogical inquiry so important for theological thinking and formulation in the twenty-first-century context.

Put succinctly, our present information age reduces theology to being one voice among many others. The question is how to make universal claims

1. Yong, *Spirit-Word-Community*; my doctoral dissertation was published as Yong, *Discerning the Spirit(s)*.

2. E.g., Kinast, *Theological Reflection*.

1

when very few are paying attention. There are 1) methodological challenges related to our postfoundationalist context, 2) intra-Christian disagreements related to the accelerating fragmentation of the Christian world, 3) an increasingly diversified public square related to our postsecular situation, and 4) a cacophony of many religious voices trumpeted in our postmodern environment. The four parts of this volume address, respectively, each of these challenges, and suggest, in conversation with our twelve interlocutors, that a pneumatological and dialogical approach can turn these obstacles into opportunities for contextual reflection and global Christian witness.

The dialogical approach manifest in the pages to come signal a fundamental Christian virtue—that of respecting the voices of others—while attempting to model how theological inquiry might proceed in this way.[3] It also presumes that there is a biographical and narrative dimension to the theological task, and therefore seeks to not only depict but also to conduct theological inquiry in such a performative mode.[4] Herein, dialogue is not only said to be integral to theological method, but shown to be so as well. This introduction identifies the animating (autobiographical) concerns behind each of the chapters while situating them vis-à-vis these overarching issues.

THE POSTFOUNDATIONALIST TURN: ON EPISTEMOLOGY AND THEOLOGY

The debate regarding foundationalism continues to rage. The question of whether there are epistemic, anthropological, or other ontological foundations upon which human thinking inevitably proceeds is an important one, since an affirmative answer would suggest human disagreements can be adjudicated across cultural, religious, and other lines, while a negative response would indicate that there are incommensurable discourses that leave people groups in relative isolation, even if globalization might bring more and more of them alongside each other. Perhaps more importantly for Christian theologians, the rejection of all types of foundationalism implies that Christian faith is one form of life and set of beliefs among many others, each with its own internal justifications. Numerous options have emerged across this spectrum in response to these matters, even if few would resort

---

3. Here I agree with William James McClendon Jr., who has argued for *Biography as Theology*; see ch. 4 within.

4. Narrativity, especially of the testimonial sort, is central to the pentecostal tradition that informs my thinking; see Cartledge, *Testimony in the Spirit*, 15–18.

to the Cartesian version of foundationalist warrant dominant during the early modern period.[5]

The three essays in Part I of this volume take up the gauntlet hurled by the turn from foundationalism. They argue that the pneumatological imagination invites recognition of a set of what might be called shifting foundations that recognize the multiplicity of starting points any dialogical encounter must be prepared to engage. Such a posture avoids a self-destructive epistemological and philosophical relativism while providing theological justification for considering the possibility that there are a multiplicity of entry points into dialogical interaction. Put alternatively and perhaps more constructively, the pneumatological imagination not only allows but in a sense also insists that we inhabit our historically situated particularity, though not at the expense of the possibility that what is known and believed potentially has universal applicability.

My primary interlocutor amidst this set of three essays is the American philosopher Charles Sanders Peirce (1839–1914). I was introduced to Peirce in a spring 1997 seminar with Robert Cummings Neville (my *doktorvater*), wherein we wrestled with Peirce's legacy in contemporary philosophy and theology.[6] Chapter 1 introduces Peirce's ideas in conversation primarily with contemporary evangelical theology. My attentiveness to the evangelical theological horizon was then driven by my seminary education into an evangelical context and the anxieties stoked within that domain when the theological conviction, confidence, and certainty it cherishes are confronted with the postfoundationalist turn. Historically conscious evangelicals have wrestled with what might be called the scriptural foundationalism of conservative Protestantism, even as the recourse to "tradition" seems to trade in one set of putative foundations for another that is no less stable. Peirce gave me the tools to see beyond the binary of either foundationalism or relativism. His triadic and pragmatic semiotic also helped me realize that there were Trinitarian and pneumatological implications and that these could facilitate theological engagement across various spectra (e.g., theology as a public enterprise, in light of Peirce's fallibilism; theology and science, the interface of which Peirce also navigated; the evangelical-ecumenical divide, given Peirce's own Episcopalianism, however unconventional it may have been). Peirce did not devote any attention to things pneumatological, but

---

5. See, e.g., the argument that Christian faith cannot dispense with "foundations" altogether by Eduardo Echeverria, "Revelation and Foundationalism."

6. The previous semester, my first in the PhD program, I had written another seminar paper—later published as "Tongues of Fire in the Pentecostal Imagination"—that utilized Peircean semiotics to illumine pentecostal glossolalia.

my own emerging pneumatological imagination told me that there were connections to be mined.[7]

The second chapter, written in 2002, especially brings the pragmatic dimensions of Peirce's thought onto the contemporary stage. Peirce worked incessantly to distinguish his pragmatism from that of his colleague William James's—the former being concerned that the latter's version could be used instrumentally and utilitarianly to justify any means—and thereby developed his ideas within a robust metaphysical and ontological framework. Once I acknowledged to myself that I had to come to grips with the pragmatism inherent in my own pentecostal tradition,[8] I realized Peirce's triadic semiotic both undergirded as well as disciplined pragmatist inclinations to engage thoughtfully and critically with reality. I thus felt drawn almost inexorably to the work of contemporary pragmatist philosopher Richard Rorty (1931–2007), one of the more celebrated pragmatist thinkers at the time I produced the first draft of the essay. Rorty also defended a non-foundationalist approach—but, accentuating the naturalistic strand converging with and coming out of Peirce's expansive *oeuvre*, his conclusions leaned toward agnosticism (at best) or atheism (at worst) regarding religion. I am not opposed to a good dose of naturalist philosophy as an antidote to hyper-supernaturalistic notions, although I think the naturalism/supernaturalism divide is a more quintessentially modern binary than either side recognizes.[9] Of more interest to me was how to rescue what is valuable in Peirce's pragmatism from the Rortyean interpretation in order to justify and enact the kind of conversation that Rorty applauded, but from which he excluded religious or theological contributions. If for Rorty religion and theology are conversation stoppers because of their alleged dogmatisms, for me his version of pragmatism neither motivates nor sustains conversation in the public domain. Hence Rortyean postfoundationalism jeopardizes such public interaction and tolls the death knell for theology—unless we can find ways to speak intelligently beyond our tribal interests. Peirce again seems to have resources that Rorty chose not to retrieve because they smacked (to Rorty) of the unenlightened intuitions that those moving into the third millennium had to leave behind. Still, there is much to learn from the Peircean-Rortyean stream of pragmatism for contemporary theology's navigation of the local and the global—the particular and the universal—even if most

7. My *Spirit-Word-Community*, esp. Parts I and II, expanded on Peirce's categories in both pneumatological and Trinitarian directions.

8. As argued by Wacker, *Heaven Below*.

9. See Yong, *Spirit Poured Out on All Flesh*, ch. 7.

theologians will leave behind Rorty's skepticism regarding things religious and theological.

The late Jesuit theologian Donald L. Gelpi (1934–2011) was keenly attuned to the need to rethink the North American theological tradition in conversation with its greatest thinkers, from Jonathan Edwards (1703–1758) on through Alfred North Whitehead (1861–1947), a line that for him certainly included Peirce. I first began reading Gelpi in the spring of 1997 and was astounded to discover that he was deeply informed by the charismatic renewal movement in the Roman Catholic Church and even devoted much of his early work to developing a philosophical construct for Christian experience that took seriously charismatic spirituality. Gelpi also engaged Peirce's semiotic substantively, finding loose correlations between his triadic pragmatism and a pneumatologically robust Trinitarian faith and praxis, all of which inspired me as a budding pentecostal theologian to attempt to understand ("master" is too ambitious a word to apply to someone as obscure as Peirce) the pentecostal experience better, at least philosophically, if not also theologically. What I began to realize after reading Peirce and Gelpi was that what began as a quest for a postfoundationalist theology—which for me meant not necessarily non-foundationalism but a shifting foundationalism, as this book will make clear—turned out to also render plausible pentecostal-charismatic spirituality and practice in a post-Enlightenment world. When my good friend James K. A. Smith founded the Philosophy Interest Group in the Society for Pentecostal Studies in 2001, I wrote up an essay the next year—now chapter 3 of this volume—for the annual meeting, introducing the benefits of engaging Gelpi in order to ponder more deeply and philosophically, not to mention theologically and practically (read: pragmatically, in the Peircean sense), about pentecostal experience. Gelpi taught me, in part through Peirce, how orthodoxy and orthopraxy were conceptually and theologically intertwined. Here was a theologian with a profoundly charismatic world view and way of life who imbibed the particularity of the North American philosophical tradition, yet modeled the plausibility of a robust theological and ethical program with implications beyond this continental and even hemispheric context. Although I had been living with Gelpi for longer than Rorty, and even though the Rorty chapter (2) was written (shortly) after this Gelpi chapter (3), the latter rounds out this first part of the book since it also serves as a window into my efforts to render more sturdy and robust the bridge I had struggled to construct during graduate school between my early and initial philosophical work and my pentecostal identity.

THE POST-CHRISTENDOM ERA:
A "PENTECOSTAL" RETRIEVAL

There is some chronological and thematic overlap between the essays in this section and those of the preceding, since chapter 4 was written in 2001 (before the Gelpi and Rorty essays) and since my dialogue with Gelpi is with a fellow pentecostal-charismatic theologian, unlike my dialogue with James William McClendon Jr., a Baptist (I doubt "Bapticostal," although I do not know for certain) theologian. However, I have placed the Gelpi chapter in part I because he worked explicitly with Peirce; my conversation with McClendon belongs better in this "post-Christendom" section. McClendon, whose Baptistic roots are lodged deep within the Radical Reformation tradition, espouses a post-Christendom mentality less characteristic of Gelpi the Catholic theologian. Hence McClendon's Baptist theology aligns better with the post-Christendom and even sectarian impulses—here meant descriptively rather than pejoratively—motivating the "come-outism" of especially early modern pentecostal movements.

Remember that my time as a graduate student (from 1989 to 1998) was one during which the whole notion of a *pentecostal theology* was still an oxymoron. Pentecostals were known for their spirituality and even missionary zealousness, and this, combined with their long history of anti-intellectualism[10]—which has roots in the fundamentalist reaction to the modernist developments at the turn of the twentieth century—had by this time produced missiological treatises and even a spiritual theology. But a pentecostal theology remained foreign. My own halting efforts to think theologically as a pentecostal during this time were focused in my PhD thesis on what that meant for living in a religiously pluralistic world. Along the way I realized that any pentecostal theology worth its name had to be globally informed, since pentecostalism had been emerging as the Christianity of choice, so to speak, in the majority world.[11] Yet it was also the case that precisely this type of renewalism was at the vanguard of the emerging world Christianity.[12] Hence the global expansion of pentecostalism appeared to have coincided, if not mapped onto, the arrival and maturation of Christianity across the global South.[13] If the center of gravity had been gradually if not inexorably shifting from the Euro-American West to Asia, Africa, and Latin America, pentecostal-charismatic Christianity was as much to blame (for

---

10. See, e.g., Nañez, *Full Gospel, Fractured Minds?*

11. E.g., Hollenweger, *Pentecostalism.*

12. As documented by Jenkins, *The Next Christendom.*

13. E.g., Johnson and Ross, *Atlas of Global Christianity.*

those seeking culpability) as anything else. A post-Western Christianity was characterized by renewalism; simultaneously, a post-Christendom world, following the demise of modern European and North American colonialism, was one in which Christianity was also emerging with vigor and vitality in postcolonial states starting in the second half of the twentieth century.

Pentecostal theology, therefore, if it was indeed going to be theological rather than merely about spirituality or solely missiological, had to be global—not in the sense of being politically hegemonic, as Christianity had been in the Western world in the millennium or more after Constantine, but in the sense of being attentive to and informed by its plurality of voices, experiences, and forms after the dissolution of Christendom. Paradoxically, then, pentecostal theology in particular, if not Christian theology in general, had to be international on the one hand, but also radically local and particular, informed by all of its diversity on the ground, on the other hand. I have argued elsewhere that Christian unity in diversity and vice versa is grounded in the many tongues of the Day of Pentecost,[14] and the three chapters in part II further triangulate this theme from three angles.

First, my dialogue with McClendon introduced me to a post-Christendom theology that had been struggling for articulation for almost 500 years since the days of the Radical Reformation. The Anabaptists, of course, did not think the magisterial reformers were going far enough in their protests against the official church, but they rested their argument more on the call to discipleship echoed in the Gospels than on the proclamation of justification retrieved from St. Paul. Theirs was a post-Christendom theology not least in the political sense of drawing a sharp line between the church and the state (which is consistent with contemporary pentecostal inclinations about the church-state relationship, or lack thereof, as the case may and should be, so they feel), but also in the theological sense of following Luther's priesthood of the believer to its logical conclusion, so as to insist on believers' adult baptisms following Christian confession. If Luther's priesthood of all believers was grounded in the Pauline doctrine of justification, the Anabaptist version was rooted in their restorationist hermeneutic focused on the life of Jesus and the earliest apostolic community. McClendon's Baptist retrieval of the Anabaptist this-is-that resonance with the apostolic experience is paralleled by the pentecostal adaptation of restorationist commitments precipitated by the Radical Reformation. And if Peircean pragmatism supported the Gelpian orthodoxy-orthopraxy interconnection, McClendon's post-Christendom theology grounded orthodoxy (right believing) in ethics (right practices), following the ethics of Jesus. This was certainly consistent with

---

14. As developed in Yong, *Spirit Poured Out on All Flesh.*

pentecostal instincts about *doing* what the apostles did, not just *believing* what they believed. Interestingly, the baptist emphasis on the freedom of the believer's conscience (so as not to be bound by a state-supported orthodoxy, among other constraints on religious liberty) that produced a multiplicity of baptist churches, not to mention denominations, has in the last century given way to a pentecostal pluralism, even as the latter's tendency to multiply and diversify is often described negatively in terms of fragmentation in the contemporary media. In any case, if the Radical Reformers and those following that train of thought were the most resistant to the mechanisms of Christendom in the sixteenth century, pentecostals and those caught up in the global renewal movement are most resistant to the Christian status quo, whatever and wherever that may be in the present time. McClendon's Baptistic vision for Christian theology at the turn of the twenty-first century thus provides a helpful mirror for the emerging pentecostal theology for the third millennium.

If McClendon's project helps to ground a pentecostal theology post-Christendom, the work of Finnish pentecostal Veli-Matti Kärkkäinen provides the constructive fodder for such a task. I first met Kärkkäinen in 1998; he was completing his *habilitationsschrift* and I my PhD, and I marveled in the years thereafter at his prolific scholarly productivity.[15] I turned my attention to engaging his work in 2005 since by that time he had emerged indisputably as the most renowned pentecostal theologian anywhere, with ten books or monographs written, all in fewer than ten years! And note that in the less than ten years (as of the time of this writing) since I wrote on his work, Kärkkäinen has not only edited a half-dozen or more volumes, but also published another three books, not including two more of an anticipated five-volume systematic theology.[16] So my review essay can be considered no more than a very preliminary report on the work of a theologian who, even after completion of his current mammoth project, can still be anticipated to write a magnum opus. Yet as I try to show in chapter 5, the methodological trajectories of Kärkkäinen's present work were already charted in his first ten books—one that was global in perspective, deeply marked by pentecostal intuitions and pluralism, and respective of difference while being doggedly ecumenical rather than incoherently heterogeneous. Therein were features of constructive Christian theology taking up the

---

15. I was blessed to make a small contribution to it by gathering and editing a set of his essays for publication: Kärkkäinen, *Toward a Pneumatological Theology.*

16. See Kärkkäinen, *The Trinity; Holy Spirit and Salvation; Holy Spirit.* The five-volume systematics is titled *A Constructive Christian Theology for a Pluralistic World*, Volume 1 being *Christ and Reconciliation*, and Volume 2 being *Trinity and Revelation*; the rest of the volumes are anticipated to be released annually from 2015 to 2017.

opportunities and engaging the challenges of Christian faith in the third millennium, global precisely in its attentiveness to the many tongues of local contexts. As importantly, Kärkkäinen modeled for me that respectful dialogue could occur not only across Christian divides but also in a religiously pluralistic world, without abandoning the missionary posture that is the *raison d'être* of Christian faith and identity. It was around this time (from about 2005 onwards) that, inspired by Kärkkäinen's work, I began to publish specifically on missiological themes as a systematician.[17]

I have already mentioned my good friend Jamie Smith. He was trained philosophically at Villanova (under John Caputo), yet has always had deep theological interests, whereas I was trained theologically at Boston (under Robert Cummings Neville) but have always had an abiding philosophical inquisitiveness. Jamie approaches the postfoundationalist turn (outlined in Part I of this volume) using continental philosophical resources, while I do so following the North American philosophical tradition. His pentecostal identity has long been shaped by the Reformed tradition (part of his graduate training was at the Dutch Reformed-dominated Institute for Christian Studies)—so much so that he calls himself a Reformed-Charismatic[18]— while mine is embedded in the classical pentecostalism of my upbringing. Chapter 6 was originally inspired by Jamie's third book, an introduction to the Radical Orthodoxy (RO) theological movement. In that chapter you will see why I think RO provides an alternative for contemporary theology, albeit one that needs the post-Christendom sensibilities of pentecostal theology and spirituality. Jamie published a response to my original essay, and we have since continued to work on other projects together.[19]

THE POSTSECULAR MILIEU: THEOLOGY AND RELIGION IN A WORLD OF SCIENCE

Discussion of Radical Orthodoxy provides a nice segue way into Part III because of RO's insistence that we now live in a postsecular age. RO means by this that the claims of a preceding generation that modernization and secularization will spell the end of religion are increasingly being recognized as hollow, and that rather than the disappearance of religion, we have

17. See a collection of these in Yong, *Missiological Spirit*.

18. See the "Introduction" of James K. A. Smith, *Thinking in Tongues*.

19. See Smith, "Spirit, Religions, World"; cf. not only our coedited *Science and the Spirit* but also our coedited book series, Pentecostal Manifestos, published by Eerdmans, which, as of early 2014, has released six volumes, with three more under contract.

seen its global intensification.[20] But if religions remain vital in a postsecular world, the course of modernization has not yet been fully run. What I mean is that the advance of science, technology, and medicine marches on. Post-secularity does not mean the abandonment of science, but its intertwining with religion rather than the overcoming of either one by the other. In this postsecular context, science and religion continue to expand, sometimes alongside each other, other times in competition with and against each other.

If Part I of this book focuses on the philosophical and epistemological dimensions of doing theology and Part II engages with the questions of universality (of Christian faith) and particularity (of pentecostal and other variations), then Part III focuses on how scientific method compares or contrasts with theological method. If modernity privatized religious— and Christian—modes of thinking as compared with the presumed publicness of secular thought, then whither belongs theological reflection in a post-secular time? How can religious and theological articulation be public when science remains the *de facto lingua franca* in the present situation, and how can Christian theology make universal claims in a world dominated by sci-entific universalism? In some contexts it seems as if science is opposed to religion and vice versa. I postulated, however, that science and religion are complementary—since all truth is God's truth—and so sought a theological method that could support the quest to discern such complementarity.

The chapters in this part of the volume come at these questions in conversation not only with Christian thinkers but also with Buddhist inter-locutors. This is not only because observation of how those in other faiths are navigating the postsecular turn provides mirrors for considering the opportunities and pitfalls along the Christian path, but also because any response to the scientific hegemony will only be stronger when fortified across religious lines. On the other hand, as should be clear, I do not see sci-ence only as an enemy to be overcome. Rather, the way forward can only be a dialogue between science and theology, even if, as is the case in the three chapters here, it is mediated in part interreligiously. Hence the dialogue of theological method opens up in a postsecular context to a trilogue, one that involves two (or more) faith traditions in conversation with science.

My graduate education in the 1990s had already convinced me that the future of Christian theology could only unfold dialogically with the advance

---

20. This shift of awareness is nowhere more clearly reflected than in the work of Harvey Cox, who, in the 1960s, predicted the demise of religion in his *Secular City*, but thirty years later heralded the pentecostalization of religion with his *Fire from Heaven*. See also Wariboko, "Fire from Heaven," and Cox, "Response to Professor Nimi Wariboko."

of human knowledge in general, and that the latter is fundamentally carried out by scientific enterprise. However, I did not seriously begin engaging the theology and science discussion until about 2004. My time as the visiting Brueggeman scholar at Xavier University in Cincinnati that fall included the opportunity to team-teach a graduate course on science and religion with Jesuit theologian Joseph Bracken,[21] as well as the chance to meet John Polkinghorne, the Anglican scientist-theologian, at a conference funded by the Templeton Foundation.[22] Out of this came an immersion into the works of the latter and what is now the seventh chapter of this book. My reading of Polkinghorne, starting with his then most recent book *Science and the Trinity: The Christian Encounter with Reality*, helped me on two fronts. First, it helped me to understand how to navigate not only the local (putatively, of religion) and the global (allegedly, of science), but also the ideal (of religiosity) and the empirical (of scientific inquiry). Second, it prompted me to reconsider how the theology and science discussion, which heretofore had proceeded largely in general theistic terms, was amenable to a more explicitly Trinitarian perspective and hence also inviting of a more robust pneumatological contribution. Yet is also showed me that any theological method fit for the third millennium will have to be both broad enough and sufficiently flexible to engage with the dynamism of the scientific imagination. It's not just that science keeps changing its mind while Christianity dabbles in truths once-and-for-all delivered to the saints; rather, scientific understandings and Christian truth claims are both stable in some respects and fluid in other respects, always open to greater clarification and understanding, not least in a postsecular milieu.

In this same postsecular space, however, those in other faiths are also engaging with what might otherwise be a scientific hegemony. Chapters 8 and 9 of this book observe Buddhists entering the postsecular but no less scientifically dominated world. Two points should be mentioned about the Christian-Buddhist conversations in this part of the book. First, if the postsecular mind allows—if not invites—religious faith in the public sphere, then it should also be open to a Buddhist presence in this domain; however, postsecularity may not presume all religious voices are equal—arguments will still have to be made. Yet in both cases examined—that of His Holiness the Dalai Lama and that of one of his translators for a time, B. Alan Wallace—Buddhists across that spectrum of traditions will fault them for not being more amenable to the advances of science and how they might

---

21. A few years later, I published "A Catholic Commitment to Process Cosmology."

22. The conference proceedings included essays by Polkinghorne and myself published in Welker, ed., *Work of the Spirit*.

eliminate implausible Buddhist convictions on the one hand and, on the other hand, for not holding on more steadfastly to foundational elements of Buddhist teachings as well as practices. Second, however, if Christians cannot ignore science in our postsecular environment, then we also cannot ignore other religious voices in this same space. Hence the two case studies of Tibetan Buddhist arrivals in modernity provide dialogical springboards for considering the nature and scope of Christian theological method for a postsecular world.

Before moving on, I should clarify: my interaction with Buddhist traditions indicates neither that they are more important than Christian engagements with other faiths nor that they are indispensable to the Christianity-science–other-religions trilogue. Rather, I have focused on Buddhism only because it, of all the East Asian traditions that piqued my interest in graduate school, has remained with me over the decades.[23] The ongoing religion and science discussion will benefit from a multiplicity of faith perspectives at the conversation table.

THE POSTMODERN SITUATION: CHRISTIAN WITNESS AMIDST MANY RELIGIONS

In many respects, the task of doing Christian theology in the pluralistic world of the twenty-first century has driven much of my work. As already indicated, my doctoral dissertation grappled with how to formulate a distinctively pentecostal and yet faithfully Christian approach to religious pluralism, the interfaith encounter, and the interreligious dialogue, and the immense challenges confronting these tasks have followed me throughout my career to date (as my comments above on Part II delineate), even when I have attempted to engage with other important themes and areas of the theological landscape.[24] The issues of postfoundationalism (as should be clear from the preceding introductory remarks and the following Part I) have to do with how to make universal Christian truth claims from our perspectively limited contexts, even as the discussion of religion and science includes, if not mandates (as indicated in the preceding remarks and to be unfolded in Part III within), working both with and alongside, if not also against, those in other faiths engaging these issues in a postsecular arena.

23. More recently, I have published two books in this area: *Pneumatology and the Christian-Buddhist Dialogue*, and *The Cosmic Breath*.

24. So it is not without reason, then, that many of the authors in Vondey and Mittelstadt, eds., *Theology of Amos Yong*, use my theology of religions as a springboard for engaging with the various loci my work has touched upon.

One of the unavoidable challenges of our present time is how to bear adequate Christian witness in a world of many faiths.

Our late modern or postmodern situation accepts all perspectives as true or valid for the perspective holder,[25] at least in part in reaction to the modernist or Enlightenment elevation of scientific reason over non-Western ways of knowing. If liberal theological traditions have presumed there is a common core to the many religions of the world, postliberal reactions (including Radical Orthodoxy), however these may be defined, have accentuated the particularity and distinctiveness of each faith. Where the former tends to elide the differences, the latter minimizes their commonalities. Amidst this late and postmodern vortex, how can Christian theology move forward? More pointedly, are there good theological reasons for whatever is determined as a plausible way forward, or are these merely pragmatically or politically driven?

My pentecostal starting point has from the beginning wagered on a pneumatological intervention in potentially charting this *via media*. Such a pneumatological engine promises to deliver a dynamic, shifting foundationalism that navigates between the Scylla of Cartesianism and the Charybdis of relativism while also opening up dialogues between religions and between science and religion to trilogues, flowing in multiple directions between the various sciences and the many religions. In our postmodern context, my wager is that this empowers Christian witness even as it enables Christian hearing of, and perhaps also learning from, the testimonies of others. This acknowledges the perspectivism of religious knowing while avoiding the relativization, isolation, and privatization of religious beliefs.

The three chapters in the final part of this book, written in the winter of 2011, the winter of 2012, and the fall of 2012 respectively, bring us full circle to engage with the foundational issues of Christian theological method in the global context of religious pluralism. Chapter 10, on the work of Jesuit Hindologist Francis X. Clooney, provides a model for how to engage the beliefs of other traditions, in particular those of the Indian subcontinent. More precisely, Clooney unveils how comparative theology might proceed in the twenty-first century postmodern context when engaged with the textual traditions of the Hindu faith. Yet in this context, there is no honest

---

25. I have preferred talking about late modernity rather than about postmodernity, as exemplified in my *Theology and Down Syndrome*; the latter, "postmodernity," presumes too much both about what modernity means and that we have passed it up completely, while the former, "late modernity," recognizes that the processes of modernization remain inviolable, at least with respect to scientific inquiry, technological advance, and medical praxis. However, I use "postmodern" in order to preserve the rhetorical parallels for the four section titles in this book.

encountering of the other texts without some kind of openness to the praxis they presume and prescribe as well. This means that faithful reading is not just an intellectual or cognitive affair, but also practical and affective. If our postfoundationalist epistemology combines orthodoxy and orthopraxis, our postmodern encounter between faiths complicates matters through the inclusion of orthopathy, the role of right feelings that shape approaches to religious texts even as the practices and ways of life reflected in such texts in turn shape devotees' passions and desires. My engagement with Clooney's body of work, however, had already been prepared for in my work as a pentecostal theologian, which presumes the orthodoxy-orthopathy-orthopraxy triad precisely because religious belief and religious life are funded by religious feeling via the pneumatological imagination.[26] This does not make the work of sympathetically engaging other faiths any easier; but it does invite Christians to consider how to think theologically in a pluralistic world, neither merely polemically against nor only imperialistically with those in other traditions, and to proceed dialogically, both challenging yet also being transformed by the mutual encounter. For Clooney, such dialogue emerges out of what he calls dual-religious-belonging: the capacity to enter into and in some important respects inhabit the faith path of others in order to return enriched for the task of Christian theological reflection.

But is such dual religious identity either possible or desirable? Clooney's work will no doubt leave many Christians behind, even those who are seeking a way forward in our postmodern times. The challenges should not be underestimated. Put otherwise, how in our postmodern condition can we cease our colonial practices of domesticating religious others for our own purposes without simply privatizing religious belief and praxis as incommensurable subjectivities? Dutch Reformed anthropologist André Droogers's study of global pentecostalism, especially its spirituality of encounter with the transcendent Holy Spirit, has contributed to his theory of methodological ludism, the human capacity to both suspend one aspect of their identity or reality in order to engage another, and to sometimes embody both views simultaneously. If such a ludic stance is possible, it may also be plausible for the theologian to embrace both Barth's *Nein!* and Tillich's correlation, if not at the same time and in the same respects (although even this might be possible!), then at least successively, albeit no less really. More expansively, perhaps Gelpi's Peircean and charismatic pragmatism, Smith's Reformed and Radical Orthodoxy, Kärkkäinen's ecumenical theology, Polkinghorne's and Tibetan Buddhists' scientific theologies, etc., can all inform some kind of dual- or multi-religious stance that both bears faithful

26. See also Yong, *Spirit of Love*, esp. ch. 5.

witness to the gospel and yet respects and even is informed by the testimony of those on the other side. Might some—if not most—of my readers declare this impossible?

Perhaps not. The twelfth chapter is a lengthy review essay, with minimal notes, of evangelical-Reformed theologian and missiologist Benno van den Toren's *Christian Apologetics as Cross-Cultural Dialogue*, which actually attempts to articulate a kind of Barthian postfoundationalism that takes cross-cultural dialogue seriously, not merely as a ploy for the Christian mission. Some might think van den Toren's task ultimately unmanageable; however, I suggest the pneumatological approach developed in the pages of this volume not only fits such an agenda but is actually needed to bring about its achievement. Such a pneumatological imagination enables the capacity to speak in the tongues and languages of others (Clooney), but also to anticipate fulfillment in Christ (van den Toren); such a pneumatological orientation also empowers the capacity to hear the testimonies of others, sometimes stereophonically (Droogers), even as it facilitates dialogue across religious, cultural, and other lines (van den Toren).

The preceding has provided some autobiographical perspective on the essays within and how they document the emergence and coherence of such a pneumatological and dialogical approach to the task of doing theology in the present time. This book as a whole attempts a cumulative argument for theological reason—more specifically, a pneumato-theological methodology—suited to the postfoundationalist, post-Christendom, postsecular, and postmodern world of the twenty-first century. I will return in the concluding chapter to summarize the results and present an updated statement about where the discussion is at. For now, welcome to the conversation.

PART I

The Postfoundationalist Turn

Epistemology and Theology
after the Enlightenment

CHAPTER 1

The Demise of Foundationalism
and the Retention of Truth

What Evangelicals Can Learn from C. S. Peirce

IN A RECENT ESSAY entitled "The Postpositivist Choice: Tracy or Lindbeck?," Richard Lints suggests that there are basically two methodological options available to contemporary theology: either the postmodern approach that highlights the public or universal character of theological rationality or the postliberal emphasis on intertextuality, narrative, and the cultural-linguistic framework of all knowledge.[1] Although Lints writes from within the evangelical tradition, a movement well known for taking a stand for the truth, he refrains from offering an answer to the question posed in the title, preferring instead to provide a descriptive survey of the two options.[2] As part of his account, he discusses the two central issues that characterize the present situation, which postmoderns and postliberals deal with in their own ways. The first is the demise of what he calls "epistemic foundationalism"; the second and related issue is the nature of and criteria for truth. The problem is that the death of foundationalism appears to have relativized all truth claims, resulting in a debilitation—if not paralysis—of theological thinking.

---

1. Lints, "The Postpositivist Choice."

2. Perhaps Lints was reticent because of the American Academy of Religion audience. He concludes by calling himself an "antimodern" but leaves this suggestion undeveloped. I fail to conceive how one can be "antimodern" (see my review of Lints's colleague at Gordon-Conwell, David Wells, and his work *No Place for Truth* and *God in the Wasteland*), but to the extent that I understand his protest against modernism, I believe my proposal in this chapter is compatible with his "antimodernist" vision.

19

Because of their insistence on the importance of truth, some evangelicals have continued to reject the validity of the anti-foundationalist critique. Those who have acknowledged its legitimacy have generally elected in turn what Lints has described as the postliberal option. I do not think that evangelicals can remain intellectually viable if the former strategy of resistance continues, nor do I think that the latter postliberalism *by itself* is an adequate methodological response since it in turn poses new dilemmas. At the same time, I do think that a variety of answers to Lints's question are not only possible but also potentially workable for evangelical thinkers. One clue to a possible solution lies within the scope of Lints's essay and conjoins the two issues he takes to be of central importance. I shall argue that the demise of foundationalism does not entail the rejection of truth. On the contrary, with the help of C. S. Peirce, the founder of American pragmatism, I hope to show that the evangelical insistence on truth in its strongest form can be retained even if knowledge is admitted to be foundationless.

My argument will proceed in three sections. First, I will briefly elaborate the contemporary evangelical theological situation with respect to foundationalism and truth. I will then look at how Peirce's pragmatism allowed him to hold to a fallibilistic epistemology even while maintaining a correspondence or propositional theory of truth. Section three will consist of an attempt to defend Peirce's method as compatible with, or at least not essentially opposed to, evangelical beliefs and sensibilities.

EVANGELICALS, FOUNDATIONALISM, AND TRUTH

Although it is widely agreed upon that foundationalism is dead, it is important to determine exactly what kind of creature it is that so many have laid to rest. In fact, if one is attentive to the various responses to the anti-foundationalist critique, one would have to agree with Timm Triplett that "work on foundationalism is flourishing."[3] In terms of the feasible options for evangelicals, however, it is important only that we distinguish between classical and minimal, or weak, foundationalism. The former is that which has been rightfully traced to the Cartesian quest for certainty: all knowledge consists either in immediately justified or self-evident beliefs, or is mediately based on such beliefs. The latter has a variety of formulations, including that proposed more recently by Reformed thinkers such as William Alston and Alvin Plantinga. They have insisted on a different sort of

---

3. Triplett, "Recent Work on Foundationalism," 93. Triplett's survey identifies no fewer than twenty shades of foundationalism (!), and includes a valuable bibliography of contributions from 1975–1987.

"foundation," one that is "properly basic" and unjustifiable on evidentialist grounds but which emerges out of doxastic (belief forming) practices and is therefore warranted and not irrational.[4] While the merits of minimal or weak foundationalism in all its variations are still being debated, classical foundationalism has, even among evangelicals, fallen on hard times.[5]

Evidence of this evangelical reaction against classical foundationalism can be seen in at least two forms. Some are protesting against foundationalism either by aligning their theory of knowledge with that of the Reformed epistemologists, or by providing a clear epistemological critique of respected conservative evangelical thinkers.[6] Others have realized that an internal critique remains incomplete without a viable option. These protestors have been led to some form of what Lints has called postliberalism. This group embraces an assortment of evangelicals from a broad spectrum, including John Yoder, Stanley Hauerwas, James William McClendon, Nancey Murphy, Clark Pinnock, Stanley Grenz, Gabriel Fackre, Henry Knight III, and others, all of whom have been attracted to the postliberal emphasis on

---

4. "Minimal Foundationalism" is William Alston's term, from his *Epistemic Justification*, 39–56, while "Reidian Foundationalism," following the Scottish philosopher, is Alvin Plantinga's, in *Warrant and Proper Function*, 183–85. Alston also distinguishes between *iterative* and *simple* foundationalism (*Epistemic Justification*, 19–38), which correspond to Cartesian and his own minimal foundationalism respectively. For Plantinga's foundationalism, see his "Reason and Belief in God." For a more detailed elaboration of a "doxastic practice" approach to epistemology, see Alston, *Perceiving God*, 146–83.

5. For an assessment of Plantinga's foundationalism, see, for example, D. Z. Phillips, *Faith After Foundationalism*, 3–130. Tilley, "Reformed Epistemology and Religious Fundamentalism," notes that on Alston's and Plantinga's premises, the "basic beliefs" of fundamentalists are just as warranted as that of Reformed Protestantism. While the "basic beliefs" may indeed be justified, the question of whether or not the contents of these beliefs are true is quite another matter. I mention the Reformed alternative for two reasons. First, the Reformed epistemologists' notion of "basic beliefs" finds an analogue in Peirce's indubitable beliefs, a point I will return to below. Second, it is important to note the departure of this theologically conservative group from classical foundationalism; this creates another option for evangelicals looking to rethink their epistemology. Generally, however, it will be seen that evangelicals have preferred the postliberal option. My proposal looks to draw from both alternatives while further investigating the question of truth.

6. Thus theologians like Carl Henry, Stuart Hackett, Gordon Clark, Ronald Nash, and Kenneth Kantzer have been chided for actually distorting their foundations or working with non-foundationalist tools; see Topping, "The Anti-Foundationalist Challenge to Evangelical Apologetics," and Clapp, "How Firm a Foundation." It is clear, for example, that Hackett is a weak foundationalist who acknowledges the arbitrariness of his starting points and indicates his vulnerability to correction (*The Reconstruction of the Christian Revelation Claim*, 25).

the narrative structure of Christian faith.[7] The essence of postliberalism as articulated by these thinkers is that Christian doctrine and theology has its own internal logic, which is sustained by the biblical textual tradition and which finds its meaning and purposes within the practices of the Christian community. While not all have consciously adopted the label postliberalism as their own, it suffices for the purposes of this chapter that many of these thinkers have in fact been attracted to narrative theology. To the extent that they have, they can be adequately classified according to Lints's definition.

The problem which immediately surfaces is that of truth. Evangelicals have generally been staunch defenders of a propositional view of truth, wherein what is asserted corresponds to an objective reality or state of affairs.[8] This correspondence theory of truth has ancient roots in Plato and Aristotle, and presupposes that there is an external world apart from the human knower. How, then, can the correspondence of our ideas to the outside world be measured? This was the question that vexed Descartes, among others. He attempted to bridge the dualism between the knower and the known by following a process of methodical doubt in search of that which could be known with certainty. Descartes concluded that his *cogito* was that on which he could erect a viable theory of knowledge: all knowledge is either inherently justified on self-evident or incorrigible beliefs (eminently rational) or else founded on such beliefs (i.e., the *cogito ergo sum*). Later Enlightenment thinkers who built on Descartes's foundation assumed this as a universal rationality. The result of this was the enthronement of Reason. There were others, however, who were not so optimistic about these matters. Skeptics such as Hume questioned the connection between knower

7. All of those named have elaborated and defended their postliberal option in easily accessible sources. Other representatives can be found in Thiel, *Non-foundationalism*, 38–78, along with essays in Phillips and Okholm, eds., *Nature of Confession*, and in Hauerwas, Murphy, and Nation, eds., *Theology Without Foundations*.

It is important to note, however, that narrative theology is not a homogeneous movement and that even postmoderns like Tracy are "narrativists," albeit, as Gary Comstock puts it, "impure" ones ("Two Types of Narrative Theology"). According to Comstock, "pure" narrativists like Lindbeck take a Wittgensteinian approach to religion and see each tradition as a coherent cultural-linguistic system which is basically immune to outside criticism, while "impure" narrativists like Tracy, Paul Ricoeur, Julian Hartt, and Sally McFague have been inspired by Gadamerian hermeneutics and emphasize the necessity of the ongoing conversation between narrative traditions and others in the quest for correlation. For this reason, and also because Tracy and other "impure" narrativists have never considered themselves fundamentally "narrative" theologians, I think it more useful to follow Lints's distinction between "postmodern" and "postliberal."

8. This has been defended at length by the doyen of evangelicalism, Carl F. H. Henry, throughout the six volumes of his *God, Revelation and Authority*. See also Netland, *Dissonant Voices*, especially 112–33, and Corduan, *Reasonable Faith*, 39.

and known as well as the notion of the *cogito* itself, and others like Nietzsche objected to the idea of a universal rationality. This thoroughgoing critique of adequate epistemic grounds and universal first principles led in turn to the view of knowledge as subjective, contextual, and relative. In the contemporary scene, the "deconstructive" postmodernism of Derrida and Rorty is the "mature fruit" of this anti-foundationalism. In this framework, it is denied that reality in itself can be objectively and infallibly known; as such, the propositional understanding of truth as correspondence is no longer tenable.

Conservative evangelicals have attempted to ignore the demise of foundationalism in part because of the implications of such for truth. Their concern is that the doors to a complete relativism would be opened if propositional truth were dispensed with.[9] Other evangelicals, however, have been sufficiently touched by the anti-foundationalist critique to be aware of "the inadequacies of propositionalism."[10] The human capacity for knowing is not only circumscribed by cultural context, but also limited by sin and the fall. As such, there is neither an Archimedean vantage point of knowledge, nor is there a sturdy foundation underneath. All knowledge is undeniably tradition dependent. This explains, in part, the popularity of postliberal theology. Its emphasis on the narrative character of knowledge has attracted many a thinker across the evangelical spectrum.

The elusiveness of truth within the postliberal framework has not, however, gone unnoticed. The question is that of truth as correspondence versus truth as coherence. In the postliberal view, truth is understood in terms of coherence in that Christian doctrine and theology are meaningful only within their own internal framework. But this raises some difficult questions about the nature and reach of Christian truth claims. What then becomes of its applicability to those lacking the Christian community? Would postliberal theologians be willing to admit that Christian truth thereby becomes no more than a function of or appendage to the Christian narrative? How are postliberals to defend the truth of their claims apart from this story when, according to the Magna Carta of postliberalism, George Lindbeck's *The Nature of Doctrine*, doctrinal or theological truth is primarily intrasystematic and performative rather than ontological or propositional?[11] One of the surprising affinities that the postmodern approach of Tracy and others has with fundamentalism and conservative evangelicalism is that both have a much stronger view of truth as the correspondence (in Tracy's terminology,

---

9. This is the concern articulated by Netland in *Dissonant Voices*, 112–96.

10. The title of chapter five of Henry H. Knight III's *A Future for Truth*, 86.

11. Lindbeck, *Nature of Doctrine*, 47–52 and 63–72.

correlation) between ideas such as doctrinal and theological propositions to reality. The difference is that in Tracy's case, the external confirmation of truth has to run the gamut of human experience pluralistically considered. In the postliberal view, however, truth as correspondence has for all intents and purposes been vanquished in favor of truth as coherence. The result has been that truth can no longer be universally asserted, but is only meaningfully embedded within particular traditions. More specifically, truth as Christians consider it is relative to the Christian narrative. Conservative evangelicals see this as a step in the direction of the complete relativism of deconstructionism, and have been rightly concerned. But this difficulty has not been overlooked by proponents of evangelical postliberalism either.[12]

It is here that I wish to reintroduce the pragmatism of Peirce. Evangelicals for the most part have not paid serious attention to Peirce. When they have noticed him, they have been misled by identifying him with the form of pragmatism espoused by his more famous contemporary, William James.[13] While there are undoubtedly other resources from which evangelicals can draw in attempting to maintain their commitment to truth in a postfoundationalist era, Peirce's ideas are situated strategically at the intersection of epistemology and truth. As Guy Debrock and Menno Hulswit, Peirce scholars, inform us, "Indeed, pragmatism, and more specifically, Peirce's own brand of pragmaticism, a term which he invented in order to distance himself from other forms of pragmatism [like James's], may well provide the key to an epistemological theory which avoids the pitfalls of both foundationalism and relativism."[14] Peirce's escape from both pitfalls may prove to

12. E.g., the essays by Jeffrey Hensley and David Clark in Phillips and Okholm, eds., *Nature of Confession*, and Nancey Murphy, "Textual Relativism, Philosophy of Language, and Baptist Vision." Yet Murphy's narrativist reconstruction of truth fails if not considered as potentially universal (Yandell, "Modernism, Postmodernism").

13. For example, Peirce receives passing mention in Erickson, *Christian Theology*, 1:43–44, where he concludes that "it is difficult to assess the truth and validity of pragmatism, for the writings of Peirce, James, Dewey, and others contain such a variety of viewpoints" (Erickson, *Christian Theology*, 1:4). The only extensive evangelical engagement of Peirce I am aware of is Glenn Galloway in his essay "Peirce and Postmodern Evangelical Hermeneutics." In this, a revision of chapter five of his doctoral dissertation, Galloway highlights the difference that Peirce's triadic sign makes for postmodern evangelicals when compared to the dyadic approach of both deconstructive postmodernism and conservative evangelicalism (Galloway's PhD dissertation is "Efficacy of Propositionalism").

14. Debrock and Hulswit, *Living Doubt*, ix. Thomas Olshewsky's essay in this volume, "Realism and Antifoundationalism," is an argument similar to mine against the historicism of Rorty and the relativism of poststructuralism. The work that he and others are doing to distinguish the contributions of Peirce from those who have come after him within the pragmatist tradition (e.g., Mead, Dewey, Lewis, Carnap, Morris, Quine, and Rorty) has been important for the retrieval of the nonrelativistic founding

be a valuable resource for contemporary evangelicals who are attempting to reconstruct a non-foundationalist theology without jettisoning the idea of truth as correspondence. It is therefore necessary, given the objective of this chapter, to summarizes aspects of Peirce's technical philosophy. But insofar as evangelicals have not heretofore seriously considered his work, the following can perhaps also serve as a useful introduction to Peirce given the concerns and commitments of evangelical theologians.

PEIRCE AND THE CRITIQUE OF CLASSICAL FOUNDATIONALISM

Charles Sanders Peirce (1839–1914) always considered himself first and foremost a logician, even if he was a proficient scientist, renowned mathematician, original philosopher, and noted semiotician.[15] Peirce's relevance to the "postpositivist" situation characterized by Lints can be better understood when it is realized how Peirce anticipated and was perhaps one of the first American thinkers to launch a wholesale critique of modernity and Enlightenment rationality.[16] Peirce was a key transitional figure between Edwards and Emerson on the one hand, and the "golden age" of American philosophy at Harvard on the other.[17] Gifted with an encyclopedic mind, he was able to contribute not only to the elaborate metaphysics of Royce and the philosophical psychology of James, but to other fields of knowledge and their emergence as academic disciplines as well. Educated in the wake of Darwin's evolutionary theory, Peirce's philosophic interests were shaped by late nineteenth-century developments in the world of the sciences. In this climate, he was inevitably directed to ask questions about the nature of scientific knowledge and its relation to the functions of the mind. This led him even before the age of thirty to an intense study of the history of philosophy and of Kant, who had earlier asked similar questions. Because he never published a systematic treatise integrating his complete vision, he

---

intuitions of the movement.

15. Biographical details can be found in Brent, *Charles Sanders Peirce*. Note that what follows will be a thematic rather than historical exposition of Peirce's philosophy; the latter is itself a fascinating topic, but my focus in this chapter is to lift up some aspects of Peirce's mature philosophy and bring them into a dialogue with contemporary evangelical theology.

16. Other discussions of Peirce as nonmodernist include Robert Neville's *Highroad around Modernism*, 25–52, and Peter Ochs's lead chapter of *Founders of Constructive Postmodern Philosophy*, 43–88.

17. Cf. Bruce Kuklick's discussion of Peirce's role in inaugurating the "Golden Age at Harvard" in Kuklick's *The Rise of American Philosophy*, 104–26.

was rather neglected until the posthumous appearance of his *Collected Papers*.[18] Since then, however, an enormous body of secondary literature has emerged, as well as a society devoted to the interdisciplinary interpretation of his work. Rather than rehearsing the technical details of Peirce's thought, I want to look at his philosophy in anticipation of the dialogue with contemporary evangelicalism that follows. I will therefore lift up elements of Peirce's fallibilism and theory of truth and discuss them both within the broader framework of his pragmatism.[19]

Peirce's fallibilism took shape in the light of his conviction that the Cartesian quest for certainty was a mistaken enterprise. Whereas the Cartesian *cogito* presupposed a dualism between knower and known, Peirce rightly saw a continuity between the two.[20] In fact, Peirce rejected the individualism and atomism inherent in Cartesianism and suggested a continuity in the world itself. This is reflected in the fact that our knowledge of the world arises in our continuous experience of it. This experience consists of two aspects. The first aspect Peirce termed the *perceptual judgment*: the uncontrollable operation of grasping, assenting, and acting on sensation. This primary stuff of experience played a similar role in Peirce's epistemology as the notion of the *sense datum* did for the older British empirical philosophers. However, against their atomistic conception of *sense datum*, Peirce anticipated James's theory of mind as a "stream of consciousness" and regarded perceptual judgments as a continuous current of inferences.[21] Being continuous, they are abstract, vague, and not segregatable, thus making them uncontrollable, uncriticizable, and indubitable in and of themselves.[22]

---

18. Unless otherwise indicated, references to Peirce will be from his *Collected Papers*, and noted within parentheses in the text according to the convention of Peirce scholarship in the form of *v.p*, denoting volume and paragraph number; all italics within quotations from Peirce are his emphases.

19. This exposition of Peirce is very selective. Those interested in following the details of Peirce's philosophy can consult my references in the notes both to his work and to the secondary literature.

20. Peirce's critique of Cartesianism was most thoroughly explicated in two early essays in the *Journal of Speculative Philosophy* (1868): "Questions Concerning Certain Faculties Claimed for Man" and "Some Consequences of Four Incapacities." Briefly, he argued that Descartes's methodological and universal doubt was impossible, that the individualism of *cogito ergo sum* was unreasonable, that thinking proceeded in a spiral rather than in the Cartesian line, and that dualism leaves things ultimately inexplicable (5.264–65). I agree with Susan Haack that Peirce's second critique of Descartes was the most effective ("Descartes, Peirce and the Cognitive Community").

21. That perceptual judgments are inferences is an important point, one which I will return to below.

22. In holding to the existence of indubitables, Peirce approved of this aspect of Reid's philosophy of common sense. Peirce clearly read and admired Reid's work (5.444),

Yet Peirce understood that even while perceptual judgments are not consciously identifiable and dubitable, a fallibilistic epistemology requires that they be open to correction.[23] This led him to identify a second aspect of experience, which he called *perceptual facts*. These are the controlled cognitions or ideas which follow upon perceptual judgments. He described them as "the intellect's description of the evidence of the senses, made by my endeavor. These perceptual facts are wholly unlike the percept, at best; and they may be downright untrue to the percept" (2.141). This is the case because perceptual facts are not immediate but temporally removed from perceptual judgments, and therefore inferentially dependent upon memory. Memory, however, is fallible, and since perceptual facts in their final form are propositions produced by controlled cognition, thinking can only grasp reality partially and inexactly.[24]

Peirce's fallibilism, along with central elements of his epistemology such as perceptual judgments and perceptual facts, have to be understood within the broader framework of his pragmatism. What, however, did Peirce mean by pragmatism? Simply put, pragmatism for Peirce was a method for ascertaining and articulating the meaning of anything. These concepts are clearly explicated in two of Peirce's most important and widely referenced

---

and insofar as he also held to the indubitability of perceptual judgments, can be said to have anticipated Plantinga's retrieval of this aspect of Reid's thinking as well. In a certain sense, then, Richard Robin is correct to call Peirce a "foundationalist" (Robin, "Peirce on the Foundations of Knowledge"). Where Peirce differed from Reid, the classical foundationalists, and the Reformed epistemologists, however, was in denying immunity to and positively criticizing these "basic beliefs." He called his own philosophy "Critical-Commonsensism" (5.497–501), by which he meant to distance himself from Kant's unknowable *Ding an sich* (5.452, 525), and from Reid's and Dugald Stewart's Common-Sensism. His quarrel with the latter was that it did not develop a means by which to address the emergence and resolution of doubts that arise from experience: "the Common-Sensism now so widely accepted is not critical of the substantial truth of uncriticizable propositions, but only as to whether a given proposition is of the number" (5.497).

23. Since all knowledge is fallible, Peirce insisted that "there are three things to which we can never hope to attain by reasoning, namely, absolute certainty, absolute exactitude, [and] absolute universality" (1.141; cf. 5.587); and, further, "if exactitude, certitude, and universality are not to be attained by reasoning, there is certainly no other means by which they can be reached" (1.142). Let's see how this plays out as we proceed.

24. The word "reality" is pervasive throughout the Peircean corpus. I will elaborate on what it means for Peirce as we proceed. Suffice it to say at this juncture that reality is what we encounter and that which our thinking attempts to comprehend. For an exhaustive discussion of the relation of knowledge and reality in Peirce's philosophy, see Part Two of Hookway, *Peirce*.

papers, published in *Popular Science Monthly* in 1877–78: "Fixation of Belief" (5.358–87) and "How to Make Our Ideas Clear" (5.388–410).

In the first paper, Peirce argued that the path of inquiry is best accomplished methodologically by scientific investigation. He rejected the method of tenacity (which grasps a desired end regardless of outside influences or resulting consequences), the method of authority (which subjects itself sometimes uncritically to the powers that be), and the *a priori* method (which claims to be reasonable when oftentimes it is no more than an expression of intellectual taste). Instead, Peirce advocated a method "by which our beliefs may be determined by nothing human, but by some external permanency—by something upon which our thinking has no effect" (5.384). The objective of pragmatism was to get at the truly real.

Part of fully understanding one's method and objective, however, involves its adequate articulation. If it is the truth of reality that shapes our beliefs, Peirce then sought to know how it is that we can attain proper beliefs. This is the subject of "How to Make Our Ideas Clear." Peirce outlined the process by which beliefs are formed. It begins with an initial awareness of something, proceeds to remove doubts regarding the thing, and concludes with the establishment of habits of action relative to the object of belief. This led Peirce to define the meaning of anything as the habits it involved. He put it this way in his famous Pragmatic Maxim: "Consider what effects, that might conceivably have practical bearings, we conceive the object of our conception to have. Then, our conception of these effects is the whole of our conception of the object" (5.402).[25] If effects are inconceivable for anything, such a "thing" is probably meaningless and, as such, neither true nor false. To get at the truth of anything is to formulate a hypothesis about its effects. True beliefs are those reached when the effects predicted are borne out in experience. This leads to *full beliefs*, that upon which we are willing to risk ourselves, in contrast to mere *opinions*. Opinions that do not lead even to insignificant actions probably either mean that hypotheses about them have not been properly framed or that there is no truth to them.[26]

25. Peirce added in a footnote that his Pragmatic Maxim was "only an application of the sole principle of logic which was recommended by Jesus; 'Ye may know them by their fruits,' and it is very intimately allied with the ideas of the gospel" (5.402, n.2). Volume V of the *Collected Papers* is titled *Pragmatism and Pragmaticism*. There is a voluminous secondary literature on Peircean pragmatism. A useful and concise survey is Knight, *Charles Peirce*, 45–68.

26. Peirce's religious example of a meaningless doctrine was transubstantiation (5.401, 541). At the same time, this did not imply his rejection of meaningful religiosity, since Peirce was a fairly traditional theist. As will be discussed below, he held to the reality of thirds or generals, leading him to posit criteria of verification or falsification that was quite unlike the materialism of Comte's positivism (5.597) and the later

The substance of these two early papers, however, could have been understood as being merely descriptive. Perhaps people use the scientific or pragmatic method of inquiry simply because of intellectual taste. Peirce saw that in order to demonstrate the truth of pragmatism, he had to show that it was normative for the process of thinking. This was a lifelong task that finally emerged in his mature philosophy, most completely expressed in his 1903 Lectures on Pragmatism at Harvard.[27] Rather than analyzing the psychological aspects of pragmatism, Peirce sought in these lectures to establish its logical basis in order to argue for its truthfulness.[28] What motivated his inquiry into the logic of reasoning was the question of how the process of experience enabled the mind to engage the world and understand it truly, or how the signs with which the mind worked mediated reality accurately. In order to answer these questions, however, Peirce recognized that he had to develop a metaphysics. This too was a subject with which he had struggled since his early efforts to reformulate Kant's categories.

Peirce therefore devoted lectures two through four to an elaboration of his categorical scheme. He had come to understand reality in terms of three fundamental categories which he termed *firstness*, *secondness*, and *thirdness*. *Firstness* is pure potentiality, the simple quality of feeling, that which makes a thing what it is in and of itself. *Secondness* is the element of struggle or of brute, resistant fact, that by which a thing is related to others. *Thirdness* is what mediates between firstness and secondness, the universals, laws, generalities, or habits that ensure the continuity of the process of reality.[29] Peirce considered these categories to be universally applicable to all phenomena,

---

stringent analytic philosophy.

27. I greatly benefited from a recent commentary on these lectures edited by Patricia Ann Turrisi in *Pragmatism as Principle*.

28. To distinguish his pragmatism from that of James's, Peirce queried, "what is the *proof* that the possible practical consequences of a concept constitute the sum total of the concept?" (5.27). Peirce's problem with James was not so much the latter's theory of truth—James was an epistemological realist just as Peirce was (see James's *Meaning of Truth*, 217–20)—as it was James's equation of truth with meaning. Peirce wanted to keep both distinct. There were other differences as well, perhaps related to vocation and temperament. James was a metaphysical nominalist, ethical utilitarian, cosmological pluralist, and psychologist-turned-philosopher; in contrast, Peirce was a realist, normativist, synechist, and scientist-logician. As such, he was always after the logic of both thought and action (5.429). Smith's *Purpose and Thought* delineates differences among the early pragmatists.

29. The import of thirdness in Peirce's philosophy should not be underestimated. It signaled his revolt against nominalism—its denial of the reality of laws or generals. It was this error, Peirce insisted, which plagued all of modern philosophy since Ockham (cf. his discussion of nominalism in 1.15–26).

irreducible, able to comprehend all other categorical distinctions, and not only descriptive of reality, but reality itself.[30]

Peirce's reformulation of the categories yielded some significant insights into the nature of experience and reasoning. Whereas the history of Western thought has generally attempted to comprehend epistemology in dyadic terms resulting in the well-known dualisms of knower and known, subject and object, and the like, Peirce explicated such within a triadic framework that combined experience and cognition. Proceeding from perceptual judgments, human cognition typically involves three types of reasoning, all of which are inferential: *abduction, deduction,* and *induction. Abduction* is the emergence of a broad inference, a hypothesis, what ensues from the general classification of perceptual judgments. *Deduction* is the prediction of what should follow from the hypothesis. *Induction* is the concrete, piecemeal testing of the deduced predictions to see if the hypothesis holds in reality. What is important here is the basic continuity between perception and abduction. From a phenomenological analysis of perceptual experience, Peirce was led to see that perceptual judgments or sensations are the continuous activity of engaging with brute singulars or secondness by which the mind registers the general or vague features of the world. Our sensation of a table is fundamentally of the laws to which things such as tables conform: hardness, coarseness, color, etc. As such, we can see that perceptual judgments are thirds that connect our sensations with the world.[31]

30. This is an unfortunately brief summary of 1.300–53. Discussions of Peirce's categories can be found from almost all of his commentators. He mentions numerous other examples to support his triadic categories, including: freedom, fact, continuity; feeling, volition, cognition; quality, reaction, representation; presentness, struggle, law; the Kantian categories of unity, plurality, and totality, and possibility, necessity, actuality; and the Hegelian categories of thesis, antithesis, and synthesis—so long, Peirce insisted, as the second was not overwhelmed by the third. Note also the fascinating discussion by Sandra Rosenthal of how Peirce could consider his categories fundamental yet fallible (*Peirce's Pragmatic Pluralism,* ch. 4, esp. 77–88).

31. It is therefore arguable that Peirce's is a naturalistic epistemology, if by this we mean the continuity between mind and reality (see Maffie, "Naturalized Epistemology"; cf. Plantinga's use of "naturalistic epistemology" within an explicitly theistic framework in his *Warrant and Proper Function,* 194–238). The history of science and the advance of knowledge also led Peirce to this conclusion. Since abduction is based on inference and all hypotheses are actually guesses, and since false hypotheses are infinitely far greater numerically than true ones, our remarkable guessing ability can be seen as evidence of the adaptation of the mind to the world (5.591, 6.417, 7.39, 46). While Peirce drew from the terminology of Darwinian evolution in calling this ability Insight or Instinct (5.173, 7.687), he did not succumb to the Spencerian materialistic or mechanistic interpretation of the universe. Rather, this led him to the view that both the world and humanity are signs to be interpreted (5.119, 314), which is in turn suggestive of the theological doctrine of the *imago Dei* (5.588, cf. 6.307); cf. also Miller,

From this discovery, Peirce determined that vagueness, generality, and inference are replete throughout both experience and the process of reasoning. Abduction is thereby connected with perception and occurs continuously with it because of the "interpretativeness of the perceptive judgment" (5.185); in fact, Peirce specifically said that a percept or sensation "fulfills the function of an hypothesis" (5.291). The various hypotheses are refined in perceptual facts, deductively theorized, and then tested in more specific ways. Those that prove themselves reliable guides for the course of experience are solidified into habits of thought and action. The process of thinking, then, is nothing more or less than the drawing of inferences from the generalities of sensations, and the continuous filling in the blanks or making determinate the vague aspects of these perceptual judgments, both by connecting them with previous cognitions and by integrating novel experiences through the ongoing process of reasoning.[32] Because generality or thirdness "pours in" upon us continuously in the form of sensation, percepts and perceptual judgments are codified over time as mental signs (interpretations) that grasp the laws and habits of things. This in turn enables us to understand and engage the world. All human experience, from the percepts of feeling to perceptual judgments and on through the entire process of cognition, is therefore wholly semiotic. But, it also follows that since cognition is nothing but inferences from the vague signs of perception, and since there is, at least potentially, an infinite series of interpretations that follow upon the presentation of a sign, all knowledge can only be provisional. This is the case because inductive reasoning can only engage in a finite number of experiments even if extended indefinitely. Reflecting this fallibilism, Peirce thus admonished the investigator to be watchful for exceptions to the rule. Barring the surprises of experience, thinking proceeds in smooth continuity from perception through to action. Peirce summarized the fundamental tenets of his philosophy in the concluding Lecture on Pragmatism in this

---

"Theological Implications."

32. Peirce puts it this way: "Perceptual judgments contain general elements, so that universal propositions are deducible from them. . . . The perceptual judgments are to be regarded as an extreme case of abductive inferences, from which they differ in being absolutely beyond criticism. The abductive suggestion comes to us like a flash. It is an act of insight, although of extremely fallible insight. It is true that the different elements of the hypothesis were in our minds before; but it is the idea of putting together what we had never before dreamed of putting together which flashes the new suggestion before our contemplation" (5.180). That perceptual judgments are thoroughly general and put us in touch with the laws and habits that structure reality is, in my opinion, one of the most important of Peirce's insights. As Robert Corrington comments, "If these beliefs were anything *but* vague, they would make it difficult for the self to function in a variety of situations, each with its own complex variables" (*An Introduction to C. S. Peirce*, 55, emphasis Corrington's).

way: "The elements of every concept enter into logical thought at the gate of perception and make their exit at the gate of purposive action; and whatever cannot show its passports at both those two gates is to be arrested as unauthorized by reason" (5.212).

The essence of pragmatism therefore follows the logic of abduction. Pragmatism is the process of inquiry that seeks to establish firm beliefs about reality from the inferences of perceptual experience. The pragmatic elucidation of truth asks the question: what can be expected to follow from a true hypothesis? The logic of pragmatism is that the vagueness of perception and perceptual judgment lead us to formulate equally general inferences (abductions), from which more specific predictions are made (deductions), which are in turn finally tested in a variety of ways (induction). If confirmed, inductive experience is shaped into provisional habits that inform our actions. As Peirce put it, "the only method of ascertaining the truth is to repeat this trio of operations: conjecture; deductions of predictions from the conjecture; testing the predictions by experimentation" (7.672). It follows that only the surprises arising from experience jolt us from our habituatedness, trigger doubt, and return us to inquiry.

Both perceptual judgments and perceptual facts are thus synthesized in our minds in such a manner so as to form habits that enable us to engage our world. So long as things are encountered as anticipated, our habits of thought and action are solidified and confirmed. They begin to be consciously criticized, however, when we are surprised by the unexpected. Such surprises raise doubts that inhibit our ability to function in the world.[33] This leads us to a process of inquiry that has as its goal the resolution of doubt and the establishment of a new mode of belief and action. This new *modus operandi*, however, will be satisfactory only if it enables us to engage the world successfully. This requires that we understand our relation to the world truthfully. In this way, that which is experientially indubitable in per-

---

33. *Surprise* and *doubt* are both important concepts in Peirce's epistemology. The former, Peirce said, "is very efficient in breaking up association of ideas" (5.478; cf. 5.512), and what surprises is precisely our being shocked by an unexpected experience of reality (1.336). The latter Peirce contrasted with *belief*. Whereas belief was understood as a self-satisfied habit, *doubt* was defined as "the privation of a habit" (5.417), or as that which "really interferes with the smooth working of the belief-habit" (5.510). Peirce insisted, however, that genuine doubt exists not in the laboratory of thought but is rather the "uneasy and dissatisfied state from which we struggle to free ourselves [in order to] pass into the state of belief" (5.372). As an example of how the experience of the real duality of secondness caused surprises and raised doubts, Peirce described how the subjective idealist walking down the street and musing about idealism is unable to persist in denying the reality of the external world after being staggered by the flying fist of a drunkard. "What has become of his philosophical reflections now?" Peirce asked (5.539).

ceptual judgments can be and is cognitively dubitable when propositionally asserted as perceptual facts and tested against experience. As Peirce said, "the scientific spirit requires a man to be at all times ready to dump his whole cartload of beliefs, the moment experience is against them" (1.55). Hence Peirce's fallibilism.[34]

The preceding discussion has hinted at how Peirce understood all knowledge to be fallible, even while he believed it could be truthful. This connection, however, needs to be elaborated upon. Important for our purposes is that the Peircean corpus provides abundant evidence that he viewed truth propositionally, and that such propositions connect our cognitions with reality.[35] This is the case in part because Peirce was convinced that truth is exclusively propositional. Any real proposition, as a semiotic relation, must be categorically triadic. In itself (as a first), a proposition is a sign that stands against an object (a second) and is capable of determining an interpretation (a third). The interpretation either gets at the relation between the sign and the object correctly or it does not. This is what allowed Peirce to say "every proposition is either true or false" (2.327). But because our initial perceptual judgments are vague, they have to be rendered more precise by the many respects or perspectives of interpretation. Propositional

---

34. Simply put, then, *fallibilism* is "the doctrine that our knowledge is never absolute but always swims, as it were, in a continuum of uncertainty and of indeterminacy" (1.171). It is important to note, in the words of Robert Almeder, that "Peirce's denial of the existence of absolute individuals provided the logical foundation for his doctrine of the indeterminacy of meaning" (*Philosophy of Charles S. Peirce*, 18).

35. From an unpublished manuscript dating from about 1905, Peirce begins rhetorically: "So what is truth? Kant is sometimes accused of saying that it is correspondence of a predicate with its object. . . . He calls it a nominal definition, that is to say, a suitable explanation to give to a person who has never before seen the word '*Wahrheit*'" (from Manuscript 283, 39, in the microfilm edition of Peirce's unpublished papers located in the Widener Library at Harvard University; quoted in Misak, *Truth and the End of Inquiry*, 128). Yet Peirce did go on to unequivocally endorse the correspondence theory. In the following brief explication of Peirce's notion of truth, however, we would do well to keep in mind the complexity of his thought. Peirce did discuss theories of truth in general and truth as correspondence specifically in 5.549–73. At the same time, Robert Almeder has documented "Peirce's Thirteen Theories of Truth." H. S. Thayer, however, has pointed out the two definitions most widely regarded as "Peirce's theory" are: "The opinion which is fated to be ultimately agreed to by all who investigate, is what we mean by the truth, and the object represented in this opinion is real. That is the way I would explain reality" (5.407); and, "Truth is that concordance of an abstract statement with the ideal limit towards which endless investigation would tend to bring scientific belief, which concordance the abstract statement may possess by virtue of the confession of its inaccuracy and one-sidedness, and this confession is an essential ingredient of truth" (5.565) (cf. Thayer, "Peirce on Truth," 124). The import of these definitions will be clear as our discussion continues. For an insightful overview of Peirce's ruminations on truth in the philosophical context of his time, see Altshuler, "Peirce's Theory of Truth."

signs thus function by addressing and creating in our minds other, more developed signs or interpretations, and so on, potentially *ad infinitum*. A true proposition, Peirce explained, meant that

> every interpretation of it is true. . . . When we speak of truth and falsity, we refer to the possibility of the proposition being refuted; and this refutation (roughly speaking) takes place in but one way. Namely, an interpretant of the proposition would, if believed, produce the expectation of a certain description of precept on a certain occasion. The occasion arrives: the percept forced upon us is different. This constitutes the falsity of every proposition of which the disappointing prediction was the interpretant (5.569).

This, then, is what allowed Peirce to claim that thought has access to the truth of reality. "Truth is the conformity of a representamen to its object, *its* object, ITS object, mind you" (5.554). For Peirce, far from truth being subjective, all truth is supremely objective in that there is a correspondence relation between propositions and reality. The difference is that Peirce recognized the complex operations of thinking. He understood that the correlation of our assertions with reality takes place not directly, but only by means of a semiotic process of interpretation. This process is a triadic relation between signs, objects, and interpretations, which arise from various experiential perspectives. These respects of interpretation yield successively more determinate aspects of previously less determinate signs.

Two other aspects of Peirce's theory of truth need to be mentioned. The first is his insistence that the context of inquiry is always a community of inquirers and never an isolated individual. Although Peirce fully acknowledged the provisional nature of all knowledge, he rejected Kant's idea that reality is an unknowable thing-in-itself. Peirce preferred instead to speak of practical certainty and to rely on the accumulated wisdom of human experience and the consensus of the community of inquirers to establish both truth and reality. As he observed, the real is that which "sooner or later, information and reasoning would finally result in, and which is therefore independent of the vagaries of me or you. Thus, the very origin of the conception of reality shows that this conception essentially involves the notion of a COMMUNITY, without definite limits, and capable of a definite increase in knowledge" (5.311). This is especially the case since the idea of truth entails something being the case regardless of our own particular wishes or desires.

The second aspect of Peirce's notion of truth that needs to be mentioned is truth as that to which opinion converges in the infinite long run.

While Peirce's use of the word *opinion* is deceiving in that it connotes numerous possible subjective formulations of truth, it should be noted that any particular opinion is always potentially *final*, thus denoting singularity. Even if there is the notion of truth as an ideal limit in Peirce, this does not mean that truth is only an eschatological notion and can never be accessed.[36] Because inquiry is the process of settling beliefs, the process of inquiry can terminate whenever particular questions cease to generate doubt, or when satisfactory answers are formulated. In such cases, the community of inquirers has reached a "final opinion": which "truths" are usually conveyed in textbooks (cf. 8.43). The fact that any question may be later reopened by the community of inquirers is evidence that later experience calls into question prior conclusions and that doubt has once again arisen; this is unavoidable given the fallibility of all knowledge.

In sum, getting at the truth involves the logic of reasoning, the continuous fallible activity of a community of inquirers, beginning physiologically with vague perceptual mental signs, proceeding cognitively via abduction, deduction, and induction to render them more completely determinate, and while never getting thought to correspond directly to its object, always increasingly approximating this concordance through the potentially indefinite process of inquiry, which terminates when a certain degree of action is made possible and doubt is minimized. The proof of pragmatism, as Peirce understood it, lies in its following the logic of reasoning. This logic enables the community of inquirers to decipher signs of themselves and the world, interpret experiences, clarify meanings, understand intellectual concepts, be habituated to reality, and apprehend truth.

Before we launch the dialogue between Peirce and contemporary evangelicalism, however, it might be useful to ask where his method of inquiry led with regard to his personal religion.[37] The "results" are most clearly seen in his 1908 essay, "A Neglected Argument for the Reality of God" (6.452–93). The "neglected argument," it should be noted, is really a nest of three arguments. These can be distinguished as the Humble Argument, the Neglected Argument proper, and what I will call the Logical Argument. Peirce began with a discussion of "musement," the free-flowing

36. Cf. the excellent discussion of Peirce's notion of truth as "final opinion" and limit ideal by Thayer, "Peirce and Truth."

37. There is an extended discussion of "religion" in the second half of Volume VI of the *Collected Papers*. At the same time, an enormous body of secondary literature has also developed on this topic. Two valuable book-length discussions are Orange's historical account, *Peirce's Conception of God*, and Raposa's thematic *Peirce's Philosophy of Religion*. Other important articles which I found helpful are Potter, "Vaguely Like a Man"; Clarke, "Peirce's Neglected Argument"; Smith, "Peirce's Religious Metaphysics"; and Raposa, "Peirce and Modern Religious Thought."

meditation all human beings periodically engage in. He suggested that pro-longed musement on the three universes (the three categories) of quality, brute actuality, and the relation between the two inevitably results in the hypothesis of God's reality as creator of the world.[38] This was Peirce's solution to the problem of the one and the many. He admitted that his Humble Argument was very similar to ancient argument from design. That the idea of God is what any reflective muser eventually stumbles upon was, for Peirce, a fact that theologians and theistic apologists throughout the centuries had overlooked. This was therefore a second theistic argument, what Peirce called the Neglected Argument proper. The final Logical Argument is the consideration of the Humble Argument as an exemplification of the process of reasoning. The hypothesis of God's reality which dawns on the muser is usually tested and confirmed both deductively and inductively. As with any other "experiment," the results of these tests will be fallible on the one hand, especially if specified in detail (i.e., as in saying what the divine attributes are), even while on the other hand being open to greater and greater clarification by the community of inquirers. It is important to remember here that Peirce understood the mind to be attuned to reality. This was what enabled the growth of knowledge. Because "the mind works by final causation, and final causation is logical causation" (1.250), it should not be surprising that he hypothesized God to be both the aboriginal creator of the world as well as the telos of its concrete development. It seemed right to Peirce that inquiry, in the infinite long run, would come closer and closer to a correct knowledge of God.

PEIRCE AND EVANGELICAL ORTHODOXY

Much more can and needs to be said about Peirce's semiotic theory—the categories, epistemology, and theism. Yet the question that needs to be addressed after this exposition of Peirce is why evangelicals should pay serious attention to this thinker. Perhaps a prior complex of questions needs to be negotiated before a more concrete dialogue on theological method can be attempted. Can evangelicals learn from someone whose presuppositions and assumptions are altogether different from their own? Is the idea that all knowledge is fallible compatible with evangelical intuitions? Is Peirce's

---

38. Peirce preferred to speak of God's reality rather than existence since the latter referred to the second universe of matter and actuality. Gary E. Kessler argues that Peirce was mistaken in not taking into account the role of cultural constraints in musement ("A Neglected Argument"). This is an important point which I will briefly allude to later.

revised notion of truth as correspondence—tempered by the infinite long run—close enough to evangelical commitments? How does the link between propositionalism and the thoroughly semiotic nature of interpretation as articulated by Peirce square with evangelical notions of revelation and the hermeneutical process? The problem that many evangelicals would conceivably have with all of these Peircean doctrines is that adherence to them would appear to place one on the slippery slope toward theological liberalism and relativism.

Partly in defense of Peirce and partly in order to not terminate the dialogue before it has even started, let me respond very briefly to these concerns. First, the combination of propositionalism and the process of interpretation in Peirce is suggestively analogous to the evangelical commitment to Word and Spirit, the two forms of divine self-communication. The Word is the concrete revelation of God, most clearly seen in the incarnation and secondarily in the biblical witness. The Spirit is that elusive revelation of God, whose comings and goings are like the wind, and beyond our ability to define with precision (cf. John 3:8). Together, the relationship between Word and Spirit is one of the central tensions in Christian theology. Second, truth as correspondence in its strongest form can be understood literally only in an eschatological sense. It is biblically attested by St. Paul's declaration that "now we see but a poor reflection as in a mirror; then we shall see face to face. Now I know in part; then I shall know fully" (1 Cor 13:12). The God who says, "I am who I am" is also the God who will be.[39] There is room here for Peirce's notion of truth as that which reveals itself in the infinite long run. Finally, Peirce's fallibilism is not a mere assertion, but rather a rigorously formulated doctrine set within an epistemological, psychological, and metaphysical framework. It is therefore important to distinguish the type of "relativism" entailed by Peirce's fallibilism from that espoused by other "deconstructive" pragmatists such as Rorty. Whereas the latter advocated a form of polite conversation as the only option since truth is relative and finally inaccessible, the former emphasized the fundamental purpose of inquiry as the attainment of truth. Given their more robust doctrines of sin and the fall, evangelicals should be some of the first rather than the last to embrace fallibilism and dispense with epistemological foundationalism. That all knowledge is partial and open to correction should be the hallmark of an evangelical theology articulated in a posture of humility before others and especially before God. Evangelicals can and should acknowledge the fallibilistic nature of knowledge and the relative or contextual form of all

39. "I will be what I will be" is a valid alternate rendition of the Hebrew in Exodus 3:14 (NIV marginal note); cf. Peirce's notion of reality as that which belongs to or appears in the future (8.284).

interpretation, without surrendering to a skeptical or nihilistic relativism with regard to truth.

With these preliminary remarks in hand, I wish to take up in the remainder of this chapter the two issues central to evangelical theology and perhaps most succinctly and formidably expressed in the doctrinal creed of the Evangelical Theological Society (ETS): "The Bible alone, and the Bible in its entirety, is the Word of God written and is therefore inerrant in the autographs. God is a Trinity, Father, Son, and Holy Spirit, each an uncreated person, one in essence, equal in power and glory." These are the doctrines of Scripture and of the Trinity.[40] I will deal with the latter first, although with each, I hope to show that Peirce is at least not incompatible with evangelical beliefs.

In the first place, it is important to note that Peirce was clear regarding his belief in God. He also rejected the Unitarianism of his father, Benjamin Peirce, the noted mathematician and astronomer, as is evidenced by his decision to remain a communicant in the Episcopal Church all his life. Yet because he believed that the word *God* was vague even to an extreme, Peirce was leery about the ways in which theologians had attempted to specify the concept and by which they had managed to render a practically understood term theoretically and theologically confusing. I am convinced, however, that there are fruitful insights to be gained in any effort to understand the doctrine of the Trinity if close attention is paid to Peirce's triadic categories. This is especially the case since Peirce regarded personality in part as the consciousness (thirdness) mediating feelings and qualities of feelings (firstness) with brute matter (secondness). This enabled him to comprehend God as supremely personal.[41] The idea of God as Alpha (first), Omega (second), and the process of evolution in between (third) was also considered by Peirce to be "essentially that of Christian theology, too" (1.362, n.1). A further analogue that comes to mind is Augustine's doctrine of the Holy Spirit as the bond of love between the first two persons.[42] Much more thought needs to be given to these matters. I am simply pointing out the potential resources inherent in Peirce's personalistic theism as an alternative to the

40. I think that these are doctrinally axiomatic to broad evangelicalism even if many within this larger community would take issue with the specific wording of the ETS statement. At the same time, however, any headway made at these points of highest tension will be suggestive of the promise in continuing the dialogue.

41. See the evidence for this gathered by Donna Orange in her *Peirce's Conception of God*, where she argues that Peirce is far closer to the personalistic God of traditional theism than to the finite God of James (or, for that matter, to the impersonalistic God of contemporary Peirceans like Robert Corrington and Robert Neville).

42. See Yong, *Spirit-Word-Community*, ch. 2, for further explication.

many other Peircean and non-Peircean contemporary reconstructions of the doctrine of the Trinity, based as they are upon impersonal categories that evangelicals would not endorse.

The evangelical adherence to the inspiration and inerrancy of Scripture seems at first sight to be problematic. Yet note the qualification of inerrancy to the original autographs; there is already even in this doctrinal statement a recognition of the finitude and hence fallibility of all human endeavors, including that of the transmission of Scripture. More important, however, is the implied dissonance between Peirce's scientific method and evangelical theological method. Whereas the apparent claim of evangelicals that theology must begin from the Bible would appear to conflict with Peirce's relegating the method of authority to second rank at best, I want to show that this discrepancy is much more a surface distinction than an essential one. I will do this by briefly commenting on the doctrine of the Wesleyan quadrilateral—that theology proceeds upon Scripture, tradition, reason, and experience—a model accepted by more and more evangelicals.[43] I will take up the elements of the quadrilateral in reverse of their usual order, since I think that the most problematic point is best handled after discussing the other three.[44]

Most evangelicals would agree that theology should not be completely divorced from experience and reason. To be sure, God is not nature or the world, but insofar as evangelicals believe that religious experiences are real encounters with God, these experiences can contribute in shaping and leading us to a deeper and more sure knowledge of God. Further, since many evangelicals are in agreement that the autonomy of reason is a misguided

43. Thorsen, *Wesleyan Quadrilateral*; see also the statement of a theologian respected among evangelicals, Albert Outler: "If we are to accept our responsibility for seeking *intellecta* for our faith, in any other fashion than a 'theological system' or, alternatively, a juridical statement of 'doctrinal standards,' then this method of a conjoint recourse to the fourfold guidelines of Scripture, tradition, reason, and experience, may hold more promise for an evangelical and ecumenical future than we have realized as yet" ("Wesleyan Quadrilateral—In John Wesley," 16–17). I find additional support for using Peirce in this way from Michael Raposa, who has himself coined a new term to describe Peirce's method of inquiry: *theosemiotic*. For Raposa, "Peirce's theory of inquiry supplies the rubric for what is, in essence, a complex theological method" (*Peirce's Philosophy of Religion*, 144). Let's see how this method compares with that recognized by evangelicals.

44. The alert reader will notice that whereas I began by proposing a dialogue between Peirce and a more Reformed version of conservative evangelicalism as exemplified by the general orientation of members in the ETS, I am now suggesting that such a dialogue may best be mediated by recourse to a theological method that is growing in prominence in the larger evangelical community. In doing so, however, I am hopeful not only to be sensitive to the plurality within the evangelical camp but also to engage the broader tradition with Peirce's ideas.

experiment in the history of thought, experience and reason are understood as two poles of the same process, in ways similar to that which was articulated by Peirce a century ago. Upon reflection, the value of Peirce's theory of experience and cognition for shedding light on the way we think, both practically and even theologically, cannot be disputed. The religious imagination also begins abductively, formulating hypotheses for reflection and criticism by others. Some of the results are eventually canonized as dogma by the community of theological inquirers, but these are always subject to later revision or even denunciation. This is consistent with the way we as religious individuals in communities actually formulate our theology. We begin with the vagueness of the concept, make it more determinate, and always revise it in light of later experiences.

This constant revision becomes increasingly relevant in assessing theological truth claims. It is especially so for those claims that have references other than strictly theological ones. The claim regarding the historical resurrection of Jesus is a case in point. This is a doctrine strenuously insisted upon by evangelicals. As implausible as the claim may be to the modern mentality, nevertheless, the only possible falsifying evidence is the production of the corpse of Jesus. Apart from this, the claim of the resurrection is the exception that Peirce warned us about, which is sustained by a certain degree of historical evidence and a massive traditional consensus. Meanwhile, the viability of the concept of resurrection has been recently reopened by the Omega Point theory as developed by the Tulane University physicist Frank Tipler. Tipler's Omega Point theory merits attention in this context if for no other reason than that it is an eschatological theory based on the infinite long run. It has been forged in part in dialogue with theologians like Teilhard de Chardin and Wolfhart Pannenberg, the latter being well known for his theory of *prolepsis*: the means by which the future affects the past.[45] When coupled with Peirce's insistence that "the mind works by final causation, and final causation is logical causation" (1.250), and that "the rational meaning of every proposition lies in the future" (5.427), to deny the possibility of the historical resurrection is to not only commit an unpardonable sin, but also violate Peirce's First Rule of Reason: "Do not block the way of

45. Tipler, *Physics of Immortality*. Tipler's theory has not, of course, gone uncriticized (e.g., Stoeger and Ellis, "Response"); but see also the two symposia in *Zygon: Journal of Religion and Science*, 30, nos. 2 and 3 (1995), which feature responses by Frank Birtel, Hans-Dieter Mutschler, Donald York, and Pannenberg himself. I mention Tipler not because I think he is right but because I think the evangelical case can only be strengthened if we enter into earnest discussion and strenuous debate with the larger theological public, one which includes secularists, those in other religious traditions, and even atheists!

inquiry" (1.135).[46] Evangelicals should not be content with a fideistic stance regarding the resurrection, but should join in the process of inquiry as to its historical credibility by utilizing more than just the historico-grammatical methods of textual interpretation at their disposal.

A point that has not been emphasized so far should be brought out at this time. Peirce did distinguish the arena of science from what he considered to be "vitally important topics." Science, he insisted, was concerned primarily with the truth, and only secondarily with practical instrumentality. In other words, Peirce distinguished between theory and practice. While the former should always be governed by the scientific method, in practice, and especially in matters of life which are of vital importance, "the wise man follows his heart and does not trust his head" (1.653). This is because "common sense, which is the resultant of the traditional experience of mankind, witnesses unequivocally that the heart is more than the head, and is in fact everything in our highest concerns, thus agreeing with my unproved logical theorem" (1.654). In this vein, he also acknowledged the role of human conscience. In the "Additament" to his "Neglected Argument" (1910), he asked bluntly, "Where would such an idea, say as that of God, come from, if not from direct experience? . . . open your eyes—and your heart, which is also a perceptive organ—and you see him" (6.493). Yet, Peirce lamented that books on the philosophy of religion, and by implication, theology, had been distorted by the intellectualist "who in his preface offers you his metaphysics as a guide for the soul, talking as if philosophy were one of our deepest concerns" (1.654). This is not to say, of course, that Peirce disdained speculative philosophical theology. His own theology was a highly speculative one; the characteristics of his theism were left purposefully vague. What is important is that Peirce reserved a place for the conservatism of tradition.[47] His rationalism and empiricism was thus tempered by his fallibilism, and connected to his theory of the communal aspect of truth. Peirce insisted that "truth is public."[48] Inquiry leads from individual opinion to communal

46. While Peirce admitted that "miracles are intrinsic elements of a genuine religion" (6.446) as part and parcel of his doctrine of *tychism*—that novelty and chance are elements of the world—he denied that the scientific method could ever prove or disprove miracles (1.90, 6.514). For further discussion, see Ayers, "C. S. Peirce on Miracles."

47. As William Davis puts it, "one of Peirce's most fundamental theses was that human reason is so weak that no individual ought to place overweening confidence in any truth he has discovered unless he can persuade all candid minds to agree with him (a thing most easily done in mathematics and accomplished only with great difficulty in most other fields)" (*Peirce's Epistemology*, 127).

48. Letter to William James, 13 June 1907, briefer version quoted in Perry, *Thought and Character*, 291.

or the more or less intersubjective consensus of all who care to engage in the disputed matter.

Evangelicals should applaud this pietistic, communal, consensual, and conservative element of Peirce's method of inquiry. What is important is that the community of investigators not hold its traditional consensus out as incorrigible like narrative communities potentially do. This is important since the fact that Christians have been bound by their consensus around a lengthy tradition has not prevented a diversity from developing around this unity. As is well known, there are at least three large-scale Christian stories: those of Orthodoxy, Catholicism, and Protestantism. The narrative of evangelical theology is but one within the last category, and is in itself surely not homogeneous. While each story can be fully coherent in itself, the question of theological truth demands that truth claims not just be asserted as such but that they engage universally, both within and without the broad contours of the Christian community—the boundaries of which, we must be reminded, are fluid rather than static—and that counterclaims be taken into consideration. So while the evangelical insistence on contextualizing the gospel message is therefore an important element of the *evangelion*, what is crucial is that truths of the gospel not distort the truths in other narrative traditions, and that both sets of truths—established beliefs about what is real—be rendered comprehensible together. Whereas evangelicals are finding creative means to acculturate the gospel, we are slower to develop means by which to acknowledge and lift up truths found in other traditions. We are slower still in acquiring more comprehensive theological frameworks with which to harmonize these truths.

If, however, evangelicals participate in the larger process of inquiry, one of their primary concerns will be establishing criteria for adjudicating truth claims. Final appeal cannot be made to that which is the product of finite rationality that is corrupted by the fall. Appeal is therefore made to Scripture or divine revelation. Here we come to the crux of the matter.

Peirce did consider the possibility of whether revelation may provide certain knowledge (1.143). While he did not think that it was philosophically possible to dismiss the idea of revelation, still, philosophy that proceeds upon reasoning can never establish certainty. On the other hand, even if revelation were divinely inspired, it is subject to human distortion. Further, the questions that arise as a result of the awareness of other canons and other claims to divine revelation cannot simply be dismissed, no matter what authority is claimed (5.381). For those who fear that the doctrine of fallibilism undermines religion, Peirce responded that "I can only say I am very sorry. The doctrine is true;—without claiming absolute certainty for it, it is *substantially* unassailable" (1.151). While acknowledging that dogmas such as the prohibition against murder are "practically and substantially infallible" (1.151), he did not think the church had any use either for mathematical or scientific infallibility.[49] Elsewhere, Peirce suggested that practical infallibility was "the only sense of the word in which *infallible* has any consistent meaning" (1.661). Thus, while Peirce was by no means reliant on the authority of any institution or church, he did grant a place for such within the structures of knowledge.

At the same time, evangelicals cannot, of course, surrender the centrality of Scripture without compromising their *raison d'être*. A more detailed assessment of the compatibility between the evangelical insistence on the priority of Scripture as the word of God and Peirce's method of inquiry would involve an application of the semiotic theory to the doctrinal statement. Questions like "What is the logic of the statement?"; "What are its referents and interpretants?"; and "What are its pragmatic implications?" would need to be investigated. The Bible as symbol must also be analyzed, and specific biblical statements that evangelicals appeal to as textual support for the doctrine of Scriptural priority and which at least on the surface seem to preclude other methods for accessing doctrinal and theological truth should be taken into consideration and subjected to semiotic analysis. Such considerations would be at the heart of a more complete dialogue between Peirce and evangelicals on the role of Scripture in religious knowledge.

Yet it is fair to say that for some (i.e., those raised as Christians), Scripture forms a part of what Plantinga and Alston call "basic beliefs," which are indubitable to some degree even in the Peircean sense. To pursue this line of thought, however, we would also need to acknowledge that the reading and comprehension of Scripture is a semiotic and interpretative activity,

---

49. With regard to analytic or mathematical truths, Peirce asked, "*how do you know* that *a priori* truth is certain, exceptionless, and exact? You cannot know it by *reasoning*. For that would be subject to uncertainty and inexactitude. Then, it must amount to this that you know it *a priori*; that is, you take *a priori* judgments at their own valuation, without criticism or credentials. That is barring the gate of inquiry" (1.144). Peirce did not deny that two plus two equals four, but distinguished between absolute and practical infallibility (4.237). Absolute infallibility "does not belong to the multiplication table" (2.75) due in part to the essence of mathematics as the study of pure hypotheticals (4.232–33, 5.567), but more so to the possibility of human error in calculation (4.478). Further, it does not follow from necessary truths that they are known with absolute certainty since the inconceivability of their denials can never be definitively confirmed (2.29). In another place, he notes that "we hope that in the progress of science its error will indefinitely diminish, just as the error of 3.14159, the value given for π, will indefinitely diminish as the calculation is carried to more and more places of decimals. What we call π is an ideal limit to which no numerical expression can be perfectly true" (5.565). Cf. also Sandra Rosenthal's discussion in *Charles Peirce's Pragmatic Pluralism*, 21–24.

one which is subject to greater and greater understanding and precision. Evangelicals who would insist on the Reformation motto of *sola Scriptura* would need to articulate a theory of experience over and against that of Peirce's that would enable them to say how we can come to a knowledge of Scriptural authority, trustworthiness, and inerrancy apart from what Peirce called the logic of reasoning and without running the gamut of the infinite long run. In other words, they would have to resort to either a fideism or a strong foundationalism of sorts, neither of which is desirable or particularly helpful. The value of Peirce's epistemology, perhaps delineated in far too much detail earlier, should now be evident. Human knowledge is intrinsically fallible given the epistemic process; yet this does not lead to skepticism or relativism, since our knowing aims for an accurate and truthful engagement with the world.[50]

What can be agreed upon at present is that the consideration of Scripture as a starting point for theological reflection does not entail that Scripture be utilized as a proof text, regardless of what the other sources of theology tell us. Evangelicals more than anyone should believe in the essential trustworthiness of Scripture precisely because its truth can only be corroborated and never disconfirmed by reality. Do evangelicals fear that reality and scripture can actually be at odds? The respected evangelical missionary Lesslie Newbigin, in attempting to outline the basis for a Christian conception of the gospel as public truth, suggested that the proper response to skepticism is not an appeal to more foundational beliefs or more ultimate realities, but living and publishing the truth and putting it to public test.[51] This is not far from Peirce's notion of a community of inquirers attempting to make its ideas clear. Christian truth can never be insulated from criticism; rather, its narrative must constantly be reassessed. Its coherence must be tested against that of other narratives, both within and without the Christian community, and whether or not it corresponds with reality must be demonstrated by reason and experience. At the same time, of course, Christian truth is eminently useful, and it is by living it that we can "taste and see

50. Of course, the ultimate test of evangelical fallibilism is our openness to entertaining the hypothesis that the Bible may not be the revealed word of God after all. This is the question that my teacher and Peircean scholar, Robert Neville, posed in response to an earlier draft of the paper which was the foundation for this chapter. My initial reply is that such should theoretically be possible. Yet, I cannot see any chain of circumstances which would cause an upswell of doubt such that further inquiry would not be able to resolve. In this sense, I would follow Peirce in dismissing such a potentiality as a "paper doubt" and set about dealing with the issues that demand our faithful attention such as attending to my children, preaching the Gospel, famines, global warming, and the like.

51. Newbigin, *Truth to Tell*, 33–35.

that the Lord is good" (Ps 34:8, NIV). Just as theological argumentation, like all other kinds of argumentation, does not proceed upon isolated threads of thought but upon interwoven strands of a complex of arguments, so also an evangelical theology should enable a critical correlation of Scripture, tradition, reason, and experience to attain true representations of God and the world.

Insofar as our primary objective has been to see how Peirce can be of assistance in our own task of negotiating the demise of foundationalism even while retaining a strong form of truth, this "dialogue" would finally stall if we did not at least briefly inquire into the ways in which evangelical theology may possibly complement or even correct the Peircean vision. We can, of course, begin by recognizing Peirce for what he was: a child of his age. While he was initially optimistic about the progressive evolution of the world toward concrete reasonableness, later in life he freed himself from the illusion that inquiry would continue endlessly since "the existence of the human race, we may be as good as sure, will come to an end at last" (5.587). From an evangelical perspective, we can also ask if the Peircean notion of the "community of inquirers" would have profited from a consideration of the history of the science of theology, given the perennial theological mode of investigation as that of faith seeking understanding. This would have enabled Peirce to give a more nuanced account of the process of inquiry rather than leaving the impression—which he oftentimes did—of science as driven purely by a disinterested quest for truth. Further, why did Peirce fail to give more serious thought to the idea of divine revelation in spite of the plausibility of such a concept within the overall framework of his philosophical theology and personalistic theism? And finally, although Peirce was correct to note that the human mind must indeed be attuned to reality in order to have stumbled upon so many correct hypotheses throughout the history of thought and of science, he overlooked at the same time the many wrong abductions, some of which produced results detrimental to the human race. Not all musers have come up with a clear notion of God. Some think they have experienced *satori,* or Buddhist enlightenment, while others have arrived at an ultimately radical evil—the Holocaust immediately comes to mind. This shows that there is always the possibility of a demonic element in the process of reasoning that lurks in the corners of the human mind. Our reasoning is undeniably tainted, and such recognition is at the root of the evangelical insistence on the fact of human finitude and on our need for the divine initiative. Many elements of Peirce's thought have been discarded or revised in the light of later findings, even as I am sure that a sustained engagement of Peirce with evangelical theology would bring other revisions and even dead ends to light. These misgivings aside, however, I see no good reason why evangelicals cannot learn and profit from Peirce in a mutual dialogue.

The general thesis of this chapter has been structured at least in part in response to the question posed by Richard Lints. I have argued that evangelicals do not have to choose between either the postmodernism of Tracy or the postliberalism of Lindbeck, nor is their only other alternative the antimodernism of Lints himself, whatever that may be; rather, the best of postmodernism and postliberalism should be put to work in the reconstruction and reformation of evangelical theology. I have argued that evangelicals are fully justified in their acceptance of non-foundationalism, and even in their attraction to narrative or community- and tradition-based forms of theology, so long as they do not think that these basic forms are infallible or immune from public criticism. Evangelicals may in this regard learn something from Peirce, whose non-foundationalism served as the basis for a fallibilistic epistemology that did not sacrifice the category of truth or truthfulness. Rather, his theory of experience and cognition allowed for the pursuit of truth within the context of a community of inquirers.[52] Of course, many aspects of Peirce's philosophy have been and continue to be disputed by those who know it well. But that is as he would have wanted it to be, and it is in the hopes that evangelicals can contribute another voice to this quest for truth that this essay is submitted.[53]

52. Other evangelicals have reached similar conclusions via different paths, including Kelvin Jones, "Formal Foundation," who argues for the abductive power of Scripture when applied to ontology.

53. This paper is dedicated to the memory of my friend, Stan Spicer (d. July 1999), whose patient reading of this and other articles published in the infancy of my professional career has saved an aspiring theologian from numerous grammatical blunders and conceptual confusions. (Stan, I will miss your friendship, humor, wisdom, intellect, cultural commentary, theological insight, and personal encouragement). Thanks are also due to Eben Yong for reading and commenting on earlier versions of this paper, and to Roger Olson (former editor of *Christian Scholars Review*) and the anonymous reviewers of the journal for their many detailed and helpful criticisms of previous drafts. It goes without saying that any remaining errors of fact or interpretation are mine alone.

CHAPTER 2

Pragmatist and Pragmaticist Trajectories for a Postmodern Theology

PRAGMATISM, EVEN IF LIMITED to its specifically North American and philosophical trajectories, is quite diverse.[1] Not only are pragmatist philosophers working in various areas—e.g., philosophy of science, linguistics, logic, social theory—but they are also debating issues of validity and legitimacy regarding developments within the tradition itself. It is inevitable that the classical pragmatism of Peirce, Royce, and James would have inspired a wide spectrum of philosophical projects, and that these would have been extended by the legacy of "middle pragmatists" such as Dewey, G. H. Mead, C. I. Lewis, and the Chicago School.[2] Even so, pragmatism was eclipsed during the middle of the twentieth century by logical positivism and analytic philosophy, only to be revived as a viable philosophical position in recent years by the emergence of neo-pragmatists like Hilary Putnam, Jeffrey Stout, and Richard Rorty.[3] But this last form of the movement has drawn

1. Thayer, *Meaning and Action,* discusses both European influences on the development of American pragmatism and British and Italian versions of pragmatism that developed during the late nineteenth and early twentieth centuries. Thayer's focus on the philosophical traditions of pragmatism means that he says little, if anything, about the forms of pragmatism that have emerged in the fields of communications, literature, politics, education, and law. Some of these areas are covered in Moore, *American Pragmatism,* and Diggins, *Promise of Pragmatism.*

2. See Rucker, *Chicago Pragmatists.* The nomenclature of "middle pragmatism" is drawn from Auxier, "Decline of Evolutionary Naturalism."

3. See, e.g., Avery, "Three Types," Gunn, *Thinking across,* and Goodman, ed., *Pragmatism.* My focus in this chapter will be on American neo-pragmatism, rather than the

vigorous responses, including some that have gone so far as to suggest that the neglect of Peirce and the purposeful misreading of James and, especially, Dewey by individuals like Rorty places neo-pragmatic thinkers outside the pragmatist tradition altogether.

My purpose in this chapter is to explore the potential contributions of American pragmatism to Christian theology in the postmodern world. Within this broader framework, then, we have not one but three heavily contested concepts or categories: pragmatism, postmodernism, and Christian theology.[4] How then should we proceed?

My strategy (the details of which will be defended along the way) will be to begin by taking up the neo-pragmatist challenge to Christian theology in our (postmodern) times by focusing our initial reflections on the work of Rorty, especially his polemic against philosophic method. From this, a sketch of a post-Rortyean—the equivalent of a post-neo-pragmatic—theology will emerge, that can be seen to dovetail nicely with postmodernist intuitions. What this leaves us with, however, are two distinctive redescriptions of our contemporary situation: one Rortyean and atheological, and the other post-Rortyean and theological. I suggest that one way of adjudicating these issues is by returning to the pragmaticism of Peirce, the unanimously acknowledged founder of American pragmatism. My hope is that so doing will also purchase for us the means to develop a truly viable and coherent postmodern theology for our time.

THE NEO-PRAGMATIST VISION OF RICHARD RORTY

On first thought, engaging the work of Richard Rorty (1931–2007) with its naturalistic and atheistic presuppositions would seem to be counterproductive if one's objective is to explore the question of how pragmatism intersects with Christian theology in our postmodern world. It would seem to be more fruitful to chart the ways in which theologians have drawn from and interacted with other strands of the pragmatist tradition. Yet I would urge

---

work of Continental thinkers like Jürgen Habermas and Karl-Otto Apel.

4. On Christianity—and, by extension, Christian theology—as a "heavily contested concept," see Sykes, *Identity of Christianity*. In one sense, everybody recognizes what we all mean by postmodernism. In other senses, however, postmodernism as a technical term is still under negotiation. I use it in the generic sense to identify the many ways in which contemporary theology senses the need to go beyond modernism even if the directions forward are not agreed upon. Perhaps our time may be better defined as "late modernity"—see, e.g., Neville, *Religion in Late Modernity*—but argument for that would take us well beyond the framework of this chapter. (See also Yong and Heltzel, "Robert Cummings Neville," esp. 29–34.)

that Rorty's neo-pragmatism not be neglected by theologians for a number of reasons. First, over the past generation, Rorty has emerged from the obscurities of mid-twentieth-century analytic and linguistic philosophy as a public figure in philosophical and cultural circles in twenty-first-century America. Even if his neo-pragmatist vision has not gone unchallenged, his fame is practically unparalleled among contemporary philosophers and his influence widespread.[5] In fact, generic keyword searches of any academic library database will reveal that about 10 percent of all items catalogued under pragmatist philosophy (and its cognates) are associated with Rorty in some way. Even more important, about half of all items catalogued under neo-pragmatist philosophy in the Online Computer Library Center First-Search databases are linked to Rorty or are responses to his work. Clearly, those wishing to reclaim the pragmatist tradition for theology will need to engage with Rorty's neo-pragmatism, at least to some degree.

This leads, second, to the further observation that such engagement is already taking place, albeit along different trajectories. This is specifically the case amidst the circles of theological liberalism where the ideas of Rorty in particular and neo-pragmatism generally are being developed in naturalistic directions.[6] In addition, however, other theological trends seem to be at least open to the kind of nonrealist philosophical assumptions long advocated by Rorty. Current movements like postliberalism and narrative theology have been understood by some along these lines, and influential theologians like Don Cupitt and D. Z. Phillips clearly advocate a nonrealist theological perspective. To engage with Rorty on this point from more realistic metaphysical and ontological presuppositions would therefore get at a wide range of issues presently debated in the theological world. And for those interested in this task, I suggest one way forward would be the retrieval of the pragmatist tradition, one trajectory of which Rorty's has been the leading voice.

But, finally, engaging Rorty is important because whereas there has been some attempt to do constructive theology with aid from the classical pragmatist tradition, Rorty's project has been consistently deconstructive. In that sense, his neo-pragmatist vision compares with the

---

5. See, e.g., Kolenda, *Rorty's Humanistic Pragmatism*; Malachowski, ed., *Reading Rorty*; Nielsen, *After Demise of Tradition*; Saatkamp Jr., ed., *Rorty and Pragmatism*; Langsdorf and Smith, eds., *Recovering Pragmatism's Voice*; Pettegrew, ed., *A Pragmatist's Progress?*; and Brandom, ed., *Rorty and His Critics*.

6. See, e.g., Anderson, *Pragmatic Theology*; Davaney, *Pragmatic Historicism*; and Hardwick and Crosby, eds., *Pragmatism, Neo-pragmatism, Religion*, many of the contributors to which are neo-pragmatists associated with the theological liberalism of the Highlands Institute conferences and seminars.

post-ontotheological turn in contemporary continental (especially French) philosophy. I suggest that insofar as the conversation between deconstruction and theology is now in full swing, engaging Rorty's neo-pragmatism would provide a distinctively American perspective on this wider discussion about the significance of contemporary postmodernism. And, if this conversation with the more radical neo-pragmatist vision of Rorty is even moderately successful, then the possibility of and prospects for an in-depth encounter between the broader American pragmatist tradition and Christian theology would indeed be secured. And what we would find in this case, I will argue, is a truly constructive kind of postmodern theology that gets us beyond mere "storytelling" to engaging with the world.

The question, however, is how such a constructive result can come from a conversation between contemporary theology and Rorty's project. This methodological issue is an important one since Rorty argues in the tradition of James and Whitehead that religion is what human beings should do in and with their solitariness. In distinguishing sharply between the public sociopolitical sphere of human intersubjective relations and the private religio-aesthetic sphere of individual and communal life, religious ideas are thereby either prohibited from the public square or admitted only if relatively innocuous regarding public issues. Attempts to bring religious topics into public conversations are therefore seen by Rorty to be "conversation stoppers."[7]

But is it the case that only religious and theological convictions end conversations? While not denying that they often do, in Rorty's case, the charge is seemingly ironic given his own stance against method. Here, Rorty builds specifically on recent developments in philosophy of science—e.g., by Kuhn, Toulmin, and Feyerabend—and in turn to hermeneutics.[8] In both cases, the demise of foundationalism means that there no longer exists an indubitable starting point for inquiry, and that rigidly defined operational methods are better understood as social conventions rather than as the keys to social or scientific advances. Progress in science and philosophy is understood in this new paradigm not as constrained externally by either reality (vis-à-vis the sciences) or truth (vis-à-vis philosophy), but as pragmatically motivated to enable better human coping. (For Rorty, the concept "true" is nonexplanatory; rather, it denotes the practical-causal relationship

7. See Rorty, "Religion as Conversation-Stopper," ch. 11 in his *Philosophy and Social Hope*.

8. See Rorty, *Philosophy and the Mirror of Nature*, Part Three. See also his "Science as Solidarity" and "Pragmatism without Method," both in *Objectivity, Relativism, and Truth*, 35–45 and 63–77 respectively. On Kuhn, see "Thomas Kuhn," in Rorty, *Philosophy and Social Hope*, 175–90.

between organisms and environments.) In fact, both disciplines are seen to operate according to differing human conventions and procedures, and not according to their own strictly defined logic. As such, following the later Wittgenstein, they are on one level incommensurable language games, the disparity of which needs to be respected even if both contribute in the long run to human happiness.[9] Rationality is redefined from being methodical to being morally virtuous—i.e., being tolerant and persuasive rather than forceful.[10] The implications for the conversations—philosophical and otherwise—Rorty wishes to continue include: movement from polemics to edifying chitchat; utilization of narrative redescription rather than critical argumentation; an ironic stance which draws from various traditions of discourse in an ad hoc way for purposes at hand, viz., to enable the speaker to do what she wants to do and get what she needs most efficiently. All of this follows inevitably from our postfoundationalist awareness that there are no mutually agreeable starting points or rules of engagement which must of necessity govern our interactions.[11]

In order to see the implications of this move, we need to take a short detour and get a close-up view of Rorty's philosophic "method" in action. His intention is to expose the pretenses of what he calls the Philosophic (capital P) tradition. Metaphysical, ontological, and epistemological questions from Plato through to Descartes, Kant, and modern thinkers have been misled by a representationalist view of language and ideas. Philosophy (with the capital P) has therefore been concerned to get things right, to access the truth, to accurately re-present reality in words. But what if all our efforts to check our words with reality itself fail since reality is linguistically engaged? What if all our endeavors to confirm the truth of our words lead only to other words rather than to reality itself? How will philosophers recognize solutions to their debates or successes regarding their reflections and hypotheses if all criteria are linguistically formulated, and all appeals to reality are linguistically mediated?[12] If this is the case, then the Philosophic quest has, for the most part, been wasting its time attempting to get to re-

9. See "Keeping Philosophy Pure," in Rorty, *Consequences of Pragmatism,* 19–36, and "Wittgenstein, Heidegger" in Rorty, *Essays on Heidegger and Others,* 50–65.

10. More recently, Rorty has defined moral progress as "a matter of wider and wider sympathy"; see his "Ethics without Principles" in *Philosophy and Social Hope,* 82.

11. My exposition of Rorty's anti-foundationalism does not mean to ignore the fact that there are viable counter-arguments; see, e.g., Triplett, "Rorty's Critique of Foundationalism," and Moser, "Does Foundationalism?"

12. This valid Peircean point is one of the primary theses of *Philosophy and the Mirror of Nature,* which Rorty saw as following from the difficulties that the linguistic turn in philosophy generated; see Rorty's "Metaphilosophical Difficulties."

ality or truth behind or beyond language. So how does Rorty accomplish this deconstruction of the Philosophic tradition? He realizes that he is in a catch-22. To undermine the tradition, he needs to engage Philosophy on its own terms and find it wanting. Yet to do so is to be constrained by the tradition's terms and categories and in that sense to perpetuate its discourse.[13]

Rorty's solution in *Philosophy and the Mirror of Nature* (1979) is to retell the history of Philosophy as built upon the mistaken quest for truth and reality behind language. As such, Philosophy is a provincial Western construction dominated first by ontotheological speculation and then by scientism, and followed consequentially by foundationalisms and dualisms of all kinds. Our Philosophical problems are therefore of our own making, mostly the result of our having simply changed the subject since we presented ourselves with insoluble questions. Philosophy should therefore be revisioned as one genre of discourse interconnected with other genres (the sciences included[14]) in the human conversation, and as serving primarily private functions of self-making and self-expression—what Rorty calls post-Philosophical philosophy—rather than the realm of public interests. Given the lack of finality and closure to philosophical conversation, then, we need to embrace the pluralism and historical situatedness of our vocabularies, and be cautious about the mirroring metaphors we use when exercising rhetorical power. In short, we need to shift from talk about correctness of representation to talk about warranted practices instead.

Now whatever we make of Rorty's project—keeping in mind both the somewhat misleading generalizations of the preceding paragraphs and that criticisms of Rorty's project have not abated since the publication of *Philosophy and the Mirror of Nature*—clearly he has deployed the discourse of Philosophy for his own purposes precisely by redescribing it as driven by inner contradictions. The result is an exposé of its questions as non-questions, and an argument for a post-Philosophical philosophy of edifying conversation for its own sake. If critics charge Rorty with impropriety in his retelling of the history of philosophy, he can respond that he is not providing argument

---

13. Recognition of this dilemma pervades Rorty's corpus; see, e.g., *Essays on Heidegger*, 94–95. Clearly, Rorty has rather arbitrarily lumped all he does not like about the philosophic tradition into Philosophy. But, as will be clear momentarily, he is intentionally re-presenting the tradition in this way to accomplish his own philosophical agenda. To correct Rorty's reading of Philosophy as a misrepresentation is beyond the scope of this chapter.

14. For Rorty's redescriptions of philosophy, literature, and science in a nutshell, see "Texts and Lumps," in *Objectivity, Relativism, and Truth*, 78–92, where he urges that philosophical ideas and doctrines need to be assessed in ways similar to the analysis of lumps by scientists and the analysis of texts by literary critics in order to be worth their philosophical salt!

but simply narrating another (better) way of envisioning the tradition (and is that not what all historical reconstruction is at least in part about?[15]). If other critics then dismiss Rorty's neo-pragmatism as an illegitimate exercise of poetic, literary, and rhetorical license, he can complain that they are not taking his Philosophic (re)descriptions seriously. His point, however, is to negate the inextricable conundrums of Philosophy in order to make room for philosophy understood as private conversation in liberal, democratic societies.

Undoubtedly, the genius of Rorty's approach has been confirmed repeatedly over the past twenty-plus years given the widespread hearing his project has gained. But, ironically, this demonstrates my point that while designed to fuel conversation in democratic societies, Rorty's attempts to promote "edifying discussion" could just as well terminate engagement prematurely.[16] Insofar as he neither provides nor wishes to present arguments for his proposals, how can his views be engaged? More to the point, because Rorty's "arguments" are made through large-scale historical reconstructions, he "resolves" the traditional problematics in ways similar to what he claims the Philosophical tradition has done: precisely by changing the subject and redefining them away. The differences are twofold. First, Rorty (and, by implication, ourselves) has finally recognized Philosophical problematics and pseudo-questions. Second, while the tradition has attempted to do Philosophy by drawing upon witnesses (in the Philosophical tradition) to build an argument, Rorty's retrievals of previous thinkers and his appropriation of the work of peers and colleagues are ad hoc—what Rorty, following the literary critic Harold Bloom, calls "strong misreadings"[17]—consciously incorporating and weaving in ideas conducive to his own vision even while ignoring or explaining away counterpositions. Hence, only with difficulty

15. See Rorty's "Inquiry as Recontextualization: An Anti-Dualist Account of Interpretation" in *Objectivity, Relativism, and Truth*, 93–110, and "Historiography of Philosophy: Four Genres" in Rorty, *Truth and Progress*, 247–73. The latter piece discusses historical reconstructions; rational or systematic reconstructions; *Geistgeschichte* as canon formation (e.g., Hegel); and finally, the dubious and generic doxographies we can do without. Rorty sees the first three as combining to enable human beings to use the past to cope with the present and the future.

16. I am grateful to James K. A. Smith for helping me see this point. See also Comay, "Interrupting the Conversation," for an assessment of Rorty the conversation stopper.

17. "Strong misreadings" are accomplished by textual critics who do not seek to understand texts on their own or their authors' terms. Rather, the critic "simply beats the text into a shape which will serve his own purpose. He makes the text refer to whatever is relevant to that purpose. He does this by imposing a vocabulary—a 'grid,' in Foucault's terminology—on the text which may have nothing to do with any vocabulary used in the text or by its author, and seeing what happens" (Rorty, *Consequences of Pragmatism*, 151).

can Rorty be critically engaged.[18] He can always counter that the criticism succeeds only if based on the presuppositions that his redescriptions have exploded. Failing that, Rorty can continue to change the subject, call upon a different set of criteria, play off other aspects of the thinkers and sets of ideas under discussion, or expand the scope of the story that needs retelling.[19] At the end of the day, if Rorty has his way in redefining moral virtuosity as tolerance, there will be no possibility for authentic engagement since public conversation can only proceed among those of like minds who either already agree on the contours of the story and the validity of the criteria, or have agreed to tolerate opposing ideas as private opinions unworthy of public dispute. Is it not, then, Rorty's neo-pragmatism that has terminated the conversation abruptly?

But engage Rorty we must, if only at the level of the thought experiment that follows. To do so, however, we need to take Rorty seriously on his own terms so as to minimize the risk of his changing the subject, etc. I propose to do this by taking his advice and following out the consequences of central neo-pragmatist ideas for religion and theology. The conviction I share with Rorty, and which we both derive from Peirce, is that human beliefs are habits of activity, and that the clarity of ideas can only be achieved by following out their consequences. In this case, of course, my habits as a religious person and as a theologian are going to lead me to read Rorty religiously and theologically. Here, I admit to following Rorty's example of selectively rereading his ancestors and peers according to his own purposes. But insofar as the driving question for me is what pragmatism contributes to theology in our (postmodern) world, to that extent I hope to draw constructively from Rorty's neo-pragmatist project. Following out the consequences of pragmatism therefore requires me to take one of those consequences— Rorty's neo-pragmatic vision—seriously, precisely in order to be able to trace the kinds of habits and actions that it has spawned and nurtured, and to assess the viability of pragmatism in all its complexity for theology. As such, I seek what Peter Ochs, following Peirce, has called a "performative solution" to the question that drives this chapter, motivated by the conviction that only by doing—in this case, the activity of theologizing—can the

18. David L. Hall makes these points clear in *Richard Rorty*, esp. 4–6 and 138–40.

19. Rorty advises: "When you find yourself at an argumentative impasse, baffled by your opponent's refusal to stop asking questions which you think you really should not have to answer, you can always shift the ground by raising questions about the vocabulary he or she is using. You can point out that the issue is biased in one's opponent's favor by the unfortunate jargon which has developed, a jargon which gives one's opponent an unfair advantage. You can use historical narratives to show why the issue previously discussed is moot and why it needs to be reformulated in terms which are, alas, not yet available"; see Rorty, "Philosophy without Principles," 135.

divergent, seemingly contradictory, and perhaps broken practices emergent from the religious intuitions of both classical and new pragmatisms be repaired.[20]

TOWARD A POST-RORTYEAN AND POSTMODERN THEOLOGY

Our goal in this section is to sketch the contours of pragmatist theology in dialogue with Rorty's neo-pragmatism. The "post-Rortyean" locution therefore plays a double role, calling attention to what a pragmatist theology might look like following after Rorty on the one hand and yet specifically retrieving theological discourse against Rorty's atheistic presuppositions on the other. The result, it will be seen, also holds promise for Christian theology in our postmodern situation.[21] But beware that I intend here to employ a strong misreading of Rorty's project, and to do so in order to suggest connections with various developments in the contemporary theological scene. I am aware that the proposed connections are both underdeveloped and unargued, but do so precisely because I believe the linkages can be made and that Rortyean insights can be retrieved and reappropriated in a Rortyean way in dialogue with a number of recently emergent theological projects. The reader will need to determine in the process whether such a reading can be fair to Rorty and retain its theological integrity at the same time. In what follows, then, I delineate a post-Rortyean, postmodern, and pragmatist theology in five theses, and then raise the question of how such a theological use of Rorty's neo-pragmatism can be justified given his atheistic secularism.

---

20. Ochs, "Sentiment of Pragmatism."

21. A good beginning toward a post-Rortyean and post/modern theology is Greenway Jr., "Richard Rorty's Revised Pragmatism." Greenway provides a very sympathetic account of Rorty's neo-pragmatism, and suggests ways in which elements of Rorty's views on truth, language, argument, reason, knowledge, and tradition could inform Christian understandings. Yet in the end, Greenway finds Rorty's neo-pragmatism deficient at key points—e.g., his neo-Sartrean humanism; his problematic modernistic assumptions (despite all of his diatribes against dualism, his world view is nevertheless shaped fundamentally by a reaction to/against transcendence, and imbued with modernist ideals/notions of individualistic self-creation and self-authentication); and his axiological solipsism, which leaves him unable to recognize the other as other and therefore does not have the capacity to fulfill his vision of human solidarity—and draws from Charles Taylor's holistic approach that seeks to sustain rather than collapse the tensions between immanence and transcendence precisely through finding eschatological hope in the Judeo-Christian faith. I will return to some of Greenway's criticisms later.

The first three theses of a post-Rortyean pragmatic theology derive from his description of pragmatism as being non-essentialistic, non-dualistic, and non-foundationalistic.[22] Briefly, Rorty's *non-essentialism* is the doctrine that things and realities are what they are *only* in relationship to other things and realities. More specifically, with regard to human beings, they are what our languages identifies them to be, keeping in mind always that as our vocabularies change, so also does our understanding of things. Here, we are at the heart of Rorty's nominalism and antirealism (or nonrealism).[23] As already mentioned, there is no getting behind our languages to the intrinsic essence of things in themselves. Kant's doctrine of the *noumena* was a colossal mistake comprehensible only within the framework of the representationalist theory of knowledge. This leads, second, to pragmatism as *non-dualistic*, especially with regard to the lexicon handed down by the Philosophical tradition. If no valid distinctions can be drawn between reality itself and language (or linguistic schemes, or the categories), neither can meaningful distinctions exist between phenomena and noumena; between "for itself" and "for us"; between is and ought; between facts and values; between objects and subjects; between ontology and epistemology; between the transcendent and the empirical, etc.—except, of course, conventional distinctions for purposes of edifying conversation. The web of interrelatedness in which we find ourselves is suggestive here of a holist view of reality and of human understanding of it. Here, we come to Rorty's coherentism and rejection of the correspondence view of truth. Rather than getting at the truth or at reality as it is, pragmatism as anti-dualism is best understood as "an attempt to serve transitory purposes and solve transitory problems."[24]

22. Rorty, "Pragmatism, Relativism, and Irrationalism," in his *Consequences of Pragmatism*, 162–66. See also the three essays in Part II of *Philosophy and Social Hope* for an elaboration on these features of pragmatism.

23. Herein lay the roots of Rorty's nominalism. Following Wittgenstein's notion of vocabulary as tools, language is similarly conceived as different sets of tools for different purposes: "For we nominalists think that the realm of possibility expands whenever somebody thinks up a new vocabulary, and thereby discloses (or invents—the difference is beside any relevant point) a new set of possible worlds" (*Essays on Heidegger*, 127).

24. Rorty, *Philosophy and Social Hope*, xxii. But it is also important to note Rorty does not deny the correspondence theory totally. He notes only the triviality of its level of applicability—e.g., "the cat is on the mat"—pointing out its incapacity to provide justification for large-scale, metaphysical, world view, and theological theories: "At this level of abstraction, concepts like truth, rationality, and maturity are up for grabs. The only thing that matters is which way of reshaping them will, in the long run, make them more useful for democratic politics. Concepts are, as Wittgenstein taught us, uses of words. Philosophers have long wanted to understand concepts, but the [Marxist] point is to change them so as to make them serve our purposes better"; see Rorty,

Finally, pragmatism's *non-foundationalism* emphasizes the radical contingency of all starting points.[25] Rorty is especially concerned with undermining both transcendentalist a priori and empiricist a posteriori approaches as giving indubitable and certain epistemic results. As a pragmatist, however, he denies that either skepticism or relativism ensues, since these assume both the epistemological representationalism that Rorty denies and a neutral ground from which to discern the relativity of all linguistic and conceptual schemes, which Rorty rejects as unavailable.[26] Rather, as he repeatedly emphasizes, the cash value of beliefs lie in the habits of successful action they inculcate.

From this, thesis 1: a neo-pragmatist theology would read Rorty's non-essentialism as emphasizing the intrinsic interrelatedness of all things. Things exist in a web of relationships, horizontally with one another, and vertically in relationship with and dependence upon God. God, in this view, is intimately related to creation, especially as revealed in the incarnational and pentecostal narratives. Thus, no thing or reality exists in, of, or for itself; such can only be nonbeing. Rather, the clue to reality's form and structure is to be intuited from the theological vision of God as triune relationality. The ancient doctrine of *perichoresis,* which envisions the divine life as constituted by three relationships, enables our own transition from an Aristotelian metaphysics of substance toward a Trinitarian (and postmodern) metaphysics of relationality.[27] Things, persons, realities, etc., are what they are precisely through their relational configurations.

Thesis 2: a neo-pragmatist theology would also emphasize the ontological and epistemological holism that emerges from Rortyean non-dualism. Ontologically, the unity of the world is a corollary of its createdness by God. Epistemologically, the beautiful, the true, and the good cannot be sundered for theological reasons. To be related to God therefore is to participate in the divine life; to know God personally in and through Jesus Christ, who is the way, the truth, and the life; to love God with all our heart, mind, and

---

"Universality and Truth," 25.

25. Argued in detail in *Philosophy and Mirror of Nature* and in Part I of *Contingency, Irony, and Solidarity.*

26. See Rorty, *Consequences of Pragmatism,* 166–69, and *Truth and Progress,* 51. Rorty's claim, "[A] belief can still regulate action, can still be taught worth dying for, among people who are quite aware that this belief is caused by nothing deeper than contingent historical circumstance," is the fundamental premise of his *Contingency, Irony, and Solidarity* (Rorty, *Contingency, Irony, and Solidarity,* 189).

27. The emergence of relationality as axiomatic in contemporary theology is widespread. Representative studies include Oliver, *Relational Metaphysic*; Jansen, *Relationality and God*; Loder and Neidhardt, *Knight's Move*; Peters, *God as Trinity*; Grenz, *Social God and Relational Self*; and Shults, *Reforming Theological Anthropology.*

strength, and to love our neighbor as ourselves.[28] As such, neo-pragmatic theology would be just as impatient as Rorty regarding the abstract, technical, and finally useless jargon bequeathed both by the Philosophical and classical theological traditions, especially as mediated through the dualistic presuppositions of the modern period.[29] Alternatively, the Kierkegaardian and Polanyian notions of personal knowledge become much more attractive, as do feminist and environmentalist perspectives, with their emphasis on holistic and participatory epistemologies.

Thesis 3: a neo-pragmatic theology would embrace Rorty's non-foundationalism as starkly depicting the contingencies and fallibilism of the human interpretive situation. Conditioned as we are by our historical situatedness and fallenness, we see through a glass dimly the light of divine self-revelation, which will be fully illuminated only in the eschaton. The neo-pragmatic–non-foundationalist conviction suggests that any starting point—whether, for example, any of the stools of the Wesleyan quadrilateral of Scripture, tradition, reason, and experience—turned into the ultimate theological foundation results in idolatrous compromise—again, to follow the example, of fundamentalism, traditionalism, liberalism, etc., respectively. We should thus acknowledge we proceed from within the hermeneutical circle rather than presume to do theology from any allegedly neutral, universal, or ahistorical vantage point. Life in the Spirit requires that theological method continuously negotiate the tensions between Scripture, tradition, community, the demands of reason, etc., rather than establish any one as more foundational than the others. This accurately describes our increasing awareness of the new era that has arisen in theology. Rorty's arguments against method can be understood as reflecting intuitions that the old ways of philosophizing have broken down. So also does the contemporary concern with theological method reflect our own attempts to legitimate the ways we do and should theologize in our postfoundationalist (and postmodern) times.[30]

---

28. See, e.g., Clark, *To Know and Love God*, esp. chs. 7 and 12.

29. Thus it is that Rorty sees his own program of deconstruction as ultimately curative and healing, tearing down roadblocks previously set up so as to enable our recovery from the wounds of dualism inflicted by the Platonist and modernist traditions such as epistemological skepticism, transcendental idealism, absolute idealism, logical constructionism, and phenomenology (see *Truth and Progress*, 109 and 154). On this point, then, Roger Lundin's assessment in "Deconstructive Therapy" is on the mark, even if it is more a cultural than substantively theological analysis.

30. The proliferation of books on method in a postfoundationalist world is staggering. I interact with the literature and defend a moderate Peircean kind of foundationalism which I call "shifting foundationalism" in my *Spirit-Word-Community*.

From all of this, thesis 4: a neo-pragmatic theology enables us to give more specific and theologically substantive meaning to the notion of language's irreducible centrality, especially its narrative structure. Here, I am referring not only to Rorty's claim that there is no getting behind language to any nonlinguistic reality, and that it's language all the way down;[31] In addition, a neo-pragmatic theology's hermeneutics of suspicion against the (essentialistic, dualistic, and foundationalistic) discourses of modernity sustains the recovery of language as set within a narrative framework as a (if not the) primary medium of engagement. Here, Rorty's strategic deployment of narrative redescription is paralleled by the turn to narrative in theology during the past generation.[32] Abstract rationalism is hereby replaced with concrete narratives and personal testimony which are better able to recontextualize the biblical genres. Rorty's notion of "strong misreading" can itself be understood as the means through which the redemptive reconstitution of human lives and communities is accomplished. The biblical message is nothing if not the good news that our own stories, traditions, and memories are not what we have made them out to be, because they are given new significance in the story of Jesus Christ.[33] While I would agree with those who see this as an opportunity for Christians to reassert their rightful place in the (postmodern) public square alongside other (communal and personal) narratives, this does raise the question of what Rorty calls "ethnocentrism" for a neo-pragmatic theology.

Given the interconnectedness (theological and otherwise) sketched here between narrative saying and doing, thesis 5: a neo-pragmatist understanding "grounds" and judges Christian beliefs not primarily by its propositional claims, but by its social and communal praxis. This reflects two related neo-pragmatist convictions. First, we should change the question from "How should we describe them?" to "What should we *do* about such intuitions?" After all, the achievement of consensus (a communal language of solidarity), if possible at all, will be accomplished practically, not philosophically: "by acts of making rather than of finding."[34] Second, however, given our postfoundationalistic situation, our beliefs and prac-

---

31. Most clearly elaborated in Rorty, "The World Well Lost," in *Consequences of Pragmatism*, 3–18.

32. Beginning with McClendon Jr., *Biography as Theology*, and Frei, *Eclipse of Biblical Narrative*.

33. Here, I agree with James K. A. Smith that the biblical story avoids the postmodern critique of metanarratives because the latter are founded upon the (modern) confidence in reason while the former are testimonies (of communities) from faith to faith; see Smith, "Little Story About Metanarratives."

34. Rorty, "Pragmatism and Philosophy," in *Consequences of Pragmatism*, xxx–xxxi.

tices are inevitably socially and communally formed and influenced. Rorty encourages us to embrace this as part of our unavoidable ethnocentrism,[35] the fact that we possess no ahistorical God's-eye-view on things. Theory, in short, is borne out in social, communal, and liberative practice.

"Amen to this!" the neo-pragmatist theologian should say. I would read Rorty's "ethnocentric turn" as participating in the larger reaction to the Cartesian and Kantian turns to the subject. Here, neo-pragmatism's way was paved by the earlier Peircean, Roycean, and Meadean turns to the community, even as it finds expression in contemporary socio-ethical and communitarian theologies. But more specifically, communities are not only sites of ideas, but also spaces of habits, practices, and ways of being in the world. As such, the beliefs and doctrines of theological communities emerge from and find their justification and warrant in their liturgies, piety, activities, and ethical relationships, rather than the other way around. In this case, Christian theology in our time needs to be accountable not to some standard of rationality or set of criteria extrinsic to itself, but rather to the liberative practices and activities of Christian communities.[36]

Yet at the same time, this awareness of the centrality of communal praxis to theology should also sound an alarm, since the growing irrelevance of Christian thinking could be due to the fact that Christian communities are increasingly secularized.[37] I am thinking, for example, of our reliance on medicine rather than on divine healing; our dependence on technology rather than on prayer; our scientific rationality rather than pervasive God-consciousness and piety or transformative action. This being the case, the loss of faith is just as much, if not more, a matter of social and communal praxis as it is a matter of maintaining intellectual integrity in our (postmodern) world. In fact, cognitive dissonance is precisely the result of the failure of the practices of the church to mediate genuinely liberating

35. "To be ethnocentric is to divide the human race into the people to whom one must justify one's belief and the others. The first group—one's *ethnos*—comprises those who share enough of one's belief to make fruitful conversation possible. In this sense, everybody is ethnocentric when engaged in actual debate, no matter how much realist rhetoric about objectivity he produces in his study" (Rorty, *Objectivity, Relativism, and Truth*, 30).

36. Thus the importance here of Pietist, experiential, and liberation theologies. In addition, however, mainline theological reflection is increasingly acknowledging the centrality of social practices to Christian doctrine. See, e.g., Hütter, *Suffering Divine Things*; Buckley and Yeago, eds., *Knowing Triune God*; Volf and Bass, eds., *Practicing Theology*; and McClendon Jr., *Systematic Theology*, Vol. 1: *Ethics*. For my own analysis of McClendon's project, see Yong, "'Baptist Vision' of McClendon, Jr."

37. I am indebted to Robbins' "Belief in God" for the general point I am making in this paragraph.

engagements with the divine. In short, what Christian theism needs is to re-envision how our social practices might enable us to experience God in authentic ways, such that our behaviors revitalize theistic language in our time instead of our persisting with such language uncritically, sentimentally, and mechanically.

At this point, it will be clear that I have accomplished a strong (!) misreading of Rorty's neo-pragmatism by bringing it into dialogue with especially recent developments in Christian theology. By doing so, I can be said to have either baptized neo-pragmatism for theological purposes or recontextualized theology within a neo-pragmatic framework (or both). I have previously justified such an approach as imitating Rorty's own procedure of ad hoc narrative redescription. The five theses proposed are not in any particular order of importance or significance, and are not designed as an argument either against Rorty or toward achieving any particular goal, except to explore the question: what would theology in our postmodern world look like in dialogue with at least this one stream of American pragmatism?

The result, however, raises the question of whether or not a genuine dialogue can take place in this way. Can strong misreadings of Rorty's neo-pragmatism be respectable hermeneutically or retain the integrity of theology? This is an important question, especially in light of Rorty's anti-realism, coherentism, and avowed atheistic secularism and naturalism, among other issues. Can a pragmatic theology succeed given these presuppositions? Granted, Rorty does not insist on the incompatibility of pragmatism and theism.[38] Yet he is also clear that in his view, "there is nothing deep down inside us except what we have put there ourselves, no criterion that we have not created in the course of creating a practice, no standard of rationality that is not an appeal to such a criterion, no rigorous argumentation that is not obedience to our own conventions."[39] He explicitly says that his own project is an effort to "see what happens if we (in Sartre's phrase) 'attempt to draw the full conclusions from a consistently atheistic position.'"[40] If this is the case, then it is not so much a question of what right we have to usurp Rorty's neo-pragmatism for theological purposes, but rather a question of

---

38. In "Religious Faith, Intellectual Responsibility," Rorty writes: "Pragmatist theists are not anthropocentrists, in the sense of believing that God is a 'mere posit.' They believe that God is as real as sense impressions, tables, quarks and human rights. But, they add, stories about our relations to God do not necessarily run athwart the stories of our relations to these other things" (*Philosophy and Social Hope*, 156). See also Rorty's sympathetic comparison of Dewey and Tillich in *Objectivity, Relativism, and Truth*, 69–71, and his "Pragmatism as Romantic Polytheism."

39. Rorty, *Consequences of Pragmatism*, xlii.

40. Rorty, *Truth and Progress*, 48–49.

whether a pragmatism that is shot through with atheistic presupposition would sabotage the pragmatic-theological enterprise at its roots. Why render theology vulnerable to a counterattack from within the ranks of a post-Rortyean framework? Why even begin to "consort with the enemy" when we have been forewarned about being unequally yoked?

My response at this point, in addition to the arguments for engaging Rorty presented at the beginning of this chapter, is that the preceding ruminations take off from Rorty's "method" as much as than they do from the content of his neo-pragmatism. Of course, on Rortyean premises, there is no strict dualism between scheme and content, nor is there an essence to his neo-pragmatism that renders it immune to being kidnapped and used illegitimately for theological purposes. My license for proceeding therefore comes with at least that warning from Rorty. Yet this thought experiment with Rorty's neo-pragmatism occurs within the larger project of exploring the possibility of a pragmatic theology for our (postmodern) times. And the result, for purposes at hand, are the five theses proposed above. Should or must we, however, choose between either Rorty's neo-pragmatism or its theological rendition? If yes, how do we decide?

Certainly on Rorty's account, there is no possibility of providing definitive argument for or against either proposal.[41] Each will need to be weighed on the merits of their overall plausibility by "us" (whether it be the liberals in Rorty's camp or the theologians in mine), according to "our" best lights. Since there is no neutral ahistorical framework within which to adjudicate between these differing narratives, we can only proceed from our own ethnocentric commitments. Here, the conversation could terminate if further dialogue were deemed either impossible or without value. In fact, to even attempt to adjudicate the issues risks shutting down the conversation since criteria for assessment would need to be invoked, and such are potentially oppressive mechanisms that sin against the pragmatist—specifically, Peircean—dictum: "Do not block the path of inquiry."[42]

---

41. E.g., "On my view, the only thing that can displace an intellectual world is another intellectual world—a new alternative, rather than an argument against an old alternative. The idea that there is some neutral ground on which to mount an argument against something as big as 'logocentrism' strikes me as one more logocentric hallucination" (Rorty, *Essays on Heidegger*, 121).

42. Rorty writes (in chronological order): "On the pragmatist account, a criterion (what follows from the axioms, what the needle points to, what the statute says) *is* a criterion because some particular social practice needs to block the road of inquiry, halt the regress of interpretations, in order to get something done" (*Consequences of Pragmatism*, xli); and: "Attempts to erect 'rules' or 'criteria' turn into attempts to hypostatize and eternalize some past or present practice, thereby making it more difficult for that practice to be reformed or gradually replaced with a different practice"; and, we

But is this actually the case? What if I were to draw upon pragmatist resources to arbitrate between Rorty's atheistic neo-pragmatism and my proposed pragmatic theism? Would it violate the terms of the discussion or Rorty's neo-pragmatism to assess its theological fruits by invoking its own pragmatist criteria? I should think not. In any case, the validity of a pragmatist theological proposal lies in its fit within the pragmatist tradition. In this case, I am answerable not only to Rorty's neo-pragmatist discourse but also to the larger tradition of American pragmatism. It is thus not only permissible but in some senses incumbent upon me to make my case within this larger framework. And, I want to suggest in what follows, there are resources from this larger tradition, specifically the pragmaticism of Peirce, which enable us to do precisely what has been accomplished above: to salvage what is valuable in Rorty's neo-pragmatism for a pragmatic theology in our time.

A PRAGMATICIST HIGHROAD AROUND THE CONTEMPORARY THEOLOGICAL IMPASSE

The flowering of Rorty's neo-pragmatist vision retrieves and builds on only select trajectories of the classical tradition of American pragmatism. Of the recognized fountainheads of classical pragmatism—Peirce, James, and Dewey—Rorty's project rejects Peirce altogether, revisions James's pragmatic theory of truth, and relies most heavily on (a strong and illegitimate misreading of, some would insist) the humanistic rather than scientific side of Dewey.[43] The result is that some commentators identify two

should think of rationality "not as the application of criteria (as in a tribunal) but as the achievement of consensus (as in a town meeting, or a bazaar)," to be achieved precisely through civilized democratic processes, without referees (*Objectivity, Relativism, and Truth*, 217 and 220); finally, "Reading Kuhn led me . . . to think that instead of mapping culture on to a epistemico-ontological hierarchy topped by the logical, objective and scientific, and bottoming out in the rhetorical, subjective and unscientific, we should instead map culture on to a sociological spectrum ranging from the chaotic left, where criteria are constantly changing, to the smug right, where they are, at least for the moment, fixed" (*Philosophy and Social Hope*, 180). While I agree with Rorty that we are all historically situated—i.e., without access to context-independent criteria and norms—I disagree that this means all of our criteria or norms are unreliable or that they are context bound. Here, of course, I am presuming, against Rorty, that truth is *not only* whatever our communities of discourse will enable us to get away with. I return to this point in the last section.

43. I do not intend to adjudicate the debate concerning Rorty's relationship to Dewey. For the clearest statement of how Rorty sees his own relationship to Dewey, see "Dewey's Metaphysics," in *Consequences of Pragmatism*, 72–89. For details of the arguments for and against Rorty's use of Dewey, see Nielsen, *After the Demise of Tradition*, ch. 8; Hall, *Richard Rorty*, ch. 2; Gouinlock, "Legacy of Instrumentalism"; Gunn,

traditions of pragmatism: a methodological and realistic strand beginning with Peirce and continuing through one side of Dewey to contemporary speculatively and philosophically inclined forms of pragmatism, and a humanistic strand stretching from the other side of Dewey through to Rorty's neo-pragmatism.[44] Because my own inclinations are with the Peircean trajectory, my intention in what follows is to draw him into the conversation in order to see whether there are resources from within pragmatism itself to adjudicate between Rorty's undertaking and my own outline of a neo-pragmatic theology.

Yet I proceed with fear and trembling, knowing that Rorty's dismissal of Peirce cannot be attributed to ignorance. In commenting on the work of Peircean-inspired semiotician Umberto Eco, Rorty confessed that early in his Philosophical career, his desire to understand Peirce

> led me to waste my 27th and 28th years trying to discover the secret of Charles Sanders Peirce's esoteric doctrine of "the reality of Thirdness" and thus of his fantastically elaborate semiotico-metaphysical "System." I imagined that a similar urge must have led the young Eco to the study of that infuriating philosopher, and that a similar reaction must have enabled him to see Peirce as just one more whacked-out triadomaniac.[45]

Peirce's metaphysics was linked with his logic and scientific experimentalism—Peirce was a capable astronomer at the Harvard College Observatory and physicist at the US Coast and Geodetic Survey—and these were repudiated along with the Philosophical tradition in due course. Rorty's post-Peircean journey has thus led him to acknowledge only Peirce's anti-Cartesianism and semiotic "exaltation of language" as being of value.[46] So far as Rorty is concerned, Peirce's "contribution to pragmatism was merely to have given it a name, and to have stimulated James. Peirce himself remained the most Kantian of thinkers—the most convinced that philosophy

---

"Pragmatism, Democracy"; and Sleeper, "Rorty's Pragmatism" and "Pragmatics of Deconstruction."

44. The most elaborate argument along these lines so far is Mounce, *Two Pragmatisms*. Rescher, *Realistic Pragmatism*, esp. 64–65 and 244–49, also distinguishes between what he calls realistic and relativistic versions of pragmatism. Developments on the speculative side of pragmatism can be found throughout the pages of the *Transactions of the Charles S. Peirce Society*. See also Rescher, *Methodological Pragmatism*, and Rosenthal, *Speculative Pragmatism*. For a countering genealogy defending the Rortyean extension of classical pragmatism, see Murphy, *Pragmatism*.

45. Rorty, in *Philosophy and Social Hope*, 134. The fruits of Rorty's early labors on Peirce can be tasted in Rorty, "Pragmatism, Categories, and Language."

46. Rorty, "Response to Charles Hartshorne," 33.

gave us an all-embracing ahistorical context in which every other species of discourse could be assigned its proper place and rank."[47]

But here I am responsible not to Rorty, but to Peirce—and, I would suggest, so is Rorty. Insofar as he seeks to cultivate and nurture the edifying conversation of philosophy, he is obligated, especially after providing strong misreadings of the tradition, to attend to any forthcoming response on behalf of those he has (mis)appropriated. In what follows then, I can only very briefly outline Peirce's own response to the problematic sketched at the end of section two—regarding the issues of realism vs. antirealism; of correspondence vs. coherence views of truth; and of pragmatism and the God question—in order to push through to the question of whether or not the integrity of a neo-pragmatically-framed theology is inevitably compromised. In the process, I suggest not only that Peirce provides satisfactory responses to preserve the possibility of a convergence between pragmatism and theology today, but that he also gives us, in the words of Robert Cummings Neville, a legitimate and more viable "highroad around modernism" than that negotiated by Rorty.[48]

So, what would Peirce have to say about Rorty's antirealism? Now, while Peircean philosophers would certainly not be the only ones to reject the kind of antirealism of Rorty and others following from the linguistic turn,[49] my reading of Peirce, for the purposes at hand, is to invoke his revision of Kant's categories—the doctrines of Firstness, Secondness, and Thirdness—as providing the necessary conceptual underpinnings to pre-

47. Rorty, *Consequences of Pragmatism*, 161. Rorty's charge that Peirce remained a Kantian must surely be a conscious misreading of Peirce. While Peirce's lengthy study of Kant as a young man is well-known, that he achieved a radical transformation of Kant is also widely acknowledged: from incognizable *Ding an sich* to the infinitely cognizable; from the "transcendental subject" to the community of inquirers and their subject of ultimate opinion; from the transcendental categories to the transcendental modes of inference directed toward the long run of cognition; see Apel, *Charles S. Peirce*, esp. ix, and Okrent, "Metaphilosophical Consequences," 179. In fact, David Hall has suggested that insofar as Rorty has not taken seriously Peirce's reconstruction of Kant's categories, especially the category of the aesthetic, "it is Rorty who has remained Kantian in a manner that Peirce has not" (*Richard Rorty*, 70).

48. Neville, *Highroad around Modernism*; ch. 1 of this book is devoted to an exposition of the Peircean alternative around modernity. See also Neville, "American Philosophy's Way around Modernism," and Ochs's "Charles Sanders Peirce." Other theologians who have taken a Peircean route include Robert Corrington, Donald L. Gelpi, and Cornel West. See Corrington, *Community of Interpreters*; on Gelpi, see his *Peirce and Theology*; and on West, note Wood, *Cornel West*.

49. See, e.g., Margolis, *Pragmatism without Foundations*; Prado, *Limits of Pragmatism*; Harris, *Against Relativism*; Farrell, *Subjectivity, Realism, and Postmodernism*; House, *Without God*; and Rescher, *Realistic Pragmatism*, all of whom take the antirealism of the post-linguistic turn to task.

serve and sustain Rorty's edifying conversation. *Firstness* is pure potentiality, the simple quality of feeling, what makes a thing itself. *Secondness* is the element of struggle or of brute, resistant fact, that by which a thing is related to others. *Thirdness* is what mediates between Firstness and Secondness, the universals, laws, generalities, or habits that ensure the continuity of the things in their environing relationships.[50] All things are what they are only as Firsts, Seconds, and Thirds—viz., having self-identity independent of anything else, having a relational identity in reaction to other things, and having a meditative aspect through which they are brought into relation with other things.[51]

Rorty is correct, of course, to emphasize the web of interrelatedness that constitutes us and our place in the world. Yet his non-essentialism and nominalism is reductionistic in insisting that relations are all there are. Central axioms of Rorty's vision beg for a more robustly ontological and realistic (rather than linguistic) account of otherness than he provides.[52] The value of tolerance assumes differences between others and us, and ethnocentrism presumes the pluralism of cultures and societies.[53] "We" finds its contrast only with "they." But if relations are all there are, then how are others distinct from us? Certainly we are what and who we are precisely in relationship with others. Yet we are also not others, distinct from them. What is it that distinguishes us from them, and what is it that organizes and establishes our identities in relationship to others? In short, Rorty's account assumes a unity amidst plurality, a self-identity in relationship, a coherent "we" interdepen-

---

50. I provide a more detailed reading of Peirce elsewhere: see Yong, "Demise of Foundationalism" [ch. 1, this volume], and *Spirit-Word-Community*, esp. chs. 3 and 5.

51. Peirce, *Collected Papers*, 1.300–53, 5.41–66, and 6.32–4. Unless otherwise indicated, all references to Peirce will be according to the convention of Peirce scholarship in the form of v.p, denoting volume and paragraph number.

52. To be sure, Rorty is not denying that mountains obviously existed prior to human beings: "But the utility of those language games has nothing to do with the question of whether Reality as It Is in Itself, apart from the way it is handy for human beings to describe it, has mountains in it" (*Truth and Progress*, 72). Obviously, there are mountains that cause our descriptions of them; not obviously, there are noncausal senses in which mountains describe Reality as It Is in Itself. There is here a fine line between Rorty's antirealism and Berkeleyan idealism. Thus Alvin Plantinga is led to write that "before there were human beings, Rorty thinks, there was no such thing as the sentence '2 + 1 = 3'" (*Warranted Christian Belief*, 434). Of course, given Rorty's ironic stance, it is unclear whether he is serious or not about otherwise giving Plantinga and other readers the impression that pragmatic antirealism should lead to any other conclusions.

53. Chantal Mouffe's "Deconstruction, Pragmatism" argues that democratic politics is and should inevitably be conflictual since without conflict, a Habermasian universality or a Rortyean public consensus (for example) would erase difference, diversity, and pluralism, the former by privatizing difference and making it irrelevant and the latter by forcing consensus.

dent with but discrete from "them." He needs to acknowledge that there is self-identity (as individuals and as communities) that provides greater or lesser integration of the web of relationships that constitute us (again, as individuals and as communities), apart from which our distinctness from others is lost, even while advocating, as he does, the fact that the identity in and through which we are is constituted precisely by our relations with those (things and persons) that we are not.[54]

It is precisely this account of otherness lacking in Rorty's own neo-pragmatism that can be found in Peirce's categories. Firstness ensures that things have their own identity that make them different from other things; Secondness results in what James called "the pluralistic universe" of facts, details, particulars, individuals, exceptions, mutations, discrepancies, discontinuities, fissures, ruptures, faults, etc.; and Thirdness ensures that there are generalities and laws that govern the interactions and relationships within the pluralistic universe so as to ensure its consistency and predictability (both to greater or lesser extents), sustain engagement, and enable inquiry. More importantly, this kind of pluralistic pragmatism provides the metaphysical and ontological grounding not only for our everyday realist intuitions, but also for a truly methodological interdisciplinarity and communal mode of inquiry.[55] In contrast, first, to the Kantian turn to the subject and the bifurcation of the knowing self and the unknowable thing-in-itself, and second to Rorty's inconsistent ethnocentrism and rejection of things external to ourselves, Peirce affirmed that real knowledge is achievable as human beings interact with the environments in which they find themselves and check and correct their interpretations of interactions with each other as perspectives are gained over time. Here, Peirce's pragmatism understood that we are influenced by things and other persons precisely by having our activity shaped in interaction with them. So this acknowledges Rorty's causal account of language's relationship to the world without succumbing to the antirealist position. On the contrary, something like Peirce's pragmatism enables and requires us to take both the world and one another seriously.[56]

---

54. For a contemporary restatement of Peirce on this point, see Robert Cummings Neville's theory of identity as comprised, irreducibly, of both essential and conditional features in his *Recovery of Measure*, esp. ch. 5.

55. See Rosenthal, *Charles Peirce's Pragmatic Pluralism*; Singer, "Pragmatism and Pluralism"; and Smith, "Community and Reality."

56. Apart from which, as argued by Geras in *Solidarity in Conversation*, Rorty's vision for a liberal and democratic society crumbles. Further, from explicitly Christian theological perspectives, a realistic theological anthropology provides the needed addition to Peirce's ontology of otherness which strengthens its capacity for ideological critique and resistance; on this point, see Echeverria, "Do Human Rights Spring . . . ?"

This leads, naturally, to Peirce's response to Rorty's coherentist view of truth. From the foregoing, it should be discernible that Peirce assumed some sort of coherentism in his insistence on knowledge as accumulated communal discovery and wisdom. More specifically, truth is that to which opinion converges in the infinite long run. Yet Peirce said much more about truth than this.[57] He also viewed truth propositionally, and posited that such propositions connect our cognitions with reality: "Truth is the correspondence of a representation with its object."[58] But having rejected the Cartesian intuitionism that grounded knowledge in self-evident and direct intuitions of external reality,[59] Peirce realized that while propositions emerge from perception and experience and correspond in a dyadic fashion to reality, they do not function in that same dyadic manner. Rather, any real proposition, as a semiotic relation, must be categorically triadic. In itself (as a First), a proposition is a sign that stands against an object (a Second) and is capable of determining an interpretation (a Third). The interpretation either gets at the relation between the sign and the object correctly or it does not. This is what allowed Peirce to say "every proposition is either true or false."[60] But any attempt to determine a proposition's truth or falsity—the dyadic correspondence between the proposition and reality—is another triadically structured proposition: an interpretation.[61] Propositions thus function by addressing and creating in our minds other, more developed signs or interpretations, and so on, potentially *ad infinitum*. A true proposition meant that

> every interpretation of it is true. . . . When we speak of truth and falsity, we refer to the possibility of the proposition being refuted; and this refutation (roughly speaking) takes place in but one way. Namely, an interpretant of the proposition would, if believed, produce the expectation of a certain description of precept on a certain occasion. The occasion arrives: the percept forced upon us is different. This constitutes the falsity of every proposition of which the disappointing prediction was the interpretant.[62]

57. Much has been written on Peirce's theory of truth. For starters, see Peirce's paper on "Truth," 5.549–73, and Almeder, "Peirce's Thirteen Theories."

58. Peirce, *Collected Papers*, 5.553–54.

59. For Peirce's rejection of Cartesianism, see his "Consequences of Four Incapacities," 5.264–317.

60. Peirce, *Collected Papers*, 2.327.

61. Rorty himself actually admits as much when he writes, "Granted that the criterion of truth is justification, and that justification is relative [to an audience's likes, purposes, wants, needs, and situation], the *nature* of truth is not" (*Truth and Progress*, 3).

62. Peirce, *Collected Papers*, 5.569.

This, then, is what allowed Peirce to claim that thought has access to the truth of reality. But Peirce's was not a naïve realism, in that he recognized the complex operations of thinking. He understood that the correlation of our assertions with reality takes place not directly, but only by means of a semiotic process of interpretation,[63] and this process is a triadic relation between signs, objects, and interpretations which arise from various experiential perspectives. These facets of interpretation yield successively more determinate aspects of previously less determinate signs.[64] It is clear that Peirce realized long before Rorty that there is no getting behind language to reality "itself." The difference is that Rorty the neo-pragmatist deconstructionist provides no means of adjudicating the differences of interpretation apart from, ultimately, the will to power,[65] while Peircean fallibilism always holds out the possibility of an emergent resolution produced by the continued intersubjective engagement of the communities of disagreement with the object(s) of interpretation.[66] So even here, we see that Peirce's affirmation of a theoretical correspondence between language and reality avoids the undesirable results of modernity's debates about truth—whether Kantian agnosticism, neo-pragmatic skepticism, or even fundamentalist literalism—instead leaving the legacy of pragmatism as a "pragmatic conception

---

63. The most in-depth recent exposition is Short, *Peirce's Theory of Signs*.

64. This is why it does no good to defend the correspondence theory of truth by saying that a declarative proposition "describes a state of affairs, and does so by agreeing with—as opposed to contradicting—objective reality" (Groothuis, "Postmodernism and Truth," 272). From a Peircean perspective which agrees with the notion of truth of correspondence, such tactics only beg the (Rortyean) question about how we can access objective reality apart from language to check the equivalence.

65. Thus Rorty admits that at the end of the "conversation" between liberals and bigots or between Rortyeans and the Nazis, "We may both have to reach for our guns" ("Universality and Truth," 13–14).

66. For more on the difference between Peirce and Rorty on this point, see Eco, "Unlimited Semeiosis." But is Peirce's fallibilism viciously incoherent since such a claim regarding fallibilism would have to be infallible itself? Rorty's response is that, "The question of whether the pragmatist view of truth—that it is not a profitable topic—is itself *true* is thus a question about whether a post-Philosophical culture is a good thing to try for" (*Consequences of Pragmatism*, xliii). Peirce himself avoided this charge by describing the doctrine of fallibilism not as a truth claim (a proposition or belief) but as a defining condition of propositions: "But you will say, I am setting up this very proposition as infallible truth. Not at all; it is a mere definition. I do not say that it is infallibly true that there is any belief to which a person would come if he were to carry his inquiries far enough. I can only say that that alone is what I call Truth. I cannot infallibly know that there *is* any truth"; see Peirce's letter to Lady Welby, 23 Dec. 1908, in Hardwick, *Semiotic and Significs*, 73; emphasis Peirce's. My own response is to say that a fallibilist simply holds that any particular belief may be wrong and in need of revision, not that all beliefs are possibly wrong.

of knowledge and value as modes of action subject to testable terminations in experience and guided by predictable properties of the physical world."[67]

But what is needed is a more precise account of how the world or reality measures our interpretations truthfully—in Rorty's terms, how the environment causes organisms to develop efficient and satisfying habits of action. And such an account will not be available apart from a fully developed philosophy of nature. Here, Peirce's scientific realism, which launched early pragmatists such as Dewey on the quest for a scientific understanding of nature, comes back into focus. For Peirce, as for Dewey, reality renders human interpretations normative through our semeiotic interactions with it. This is no intuitive picture or mirror theory of truth ably criticized by Rorty. Rather, truthful empirical content emerges in our engaging with and responding to the world, and in the ways which it influences and shapes our activity. What carries over are the values of the world's otherness that we need to register, heed, and respect in order for appropriate and successful habits to emerge. Insofar as Rorty and other neo-pragmatists have taken the linguistic turn toward the humanities, they have neglected the sciences and retrieved only half of the tradition of classical American pragmatism. And, given the centrality of experimentation to classical pragmatism, the interpretation of the "text" of reality needs to be restored alongside the neo-pragmatist emphasis on interpretation of literary texts.

What is interesting is that given Rorty's neo-Darwinist framework, he has overlooked the fact that the Darwinian account requires not only a causal relationship between the world and language users, but also the rejection of nominalism. A thoroughgoing "evolutionary epistemology" takes Rorty to task for ignoring the requirements of his own Darwinian presupposition, since evolutionary biology shows that organisms adapt to their environment through expectation of regularities or laws—Peirce's Thirdness.[68] What has happened is that another of Rorty's strong misreadings—in this case, of Darwin—has legitimated his doctrine of chance and disregarded the teleological suggestiveness of evolutionary naturalism precisely because Rorty is opposed to any overarching conception of meaning apart from the purposes suited to the needs of particular organisms in particular situations.[69] Now it is certainly the case that Peirce's optimism regarding truth

67. Thayer, "Pragmatism," 18.

68. For more argument on this point, see Munz, "Philosophy and Mirror of Rorty," 374–78.

69. Thus Rorty writes: "Teleological thinking is inevitable, but Dewey offers us a relativist and materialist version of teleology rather than an absolute and idealist one. . . . It pays for us to believe this [Dewey's vision] because we have seen the unfortunate results of believing otherwise—of trying to find some ahistorical and absolute relation to reality for truth to name. . . . 'Growth itself is the only moral end' is the moral theory

converging in the infinite long run reflected, in part, the power the idea of progress held over Western intellectuals in the late nineteenth century. But to expose such unwarranted optimism does not require lapsing into pessimism or embracing Rorty's anti-teleological position. It is, on Peirce's and Dewey's terms, to insist on the difference between pragmatism and the earlier empiricisms, the former emphasizing consequent phenomena and the latter antecedent ones. In other words, pragmatism is focused on the future, and requires a metaphysics of the future, of openness, of freedom, and, by extension, of responsibility.[70] In Christian and theological terms, it is to allow, following Rorty, that there is no *telos* in the sense that conversation is itself a gift (received by faith), not a means through which we will achieve our salvation, even while we can at the same time hope for the eschatological transformation of our conversation and its objects that reflects the gloriousness of what will be revealed.[71]

This raises, finally, the question of what Peirce would have said about the possibility of a pragmatic theology. We could here certainly comment at length either about Peirce's own theistic beliefs and Episcopal piety or about pragmatism as a distinct expression of what Henry S. Levinson has called "the American aesthetic tradition of spirituality."[72] What I want to focus on, however, is Peirce's own conception of pragmatism as a method of inquiry. He recollects that "pragmatism was invented to express a certain maxim of logic. . . . The maxim is intended to furnish a method for the analysis of concepts."[73] Succinctly stated, the pragmatic maxim asserts: "Consider what effects, that might conceivably have practical bearings, we conceive the object of our conception to have. Then, our conception of these effects is the whole of our conception of the object."[74] Peirce spent the better part of his lifetime exploring the consequences of this maxim for science, philosophy,

it now pays us to have, for we have seen the unfortunate results of trying to divinize and eternalize a given social practice or form of individual life" (*Truth and Progress,* 305).

70. See Dewey, "Development of American Pragmatism," 32–33.

71. Here I can do no better than grant Rorty's point (*Objectivity, Relativism, and Truth,* 27) that Peirce's notion of the teleological convergence of inquiry or of a limited ideal of truth (*Grenzbegriff*) has theological roots.

72. Levinson, *Santayana, Pragmatism, Spiritual Life,* locates the classical pragmatists in the same religio-aesthetic tradition as that of Edwards, Emerson, and Santayana. A large portion (Book II, over 200 pages) of Volume VI of the *Collected Papers* documents Peirce's thoughts about religion, including his famous "A Neglected Argument for the Reality of God." The secondary literature on this topic—beginning with book-length studies by Orange, *Peirce's Conception of God,* and Raposa, *Peirce's Philosophy of Religion*—is enormous.

73. Peirce, *Collected Papers,* 8.191.

74. Peirce, *Collected Papers,* 5.2; also 5.9, 5.14ff., and passim.

and religion. But by 1905, he noted that *pragmatism* had come to be associated predominantly with one aspect of James's theory of truth—crudely understood as that which worked[75]—and with the humanism of the British philosopher F. C. S. Schiller. As such, Peirce renamed his own system *pragmaticism*, "which is ugly enough to be safe from kidnappers."[76]

Now it is undoubtedly the case that given the large corpus of Peirce's writings, his idea of pragmaticism as principle of logic intended for the analysis of concepts has come to be associated with some of the other elements of his system, such as his theories of meaning and truth, his semiotics, and even his metaphysics as a whole.[77] My point is to suggest that while atheistic presuppositions are undeniably attached to Rorty's neo-pragmatism, these are not necessarily essential to pragmatism and certainly not to Peirce's pragmaticism specifically. In fact, it could just as well be argued that Peircean pragmaticism, when viewed within the framework of his system as a whole, requires the theistic component. Yet what is interesting in this regard is that Peirce's pragmaticism goes beyond the binary oppositions of subject-object, of relativism-objectivism, and of naturalism-supernaturalism, and does so precisely by offering a triadic reconceptualization of ontology and epistemology that supersedes the disastrous Cartesian and Kantian dualisms inherent in the modern narrative, allowing for the establishment of a semiotic sufficiently sophisticated to engage religious experience and the question of theism. As such, Peircean pragmaticism offers one highroad around modernity, the viability of which is being increasingly recognized today.

By way of contrast, Rorty's neo-pragmatism finally assumes modernity's terms and conditions and thereby falls prey to its dictates rather than overcoming its liabilities. What I mean is that Rorty reacts to Kant's thing-in-itself by eliminating it rather than reconceiving the subject-object relationship. He reacts to the questionable image of mirroring in epistemology by dismissing epistemology altogether rather than reconstituting it. He reacts to the problems associated with transcendence reductionistically rather than constructively.[78] The result is a loss not only of the world, but

75. No doubt in his own way, James's writings—e.g., "Pragmatism's Conception of Truth," and *Meaning of Truth*—provided the impetus for this (mis)understanding of truth at the popular level. Yet Smith, *Purpose and Thought*, ch. 2, has also shown that James held to a basic correspondence theory of truth; or, better, a theory of truth as "dynamic correspondence."

76. Peirce, *Collected Papers*, 5.414.

77. On the various notions of pragmatism even in Peirce's own writings, see Gallie, *Peirce and Pragmatism*, esp. ch. 7.

78. On Rorty's own modernism, against all his protestations, see Greenway, "Richard Rorty's Revised Pragmatism," ch. 8; Farrell, *Subjectivity, Realism, and Postmodernism,*

also of other selves and of God. What is left is an uncritical and uncriticizable ethnocentrism on the level of public discourse erected on the shaky foundations of a narcissistic, privatized, and solipsistic individualism. This would be the return of modernity with a vengeance, an *ultramodernism* that finally marks Rorty's neo-pragmatist enterprise.

For this reason, I suggest pragmatist theology could be either modernist or postmodernist. A post-Rortyean neo-pragmatist theology would be postmodernist insofar as it correctly identifies the fallibilist, non-foundationalist sociohistorically traditioned and narrative texture of all human interpretations of the divine. At the same time, however, it would also be modernistic in certain irreducible senses delineated above, being a remnant of modernity's dualisms that remain to infect neo-pragmatism's projects.[79] Alongside the Rortyean trajectory of pragmatism, however, is the Peircean pragmaticist alternative. This would reinforce all the benefits of a neo-pragmatic theology without its liabilities. Further, it is not modernistic in eschewing modernity's treacherous dualisms, nor is it premodern in its having awakened the second naïveté against traditionalist authoritarianism. Perhaps it would point the way forward to a truly *postmodern* position in our late modern world, one that avoids modernity's (and the Philosophical tradition's) pitfalls rather than mishandling them. And if that is the case, then might not this exercise serve as one route toward reconceiving a post-Rortyean, pragmati(ci)st, and truly postmodern theological account of Christian belief and practice in our time?[80]

---

ch. 4; and Guignon, "Pragmatism or Hermeneutics?"

79. Thus it may be better to follow Richard Bernstein, who defends Rorty's neo-pragmatism by characterizing it as a practical-moral vision (with political implications) in the tradition of the Socratic virtues. For Rorty, "the moral task of the philosopher or the cultural critic is to defend the openness of human conversation against all those temptations and real threats that seek closure"; see Bernstein, *Beyond Objectivism and Relativism,* 205.

80. Another obvious route is that charted over the last thirty-plus years by Professor Donald Gelpi. I originally wrote this essay for a festschrift for Don, but it never materialized. I never had Don as a teacher formally, but early on in my doctoral studies I stumbled upon his work, and he has remained a major dialogue partner for my work ever since. From the beginning, Don has encouraged me, provided critical perspective, and, all along, continued to model what it means to be a scholar who does his work "in" and "after" the leading of the Holy Spirit. At one point, I published "In Search of Foundations" [see next chapter], both as an initial effort to digest and wrestle with his ideas and as a way of more forcefully urging my pentecostal theological colleagues to pay closer attention to his work. Later on, the Gelpian influence is clearly documented in my *Spirit Poured Out on All Flesh,* esp. chs. 2 and 7. This chapter attempts to follow, even if only at a great distance, in the footsteps of Don's adept lifelong engagement with and appropriation of the North American philosophical tradition as a Christian, Catholic, and charismatic theologian.

CHAPTER 3

In Search of Foundations

The *Oeuvre* of Donald L. Gelpi, S.J., and Its Significance for Pentecostal Theology and Philosophy

OVER THE PAST THREE and a half decades, Donald L. Gelpi, S.J., was one of the few individuals working at the intersections of theology and philosophy, and who had been, at the same time, involved with the charismatic movement (the Catholic Charismatic Renewal, in his case). Among other results has been the emergence of a systematic philosophical theology and spirituality that is imbued with intuitions derived from the charismatic experience, which continue to be appreciated as such by charismatic scholars working in these areas. In the past few years, Gelpi's overall project, begun in earnest with the trilogy of *Charism and Sacrament* (1976), *Experiencing God* (1978), and *The Divine Mother* (1984), has come into much clearer focus with the appearance of four new books, one of which is a three-volume Christology. These recent installments further develop the central themes of Gelpi's theological vision: a foundational philosophical theology based in part on the concept of conversion derived from Lonergan; a fallibilistic and communal method of inquiry adopted from Peirce; a thoroughly enculturated North American theology extracted from a prolonged dialectical and dialogical engagement with the North American philosophical tradition; and a pragmatism designed to give account of the cash value of theological and doctrinal statements for Christian formation and growth in grace.

This chapter will seek to accomplish two broad objectives. First, I wish to introduce the work of Gelpi to pentecostal philosophers, theologians, and educators because I are convinced that we have much to learn from him. I propose to do so by providing broad overviews of the central themes of Gelpi's projects (outlined above) as they have been unveiled in his most recent books. Second, I wish to demonstrate how this recent work grew out of Gelpi's earlier, more explicitly Charismatic and pentecostal reflections. To do so, I will pick out and comment at greater length during the review itself on three motifs—his foundational pneumatology, his theological anthropology, and his theological method—that connect the "earlier" Gelpi of the '70s and '80s with the "present" Gelpi at the turn of the new millennium. Along the way, I will comment as appropriate, especially in the notes, on how Gelpi's theological project intersects with, complements, or perhaps even charts fresh avenues of exploration for pentecostal-charismatic scholarship.

DISCERNING "POSTMODERNISM"

Perhaps the volume that affords us the clearest entry into the lifelong work of Gelpi is his *Varieties of Transcendental Experience: A Study in Constructive Postmodernism* (2000). In the Preface, Gelpi himself admits that while the book can be understood both as an engagement with the questions raised by postmodernity in its deconstructive modes and as a dialectical study of ideas in the North American philosophical tradition, it also serves as a loosely conceived intellectual autobiography, insofar as it presents the results of his own extended dialogue with thinkers in that tradition beginning in the late 1960s.[1] It therefore behooves us to spend a bit more time on this volume in order to discern the shape of Gelpi's thought.

Varieties has both a normative, polemical contention and a descriptive, historical agenda that are intertwined. The former is the argument that the North American intellectual, philosophical, and religious tradition offers our contemporary generation better resources than those suggested by deconstructive postmodernism to critique and respond to the rationalism, positivism, subjectivism, atomism, individualism, dualism, and nominalism bequeathed by Enlightenment modernism.[2] The deconstructionist move, especially that proposed by French philosophers like Derrida, is to eschew ontological and theological thinking, to relativize questions of truth perspectively and according to the sign systems or frames of references that are in play, to reject the stability of meaning, both textual and otherwise, and to cut the cord between language and reality itself.[3] Gelpi

---

1. Gelpi, *Varieties*, ix–x; cf. Gelpi, *Experiencing God*, 12–13.

2. This is described in detail in Gelpi, *Varieties*, Part 1.

3. Gelpi, *Varieties*, 339–40; pentecostals have begun to wrestle with such questions in earnest dialogue with deconstructive thinkers; see, e.g., Smith, *Fall of Interpretation*

suggests that the deconstructionist concerns are themselves bound up with the failures of Enlightenment thinking about these things, and that there are suggestive pathways around these dead ends cleared by North American thinkers that have not been seriously considered. What is needed is a theory of thinking that is affective, moral, and cognitive—both imaginatively and creatively—but not rationalistic; an empiricism that is pragmatistic, fallibilistic, and solidly grounded in phenomenological discernment but is not positivistic or reductionistic; a communal method of inquiry that takes the turn to community as seriously as it does the turn to the subject without being solipsistic or subjectivistic; a metaphysics that understands otherness within a relational framework without collapsing into either dualism or monism; and a critical realism that affirms language and symbols as human conventions without adopting a nominalist understanding of generality and legality. All of these combined with a semiotic theory of experience and knowledge can affirm deconstructionist convictions about the central place of sign systems in human thinking without succumbing to epistemological relativism and skepticism.

In each case, Gelpi claims to find, at least in inchoate forms, each of these alternatives within the North American intellectual tradition.[4] To demonstrate this thesis, a comparative dialectical analysis—here, Gelpi followed Lonergan's usage of dialectic as a methodological specialty involving comparison and contrast, rather than Hegel's notion of thesis-antithesis-synthesis—of the ideas emergent in this tradition is presented. Emerson's contribution was to move from a rationalistic logic toward the belief that some kind of aesthetic, creative, and imaginative intuitionism, albeit one that is also finite and biased, is present at the root of all human thinking.[5] Theodore Parker's development of Emerson's intuitionism, with the help

---

and *Speech and Theology*.

4. From where I sit, the only other theological project to take the North American cultural situation seriously which rivals Gelpi's in scope is Douglas John Hall's *Christian Theology*. The difference between the two is Gelpi's much more intensive and specific focus on the North American philosophical tradition resulting in a creative dialogue. Hall's project, on the other hand, is as much, if not more so, an engagement with Western culture generally as with the North American culture more specifically. As such, the distinctive particularities of the North American situation are oftentimes muted in his discussion of post-Western, post-Enlightenment, and postcolonial concerns.

5. See also Gelpi's extended study of Emerson in Gelpi, *Endless Seeker*. Although Gelpi's *Varieties* begins the movement toward constructive postmodernism with a consideration of Emerson's ideas, Gelpi is not oblivious to the resources available for this same project in important American thinkers preceding the New England transcendentalist. In particular, the voluminous writings of Edwards have yet to be mined toward this end. For a preliminary assessment of Edwards in this regard, see Gelpi, "Incarnate Excellence."

of Kant's practical reason and Schleiermacher's notion of absolute dependence, was a step back in the direction of Enlightenment agnosticism and subjectivism, which the American thinkers were seeking to transcend. However, Parker also saw more deeply than Emerson that experience itself was a complex integration of the affective, rational, moral, and religious dimensions of human endeavor. The way to balance these realms of experience harmoniously was advanced by Orestes Brownson, whose conversion to Catholicism and study of the work of Pierre Leroux, a French political philosopher, brought about an appreciative grasp of the Catholic analogical imagination that attempts to think in "both-and" rather than "either-or" terms. Further, Brownson moved from the dualistic and dyadic conception of knowledge favored by Enlightenment nominalism and rationalism toward a synthetic and rudimentary triadic notion whereby the subject of cognition and the object of cognition are linked by the form of cognition. Finally, Francis Allingwood Abbott's contribution was to clearly recognize and identify the nominalism—both extreme, whereby universals are mere words, and conceptual, whereby universals exist only in the mind, but not in reality—that plagued Enlightenment thinking, and argue for the reality of universals in developing a more robust metaphysical realism and scientific method.

In Gelpi's account, the transitional figures in the North American intellectual tradition are Charles Sanders Peirce and, developing Peirce's ideas, Josiah Royce. In Peirce, the positive contributions of the New England Transcendentalists and Abbott's scientific theism converge and point the way toward a constructive postmodernism.[6] Now, it is not the case that Peirce systematically studied his Transcendentalist predecessors and engaged in serious dialogue with them. Gelpi clearly points out that his dialogue partners were, instead, Duns Scotus, Descartes, Hume, Locke, and especially, Kant. At the same time, it is also undeniable that Peirce imbibed the transcendentalist tradition from their trafficking through his home as a youth even while he engaged the American intellectual tradition as an adult with

6. Here, I need to clearly distinguish Gelpi's constructive postmodernist vision from that proposed by others such as David Ray Griffin at Claremont. Insofar as the latter's proposal derives its power from Whitehead's metaphysics, Gelpi considers it hopelessly derailed by the conceptual nominalism and bipolar dualism that infects both Whitehead's philosophy of organism and its descendants such as Hartshorne's neoclassical theism. Whether or not Griffin's version is impaled on these Whiteheadean horns is perhaps an open question. Gelpi is undoubtedly aware of work being done by Griffin and others, but is silent about this in *Varieties*. For a summary of Gelpi's critique of Whitehead, see *Turn to Experience*, ch. 3. The work of Griffin and others is best accessed through the many volumes in the SUNY Series in Constructive Postmodern Thought, edited by Griffin.

Abbott, William James, and others in the Metaphysical Club at Harvard. The result is that Peirce's work, arguably, brings to culmination the transcendentalist critique of the Enlightenment.[7] He advanced Emerson's theory of epistemic finitude and bias toward a fallibilistic theory of knowledge that understood thinking to proceed from three basic forms of inferences: abductive hypotheses; deductive clarifications; and inductive verification and falsification. In so doing, Peirce was responding not only to Emerson but also to the intuitive and universal doubt of Descartes and the deductivism, transcendentalism, and a priorism of Kant. It's not that Peirce denied the role of intuitions altogether in human cognition. He simply denied that intuitive knowing yielded an immediate subjective grasp of objective truths as Emersonian transcendentalism, Cartesianism, and Kantianism affirmed. Instead, intuitions are to be understand—here not only with Emerson but also Parker—as affective, aesthetic, and morally tinged images and inferences that contribute semiotically to knowledge.[8]

Here, Brownson's triadic conception of knowledge was given greater logical precision by Peirce's inferential semiotic: all knowledge is mediated by signs that stand for something (their interpretants) to someone (their interpreters), and do so in a potentially infinite sequence since each interpretant becomes, in turn, an objective something (another sign) with some meaning (it's interpretant) to someone (an interpreter), and so on. That knowledge involves inferential signs, interpretants, and interpreters means that inquiry is not only semiotic and involves interpretation, but is also necessarily communal, and involves the movement from vagueness to increasing specificity as initial hypotheses are clarified and tested.[9] Finally, over and against nominalism in all its varieties, Peirce advocated, with Abbot and

---

7. This thesis is also argued by my teacher, Robert Cummings Neville, in his *High-road around Modernism*, ch. 1. Given that Neville was freshly out of grad school at Yale (where he did his work under John Smith and Paul Weiss) when he began supervising Gelpi's research and dissertation writing in the mid-to-late 1960s, Gelpi's acknowledgment (*Varieties*, viii–ix) of the congruence between his and Neville's project is not surprising (see also Gelpi, *Experiencing God*, 12).

8. Pentecostal claims to knowledge have always been justified in a variety of ways, many of which stand outside the standard epistemological framework of Enlightenment rationality. The role of the affections and intuition has always been crucial in this regard. Gelpi's appropriation and revision of North American thinkers are good first steps for pentecostals wishing to think through both their epistemology and notion of intuition philosophically. Meanwhile, Steven Land has begun inquiry into an affective pentecostal epistemology in *Pentecostal Spirituality*, and Stephen Parker has laid the empirical groundwork for the role of intuition in pentecostal discernment in his book *Led By the Spirit*.

9. For my own first stab at deciphering the sign systems that nurture pentecostal glossolalia, see "Tongues of Fire."

Scotus, an epistemological and metaphysical realism, albeit one accessible to human minds through pragmatistic and communal inquiry. This was an important move because the human mind's capacity to grasp real universals mean it is able to experience the laws, habits, and tendencies that ground reality's processes, and hence to anticipate and thereby conform human actions with the way reality behaves. Peirce's pragmatic maxim thus defined the meaning of anything with its operational consequences and practical effects.[10]

Following Peirce's advice to study logic, the Harvard philosopher Josiah Royce developed aspects of Peirce's ideas in his own original synthesis. Royce's key contributions include his philosophy of loyalty, which served as a sustained critique of individualism, and, correlatively, his "turn to community." This latter idea was developed by Royce into a thoroughgoing metaphysics of universal community (understood in Pauline terms as the kingdom of God) whereby human relationality and interaction is mediated by the universal interpreter spirit (understood in biblical terms as the holy Breath[11]). Combining Peirce and the mature Royce, the result, Gelpi suggests, is a triadic, social, and realistic metaphysics which offers a viable philosophical alternative to both Enlightenment rationalism and religion, and to the alleged "way out" of deconstructionism that turns out to be a dead end after all.[12]

THEOLOGICAL METHOD IN A POSTMODERN WORLD

It is clear that Gelpi's sustained engagement with the North American intellectual tradition was motivated by his conviction, that it points the way forward for the postmodern mind even while, at the same time, it is conducive to the development of a sensitive and informed theology contextualized in the Yankee idiom. In *Peirce and Theology: Essays in the Authentication of*

10. As Grant Wacker has recently argued at length in his *Heaven Below*, the successes of the earliest pentecostals were achieved precisely by balancing their otherworldly interest with an intense pragmatism. That pentecostals are prone to a pragmatic mentality should not therefore be, in and of itself, a cause for concern.

11. Gelpi prefers the nomenclature of holy Breath over Holy Spirit both because it better translates the Hebrew *ruah* and the Greek *pneuma*, and because it is unburdened with the dualistic, essentialistic, and transcendental Thomist connotations that the concept of Spirit has acquired over the centuries (see *Experiencing God*, ch. 4, and *Divine Mother*, 11–13). In this chapter, I will follow his usage unless referring to the Spirit from non-Gelpian perspectives.

12. Generally speaking, pentecostal theologies of the charismata have been far too individualistic, and need to be turned toward the communal emphasis of Paul's original discussion; see 1 Corinthians 12.

Doctrine (2001), Gelpi supplements and develops his theological method originally laid out in *Inculturating North American Theology* (1988).[13] As a Jesuit, the influence of thinkers like Rahner and Lonergan on Gelpi was considerable.[14] Gelpi took seriously the latter's insistence that theology mediates between a religion and the culture in which that religion finds itself. Yet Gelpi himself had seen the need to revise or develop aspects of Lonergan's methodology with insights from the North American philosophical tradition.[15] Three in particular are noteworthy for our purposes. First, Lonergan's normative method of cognitive operations—experiencing, understanding, judging, and deciding—is reconceived from being transcendentally based toward being a semiotic process. Inductions, for example, clarify Lonergan's notion of judgment, while abductions and deductions render understanding with greater logical precision. Further, the linear character of Lonergan's cognitive operations is noted as failing to do justice to the organic and aesthetic mode of human experiential growth whereby the addition of one variable to the canvas transforms or transmutes all of the existing variables and provides a picture with a new qualitative shape.[16]

Second, Lonergan's eight functional specialties—research, interpretation, history, dialectic, foundations, doctrines, systematics, and communications—had largely been adopted by Gelpi as a sound theological method which presents recurrent operations that yield cumulative and progressive results. Those familiar with Lonergan's method realize that the first four specialties attempt retrieval of a tradition while the last four undertake reformulation. The result is that the method functions transformatively as critical praxis.[17] This connects well with Peircean pragmatism. Gelpi's contribution was not only to apply and develop the functional specialty of dialectics,[18] but to expand on Lonergan's own understanding of foundations by elaborating on the notion of conversion.[19] In particular, whereas

13. See also Gelpi, "The Foundational Phoenix."

14. See Gelpi, *Life and Light*.

15. See Lonergan, *Method in Theology*.

16. Gelpi, *Gracing*, 311–12.

17. Nancy C. Ring highlights Lonergan's method as transformation driven by critical praxis over and against Tillich's method as doctrinal disclosure directed toward critical theory; see Ring, *Doctrine within Dialectic*.

18. As in Gelpi, *Varieties*; also see his *Gracing* and *Firstborn*.

19. Lonergan's understanding of conversion as elaborated by Avery Dulles, S.J., "Fundamental Theology and the Dynamics of Conversion" (in Dulles' *The Craft of Theology*, ch. 4), should be compared with Gelpi's explication in his various works—e.g., esp. "Conversion: Challenge of Piety"; "Conversion: Beyond Impasses of Individualism," in *Beyond Individualism*, ch. 1; and *Conversion Experience*, exercises one, two, and three. For more on specifically religious conversion, see also the discussions in Rambo,

Lonergan defined conversion only in moral, intellectual, and religious terms, Gelpi understood, with the help of Edwards and others in the North American intellectual tradition, both that there are also affective conversions and that moral conversions can be specified in two directions: those related to the realm of interpersonal relationships focused on establishing authentic moral character, and those related to the realm of sociopolitical structures focused on the establishment of a just order.[20] The result is that in Gelpi's hands, foundational theology is fundamentally a systematic theology of conversion whereby religious experience is explored from normative perspectives that seek to authenticate past experiences, to provide guidance for actualizing and discerning future experiences as measured against interiorized ideals and principles, to clarify the meanings of doctrinal statements, and to ascertain their truth or falsity.[21]

Understanding Religious Conversion, and Lamb and Bryant, *Religious Conversion*.

20. Traditionally, pentecostal theologizing about conversion have focused on their debates, especially with evangelicals, around the topic of initiation. Gelpi challenges us to reflect on the notion that baptism in the holy Breath is not just an initiatory event but denotes a dispositional orientation toward being assimilated to the mind of Christ.

21. From these five forms of conversion—affective, intellectual, moral, sociopolitical, and religious—Gelpi also describes seven conversion dynamics (*Committed Worship*, vol. I, 33–55). Each form of conversion informs or transvalues (sets in a different frame of reference) the other forms—e.g., affective conversion shapes the other types of conversions, and so on. In addition to these five dynamics, Gelpi adds a sixth, that religious conversion mediates between affective and moral conversion, and a seventh, that affective, moral, intellectual, and religious conversions work together to bring about sociopolitical conversion. By the former, Gelpi means to say that religious conversion brings moral and affective conversion into a specific kind of relationship they would otherwise not enjoy. But do not all conversions bring about a qualitative transformation in the individual in meditative ways such that the other dimensions of life are transmuted, and other conversions are either effected or themselves transvalued? In fact, Gelpi says as much at one point in *Inculturating North American Theology*, 43. Why, then, in these later works since *Inculturating North American Theology*, does he specify religious conversion's mediating moral and affective conversion over and against religious conversion's mediating intellectual and sociopolitical conversion, or moral conversion's mediating religious and affective conversion, and so on? The seventh dimension points out, correctly, I believe, that there is a cumulative effect whereby four realms of conversion brings about sociopolitical conversion. But again, why single out this particular causal configuration and movement? Would it not be true also to say that sometimes, moral, affective, intellectual, and sociopolitical conversion bring about religious conversion, or that there are potentially different alignments of conversions in two, three, or four realms that stimulate conversions in the remaining realms, and so on? In short, why not simply identify five conversions that are dynamically interconnected so that conversion in any one or two or three, etc., realms can bring about, transvalue, and even transmute conversions in one or more of the other realms? (See also Yong, *Spirit Poured Out on All Flesh*, ch. 2.)

Third, Gelpi made explicit what Lonergan did not: the operational procedures for authenticating the truth or falsity of doctrines,[22] and the operational procedures for authenticating the viability or implausibility of the theological methodologies or principles themselves.[23] The former build, in part, upon the various types of conversions—psychological, affective, moral, intellectual, etc.—experienced by human beings (see discussion of conversion below). The latter derive from Gelpi's distinction between a foundationalistic theology understood in the Cartesian sense as emergent from indubitable starting points, and a foundational theology understood in the Lonerganian and Peircean sense as emergent from conversion seen in all its complexity, producing beliefs and habits that are nonetheless fallibilistic and revisable. Here theology's grounding is reconceived in dynamic and eschatological terms, and not solely by appealing to faith (as in neo-orthodoxy), developing a universal and metaphysical anthropology (e.g., Kant's deductive logic, or transcendental neo-Thomism), arbitrarily closing the hermeneutical circle (e.g., liberation theology's privileging the poor), invoking the methods of phenomenology or hermeneutics (which does not allow access to questions of truth or falsity), relying on the massive data of exegesis (which focuses on meaning to the neglect of questions of significance and application), or rethinking it in dialogue with the personality sciences (where the turn to the subject ignores community and society).

THE "FOUNDATIONS" OF THEOLOGICAL ANTHROPOLOGY

The procedure of clarifying and authenticating doctrinal statements is put to strenuous test in *The Gracing of Human Experience: Rethinking the Relationship between Nature and Grace* (2001). Here, the perennially difficult theological topic of the relationship between nature and grace in philosophical and theological anthropology is worked out. Gelpi argues that reflection on this matter has been misled over the centuries by misconceptions, extremes, and foreign philosophical intrusions such as Platonic, Stoic, and Gnostic essentialism and dualism; Aristotelian substantialism; Augustinian pessimism; transcendental Thomist optimism; medieval and modern nominalism; and positivistic and subjectivistic rationalisms.[24] Again, he suggests that Peirce's triadic, social, relational, semiotic, and realistic metaphysics—as amplified by Royce's philosophy of loyalty and more robust

22. Gelpi, *Peirce and Theology*, 22–38.

23. Ibid., 55–69.

24. See Gelpi, *Gracing*, Part I.

"turn to the community"; Dewey's transactional instrumentalism, logic of deliberation, and social philosophy[25]; and G. H. Mead's social psychology—not only avoids the problems generated by these systems of thought, but also preserves means by which Christians can continue to think and speak about experiencing God.[26] Gelpi was more specific, however, in developing the metaphysics of experience he had previously adapted from Whitehead's reformed subjectivist principle—that reality consists of concrete experiencing subjects rather than of Aristotelian substances—though he later revised this conception in the direction of the triadic and realistic metaphysics of Peirce and Royce.[27] As it stands, in this approach, reality consists not of substances and accidents (Aristotle), nor only of concrete facts and abstract ideas (Whitehead), but of three irreducible types of experiential feelings that Peirce called qualities (the hows by which things are present to each other), facts (the over and againstness of things to each other), and laws (the habits and tendencies which structure things' being present to and being over and against others).[28] Lived experience (phenomenologically examined) and

25. Gelpi makes selective use of Dewey. He is wary of Dewey's nominalism and naturalism (*Varieties*, 298, 344), but nevertheless believes and argues (*Inculturating North American Theology*, ch. 5, and *Gracing*, ch. 6) that Dewey does make a significant contribution to the development of Peirce's pragmatic logic.

26. See Gelpi, *Gracing*, Part II. In 1988, Gelpi had already sketched how the North American philosophical tradition pointed the way forward for philosophical theology in the twenty-first century: it repudiated dualism and substance philosophy, rejected transcendental thinking with a dynamically structured and experientially based method of inquiry, assimilated and acknowledged rather than denied the legitimacy of religious and aesthetic experience, admitted to the dialogic and fallibilistic character of human reason over and against necessary and a priori reasoning, was concerned with pragmatic consequences, and did not opposed naturalism to supernaturalism (cf. *Inculturating North American Theology*, 11–13, and *Grace as Transmuted Experience*, ch. 1). For these reasons, Gelpi now notes: "Just to formulate a theology of supernatural grace which avoids past blunders would clear the ground for a major advance in Christian anthropology, even if that anthropology would commit new theological blunders of its own. If the new approach did err, as Peircean fallibilism insists it might, then at least the resulting errors would have the interest of speculative novelty instead of simply rehashing the same old tired heresies" (*Gracing*, 165–66).

27. See Gelpi's early trilogy; a succinct statement of his metaphysics of experience can also be found in *Turn to Experience*, ch. 5. Needless to say, the experiential orientation of pentecostalism cries out for systematic reflection, especially since, as Gelpi has repeatedly mentioned, the notion of experience is itself notoriously ambiguous. The first steps in this direction have come from a charismatic theologian who has studied under Gelpi: see Howard, *Affirming Touch of God*.

28. Peirce's phenomenological and metaphysical categories are explicated throughout Gelpi's corpus. Qualities are inefficacious conceptualities analogous to the Scotist notion of haecceity—thisness or suchness—that includes a broad spectrum of (mostly concrete) evaluative responses (like taste, touch, sight, smell, sound, visceral

what is experienced (metaphysically construed) is thereby always already triadic (qualitative, factual, and legal), social (relational both in the oppositional sense of factuality and in the participatory sense of habituality and dispositionality), and realistic (whereby generalities are not only nominal or mental constructs but legally structure and shape the hows and whats of experience).[29]

Gelpi's constructive argument is that human beings can indeed experience divine grace if in fact such grace is mediated experientially—i.e., conceptually or qualitatively, factually, and legally. He suggested that the experience of Jesus and the experience of the Breath of Jesus—in theological terms, the divine mission of the Son and the divine mission of the Breath—are the two paradigmatic experiences that reflect the divine gracing of the human condition. (Here, given Gelpi's metaphysics of experience, the "experience of Jesus" refers both to the self-conscious life of the carpenter from Nazareth on the one hand, and the interpersonal relationships understood from the perspective of others who interacted with him on the other; same for the "experience of the Breath of Jesus.") The incarnation is the human experience of the divine Son of God. Pentecost, which includes the sacramental and Charismatic formation and constitution of the ecclesia, becomes the means through which the qualities, facts, and laws embodied by Jesus are graciously extended to the human race.[30] Human beings enter into this graced relationship and environment through initial and ongoing conversion—corresponding theologically to the experiences of justification and sanctification—understood as repentance for irresponsibility toward the taking of responsibility for one's beliefs and their concomitant practices.

Yet conversion is itself a complex notion that impacts various aspects of life besides the religious dimension. Naturalistic and secularistic forms of conversion touch the affections, the intellect, and the will—the last involving

---

perceptions, emotions, moods, images, etc.). Facts are the concrete oppositions that characterize reality's physical interactions and interrelatedness (like actions which are of one thing on another, and the reactions that are thereby elicited, etc.). Laws are organic, vectorial, and dynamic tendencies that wax and wane according to the diverse processes that they negotiate, coordinate, and direct, which ground continuity in experience, and which render intelligible qualitative experience and factual relationships (e.g., as hardness in general allows us to recognize the hardness of this table, or of that diamond, and as the laws of physics enable us to predict when the interaction of heat and water produces evaporation). For early, detailed discussions, see *Charism and Sacrament*, ch. 1; *Experiencing God*, 75–78; and *Divine Mother*, 23ff.

29. For more in-depth explication of these Peircean ideas, see my "The Demise of Foundationalism" [chapter 1 in this volume].

30. Pentecostals are now beginning to take the idea of tradition and the role of the sacraments seriously—see, e.g., Chan, *Pentecostal Theology*. For an interesting move to understand glossolalia in sacramental terms, see Macchia, "Tongues as a Sign."

the moral and sociopolitical dimensions—and can occur apart from divine grace (hence Gelpi's rejection of Augustinian pessimism). Converting naturally in these areas makes one more susceptible to responding to God when confronted by the presentation of the gospel and the call to repentance. Christian conversion is therefore a specific kind of religious conversion that in turn transvalues and transforms the other kinds of conversions in the sense that the infusion of grace sets the believer in relationship to Jesus, and directs him or her to live in conformity with the values of the kingdom of God.[31] Thus affective conversion transvalued by Christian conversion—i.e., graced by the divine Breath—is infused by the theological virtue of Christian hope since the believer's affections, imagination, and emotions are imbued by the attitudes reflected and modeled by Jesus;[32] intellectual conversion transvalued by Christian conversion is infused by the theological virtue of Christian faith since the believer's cognitive processes are directed toward embodying and articulating the truth as revealed ultimately in Jesus; moral conversion transvalued by Christian conversion is infused by the theological virtue of Christian love, since the believer's will is transformed to imitate the life and deeds of Jesus. In short, while secular conversion humanizes the

---

31. There are, of course, other kinds of religious conversions. Non-Christian religious conversions would bring the convert into a relationship not with Jesus, but with the Buddha, or Atman, or Muhammad, or Tien, etc. Is it possible that such non-Christian religious conversions are pneumatologically mediated or that they bring the convert into conformity with the values of the kingdom of God apart from conscious assimilation into the mind of Christ? Clearly non-Christian religious conversions also transvalue and transform the other kinds of conversions that the individual experiences. The early Gelpi seems to endorse the main lines of Rahner's "anonymous Christianity" thesis as related to this question (see *Life and Light*, 63–68), while the later Gelpi suggests a pneumatological approach that recognizes both the possibility of the holy Breath's gracing even non-Christian religious traditions and the possibility of Christians learning from non-Christian religious others given the incarnation as a finite (i.e., inexhaustive) and sacramental (i.e., concealing as well as disclosing) revelation of God (*Firstborn 3*, esp. 406–13). At the same time, the normative significance of Jesus is affirmed in faith since Jesus' revelation of the divine experience in human, albeit sinless, form endows it with the power to measure and judge and authenticity of all other human and religious experiences (cf. Gelpi, *Gracing*, 328 and 337). My own reflections on this complex set of questions are to be found in *Discerning the Spirit(s)* and *Beyond the Impasse*.

32. Actually, Gelpi's most penetrating and rich discussion of affective conversion occurs in his *Inculturating North American Theology*, chs. 3–4, where he shows how conversion at this level includes confronting and dealing with the fears, biases, resentments, and doubts that often block authentic engagement with and appropriate appreciation of the other on its own terms. Affective conversion functions in this foundational sense to remove the inhibitions which prevent clear thinking.

person or Christian, Christian conversion christianizes the human through the persuasively transforming power of the holy Breath.[33]

In Gelpi's metaphysics of experience, essences become the qualitative hows of experiences rather than the whats.[34] Human experience is thus graced not by an essential what, but by the living Breath of God. Dualisms of all kinds—metaphysical, between mind or spirit and matter; epistemological, between knower and known, or between percept and concept; existential or personal, between self and other, etc.—are overcome with the recognition of the triadic, social, and relational character of all experience, divine and human. Nominalism is rejected in favor of a critical realism. In this way, grace is experienced by believers through the ecclesial, sacramental, and charismatic activity of the divine Breath, who assimilates them to the mind of Christ in order that they may embody his truth and activity in the world. Pessimism is muted by a recognition of the natural capacities in human experience even if such capacities are not finally salvific left on their own; thus the importance of charismatically inspired evangelism in all of its forms.[35] Finally, optimism is replaced by a critical fallibilism that opens up believers to correction in as much as they maintain an attitude of docility before the holy Breath.

But notice also that by invoking a metaphysics of experience understood within Peirce's semiotic realism, Gelpi was able to sketch the process by which doctrinal statements and beliefs that emerge from experience and are only more or less vaguely stated can be clarified, rendered explicit, and confirmed by ongoing practice. Because this process involves analysis of the theoretical and metaphysical presuppositions that undergird doctrinal assertions, far from being useless speculative efforts, metaphysical inquiry is crucial to the hypothetical exploration of the meaning of doctrine since it provides frameworks within which doctrines can be clarified, confirmed, revised, or perhaps even rejected. Of course, given the dialectic between the concrete and the abstract, the reverse movement is also possible, whereby metaphysical frameworks themselves are clarified, confirmed, revised, or rejected according to the results of empirical inquiry.[36] On this point, Gelpi

---

33. Gelpi, *Gracing*, 342.

34. This move away from Aristotelian substance philosophy connects well with the kind of relational theological thinking that younger pentecostals are exploring; see, e.g., Cross, "The Rich Feast of Theology."

35. If the idea of providing some kind of metaphysical grounding for a pentecostal theology of mission and of evangelism seems rather odd, it is for that matter no less exciting.

36. Gelpi provides some valuable guidance regarding development and continual assessment of metaphysical hypotheses as a whole (*Varieties*, 341–48, *Gracing*, 272–76).

wisely adopted William E. Hocking's principle of alteration, which suggests the need for the ongoing interplay between detailed investigations on the one hand, and reflection on one's theory of reality in general on the other, in any fallibilistically conceived effort to develop a theory of the whole.[37]

ELEMENTS OF A POSTMODERN CHRISTOLOGY

Elements of the dialectical argument in *Varieties*, the foundational argument in *Peirce and Theology*, and the (arguably) doctrinal argument in *Gracing* are systematically explicated in Gelpi's magnum opus (to date): a three-volume Christology. *The Firstborn of Many: A Christology for Converting Christians* (2001) is 1,665+ pages of text (excluding the very helpful glossaries appended to each volume, which help steer the reader through Gelpi's technical terminology) that systematically elaborates and exemplifies the conviction that the theoretical meanings of the central Christian doctrines regarding Jesus Christ are made clear in the operational consequences they lead to and the behaviors they inculcate.[38] Volume 1 lays out the methodology employed (Part 1), provides a multidisciplinary portrait of the historical Jesus (Part 2), and explores the kerygmatic Christology and the apocalyptic Christology of the Book of Revelation in light of the category of hope (Part 3). The second volume, devoted to a painstaking literary analysis of the synoptic evangelists, focuses on the question of how the gospel narratives reveal the mind of Jesus, and how that revelation mediates not only christological knowing but christological praxis. The final installment focuses on the Christology of the Johannine school as providing the transition from narrative to doctrinal Christology (Part 1), proceeds to elaborate

---

How does one go about doing metaphysics? By a) producing a "working hypothesis" driven by a root metaphor; b) abducing more particular hypotheses based on the general hypothesis; c) clarifying deductively the operational consequences of these second-tier hypotheses; d) testing inductively the clarified abductions against lived experience, and the results of scientific and scholarly studies; and e) asking repeatedly: does the metaphysical vision meet the criteriological tests of consistency (does the hypothesis exhibit logical consistency when inductively tested?), coherence (does it aspire and succeed to universality without claiming a priori necessity?), and applicability (does it serve to adequately explain any facts which might be encountered?)?

37. Gelpi, *Gracing*, xii; see Hocking, *Meaning of God*, 405–27. For an example of the application of Peirce's fallibilism to the empirical methods of science, and the science-religion dialogue about "the whole," see Austin, *End of Certainty and Beginning of Faith*.

38. Previews of Gelpi's Christology were sketched as far back as *The Divine Mother* (1984), and in that sense, the Christology fulfills a promissory note issued long ago. More recently, an overview of the Christology is presented succinctly in *Committed Worship*, vol. 1, ch. 2.

on a post-Chalcedonian Trinitarian Christology in part by identifying how other Enlightenment and post-Enlightenment Christologies are plagued by precisely the kinds of untenable philosophical presuppositions exposed in *Gracing*, and in part by reformulating the doctrines of the Trinity, the hypostatic union, and the atonement within a triadic, social, and realistic metaphysics of experience (Part 2), and concludes with a practical Christology of loving and serving as Jesus loved and served (Part 3).[39] Because there is neither space nor time here to do justice to the richness of this work, I will highlight three of its distinctive contributions to systematic christological reflection, all of which are connected to Gelpi's larger project.

First, Gelpi's multidisciplinary portrait of Jesus in Volume 1, Part 2 reflects the kind of sustained and progressive communal inquiry advocated by both Peirce and Lonergan, as well as Hocking's principle of alteration. Here, the triadic, social, and realistic construct of experience is deductively clarified and inductively tested by a wide range of empirical approaches to Jesus' finitude and humanity. His cognitive, emotional, and moral development as a human person in first-century Palestine is critically explored with the help of contemporary psychological and clinical studies such as those by Piaget, Kohlberg, Erickson, and Damon. Jesus' linguistic and social development is also critically examined with the help of Daniel Stern, Lev Vygotsky, Walter Ong, R. L. Selman, and others. The process of religious maturation undergone by Jesus is illuminated by aspects of Fowler's theory of faith development. The result is a complex philosophical anthropology and developmental psychology that lays claim not only to scientific probability but also to scientific plausibility. Gelpi writes, "That may sound disappointing; but to the best of my knowledge, no one to date has ever attempted to develop a Christology based on a philosophical construct of the human which could make even that minimal scientific claim."[40] To round out his Jesusology, Gelpi engages the findings of the recent Jesus quests in order both to understand the world that Jesus entered and to historically reconstruct the "bare facts" about his life and teachings. The result is that naïve presuppositions and misconstrued fundamentalisms are cleared away

---

39. Here, Fr. Gelpi has pointed out to me that *Firstborn* was actually written before *Gracing Human Experience* and before *Peirce and Theology*, even if all three were published in 2001. In other words, the details of Gelpi's theological anthropology in *Gracing* are derivative from the Christology of *Firstborn*, not the other way around. Further, the specificity of the method laid out in *Peirce and Theology* was sharpened by the writing of *Firstborn* even as *Firstborn* itself emerged out of Gelpi's extensive ruminations previously on theological method.

40. Gelpi, *Firstborn*, vol. 1, 251.

even while the "solid historical roots of Christian faith"[41] are evidenced and the notion of Jesus as a finite, developing human experience is confirmed.[42]

Second, Gelpi's Christology is fundamentally biblical not because it is exegetical per se, but because of the painstaking dialectical method with which he reads the gospel narratives. This dialectical reading—what Gelpi calls "linkage analysis"—involves comparison and contrasts (Lonergan's fourth functional specialty) within each and across all three synoptic Gospels, focused on the different theological frames of reference employed by the Gospel writers. Dramatic, thematic, and allusive linkages illuminate the shape of Jesus' life and the force of his teachings in order to communicate what Gelpi called "christological knowing"—i.e., the affective, intellectual, moral, and religious demands that the person of Jesus Christ makes on readers of the gospels in general and on believing Christians more specifically. The first, dramatic linkages include positive linkages across the narratives of Jesus' relationship with John the Baptizer, with the Father, and with the Breath that reveal the mind of Jesus and the ideals that believers should aim for. Negative dramatic linkages in Jesus' encounters with Satan, with the scribes, Pharisees, and priests, and with Pilate define those vices, attitudes, choices, and actions that believers ought to avoid. Ambiguous dramatic linkages presented in Jesus' relationship to the crowds and his own disciples demonstrate the ambivalence that permeates lived experience and the importance of decision in the light of the gospel story, and calls for conversion.[43] Thematic linkages focus primarily on Jesus' teaching and explicate the moral demands of Christian discipleship. Allusive linkages highlight patterns in the Gospels that present central themes, whether focused on the paschal mystery (Mark), the ecclesia and commission to the world

---

41. Ibid., 331.

42. The value of applying Hocking's principle of alternation is clear in Gelpi's multidisciplinary portrait of the historical Jesus. Pentecostals neglect such cross-disciplinary approaches to theology at great loss. However, there should also be the recognition that the diversity of global pentecostalism requires a plurality of enculturated pentecostal theologies. This pluralism is complicated by the fact that transnational and regional factors are at work in any particular area in the forging of pentecostal identities. Social anthropologists—e.g., Corten and Marshall-Fratani, *Between Babel and Pentecost*—are now engaging in detailed semiotic analyses of the various linguistic, ritual, symbolic, and material sign systems that shape institutional and individual pentecostalisms. Peirce's semiotic theory therefore has to be invoked across the board from research to communications, the last being especially crucial since Gelpi's project of developing a charismatic North American theology needs to be supplemented by indigenous historical and cultural engagements in order to craft a pentecostal theology befitting the breadth of the movement it claims to represent.

43. Gelpi's deployment of narrative theology and literary analysis connects well with the pentecostal orientation toward narrative and testimonial forms of theologizing.

(Matthew), or the presence and activity of the holy Breath (Luke). Volume two of Luke's Christology, the book of Acts, demonstrates the operational consequences that belief in Jesus—narrated in volume one specifically, but in the synoptics in general as well—brings about in the lives of those assimilated to him by the power of his Breath.[44]

On this note, it is important to specify the third and, for our purposes, most distinctive contribution of Gelpi's Christology: that it is driven by Peirce's pragmatic logic of consequences. As delineated in *Peirce and Theology*, doctrines can be authenticated only by making explicit their operational outcomes. The authentication of christological doctrine must therefore pass not only the historical test of who Jesus actually was—thus the importance of the earlier discussion on the historical Jesus[45]—but also the soteriological test of living out the ideals he embodied practically. Here lies the central import of Gelpi's insistence that the meanings of doctrinally vague propositions about Jesus Christ are specified in the ethical behaviors that true christological knowing produces. This move overcomes the dualism between theory and practice since "practice clarifies speculative intent, while belief consists in the willingness to take responsibility for the operational, practical consequences of what one affirms speculatively."[46] But note that within Gelpi's foundational theology, this bridge between theory and practice is crossed by conversion.[47] Christological knowing arises out of the initial and ongoing process of being assimilated to the mind of Christ by the holy Breath, or, in Pauline phraseology, in "putting on the mind of Christ." This is because Jesus saves precisely by living a finite and yet perfect human life, by revealing, proclaiming, and embodying in his life and death the pattern of kingdom living, and by endowing humankind with the gift of the Breath so as to empower human beings to realize, be conformed to, and

---

44. Throughout his Christology, Gelpi's method lifts up how the Spirit works through the biblical text to both remind us of what Jesus said, and to reveal Jesus as Emmanuel, God with us. For this reason alone, pentecostals should pay serious attention to the accomplishment in *Firstborn*.

[See also Yong, *Who is the Holy Spirit?*, which follows this Gelpian suggestion methodologically by working through the Book of Acts sequentially but referring back to Jesus' life and teachings in the Gospel of Luke in light of the apostolic experiences.]

45. Gelpi, *Firstborn*, vol. 1, Part 2.

46. Ibid., vol. 3, 356.

47. Gelpi is here suggestive regarding a philosophical vocabulary by which to understand how the Spirit effects transformation in the lives of believers. Here, the biblical scholarship of Wenk, *Community-Forming Power*, provides exegetical confirmation for Gelpi's hypothesis. His research into the pentecostal canon within the canon, Luke-Acts, has also shown that the encounter with the Spirit is not simply an emotional experience but one that results in inspired activity and transformative action.

in turn embody the mind of Christ.[48] In other words, salvation is not only the knowledge of certain propositions, doctrinal or otherwise, but being converted both initially and in an ongoing sense by being assimilated to the mind of Christ in the power of his Breath. In this way, as Gelpi remarked previously, "orthopraxis grounds orthodoxy."[49]

GELPI AS A CHARISMATIC THEOLOGIAN

I would like to suggest that this insight of Gelpi's reflects at least in part the motivation which has driven his own quest to understand his religious practices and experience of God, and that his research, reflection, writing, and book publications over the past three-plus decades provides a record of that process of inquiry. More specifically, I am submitting that it is his life-transforming encounter with Pentecost in 1968[50] that demanded the adjustment of his theological identity from that of being a more-or-less traditional Catholic religious to that of being a specifically *charismatic* Catholic religious. The transition is signaled implicitly by the brief discussion of the impact of the charismatic renewal on Catholic religious life at the end of *Discerning the Spirit*,[51] and explicitly in the only two volumes devoted to pentecostalism which he published shortly thereafter (*Pentecostal Piety* and *Pentecostalism: A Theological Perspective*). These volumes launched Gelpi on a research program driven by the question, "What does it mean to experience the Spirit of God?"

Gelpi's development of a metaphysics of experience in his early theological trilogy[52] reflects his intuitions at that time that the dominant themes and motifs of North American philosophical tradition held much more promise for answering this question than the transcendental Thomism in which he had been initially trained. More specifically, the metaphysics of experience derived from bringing Peirce, Royce, and Whitehead together could potentially resolve perennial conundrums in the history of theology, including those concerning the relationships between charismatic and sacramental life, between grace and nature, and between foundational pneumatology and foundational Christology. This explains why Gelpi returned to revise and develop themes from *Charism and Sacrament* in his two-volume *Committed Worship* (1993); why the theological anthropology in *Experi-*

48. Gelpi, *Firstborn*, vol. 3, ch. 11.

49. Gelpi, *Gracing*, 338.

50. Gelpi, *Experiencing God*, 11–12.

51. Gelpi, *Discerning the Spirit*, 319–25.

52. See Gelpi's *Charism and Sacrament*, *Experiencing God*, and *Divine Mother*.

encing God is expanded away from the technical jargon of Whiteheadian philosophy toward the more accessible experiential account in *The Gracing of Human Experience*[53]; and why the Trinitarian pneumatology *The Divine Mother* (1984) is complemented and completed with *The Firstborn of Many*.

Along the way so far, I have attempted to show the relevance of Gelpi's thought to pentecostals by engaging in a running dialogue between the various facets of his work and that of especially more recent pentecostal (and charismatic) scholarship. Let me now make what may be the bold claim that pentecostals (and charismatics) should take Gelpi seriously because his *oeuvre* is, to date, not only the richest philosophical explication of pentecostal-charismatic experience, but perhaps also the most original, penetrating, and systematic theological project to appear that is both deeply rooted in and pervasively imbued with intuitions derived from charismatic and renewal praxis. Thus, for example, the idea that the sacraments mediate and nurture conversion in all its dimensions—e.g., of how Christian conversion is mediated through baptism and first communion, or of how the vocational dimensions of life are sacramentally graced through marriage and holy orders—is not separated from the conviction that the sacraments are effective precisely as vehicles through which believers are assimilated to the mind of Christ according to the illuminating power of the holy Breath. This togetherness of sacrament and charism is not only made possible but actually demanded by the triadic, realistic, and social metaphysics of experience, since the Breath is experienced as providing, both initially and in the ongoing life of discipleship, the legal and habitual tendencies that form and express the mind of Jesus in the individual and in the concrete and material structures of the community of faith.[54] In a similar way, that nature assumes grace and that Christology assumes pneumatology both reflect Gelpi's conviction that orthodoxy assumes orthopraxis. I would argue that each of these insights derive, finally, from the pneumatological and charismatic starting point at the base on Gelpi's philosophical theology.[55]

53. Cf. also *Gracing*, chs. 2–3.

54. Thus Gelpi understands his own work to be directly relevant to the development of a new catechesis; both *Committed Worship* and *Conversion Experience* are intended to lay the theological groundwork for the development of an ecumenically sensitive restored catechumenate (e.g., the Rite of Christian Initiation of Adults or RCIA). On the pentecostal side, Cheryl Bridges Johns, *Pentecostal Formation*, has begun to prod pentecostals forward in thinking about how spontaneity and structure come together in spiritual formation.

55. Pentecostal reflection on a theological method that proceeds from a distinctively experiential and pneumatological starting point has begun in earnest during the past generation. Classical pentecostal approaches include Menzies, "Synoptic Theology," and Roger Stronstad, *Spirit, Scripture and Theology*. More recently proposals include

The speculative theory illuminates the logic of pentecostal and charismatic practice, even while the practices and experiences themselves cry out for metaphysical and theological explication.

How then should pentecostals respond to Gelpi's *oeuvre*? Some might resist engaging his work because of being intimidated by the philosophical apparatus he deploys. Is this too much philosophizing for pentecostals? Perhaps a decade ago, yes, as described by pentecostals like Henry Lederle who said then that Gelpi "employs such a wide range of philosophical approaches that he undercuts basic communication with most of those interested in a theology of the charismatic renewal."[56] Today, however, more and more pentecostals are seeing the need to provide theoretical accounts of their beliefs and practices. Perhaps it is the case that pentecostals today are much more sophisticated philosophically and therefore ready to take up the challenging questions posed by Gelpi's life's work. Alternatively, perhaps it is also the case that the latter Gelpi wrote in ways which are much more accessible to pentecostal scholars. Perhaps a bit of both. In any case, may the discussion continue . . . [57]

McQueen, *Joel and the Spirit*; Solivan, *Spirit, Pathos and Liberation*; Cross, "Pentecostal Systematic Theology?"; and Cartledge, *Charismatic Glossolalia*. D. Lyle Dabney is hard at work on the multi-volume pneumatological theology outlined in "Otherwise Engaged," while Frank Macchia is reformulating the doctrine of justification from a distinctly pneumatological perspective. My own efforts to begin with pneumatology and work from there to metaphysics, epistemology, and theological method have been inspired in part by my interaction with Gelpi's work during the past few years, and is available in *Spirit-Word-Community*. [See now also Macchia, *Justified in the Spirit*.]

56. Lederle, *Treasures Old and New*, 117.

57. Portions of an earlier version of this chapter were presented to the Philosophy Section of the Society for Pentecostal Studies Annual Meeting, Southeastern College, Lakeland, Florida, 14–16 March 2002. My thanks to Fr. Gelpi for his response given at this same session.

PART II

The Post-Christendom Era
and the Pentecostal Retrieval

CHAPTER 4

The "Baptist Vision" of James Wm. McClendon Jr.

A Wesleyan-Pentecostal Response

ON 30 OCTOBER 2000, shortly after completing the final pages of his *Systematic Theology*, James William McClendon Jr., Distinguished Scholar in Residence at Fuller Theological Seminary, returned home to be with the Lord.[1] The following review, reflection, and response to McClendon's "baptist vision" is written in recognition of its importance for contemporary Christian theology. At the same time, insofar as it seeks to participate in, complement, and extend the theological conversation to which McClendon had devoted his life's work, it should also be considered as a tribute to his legacy. Part one of this chapter will summarize some of the primary themes, motifs, and arguments of the *Systematic Theology*, thereby setting the stage for the dialogue to follow in part two. There, I will look in some detail at McClendon's "baptist vision," his biographical/theological method, and his theology of religions, and do so in conversation with recent Wesleyan and pentecostal theology since these are considered by McClendon as members within the family tree of the Radical Reformation.[2]

1. McClendon's magnum opus is his three-volume *Systematic Theology*: Vol. I, *Ethics*; Vol. II, *Doctrine*; and Vol. III, *Witness*. All references to these volumes will be cited parenthetically in the text simply by volume, colon, and page number; italics and emphases within quotations are McClendon's unless otherwise noted.

2. Because I did not know James McClendon personally, I can only honor his life's work by engaging seriously with his ideas. At the end of the Preface to Volume II, McClendon writes, "I point out that I have written slowly, that there is much on each page, and that slow reading is in this case the best reading. In particular, I point this out to reviewers, who are at their lovely best when they take time to read what is actually

MCCLENDON'S SYSTEMATIC THEOLOGY—
AN OVERVIEW

Theology had been previously defined by McClendon as "a science of convictions."[3] But what are convictions? They are "our persuasions, the beliefs we embody with some reason, guiding all our thought, shaping our lives" (1:23). Theology is, therefore, the "discovery, understanding, and transformation of the convictions of a convictional community, including the discovery and critical revision of their relation to one another *and to whatever else there is*" (1:23). Putting it this way, the progression of McClendon's *Systematic Theology*, from *Ethics* through *Doctrine* and concluding in *Witness*, makes eminent sense. Theology flows out of and shapes convictional practices. What Christians believe (*Doctrine*) cannot be abstracted from what they do (*Ethics* and *Witness*).

1. Ethics. McClendon begins his *Ethics* with the question of what an authentic baptist theology should be like. He lays out the hypothesis, designed to be tested throughout the *Systematic Theology*, that the marks of a distinctively baptist theology include the following features:

1. Biblicism, understood in the sense of Scripture being authoritative for faith and practice;

2. Evangelism, oriented toward mission with the understanding that genuine witness may entail suffering;

3. Liberationism, with emphasis on the individual's voluntary response to God, and on the Christian community and its separation from the state;

4. Discipleship, defined as lifelong service in acknowledgment of the lordship of Christ and signified by believer's baptism;

5. Community, understood as sharing life together in the service of and with Christ, signified by the Lord's Supper.

Drawing from Peter's connecting the pentecostal experience with the prophecy of Joel—"this is that" (Acts 2:16), this experience on the day of Pentecost being a fulfillment of that prophecy—the baptist vision also makes a similar claim. Expressed as a hermeneutical motto, this claim is a "shared awareness

---

written." I hope that I have heeded the author's request, and that such would be evident in what follows to those who knew him best.

3. From McClendon Jr. and Smith, *Convictions*, esp. ch. 7; orig. published as *Understanding Religious Relativism*.

of *the present Christian community as the primitive community and the eschatological community.* In other words, the church now is the primitive church and the church on the day of judgment is the church now; the obedience and liberty of the followers of Jesus of Nazareth is *our* liberty, *our* obedience" (1:31). These two motifs—"this is that" and "then is now"—are at the heart of McClendon's baptist vision: "The church now *is* the primitive church; *we* are Jesus' followers; the commands are addressed directly to *us*. . . . The baptist 'is' in 'this is that' is therefore neither developmental nor successionist, but mystical and immediate; it might be better understood by the artist and poet than by the metaphysician and dogmatist" (1:33).

But why begin with ethics? While McClendon acknowledges the interconnectedness between ethics and doctrine and their presupposing each other, he argues for the chronological priority of ethics over doctrine (1:42). Are not spiritual and moral instruction the center of Christian life from which emerges Christian teaching? Yet McClendon is not interested in ethics understood simply as moral decision making. Rather, building on the work of others like Stanley Hauerwas and John Howard Yoder, McClendon sees that decisions of the moral life flow out of shared convictions about the way things ought to be, and such convictions derive, finally, from the shared story that Christians participate in. Our Christian lives are or should be no more and no less than the reenactment of convictions found in the biblical story: "this is that."

It is also important to note that, for McClendon, convictions are what make persons and communities what they are. To relinquish a conviction is not simply to shed an incidental belief but to undergo a transformation of self or community into something other than what it was before. But what then about the convictions undergirding Christian morality? What, in other words, is the content of Christian convictions about the spiritual and moral life? McClendon suggests a three-stranded framework for understanding biblical morality: the sphere of the organic (the body and the material, natural, and environmental realms), the sphere of the communal (the social, interpersonal, and ecclesial realms), and the sphere of the anastatic (the resurrection, pentecostal, and eschatological realms) (1:66–67). His argument is that God is to be found in each sphere of human life, even while none of the spheres is disconnected from the others, and each includes the other two (cf. 1:186). The three-part structure of *Ethics* unfolds according to this threefold framework.

Each of the three parts, in turn, follows a similar structure. The sphere of the organic begins with the contours of an ethics and morality of the body and moves toward an ethic of sexual love. The sphere of the communal outlines a social ethics and moves toward an ethic and politics of forgiveness.

The sphere of the anastatic begins with a sketch of resurrection ethics and moves toward an ethic of peace. The movement in each case, from the general toward specificity, is mediated in the middle chapters of each part by biographical narratives that depict the baptist vision of "this is that." These biographies are by no means accidental to the *Systematic Theology*. Rather, they follow from McClendon's conviction that narratives are at the heart of identity, and that part of the theological task involves exploring how the Christian narrative and personal narratives that are far removed in space and time are interrelated.[4]

More concretely, for example, Part I begins with the narrative of the black experience of religion and morality as embodied. The next chapter, on the lives of Sarah and Jonathan Edwards, tests the ethical theory as it relates to the erotic and yet common life of Christians. The last chapter in this part discusses sexual love within the larger moral framework of multiple narrative identities. Whether it be the Augustinian understanding of concupiscence connected with the fall, the romantic myth of the twelfth-century Tristan poem, the Freudian myth of eroticism, or Robert Louis Stevenson's love story, *Catriona* (1893)—the last presented in order to illuminate the biblical story of divine agapic love—moral character, identity, and norms are shown to be derived from various kinds of narratives.

Part II, on social ethics, continues this narrative approach. Bonhoeffer's life illustrates how Christian convictions are lived out amidst difficult social and political circumstances. Without a communal environment to cultivate, reinforce, and act upon the shared Christian story, not only was Bonhoeffer's martyrdom inevitable, but the Confessing Church's resistance to the Nazi regime was bound to fail (cf. 1:207, 210). This is because it is only in communities that practices are established, performed, and maintained. Practices that go wrong or counter the redemptive model of Jesus' life become fallen principalities and powers that stand in need of correction (1:173–77, passim).

Finally, in the discussion of resurrection ethics, Dorothy Day's quest for social utopia exemplifies the socio-ethical implications of a millennial vision wedded to pacifist convictions. Yet visions and convictions are rooted in practices and narratives that persist through trying times. Day's period of engaging the world, from the Great Depression through World War II and to the later civil rights movement, is a testimony to the continuities amidst the disjunctions of a set of meaningful and lived convictions. Building on Day's biography, McClendon argues in the final chapter of this part that

---

4. This theological program was charted long before the *Systematic Theology* began; cf. McClendon Jr., *Biography as Theology*. Alongside the three biographical chapters, other section-long or paragraph-long narratives are interspersed throughout *Ethics*.

peacemaking is the set of practices that brings together all three spheres of the ethical life: the organic, the social, and the eschatological. These practices are rooted, finally, in the life and message of Jesus. As McClendon notes, it is by stories that "our lives are shaped; their narrative logic controls our use of rationality; they are the stuff of our convictions. If, then, we find our own convictions in discord, the indication is that we have not gotten our own stories straight" (1:313). Thus it is that this three-sphered ethics is a narrative ethics because "its task is the discovery, understanding, and creative transformation of a shared and lived story, one whose focus is Jesus of Nazareth and the kingdom he proclaims—a story that on its moral side requires such discovery, such understanding, such transformation to be true to itself" (1:332).

2. *Doctrine*. *Doctrine* continues the development of McClendon's baptist vision: "this is that; then is now." The driving motif in this volume is doctrine as practice: What does the church need to teach in order to be the church? McClendon's argument is that (at least in America), theology from Edwards to Martin Luther King Jr., has been "a practice about practices, a secondary practice that sought to discover, to interpret, and (provisionally) to revise the primary practices of the Christian communities it served" (2:56).

To further explore this thesis, McClendon suggests that traditional soteriological doctrines and categories be reinterpreted as practices at various stages of the Christian spiritual journey that are directed toward the eschatological reign of God (Part I). What is known as "catechesis"—which in the early church both preceded and followed baptism—concerns the practices of instruction. "Conversion" governs the practice of baptism. "Koinonia" shapes the practices of eucharistic life following the way of Jesus. "Sanctification" influences the practices of discernment. McClendon discusses these successively under the categories "preparing," "conversion," "following," and "soaring" (2:137–44). Yet each of these are dimensions of the one "salvation" that Christians experience (2:121). This salvation is the means through which believers experience the presence of Christ (the organic); through which they come into right relations with Christ and each other (the communal); and through which they enter into a new way of life (the anastatic).

Yet while practices do fund doctrines, it can also be said that doctrines also illuminate practices. McClendon's discussion of Christology (Part II) specifically focuses on the various ways in which christological doctrines illuminate Christian practices. The doctrine of the resurrection serves to structure the practice of Christian worship; that of ascension enables vision of the risen Christ (it encourages the practices of waiting and tarrying) and reception of the Spirit of Christ (it legitimates the experience of Spirit baptism); that of the pentecostal presence of the risen Christ governs the kingdom work and disciple witness of the community of Christ's followers (2:240).[5] But, at the same time (and perhaps, more importantly), resurrection, ascension, and Pentecost are not only about us and our practices, but also about God and his actions. They narrate the activities of God's own story (cf. 2:248) such that they are truthful representations of God's character and life. In this way, McClendon attempts to account for Christian theology, doctrine, and practice. But to do so, he has to resort, finally, to a "two-narrative" Christology (2:274–78) that is reminiscent of the "two-nature" Christology of Chalcedon.

This said, McClendon insists that doctrines are never only items of belief, but also structures of practices. Thus, Christology serves as an invitation to us to participate in the life of Jesus and that of his disciples. Further, the doctrine of the atonement is about the work of God through Jesus Christ; but it is also about how Jesus' sacrificial life illuminates the Christian practice of carrying the cross. Thus, the Gospel stories are about Jesus' life and his relationship to his disciples; but they also "invite contemporary readers to identify themselves with the wayward but transformed disciples of the story. The Gospels rhetorically invite readers to *become* participating disciples [by providing] the essential elements—character, plot, setting—of authentic narrative" (2:228).

Part III, on "The Fellowship of the Spirit," continues to probe the question of what kind of Christian community is appropriate to the Christian story. As expected, McClendon argues for a "free church" ecclesiology rooted in the baptist vision. Such an ecclesiology is "local, Spirit-filled, mission-oriented, its discipleship always shaped by a practice of discernment" (2:243). This hearkens to the marks of the baptist vision as detailed in *Ethics*. It assumes regular Bible reading along with communal interpretation. It is therefore pneumatic over and against Protestant or Catholic ecclesiologies that are characterized as more localized/individualized or corporate/catholic (2:341–44; I will return to this point later). Yet this is far from a sectarian (in the pejorative sense) ecclesiology. Rather, while each ecclesial voice and vision should be heard by the others, all are "provisional, awaiting future, even eschatological, completion" (2:337). In fact, McClendon's ecumenical

---

5. For an extensively developed narrative Christology of praxis that complements McClendon's efforts, see Gelpi, *Firstborn*, esp. Vol. 2: *Synoptic Narrative Christology*. Gelpi's Christology, however, should be read against his larger project of a systematic foundational theology of Christian conversion: how should Christian beliefs shape Christian life? For an overview of Gelpi's system, see Yong, "In Search of Foundations" [ch. 3 of this volume].

vision insists that each voice continues to engage other voices, including those of the Jews who are not only at the roots of the Christian community, but who also share central biblical narratives with those in the Christian way (2:345–60).

When applied to Christian worship, the baptist hermeneutical principle of "this is that, then is now" is what enables the church at worship to know itself as the church (2:385). Thus, paedobaptism is unacceptable since only adults can affirm the "yes" or insist on saying "no" to Jesus (2:394–95), and the former is absolutely necessary for true discipleship. With regard to the Eucharist,

> to say that [Jesus] is present *in a way that matters* . . . is to say that the one of whom this story tells is present in such a way that *the story continues,* present in a way that makes no sense save for the story to this point, a way that shapes the story still to follow. Hence there can be no better "honoring," no better "worshiping" of the one who meets us in Christian liturgy than recalling that story, any of its parts and especially its high moments . . . (2:378).

It also is important to emphasize that the entirety of the liturgy (and not only the formal sacraments)—including its times, structures, and spaces—not only coheres with what the church teaches, but is the means of living out and transmitting (handing off) Christian convictions.

Readers will notice, however, that McClendon appears to have deviated from his biographical theology. Where are the historical and contemporary narratives which hold together the practices and undergird the convictions of Christian doctrine? McClendon explains in the Preface that due to constraints of space (as it is, *Doctrine* is already the longest of the three volumes, reaching 536 pages), only a short section here or a paragraph there provide biographical glimpses into the life and faith of Christians. In this volume, therefore, the dominant narrative is that of Jesus Christ. Secondarily, the narrative of the church functions to illuminate the soteriological structure of Christian faith and experience. Yet this secondary narrative remains highly abstract. Put another way, it is descriptive of every Christian in a general sense (and thus functions normatively), but is of no one in particular (as readers of *Ethics* will clearly miss).

Yet it is also true to say that the combination of these two narratives—of the Gospel narrative and that of the Christian way—leads McClendon to completely restructure the traditional framework of systematic theology. Arguably, his is the most ambitious project in systematic theology to date that proceeds from the narrativist framework. As such, *Doctrine* provides new categories and new theological loci by which to grasp the important truths, beliefs, and experiences of Christians in a postmodern world.[6] This is a movement away from classical theism, if by that one means building the Augustinian-Thomistic synthesis on indubitable foundations (i.e., the doctrine of revelation), proceeding through Trinitarian theology (i.e., the doctrine of God), and culminating with eschatology (i.e., the doctrine of last things).[7] Of course, these elements are all present in *Doctrine*, but transfigured structurally, relationally, and, arguably, in terms of content, by the narrative method employed. Thus, for example, McClendon begins with eschatology and concludes with the doctrine of revelation understood in terms of the category "authority." The discussion of the doctrine of the Trinity is found in chapter seven, but is there set squarely within the Gospel narrative of the life, death, and resurrection of Jesus. On the one hand, then, those who are looking for a traditionally structured systematic theology might come away from a superficial reading of *Doctrine* feeling like they've missed out on their meal altogether. On the other hand, those who are looking to see how one baptist vision informs and shapes the enterprise of systematic theology may feel like they've been treated to a royal feast.[8]

3. *Witness.* The last volume of *Systematic Theology* reintroduces the biographical method prevalent in *Ethics* but largely missing in *Doctrine*. The driving question of *Witness* is "where and how the church must stand to be the witnessing church; that is, what must be the relation between the culture that is the church (and the larger Christian and biblical metaculture the church represents) and those cultures the church indwells, evangelizes, serves?" (3:34). McClendon's goal in this volume, broadly put, is a theology of culture.

---

6. For all of their emphasis on testimony, pentecostals have yet to produce a systematic theology in narrative form. One such Wesleyan account is available: Lodahl, *Story of God*. It is a single-volume work that focuses exclusively on the biblical narrative, thereby following its basic contours. The arrangement of the theological loci reflects this biblical shape: creation, sin, covenant, Christology, ecclesiology, and eschatology. What, if anything, do these examples—Lodahl's and McClendon's—tell us about the implications of narrative methodologies for the traditional theological loci?

7. McClendon makes the observation that, generally speaking, the scholastic and rationalistic language of classical theism remains incomprehensible to most Baptist ministers (2:300–301). This in itself marks a paradigm shift in evangelical theology today; see my "Divine Knowledge and Future Contingents."

8. [E.g., my own version is, with Anderson, *Renewing Christian Theology*, which begins each chapter with a literary examination of a biblical "character"—thus reflecting the McClendonian influence a decade later.]

Part I focuses on exploring certain aspects of contemporary culture. In successive chapters, the religious, scientific, and artistic dimensions of human life are probed as "cultural vistas." McClendon's fundamental intuition that Christian convictions require both a yes and a no to culture appears immediately in the discussion of religion that begins with Navajo culture. Navajo convictions and practices are presented across the broad spectrum of the Navajo experience, followed by a brief history of the arrival of Protestant and Catholic missionaries and their interaction with the Navajos. McClendon's assessment of Christian faith vis-à-vis Navajo religiosity is captured in a section which deserves to be quoted at length:

> For the gospel of the new that comes in Jesus Christ can only exclaim with an amen to the Navajo sense of the wholeness of life and the beauty it evinces. Would that Europeans and Anglo Americans had perceived such a wholeness sooner and more clearly! Here Navajo "religion" (or better, their religiousness) has much to teach the Christian missionaries and witnesses who come near it. On the other hand, the gospel must proclaim good tidings . . . a word of great good cheer to Navajo people who, for whatever reason, are hounded by fear of witches and dread of ghosts. . . . Thus, to repeat, the gospel is not a simple no or yes to Navajo "religion" but declares a simultaneous yes and no (3:73).[9]

This simultaneous yes and no persists throughout the remainder of McClendon's discussion of American religious culture, which includes the American Revolution, the nineteenth-century evangelical revivals, and the Social Gospel.

The chapters on science and society (written by Nancey Murphy) and on art in American culture continue to tease out the tensions between the yes and the no on the one hand, and McClendon's baptist vision on the other. Scientific discoveries affirm the intrinsic connection between the material and social strands of human experience (cf. the argument in *Ethics*) even while the theological doctrine of original sin (for example) is seen to have played a role in advances in the biological and sociobiological sciences. Further, the baptist conviction that witness perseveres through suffering provides a window into the question of natural evil. In the discussion of the visual, verbal, and musical arts, the tensions between emphasis on the empirical here-and-now world and the transcendental spiritual-sublime world is explored through the lens of the two-narrative christological notion of the hypostatic union (developed in *Doctrine*). Just as the incarnation meant the transmutation of both flesh and spirit into a "distinct biblical whole ('God

---

9. See also Yong and Zikmund, *Remembering Jamestown*, including my "Conclusion."

with us')," so does Christian art mean the transmutation of both empirical and spiritual art into a new whole as well (3:137). This chapter makes for especially interesting reading as McClendon contextualizes aesthetic theory and theology in the narratives of prominent American artists, writers, and musicians.

Part II of *Witness* is an extensive engagement with the philosophical debate about modernity and postmodernity in contemporary American culture. Structured after the argument in *Ethics*, the three chapters move from a general overview of modern philosophy through to a more specific examination of philosophy of religion in a postmodern world, mediated by an intellectual and religious biography of Wittgenstein. Here, McClendon breaks new ground in bringing to light evidence regarding the important role of Christian conversion and convictions in Wittgenstein's philosophical development. In this regard, Wittgensteinian "fideism" must be understood not as an isolated and parochial "last stand" designed to protect beliefs from outside criticism, but rather as flowing forth from and grounded in the entirety of his quiet and yet sincere Christian life, "one that weighs his [Wittgenstein's] 'wonderful life' and its basic Christian dimension into the task" (3:269). The result for the discipline of philosophy of religion at the turn of the third millennium is that there is no such thing as philosophy of religion apart from the religious convictions that are brought to bear on such philosophizing.

While I will return to the question of McClendon's philosophy of religion later, the third and final part of *Witness* does play out this movement toward a holistic Christian theology of culture and of cultural engagement. McClendon's dialectical treatment of the world's identity and Christian identity—"they measure and define each other" (3:343)—means that Christianity itself is an essentially contested concept.[10] How then can the followers of Jesus provide a distinctively Christian witness to the world? Certainly not in abstraction from the testimonies of their lived narratives, McClendon responds. It is precisely in such living narratives that the rationality of Christian convictions can be seen to be most profound and the Christian witness is felt to be most powerful because it engages rather than withdraws from or rejects the world. Of course, the plurality of cultures, religions, and experiences in the world means that the Christian witness appears as one amidst a number of "clashing stories." This means, of course, that adjudicat-

---

10. Here, McClendon builds on the work of Sykes, *Identity of Christianity*. The latter's proposal, in turn, parallels that of Robert Schreiter, who suggests that the process of contesting Christian identity requires a dialectical movement between concepts whereby one humbly submits one's claims to others even while one receives the claims of others in a self-critical fashion; see Schreiter, *Constructing Local Theologies*, 119–21.

ing conflicting narratives is both an ongoing contest of engaging one's own testimony with that of others and an eschatological anticipation intrinsic to the hope embedded in the Christian story.

In the concluding chapter of this *Systematic Theology*, McClendon applies his theology of culture to the concrete case of the relationship between Christian theology and the university. He argues that every world view, even that of "secularism," is theological in some respect because all world views make explicit the convictions of one narrative or another. Since this is the case, one cannot and should not bar Christian theology from the university. On the other hand, "Every world view, every serious examination of human convictions in light of one another *and in light of whatever else there is* (no reductionism is acceptable in this work)—all this has some claim upon the curriculum, the prominence of each claim being proportionate to its perceived value in the larger arts curriculum and in the wider culture" (3:416). Here again, the "yes" and the "no" of McClendon's baptist vision is made evident.

WESLEYANS AND PENTECOSTALS IN DIALOGUE WITH MCCLENDON

The preceding summary undoubtedly does not do justice to McClendon's 1,386-page multi-volume work. I surely do not intend to raise every conceivable point of criticism which might be raised, for at least two reasons.[11] In the first place, my concerns about McClendon's work are few; I found myself more often than not agreeing with him intuitively and theologically.[12] This leads to my second reason for only a circumscribed dialogue with

---

11. Both sympathetic and critical reviews have been published in response to *Ethics* and *Doctrine*; see, e.g., Mouw, "Ethics and Story"; Hauerwas, "Reading McClendon"; Jennings, "Recovering the Radical Reformation"; and Wood, "McClendon, Jr.'s *Doctrine.*"

12. My only real question about McClendon's project concerns the emphasis he places on the priority of narrative. I would agree with such considered chronologically—that all thought is second-ordered activity that proceeds from life experiences—but wonder about whether or not it is a nuanced enough position that takes the dialectic of thought and experience into account epistemically. In other words, to turn the questions around, do moral lives frame decision making, or does the latter constitute moral selfhood? Do narratives structure experiences, or do experiences give birth to narratives? Are the meanings of narratives equivalent to an understanding of their truths, or are narratives to be held to and assessed by non-narrativist criteria and principles? My own intuition in the matter is much more complex than McClendon's rhetoric, at least, lets on. Yet while I will deal with some of these questions incidentally in what follows, space constraints and the purpose of this review essay as a tribute to McClendon's life work prevent me from taking up these issues at any length. For discussions of some of

McClendon's opus. As a pentecostal who has received part of his graduate education in a Wesleyan environment (Western Evangelical Seminary in Portland, Oregon), my goal in what follows is to bring McClendon's achievement specifically into dialogue with the Wesleyan and pentecostal traditions. I believe this to be a worthwhile task not only since McClendon specifically includes both Wesleyans and pentecostals within his baptist vision at various places throughout *Systematic Theology*, but also because the grounds of convergence between this baptist vision and Wesleyan and pentecostal trajectories potentially makes for fruitful comparison and self-critical reflection. I will begin by exploring the inclusion of Wesleyans and pentecostals in the baptist orbit (§1), and move from there to exploring this "family" connection in greater detail by way of looking at the issue of theological method (§2). I conclude by testing the methodological proposals of all three traditions in light of their common task of theologizing Christianly in a religiously plural world (§3).

1. The Baptist Vision and the Baptist Orbit. The first observation I would like to make concerns the relationship of Wesleyan and pentecostal Christianity to McClendon's baptist vision. Certainly McClendon recognizes that these are three distinct trajectories of Christianity that have emerged since the Protestant Reformation. Accordingly, he at times distinguishes churches with their origins in the Radical Reformation from churches in the Holiness and pentecostal streams (1:19). Yet at other times he does not, as when he sets off the baptist type of ecclesial existence over and against the Catholic and Protestant (2: chap. 8, esp. 334–35, 341–44 and 364–65; 2:450); includes all "believer's churches" within the "baptist" orbit (1:34–35); speaks of the "strange voices" from the for-the-most-part silent baptist tradition (3:339–40); reflects on being oriented eschatologically to the coming kingdom of God (3:342); discusses what has traditionally been called "sanctification" and includes under his category "soaring" the Wesleyan doctrine of entire sanctification and the pentecostal experience of Spirit baptism (2:142–44); draws a parallel between baptist discipleship and Wesleyan perfect love (2:278); and agrees with Lesslie Newbigin's classification of sixteenth-century Anabaptists together with twentieth-century pentecostals as the "third force" in Christendom (2:335 and 434).[13] In each of these cases, "baptist" includes Wesleyans at one moment, pentecostals at another, both at a third,

---

these questions by advocates of narrative theology, see Goldberg, *Theology and Narrative*; Thiemann, *Revelation and Theology*; Hauerwas and Jones, eds., *Why Narrative?*; and Frei, *Theology and Narrative*.

13. McClendon here follows Newbigin, *Household of God*.

and so forth. In fact, things become significantly muddied when baptist also includes, at other moments, evangelical and fundamentalist bodies (1:19), Methodism (2:365), and other denominations in the free church tradition that are

> amorphous, and in its wholeness little known. Its communal structure, like its doctrine and morals, is known only by bits and pieces, and not as the character of one ecclesial type. Some know what it means for Pentecostals to speak in tongues; others see the point of the immersion of new members; others make sense of the practice of the Rule of Christ (Matt. 18:15–18); yet others appreciate the paradoxical claim that "this [present gathering] is a New Testament church" (2:362; brackets orig.).

Leaving aside the question of what it is that defines either Wesleyanism or pentecostalism, perhaps one way to approach the relationship between these two traditions and McClendon's baptist vision is to inquire into what exactly "baptist" means. The key clearly lies in his understanding of "baptist" as referring to any and all who are heirs of the Radical Reformation (1:19–20, 2–35; 2:45), and central to the definition of the latter is the primitivist hermeneutic of "this is that" and "then is now." In this case, of course, Wesley's biblicism and pentecostalism's primitivism appear to both qualify within the baptist orbit. But, it seems, so would the Lutheran *sola scriptura*. Other considerations therefore impinge on the definition of baptist, including those features that mark out and clearly distinguish an authentic baptist theological vision.

Clearly, however, McClendon is not undertaking either a Wesleyan or pentecostal theology, but a baptist theology. Yet his is not a parochial baptist theology, but an ecumenical one. It is motivated by the biblical narrative of what the church should be (2:371). Thus, the issue, as noted above in the discussion of ecclesiology in *Doctrine*, appears to revolve around how one understands the church. This *Systematic Theology* represents a uniquely baptist effort to bring those voices and traditions that have been on the periphery of the discussion back to the center. Here, McClendon rides the tension between particularity and universality. On the one hand, the baptist vision emerges from a historically locatable trajectory that bridges the world of the Bible and the world of the Radical Reformation; on the other hand, this vision is also ecumenical and eschatological, as evidenced not only by the various personal and communal narratives it brings together, but also by the emphasis on the anastatic (in *Ethics*), the theological priority of the kingdom of God (beginning *Doctrine*), and the ecclesial practices that anticipate participation in that kingdom (concluding *Witness*, as "Story's End";

3:371–83, esp. 379–80). Thus McClendon suggests that the various Christian identities "are justified only if they serve as provisional means toward that one great peoplehood that embraces all, the Israel of God" (3:374; cf. 2:365).

Granting this notion of eschatological provisionality, and the ecumenical orientation of this baptist theology that proceeds not from a view from nowhere but from the specificity of practices within the free church tradition, the place of Wesleyans and pentecostals within McClendon's baptist orbit seems legitimate. McClendon's project is sure to connect with the sympathies of ecumenically minded and yet convinced Wesleyans and pentecostals. Further, insofar as Wesley and early pentecostals emphasized practical Christianity over abstract doctrinal and theological speculation, the ethical priority and emphasis of this baptist vision is sure to be theologically attractive. At the same time, even conservatives within both traditions will be drawn to various aspects of this *Systematic Theology*, including its biblical commitments, its narrative structure, its evangelical and missionary thrust, and its pneumatic ecclesiology. Having said all of this, however, it is also important not to ignore the fact that Baptists are not Wesleyans or pentecostals and vice versa. In order to explore more explicitly some of the differences, I want to probe in greater detail the driving force behind this reshaping of systematic theology as traditionally conceived, McClendon's biographical or narrative methodology, and how that compares and contrasts with Wesleyan and pentecostal approaches.

2. Biographical Theology and Theological Method. The method behind the *Systematic Theology* derives from two fundamental tenets laid out at the beginning of *Ethics*: that theology is the science of convictions, and that convictions are inevitably narrative based. Building from these, McClendon insists that theology is pluralistic since it emerges from the various narratives that are brought to the theological task (1:36–37). Pluralism reigns even among baptist theologies because its two common features are emphasis on the Bible and emphasis on experience—defined as "what we have lived through and lived out in company with one another, the experience that constitutes our share in the Christ story" (1:38–39); yet this experiential approach does not open the door to relativism since theological activity is disciplined by its quest for truth (1:39–41). This leads McClendon to argue, following the patristic fathers and the Radical Reformers, for the chronological (not logical) priority of ethics over doctrine, even if both are ultimately concerned with understanding the fundamental convictions of any community (1:42–44).

These preliminary thoughts are then put to work throughout *Ethics*. In the final chapter of this first volume McClendon returns to the question of method and summarizes his case—made throughout the book—that the ethics of propositional principles, decisionism, and values all "presuppose and require some narrative, and that their Christian use presupposes and requires the Christian narrative" (1:328–29). More important, the three-stranded ethic is itself "none other than the critical analysis of the moral life of those who share in a certain ongoing real story [that of Jesus and of the kingdom of God]—a story whose link with its primitive past is established by *anamnesis* or memory, and whose link with its final end is fixed by the anticipation or hope of the sharers of the Way" (1:332). Ethics is, after all, more about the building of character and the exemplification of virtues than it is about the making of choices. The truths of character building and virtuosity are of necessity story shaped.

The same strategy of exemplifying the method and commenting on it only in the last chapter of the book is pursued in *Doctrine*. What is the theological authority behind the claims made about what the church needs to believe in order to be the church? For McClendon, "authority" is "first of all a name for the Godhead of God." The question then is how one locates "the subsidiary authorities by which God's authority takes hold" (2:456). Scripture is itself one of these proximate authorities (2:463), even if supremely normative (the traditions of the church being understood as "hermeneutical aids" [2:471]). In what might be understood as a Barthian move, Scripture's witness is understood as pointing to Christ. McClendon thus discusses the question of authority by appealing to the story of God exemplified in the person of Jesus Christ. We find that this is not just a story "out there," but a story in and through which we live, a story that lays a claim on us in one sense, but is an open invitation to us in another. More important, our living out the story validates its truth, since it enables us to affirm "this is that" and "then is now": "Here is a mystical vision, mysterious exactly because it does not deny the facts of history but acknowledges them. Our study of the original setting [e.g., the quests for the historical Jesus] does not cancel the vision but enhances its claim upon us" (2:466).[14]

---

14. Here, McClendon has the recent developments in biblical scholarship firmly on his side. Even in the debate between emphasizing the Bible as history (James Barr) over and against the canonical shape of Scripture (Brevard Childs), both sides recognize the import of the centrality of narrative. In the former case, narrative is a genre that structures the biblical events, while in the latter, narrative provides the framework for understanding canonical processes. For a discussion of the tensions involved in this particular debate, see Kermode, "Argument about Canons."

To see his narrative hermeneutic at work in what is usually categorized in traditional systematic theology under the label of prolegomena, observe how McClendon deals with the question of canonicity. His starting and ending points are the same: that *practice* secures biblical authority (2:473) and not vice versa, since it is our living the story that "displays an authority that is none other than the bidirectional love of God: 'this is how we know that we dwell in him and he dwells in us' (1 John 4:13)" (2:462). McClendon applies this narrative perspective to the question of the biblical canon, a move that allows the blending of two stories—God's and humanity's—into one. Just as the two-narrative Christology developed earlier teaches the interconnectedness of the human story and the divine, so also does a narrative perspective on the Bible enable us to see that the Scriptures are not only about God's story, but also about our own, the two stories becoming "one indivisible Book" (2:476) through the one work of the spirit of God in the unveiling of the divine-human encounter. McClendon thus sidesteps the traditional questions regarding the priority of church and tradition over Scripture or vice versa. Rather, it is precisely because the various books

> already possessed scriptural attributes—such attributes as being at once God's own story and a truly human story, as centering upon Jesus Christ, as evoking in their readers the prophetic or baptist vision—so that churches, by their recognition of these attributes, thereby revealed themselves as real churches. In this sense, their act of recognizing Scripture authenticated the church as church even while it acknowledged Scripture as Scripture. Canonicity . . . foreshadows an act that must be repeated whenever a church, Spirit-guided, uses any part of the Scriptures *as* Scripture. In this sense, the canon is not merely "open in principle," as many have said, but open in fact (2:476–77).

How does McClendon's narrative method compare and contrast with Wesleyan and pentecostal approaches to theology? While it would certainly be wide of the mark to assume that the latter two movements employ only a single hermeneutical or methodological approach, for the sake of discussion, I want to focus on the Wesleyan quadrilateral and the pentecostal pneumatic hermeneutic. Briefly, the quadrilateral emphasizes the priority of Scripture, albeit not to the neglect of tradition, reason, and experience as sources of theology.[15] The pentecostal pneumatic hermeneutic, on the other

---

15. While not explicitly identified as such by Wesley himself, the quadrilateral was exemplified in Wesley's own theological method. On the quadrilateral, see, e.g., Lodahl, *Story of God*, Part I; Thorsen, *Wesleyan Quadrilateral*; Cobb Jr., *Grace and Responsibility*, 155–76; Gunter et al., *Wesley and the Quadrilateral*.

hand, insists on the centrality of the Spirit's illumination of the Scriptures as read and experienced within the community of faith; in this sense, biblical exegesis is also always exegesis of experience or its lack thereof.[16]

McClendon's only mention of the quadrilateral is in connection with his discussion of theological authority. He agrees that Scripture, evangelical experience, and salvific community (and its practices, it should be added, all of which combine as "tradition") are appropriately understood as authorities for the theological task. What about reason, as advocates of the Wesleyan quadrilateral might add? McClendon's response is that it is a categorical mistake to identify reason as such, more properly understood as the processes of thought rather than as a site of authority (2:458–59).[17] And, given his conviction about Scripture as the highest Christian authority, both experience and tradition are normatively subordinated to it. The "God of the philosophers," for example, derived from and can only be equated with the "God of tradition" (2:316). And so, the resolution to the question of "Which tradition among many?" is to be found not in a metatradition derived from some nonexistent Archimedean standpoint, but from the practices of discipleship shaped by the biblical narratives (2:317). Accordingly, McClendon insists, "The baptist vision is more often caught from the Scriptures than taught by a tradition" (1:198).

But what about experience, evangelical and otherwise? Does not McClendon's biographical theological method act (consciously or not) as a material norm for his scriptural exegesis? How can he avoid doing so when the beginning, middle, and conclusion of his reflections build on individual and communal narratives (such as appeal to black religious experience, Jonathan and Sarah Edwards, and Stevenson's *Catriona* in the organic sphere of ethics)? McClendon's response would probably be the counter question: How can one recognize the truth of the biblical narratives apart from their instantiation either in our own lives or in those of other Christians? This would parallel the response given by pentecostal pneumatic hermeneutics

16. Here, I draw from the work of Menzies, "Synoptic Theology," and Stronstad, *Spirit, Scripture and Theology.* Dabney, "Otherwise Engaged," argues that such a pneumatocentric hermeneutic is most appropriate for the accounting of Christian convictions in a postmodern world. My own constructive proposal includes this pentecostal element, although I call it a "trilectical hermeneutic and method" instead; see my *Spirit-Word-Community.*

17. More explicitly: "reason or rationality is not understood as an authority or the authority; it is neither an authority in or on religion, nor a criterial authority for students of religion; rather it is a name for the thought processes by which we seek to maintain order in any sphere of conversation. To think is to reason, but to list thinking among one's authorities reflects either a category mistake (a misunderstanding of how the term is used) or a covert appeal to authorities one prefers to leave unnamed" (2:459).

that all exegesis proceeds not in a vacuum but from one's personal and communal experiences of God through the Spirit. This leads to the pentecostal emphasis on testimony—"Look what the Lord has done!" A similarly structured pneumatic hermeneutic, then, can be seen to animate both McClendon's baptist vision and what I have elsewhere called the pentecostal "pneumatological imagination," albeit resulting in diverse emphases.[18]

If that is the case, however, is not McClendon's baptist hermeneutic ("this is that; then is now") nothing more than primitivist or typological hermeneutic? He himself uses these labels to classify his hermeneutic at various places (e.g., 2:92, 395). If true, such a charge, frequently leveled at pentecostal hermeneutics, would seem to lead McClendon back to a fundamentalistic biblicism. That this project does not fail on this score should be self-evident, but deserves brief comment along three lines. First, McClendon's emphasis on the eschatological sense of the biblical reality runs counter to a naïve primitivism. In this regard, this baptist theologian finds himself in the company of pentecostals whose theological imagination is similarly animated by eschatological convictions.[19] Second, McClendon's "this is that" builds on a sophisticated application of speech act theory.[20] Doing so allows him to alternate emphases between the biblical narrative on the one hand and historical or contemporary narratives on the other, as appropriate to the various junctures of his argument. Thus the tension between the biblical and the ecclesial horizons is preserved.[21] Lastly, McClendon's biographical theology simply attends to a multitude of narratives, including that of the scriptural one. As previously noted, this "baptist vision" is deceiving (albeit not intentionally) in that it casts a wide net, one wide enough to include Wesleyans and pentecostals, among others. McClendon's ecumenical breadth and sensitivity means that he goes about his task of forging such a "baptist theology" in a way that will arouse few objections from those—such as Wesleyans and pentecostals—not normally considered within the baptist camp. But, on the other side, what about the possibility that McClendon's inclusiveness may alienate others whose convictions are

18. See my *Spirit-Word-Community*, ch. 4.

19. See, e.g., Faupel, *Everlasting Gospel*.

20. See McClendon and Smith, *Convictions*, ch. 3.

21. Nancey Murphy addresses this question with regard to the horizons of both the contemporary and ancient biblical audiences. She argues that McClendon's baptist vision—"this is that"—provides the hermeneutical key to understanding how the biblical words were received and practiced communally then and how they continue to be received and practiced communally today, since, according to speech-act theory, "the illocutionary force *then* is to be the illocutionary force *now for us*" (Murphy, "Textual Relativism, Philosophy of Language," 266; italics original in Murphy).

not quite as catholic? Is it the case that a narrative theological method compromises—at least potentially, if not actually—the exclusivity of Christian doctrinal claims to truth on precisely this score?

3. Testing the Methodologies: The World of the Religions. This raises the ecumenical question in all of its breadth and depth. I propose to consider this issue not only in terms of intra-Christian ecumenism, but more seriously, especially for the task of contemporary theology, with regard to interfaith relationships and the interreligious dialogue. This is an area of theological reflection that McClendon himself recognizes has serious implications for Christian doctrine and practice. At the end of *Ethics*, McClendon provides a summary of the two convictions undergirding his argument for a Christian ethics:

> [The first is that] My story must be linked with the story of a people. The other is the conviction (call it the doctrine of salvation) that our story is inadequate as well: The story of each and all is itself hungry for a greater story that overcomes our persistent self-deceit, redeems our common life, and provides a way for us to be a people among all earth's peoples without subtracting from the significance of others' peoplehood, their own stories, their lives (1:356).

What exactly does McClendon mean here? Does this "greater story" refer to the gospel story? This might be a plausible reading except for the previous sentence. Should it then be understood as the eschatological version of that story? But how can the eschatological story be "greater" if in fact "this is that"? The most obvious meaning seems to be that McClendon wishes to take with all seriousness the plurality of stories that characterize human life and existence, including those of religious others.

McClendon's own theology of religions builds on three fundamental motifs. First, following his assessment of Christian faith, all religions and religiosities are understood as "powerful *practices* that embody the life-forming convictions of its practitioners" (2:421). This move builds on post-Wittgensteinian cultural-linguistic theories of religions (like those of Clifford Geertz and George Lindbeck), and theologies of religion which emphasize their diverse practices targeting distinctive aims and teloi (like those of Joseph A. DiNoia and S. Mark Heim) (3:300–01). Second, following from the first, is the conviction that Christians can and should genuinely engage religious others in a transforming and yet critical dialogue. This is because those of other faiths are strangers dwelling within the land of faith and examining its constitution, just as once there were strangers within the gates of

Israel, and these deserve special honor for their distinctive atheist or Buddhist or Muslim or Judaic or other contributions to Christian self-understanding, although this must not be allowed to obscure their lack of the crucial element of trust in Jesus that identifies regular participants (2:33).

This leads, finally, to the soteriological question. Those who have never heard the gospel will be judged according to the light that they have. McClendon states forthrightly that this category of persons cannot be condemned in an a priori sense since "one cannot reject what one has not been offered!" (2:131). The Christian Testament's pronouncements of judgment, condemnation, and damnation "have no clear application *outside* the bounds of [the Christian] community" (2:423). In this sense, and returning to the conviction of religion as embodied practices, McClendon's baptist vision strives to preserve the undeniable exclusivity of Christian beliefs. He therefore writes that "*extra ecclesiam nulla salus* ('outside church, no salvation') is true, not in Cyprian's Catholic party sense, but in the sense that *the very meaning* of the word 'salvation' (or *salus*) in Christian use turns upon the shared life Christians take up when they come to Christ" (2:423).

But if this is the case, then how does one adjudicate conflicting truth claims across religious lines? If each religion's convictions are embodied in its practices, and if the latter are funded by their own narrative forms and structures, then how can critical and normative engagement occur? That "facts always arrive theory-laden; there are no theory-free facts, no convictionless facts, no facts save those constitutive of one story or another" (3:363) may mean that narratives can only and continuously speak past one another. What's good for me will not be good for you. The specter of relativism raises its ugly head.

Here, it might be useful to compare and contrast the results of McClendon's method with those of Wesleyan and pentecostal theologies of the religions. On the Wesleyan side, Philip Meadows brings together recent thinking shaped by Wesley's own theology of the unevangelized in a richly suggestive proposal.[22] He urges (a) a broad reading of religion that recognizes each as a complex phenomenon that eludes simplistic categorizations as either true or false or as good or evil; (b) a providential understanding of the world such that its various processes, including religious ones, are overseen by rather than outside the hand of God; (c) a gracious conception of being human that underscores the seed of the Word in the heart of every person (cf. John 1:9); (d) a christological notion of salvation that preserves

---

22. Meadows, "'Candidates for Heaven.'" The literature on Wesleyan views of the religions is growing, as exemplified in the studies cited in Meadows's article (esp. note 3). Cf. also Cunningham, "Interreligious Dialogue," and Cobb, *Grace and Responsibility*, esp. 145–53.

the life and death of Jesus at the center of the divine plan without insisting on epistemic access to these events as the *sine qua non* of being saved; (e) a dialogical approach to mission that includes interpersonal relationships and mutual social projects alongside kerygmatic proclamation; and (f) a pluralistically envisioned eschatology such that "salvation understood as the pursuit of holiness can, in fact, serve as a metanarrative to inscribe (rather than exclude) other ways of being religious, acceptable to God as means of grace with their own particular goals."[23]

On the pentecostal side, my own work in theology of religions follows a similar trajectory.[24] My concerns, however, are to emphasize insights into the structures of human religiosity from a pneumatological perspective. Thus I have called attention to the pneumatological imagination as it functions epistemically with regard to human affections and emotions, and human relationships to others and to God. This enables pneumatological categories to emerge that situate the discussion of theology of religions in a different frame of reference than one that is concerned exclusively with soteriological issues. In other words, it demands the shift in attention from the question "what of those who have never heard?" to reflections on the religions in all of their complexity as human aesthetic, ethical, and spiritual experiences. The resulting program requires nothing less than extensive dialectical, dialogical, and empirical analyses targeted toward understanding the religions comparatively—i.e., in terms of genuine rather than superficial similarities in differences—and therefore theologically.

Taken together, the Wesleyan theology of religions proposed by Meadows and the pentecostal one proposed by myself complement McClendon's own vision. Let me highlight a number of points of convergence that enable us to see these visions at work. In the first place, the baptist "this is that" retains a historical focus on how the past implicates and shapes the present, not only descriptively but also normatively. Thus the centrality of Jesus' life and death, and the testimony of the apostles, prophets, and early Christian community to that gospel narrative together function normatively both for Christian beliefs and, more importantly, for Christian practices. This connects with the Wesleyan christological inclusivism that distinguishes between the ontological and epistemic issues: Jesus' life's work and death are the basis of salvation, even if it is left open as to whether or not explicit knowledge and confession of his name is required for salvation. It also connects with the pentecostal experience of the Spirit as the experience of Jesus

23. Meadows, "'Candidates for Heaven,'" 129. On this last point, Meadows follows the richly suggestive work of DiNoia and S. Mark Heim. Note also the latter's recent *The Depth of the Riches*, which is not referenced by Meadows.

24. See, e.g., Yong, *Discerning the Spirit(s)*, and *Beyond the Impasse*.

since it is both true that the Spirit is the Spirit of Jesus and that Jesus is the sender of and the baptizer with the Spirit. In short, at various junctures, baptist, Wesleyan, and pentecostal theologies of religions are christocentric, even if they may be divided between restrictionism/exclusivism and inclusivism with regard to the question of epistemic access to that gospel.

Second, all three emphasize a robust theology of mission. The baptist vision insists that the practical theory of religions frees us to see that mission is one of the integral practices of the religion we call Christian, that without it Christianity *dis*-integrates—that is, loses its integrity. In short, to be Christian is to be on mission. Hence, the final motivation for mission need not rest in the unanswerable question of the status before God of those to whom we are sent, but rather on the far more immediate question of our own status as Christ's disciples (2:424). Similar motivations underwrite Wesleyan and pentecostal missions. The former derives from Wesley's pastoral vision of the wide world as a parish, while the latter flows from the descent of the Spirit's "power from on high." Both revolve as much around the issue of Christian obedience—flowing forth from sanctification on the one hand and from Spirit baptism on the other—as they do around the Great Commission.

This leads, thirdly, to the eschatological dimension of the baptist "this is that," which insists both that *then* ought to be *now* and that *then* also will be *in the future*. McClendon thus rightly calls attention to the fact that, "Special to each master story is the *hope of the future* that it generates" (3:359). This connects well with the sanctifying and perfect love trajectory of Wesleyan spirituality and with the eschatological orientation of pentecostal praxis. In each case, eschatology is not simply an abstract, speculative scheme, but a means of ordering one's affections, shaping one's character, and structuring the social relations of the community of faith.

But the question that arises here is that which lies at the heart of the contemporary experience of religious pluralism. It concerns the potentially arbitrary privileging of the future. Sure, all religions have eschatologies, but not all eschatologies are alike, nor do all eschatologies play similar structural or functional roles within their respective religious systems. Buddhists and Hindus, with their cyclical rather than linear views of time, certainly have master narratives that envision the future, but to discuss these futures in conjunction with "hope" is misleading because of the connotations that category has within the Judeo-Christian framework. This is not to say that Buddhists and Hindus have no hope, but that their hopes have distinctively Buddhist and Hindu flavors.

This exemplifies the problematic questions that attend to contemporary Christian theology of religions in general, and to McClendon's culturally relative perspectivism in particular (or "soft perspectivism," as he also calls it; 1:350–51; 3:52–54). A story theology inevitably runs up against other stories, other narratives, other cultures, leading to a contest of stories and a clash of narratives. McClendon resorts to a principled criteriology of love, forgiveness, and peace. He acknowledges that these arise out of the Christian master story and therefore "provide no way for our story's 'logic' to triumph over all others." Yet, they also "serve as bridges linking the concerns of the world to the concerns of Jesus' people. The Hebraic *shalom* and the Arabic *salaam*, for example, together form "a bridge by which they [Jews and Arabs] can come to respect each other's yearnings and find common way to fulfill them" (3:366). Respect means, in this context, much more than toleration, but appreciation and the willingness to be transformed. In fact, insofar as even one voice is silenced, all parties actually lose. The marginalization of the baptist voice, for example, is ample evidence that not only is that one cause "injured, but *so is every cause*" (3:339).

Here, the subtle point that emerges is that human stories are many, but also in some respects one. This finds agreement with the broad theological anthropology of Wesleyanism and the pneumatological anthropology of pentecostalism. Witness does indeed arise out of the particularity of experience, but engagement and encounter with the testimonies and stories of others is always possible. Thus, it is true that perspectivism,

> like mere relativism, acknowledges the great, contrary variety of human convictional communities, and acknowledges that the truth perceived in one is not easily translated into the truth of another community. Yet it does not theorize that there is no truth that is true. While recognizing that truth may be hard to get at, it is not dismayed. Meanwhile, perspectivism thinks it sees difficult but real ways to bring together discordant elements in the human fabric—a project about which relativism is totally pessimistic, and absolutism blithely optimistic (1:350).

This leads, finally, to that kind of interreligious dialogical encounter which the baptist, Wesleyan, and pentecostal visions all endorse. Such is missiological in intent, self-critical and transformative in practice, concerned with the question of truth, and eschatological in orientation. At their best moments, all three eschew rationalistic theologizing that neglects affective praxis and resist abstract schematizing in favor of dynamic modes of reflection; and all three attempt to creatively engage centrist theologies from their marginal positions. If this is what the baptist vision is about, I can, as one pentecostal, cast my lot with the McClendons of this world. And, I believe that I could speak also for many of my pentecostal and Wesleyan friends and colleagues. May the legacy of James Wm. McClendon Jr., encourage us in our ongoing work.

CHAPTER 5

Whither Evangelical Theology?

The Work of Veli-Matti Kärkkäinen as a Case Study of Contemporary Trajectories

It was the appearance of Veli-Matti Kärkkäinen's most recent book [as of the time of writing], *One with God: Salvation as Deification and Justification*, that occasioned the invitation to review his larger corpus in the pages of this journal.[1] My long-standing appreciation for Kärkkäinen's theological work had previously been registered in my collecting, editing, and publishing a set of his essays in book form a few years ago.[2] In the editor's introduction to that book, I noted that Kärkkäinen was fast becoming one of the more important theologians to be reckoned with in our time. He had not only already established himself as one of the leading pentecostal voices in the academy, but had also been working hard toward an ecumenical rather than merely confessional theology. In the meanwhile, the Kärkkäinen volumes that have appeared in the past few years have not only confirmed but also added to his theological reputation.

As I reflect on Kärkkäinen's wide-ranging publications across the fields of ecumenical and systematic theology and more recently in theology of religions, I am led to ask important questions about the present and future directions of evangelical theology. There are actually two sides to this question, one concerning the status of Kärkkäinen as an evangelical theologian,

1. My thanks to David Parker, editor of *Evangelical Review of Theology*, for the invitation, the opportunity, and the space for this extended engagement with Kärkkäinen's work.

2. See Kärkkäinen, *Toward a Pneumatological Theology*.

and the other concerning the contested nature of evangelical theology itself. With regard to the former issue, I will shortly attempt to make the case for why Kärkkäinen qualifies as an evangelical theologian. The latter issue, of course, is complex. The boundaries of evangelicalism and, by extension, evangelical theology, have always been debated.[3] Not surprisingly, some have suggested that evangelicals should focus not on boundary disputes but on identifying common and unifying core convictions.[4] However, attaining agreement on what elements are non-negotiable and what are adiaphora has proven elusive, especially since the diverse evangelicalism of the Euro-American West has been complexified with the recent growth of evangelical churches in the Eastern and Southern Hemispheres.[5] The present configuration of evangelicalism as a pluralistic and global phenomenon begs the question about what evangelical theology is or should be as we proceed into the twenty-first century.

In the following pages, I wish to take up this question about evangelical theology today, and do so by looking at the work of Kärkkäinen. I will argue that Kärkkäinen is an evangelical-ecumenical-world theologian in the making, and that it is, in fact, not only possible but even necessary that evangelical theology move in some of the directions charted out by him. The next three sections look at each of these three interrelated aspects of Kärkkäinen's theological work—evangelical, ecumenical, and world—followed by a critical dialogue with Kärkkäinen. I conclude in the briefer last section by asking about how Kärkkäinen's *oeuvre* to date also speaks to the possibilities and challenges regarding the future of evangelical theology in the twenty-first century.

KÄRKKÄINEN AS EVANGELICAL THEOLOGIAN

Prosecution of the thesis that Kärkkäinen is an evangelical-ecumenical-world theologian needs to begin with a look at his evangelical credentials. Resistance to this could come from two directions. For one, Kärkkäinen has identified himself first and foremost as a "Pentecostal theologian" (formerly) or "ecumenical theologian" (more recently), and much less as an "evangelical theologian." For some evangelicals, the labels "pentecostal" and "ecumenical" signify experientialism and enthusiasm on the one hand and liberalism and diminished evangelistic zeal on the other hand, and these traits are considered antithetical to authentic evangelical identity. At another

3. Stone, *Boundaries of American Evangelicalism*.

4. E.g., Fackre, *Restoring the Center*, and Grenz, *Renewing the Center*.

5. See Jenkins, *Next Christendom*, and Hitchen, "What It Means," two parts.

level, for other more conservative evangelicals, Kärkkäinen's affiliation with Fuller Theological Seminary (since 2000) also puts him outside the evangelical orbit given Fuller's historically more ecumenical and neo-evangelical reputation.[6] Yet it is his location at Fuller that would also lead most theologians in the academy to identify Kärkkäinen as an evangelical. This irony provides further justification for us to utilize the work of Kärkkäinen as a lens to explore the present state of evangelical theology and query about its future directions. I proceed to defend Kärkkäinen as an evangelical theologian along three lines: through a biographical summary of his personal and theological journey, an overview of the evangelical elements of his early theological work, and a survey of his more recent publishing record.

The second of four children, Veli-Matti was born in 1957 to Toivo and Aino Kärkkäinen, who were then faithful in the Finnish Lutheran Church. During his teen years, he made a renewed commitment to the Christian faith even as the family was in the process of affiliating with a small pentecostal congregation in his hometown of Kiuruvesi. After receiving his master's in education from the University of Jyväskylä (in Jyväskylä, Finland) in 1982 and working for a few years as a faculty secretary and lecturer at the same institution, Kärkkäinen moved with this wife, Anne-Päivi, and two daughters, Nelli and Maiju, to Pasadena, California, and enrolled in Fuller Theological Seminary's masters in theological studies program. While completing that degree (1988–1989), he pastored a small, independent evangelical church, the Finnish Christian Fellowship, in Los Angeles. Influenced by two prominent pentecostal professors at Fuller, Cecil M. Robeck and Russell Spittler,[7] he took out a membership with the Society for Pentecostal Studies in 1988, and has remained an active member ever since.[8] Upon completing his work at Fuller, Kärkkäinen returned to Jyväskylä, where he was ordained by the Full Gospel Church, a classical pentecostal denomination in Finland, and pastored a Full Gospel Church congregation there from 1989–1991.

In June 1991, Kärkkäinen moved with his family to Thailand to work as a Full Gospel missionary at the Full Gospel Bible College (FGBC) in Bangkok. At FGBC, Kärkkäinen taught a wide range of courses and also served as the college's academic dean. During his tenure, he learned to speak, read,

---

6. Marsden, *Reforming Fundamentalism*.

7. *Toward a Pneumatological Theology* was dedicated jointly to Robeck and Killian McDonald (more on him momentarily). Kärkkäinen's indebtedness to Spittler was expressed in a *festschrift* essay: "Theology of the Cross."

8. In 1994 and 1995, Kärkkäinen joined the European Pentecostal Theological Association and the European Pentecostal Charismatic Research Association, respectively. He remains an active member in these scholarly organizations.

and write in Thai.[9] Upon completing his term assignment, Kärkkäinen returned with his family to Finland, where Veli-Matti began serving at the Pentecostal Full Gospel Iso Kirja College (in Keuruu), first as professor of theology, and then in 1994 as president. During this time, he matriculated at the University of Helsinki to pursue research in ecumenical theology and dogmatics. Kärkkäinen completed his Helsinki doctorate in 1998 with a dissertation on the first three quinquennia of the Roman Catholic-pentecostal dialogue (the final draft of which he wrote as a visiting scholar hosted and mentored by Kilian McDonnell at the Institute of Ecumenical and Cultural Research at St. John's University in Collegeville, Minnesota). He then wrote his *habilitationsschrift* in 1999, focusing on the fourth quinquennium of the dialogue.

Both the dissertation and the *habilitationsschrift* have been published (*Spiritus ubi vult spirat* and *Ad ultimum terrate*). In these volumes Kärkkäinen provides a summary account of the first four rounds of the dialogue between official delegates of the Roman Catholic Church and various pentecostal scholars and theologians who have been able to participate over the years.[10] Consisting of one week of meetings a year for five years, the dialogues over the first four quinquennia included: 1) an initial phase of mutual introduction (1972–1977); 2) many of the "hard questions"—e.g., glossolalia, hermeneutics, healing, tradition and experience, Mary—between the two traditions (1977–1982); 3) an exploration of various topics related to the church and the communion of saints (1985–1989); and 4) a discussion of evangelization and mission (1990–1996). Three brief comments about the methodological, thematic, and theological aspects of these volumes are important for our purposes.

First, the research and writing of *Spiritus ubi vult spirat* ("the Spirit blows where it wills") and *Ad ultimum terrae* ("to the ends of the earth") emerged out of Kärkkäinen's immersion in the theological traditions of both modern pentecostalism and the Roman Catholic Church. To be sure, both volumes relied heavily on the Final Reports of the dialogue,[11] the theo-

---

9. Kärkkäinen also has command of Finnish, his mother tongue, Swedish, the second national language of Finland, and English and German, besides being able to read Russian, French, Italian, Spanish, and various Scandinavian languages, and having a working knowledge of the biblical and theological languages. He has and continues to publish widely in Finnish and other Scandinavian languages, especially in popular and ecclesial periodical literature.

10. Given that most classical pentecostal denominations have been suspicious of the ecumenical movement, none have formally recognized the dialogue. Pentecostal participants have not been formal representatives of their churches, and usually rely not on denominational sources of support but on either institutional or private funding.

11. The Final Reports of the first three quinquennia were published in *Pneuma: The*

logical position papers written specifically for the dialogue, and the formal recorded dialogue notes. At the same time, because Kärkkäinen's goal was not just to present a descriptive account of the dialogue but also to provide theological analysis, he took up the task of mastering the growing amount of theological literature being produced by pentecostal scholarship and post-Vatican II Roman Catholic theology. The latter not only formed the background for the Roman Catholic approach and contribution to dialogues but also allowed for and in some instances sustained the Catholic Charismatic Renewal movement. In the process, Kärkkäinen familiarized himself with the major Catholic theologians of the last two generations—Rahner, Congar, Schillebeeckx, Ratzinger, von Balthasar, Dulles, Mühlen, Sullivan, Gelpi, and others—which in turn introduced him to the breadth and depth of the Catholic theological tradition. We will see momentarily how this wide-ranging engagement with Catholic theology has served Kärkkäinen as an ecumenical theologian.

Second, Kärkkäinen's comprehensive overview of the first four quinquennia of the Roman Catholic-pentecostal dialogue meant that he was given the opportunity to engage both with the broad scope of the theological spectrum and with the particularly problematic topics dividing the two theological traditions. Over the course of the two volumes, then, we observe the emergence of Kärkkäinen the systematic theologian precisely through his grappling with the challenging issues raised by the dialogue. What is the nature of revelation and of Scripture? What are the roles of tradition, experience, and the Holy Spirit in biblical interpretation? What does Christian initiation consist of, and what role, if any, does Spirit and/or water baptism play in this experience or process? What is the nature of the church, and how do we understand the unity of the body of Christ, the apostolicity of the church, the ordination of its ministers, and the charismatic dimension of the church in relationship to the kingdom of God? What does the missionary mandate of the church consist of, and how do we define the evangelistic thrust of the church in relationship to culture, social justice, proselytism, and common witness? Throughout, Kärkkäinen deftly negotiates the tension between accurately reporting on the dialogue on the one hand, even while providing critical analysis and measured assessment on the other.

This leads, third, to the specifically theological tendencies we see emerging during this early phase of Kärkkäinen's work. While Kärkkäinen repeatedly demonstrates that he recognizes the value and truth of the Catholic perspective, he nevertheless inevitably suggests a way forward

Journal of the Society for Pentecostal Studies 12, no. 2 (1990): 85–142, while that of the fourth appeared in *Pneuma: The Journal of the Society for Pentecostal Studies* 21, no. 1 (1999): 3–88.

that strengthens rather than betrays a pentecostal theological identity in particular and a theological orientation in line with Confessing Church (Free Church) commitments in general.[12] So, biblical revelation is neither merely mediated by tradition nor merely propositional, but is personally encountered in and through Scripture (revelation's ultimate norm) by the power of the Holy Spirit; Spirit baptism is limited neither to Christian initiation nor to postconversion charismatic experiences, but may be suggestive of the fullness of Christian life marked by dynamic Christian witness; the church is neither merely a hierarchical institution nor merely a localized and organic body of believers, but a diverse communion (or fellowship, *koinonia*) of the Holy Spirit; and evangelization is neither exhausted by social concerns nor defined only in terms of personal transformation, but includes both within the wider *missio Dei* that seeks to reconcile the world to the Father through the Son in the power of the Spirit. Of course, differences remain about apostolicity (apostolic succession versus apostolic experience made available today by the Spirit), Mary (*theotokos* versus servant of the Lord), tradition (the papacy and the magisterium versus the priesthood of all believers), conversion (lifelong process versus sudden experience), and other topics. Kärkkäinen would acknowledge these impasses, but routinely call for further research.

These early volumes reflect the emergence of Kärkkäinen as an evangelical theologian. They demonstrate the possibility of engaging ecumenical dialogue in ways that compromise neither Confessing Church commitments in general nor pentecostal identity in particular. On the contrary, it is precisely in dialogue that one's theological position is deepened even while, paradoxically, a confessionally grounded and yet ecumenically generous understanding of the gospel is forged. Not surprisingly, it was also during this period of research and writing that Kärkkäinen was invited to participate in other evangelical networks: the Lausanne Committee of Finland (1994–present), the AD2000 Committee of Finland (1994–present), the International Consultation on World Evangelization (held in Seoul, South Korea, in May 1995), and the International Charismatic Consultation on World Evangelization (1998–present), just to name a few. Arguably, his work on these committees and consultations provided concrete opportunities to test out ideas forged in the theological laboratory. These early publications and his ecumenical work vaulted Kärkkäinen to the forefront of pentecostal theology in dialogue with the broader church and academy.

---

12. The Confessing or Free Church tradition derives from the Anabaptist Reformation. For overviews, see Camp, *Mere Discipleship,* and Callen, *Radical Christianity.*

It was partly on these merits that Kärkkäinen was invited to join the faculty of Fuller Theological Seminary in the fall of 2000.

Since joining the Fuller faculty, Kärkkäinen has increasingly solidified his evangelical theological reputation. This is reflected, in part, in a torrid pace of writing that has resulted in seven other volumes, including a three-part systematics textbook on pneumatology, Christology, and the doctrine of God. Throughout, Kärkkäinen has defined an evangelical theology as one that "cherish[es] classical Christianity as explicated in the creeds and mainstream confessions,"[13] and defended "the more orthodox version of Christianity as opposed to the liberal left wing."[14] Scripture is understood as the infallible touchstone for theological reflection and as the "normative source of theology and practice,"[15] and five out of his six theology textbooks (the soteriology, three-volume theology, and theology of religions) begin with biblical overviews. Further, as we shall soon see, Kärkkäinen's early exploration on pneumatological theology in the Roman Catholic-pentecostal dialogue has combined with his commitments to a high Christology to produce a robust Trinitarian framework for theological reflection. Finally, the missionary and evangelistic zeal characteristic of Kärkkäinen's pentecostal roots have not diminished, but rather found new and intensified expression in his engagement with the topic of theology of religions.

As a result of these developments during his tenure at Fuller, Kärkkäinen has become somewhat of a spokesperson for the evangelical perspective in theology. His invitation to contribute to volumes focused on bringing evangelical theology into dialogue with the wider academy reflects a growing appreciation for his evangelical commitments.[16] A recent editorial project launched with his colleague, William Dyrness, *Global Dictionary of Theology*,[17] unveils the richness of the evangelical theological landscape as it has developed around the world. To be sure, more conservative evangelicals and certainly most fundamentalists will continue to question Kärkkäinen's evangelical credentials. However, given any moderate (rather than conservative) definition of evangelical, Kärkkäinen's status as an evangelical theologian is difficult to deny.

---

13. See Kärkkäinen, *Christology*, 171; cf. Kärkkäinen, *One with God*, 81, and Kärkkäinen, *Theology of Religions*, 145.

14. Kärkkäinen, *Doctrine of God*, 192.

15. Kärkkäinen, *Theology of Religions*, 33; cf. Kärkkäinen, *Toward a Pneumatological Theology*, 26–28.

16. E.g., Kärkkäinen, "Uniqueness of Christ," "Christianity and Other Religions," and "Evangelical Theology and Religions."

17. See Dyrness and Kärkkäinen, eds., *Global Dictionary of Theology*.

KÄRKKÄINEN AS ECUMENICAL THEOLOGIAN

Kärkkäinen's ecumenical journey has continued over the years. He has been involved in the International Dialogue between the World Alliance of Reformed Churches and Pentecostals (1996–present), served as a consultant to and member of Faith and Order (Finland, 1994–2001; and USA and Canada, 2001), and participated in consultations and committees of the World Council of Churches ("Toward Common Witness," 1996; Joint Working Group between the WCC and Pentecostals, 1999–present; "Ecclesiology and Mission" Consultation, 1999–present; Theological Preparatory Consultation on Mission, 2000–present; Advisory Group for Church and Ecumenical Relations, 2000–present; and Consultation on Healing and Faith, 2002–present). All of this work has confirmed the global horizons for Christian theological reflection nurtured during his formative experiences teaching in Asia and studying and pastoring in Europe and North America. I suggest that the best way to understanding Kärkkäinen as an ecumenical theologian is precisely by grasping the worldwide scope of his theological vision. Presentation of this global sensitivity is most efficiently accomplished in a brief overview of the methodology and content of Kärkkäinen's Trinitarian trilogy, ecclesiology, and soteriology.

I begin with *An Introduction to Ecclesiology* (2002) in part because the ecumenical scope of Kärkkäinen's work is most clearly evidenced therein. There are three parts to the book. "Ecclesiological Traditions" includes discussions of the doctrine of the church in Eastern Orthodoxy, Roman Catholicism, Lutheranism, the Reformed churches, the Free churches, the pentecostal/charismatic orbit, and the ecumenical movement. "Leading Contemporary Ecclesiologists" include John Zizioulas's "communion ecclesiology" (Orthodox), Hans Küng's "Charismatic ecclesiology" (Roman Catholic), Wolfhart Pannenberg's "universal ecclesiology" (Lutheran), Jürgen Moltmann's "messianic ecclesiology" (Reformed), Miroslav Volf's "participatory ecclesiology" (Free Church and pentecostal), James McClendon Jr.'s "baptist ecclesiology" (Anabaptist), and Lesslie Newbigin's "missionary ecclesiology" (evangelical Anglican). The last part, "Contextual Ecclesiologies," overviews the non-church movement of Kanzo Uchimura in Japan, the Base Ecclesial Communities in Latin America, the feminist church (as represented by Letty Russell and Elisabeth Schüssler Fiorenza), the African independent (indigenous) churches, the Shepherding Movement (in pentecostal/charismatic circles), the new "world church" (in dialogue with the Anglican moral and political theologian Oliver O'Donovan), and the post-Christian church as "another city" (in dialogue primarily with Barry Harvey, but in the tradition of prominent theologians like Stanley Hauerwas and John Howard Yoder). Already the heavily ecumenical flavor of the ecclesiology is unmistakable.

While much could be said about Kärkkäinen's ecclesiology, its ecumenical potential, I suggest, is partly the result of the specifically pneumato-theological thread that is woven throughout the volume. Eastern Orthodoxy is not only "Spirit-sensitive," but also understands the church to be constituted by the Spirit. Post-Vatican II Catholic ecclesiology has emphasized the importance of the charisms in the life of the church (thus opening the door to the charismatic renewal in the church, for sure). Lutheran ecclesiology understands the Spirit to make alive both the Word and the sacraments. Obviously, pentecostal/charismatic ecclesiologies emphasize the church as a "charismatic fellowship."

Turning to contemporary ecclesiologists, we see a similar recurrence of pneumatic and charismatic motifs. Zizioulas emphasizes Christology and pneumatology as the dual foundations of the church. Küng writes about the church as the "creation of the Spirit." Pannenberg's is a thoroughly pneumatological ecclesiology, an understanding of the church permeated by the person and work of the Spirit. Moltmann wrote a very influential book titled *The Church in the Power of the Spirit* (ET: SCM Press, 1977). Volf focuses on the charismatic and Trinitarian structure of the church. McClendon's "baptist vision" is very similar to those of pentecostals, emphasizing the "this is that" correlation between the present experience of the Spirit and the experiences of the earliest Christians as recorded in the book of Acts. And, of course, how can one have a missionary ecclesiology such as Newbigin's without a robust pneumatology? Thus Newbigin's portrait of the church as a "community of the Holy Spirit." Pneumatic and charismatic themes are evident also in the contextual ecclesiologies, not only in the African Spirit churches, but also in the Shepherding Movement's "renewal ecclesiology."

In short, Kärkkäinen's ecclesiology is not just an introductory textbook, although it is that as well. Rather, it can also be read as providing a constructive and ecumenical ecclesiology precisely through the development of a pneumatological theology of the church. The ecumenical nature of the church is established, in this case, not politically, organizationally, or structurally, but theologically (read: pneumatologically). To draw from the biblical metaphor of the gift of the Spirit, the many tongues of Pentecost prefigure the church as a unity constituted by diversity, and hence ecclesiology, as constituted by the many gifts of the many churches and the many perspectives of her theologians.

Not surprisingly, then, Kärkkäinen's three-volume Trinitarian theology begins with the *Pneumatology* (2002). The six chapters introduce the topic, provide a wide range of biblical material, look at developments in the Christian theological tradition, present ecclesiastical perspectives (Eastern Orthodox, Roman Catholic, Lutheran, pentecostal/charismatic, and ecumenical), highlight leading contemporary theologians of the Spirit (the Orthodox Zizioulas, the Catholic Rahner, the Lutheran Pannenberg, the Reformed Moltmann, the biblical pneumatology of Michael Welker, and the evangelical Clark Pinnock), and conclude with what Kärkkäinen called "contextual" pneumatologies (drawn from recent developments in process theology, liberation theology, ecological theology, feminist theology, and African theology). It is obvious that in a relatively short volume, Kärkkäinen is simply providing a survey of the theological landscape, precisely the task of an introductory theological text.

The approach in *Pneumatology* provides various windows into Kärkkäinen's theological method. First, Kärkkäinen is attuned to the perspectivism of all theological reflection. This pluralism is not, however, a threat to the theological enterprise. Rather, theology is enriched precisely by the diversity of perspectives. This begins especially with the scriptural data, and is continued in the historical and ecclesiastical traditions. Second, drawing in part from his missionary background, Kärkkäinen recognizes that contemporary theological reflection needs to engage the wide range of perspectives outside the theological mainstream of the Euro-American West. Hence, the liberation perspectives of Latin American theologians and the spirit-world perspectives of African theologians need to be given voice. Finally, the entire tenor of Kärkkäinen's initial contribution to a Trinitarian theology is dialogical rather than polemical. In contrast to traditional evangelical theologies that either ignore or castigate process, "green," or feminist perspectives, Kärkkäinen's attitude is respectful, reflecting a willingness to learn. Those looking for explicit critical comment will be disappointed. However, those willing to read between the lines will observe that Kärkkäinen has adopted in this volume the posture previously developed in his work on the Roman Catholic-pentecostal dialogue: that discovery of critical points of difference both requires honest acknowledgment and calls for further research. This approach invigorates theology as a personal and communal journey in the Spirit: "New discoveries, new challenges, new potentialities await."[18]

A similar method and ethos pervades his *Christology* (2003). Part I presents the "many faces of Christ" in the Bible, while Part II surveys the history of Christology from the post-apostolic period through the early councils and medieval developments to the various quests for the historical Jesus initiated during the modern period. Parts III and IV overview contemporary Western and non-Western (again, Kärkkäinen calls these

---

18. Kärkkäinen, *Pneumatology*, 177.

"contextual") Christologies. The former include short chapters on Barth, Bultmann, Tillich, Zizioulas, Rahner, Moltmann, Pannenberg, Norman Kraus (of the Mennonite tradition), Stanley Grenz, and John Hick. The latter present an even wider kaleidoscope of christological ideas: process theology as represented in the work of John B. Cobb Jr., among others; various feminist perspectives; black theology as exemplified in James Cone and the South African theologian Allan Boesak; postmodernists like Mark Taylor and Ted Peters (who Kärkkäinen suggests represents an "evangelical version of postmodern christology"); Latin American liberation theology as seen in Gutierrez, Boff, Gonzalez, and Sobrino; African theology as articulated by John Mbiti, Charles Nyamiti, Aylward Shorter, and Benezet Bujo; and Asian theology as proposed by Raimundo Panikkar, Stanley Samartha, Korean Minjung theologians, and Indian Dalit thinkers. As Kärkkäinen's colleague at Fuller, Colin Brown, notes, the *Christology* is "breathtaking in scope and pace" (back cover).

Three brief comments about Kärkkäinen's *Christology* are in order. First, while Kärkkäinen is focused on the second article of the creed, his wide range of dialogue partners brings with them issues that touch on the entirety of the theological spectrum. Process thinkers have metaphysical concerns, John Hick (and others) engage in christological reflection in light of the challenges of religious pluralism, Bultmannians and Tillichians (among others) are divided over the relationship between the Jesus of history and the Christ of faith, etc. Here, the systematic thinking cultivated in his earlier work allows Kärkkäinen to present the issues clearly without losing a sense of (christological) coherence. Second, Kärkkäinen's introductory comment is also illuminating: "the most exciting feature of the current scene is the rise of contextual and/or intercultural Christologies that attempt to speak to specific local needs . . . or needs of specific groups of people (such as women or the poor)."[19] Rather than seeing this as a capitulating to a postmodern relativistic hermeneutic, I suggest that this represents actually the full flowering of an evangelical and pentecostal commitment to understanding the gospel as transculturally relevant. In this, the motivation is not merely to develop an apologetic against liberalism or any other kind of ism, but to engage the beliefs and practices of the worldwide church. This leads, finally, to Kärkkäinen's concluding suggestions for future research, which are themselves instructive: further explication of Christology in a religiously plural world; further extension and assessment of the various contextual Christologies; further inquiry into the relationship between the person and work of Christ, the latter with regard to engaging the various contexts of christo-

---

19. Kärkkäinen, *Christology*, 10–11.

logical reflection; and further reflection on the connection of Christology to pneumatology and the larger Trinitarian question regarding the identity of the Christian God. As with the pneumatology, Kärkkäinen's Christology is published but still very much in *via media*—there is always more that can and should be said.

Not surprisingly, given the many promissory notes handed on by the *Pneumatology* and *Christology*, Kärkkäinen's *The Doctrine of God* (2004) is the most ambitious and lengthy of the three books, focused as it is not only on God the Father, but also on the Trinitarian identity of God. As before, however, the goal of *The Doctrine of God* as the culminating volume of the trilogy is to bring the classical theistic tradition into dialogue with its modern/recent challengers. Again, Parts I and II focus on the biblical and historical traditions as internally pluralistic and thematically diverse, yet with a narrative coherence. Parts III and IV elaborate on familiar contemporary European theologians, and on North American theologies in dialogue with the classical tradition (secular/death of God theology, process theology, open theism, and evangelical theology). Parts V and VI explore other more "contextual" North American options (Native American theologies, African American and immigrant theologies, and feminist, womanist, and Latina theologies), and God in "non-Western perspectives" (African, Latin American, and Asian theologies). Again, Kärkkäinen is generally sympathetic in his discussion of the thirty-plus theologians he describes, even if generalizations are unavoidable given his attempt to cover as much theological ground as he does in a limited amount of space.

Yet there are also subtle but significant shifts to be observed in *The Doctrine of God*. Here, Kärkkäinen offers more of his own critical perspective, even if such is often disguised as mere commentary. So, while Tillich's theology was highly contextualized to the existentialist ethos of the mid-twentieth century, "after roughly two decades of unprecedented interest, it did not redeem its promises for continuing movement."[20] Further, the death of God theology—in its more radical form expounded by William Hamilton and Thomas J. J. Altizer—"could not sustain itself. It was criticized not only by churchgoers and the general public for introducing atheism and paganism into the Christian faith but also by serious theological critics such as Langdon Gilkey for taking the term *God* out of the sphere of Christian theology and Christian tradition."[21] Last (for our purposes) but not least (given

20. See Kärkkäinen, *Doctrine of God*, 166. Contra Kärkkäinen, however, Tillich scholarship is certainly alive and well in the theological academy. [In fact, more recently, Kärkkäinen himself has contributed a chapter, "Spiritual Power and Spiritual Presence" to a volume I am coediting on the legacy of Tillich.]

21. Kärkkäinen, *Doctrine of God*, 178; again, however, Altizer's theological

space constraints), it is asked if process theology "has been too contextual in succumbing to the framework of a pantheistic world view."[22]

The Doctrine of God concludes also with suggestions for future research along three lines. First, Kärkkäinen calls for further work on postmodern reactions to the Enlightenment. The limits of Western modernism have to be recognized. What comes after modernity, however, is still an open question. Second, the expansion of Christianity in the Southern and Eastern Hemispheres demands theological reconstruction as well. Such work should be dialogical, involving the world church, even if Southern and Eastern voices are to be privileged initially. The "exciting developments" in Trinitarian theological speculation occurring in these contexts are, in part, what fuels Kärkkäinen's optimism about the future prospects of theology. Finally, the new situation of religious pluralism needs to be grappled with theologically. A greater sensitivity to the issues raised by the diversity of religions can be noted in the *Christology* and even more so in *The Doctrine of God*.

In looking back over the Trinitarian trilogy, certain features of Kärkkäinen's theological method highlight its distinctively ecumenical flavor, including its taking seriously Roman Catholic and Orthodox perspectives. As important is the breadth of positions given space and voice in these three textbooks. While one may wonder about why only newer Eastern and Southern perspectives are labeled as "contextual," Kärkkäinen is nevertheless to be applauded for taking seriously the emerging "non-Western" voices in the theological conversation. Methodologically, Kärkkäinen is sensitive to the different sociohistorical and cultural-religious contexts within which the task of theology is pursued, and hence more open to narrative approaches to the theological task. Theologically, the doctrines of the Spirit, of Christ, and of God are dynamic and "tangible," being located within particular traditions of discourse and communities of practices. Ethically, Kärkkäinen realizes that the theological reflection has implications for sociopolitical liberation and for interreligious relationships, among other concrete realities.

In contrast to his ecclesiology and Trinitarian trilogy, Kärkkäinen's soteriology, *One with God* (2004), is less a textbook than it is a constructive theological monograph. Kärkkäinen's objective is to develop a doctrine of

---

articulations continue to command attention in the theological academy. For a recent re-statement of his position, see Altizer, "Primordial, Godhead, and Apocalyptic"; for an assessment of Altizer's recent Christology in comparison with other Christologies, see Yong, "Globalizing Christology."

22. Kärkkäinen, *Doctrine of God*, 185. Interestingly, Kärkkäinen's most critical comments seem directed toward positions commonly classified under the category of theological liberalism, much of which is in its second, third, or even fourth generation. These critical remarks are less noticeable in his discussion of non-Western theologies.

salvation that bridges not only East and West, but also Catholic and Lutheran emphases in the Western church, and toward that end he suggests that the fusion of the Orthodox doctrine of deification and the Lutheran doctrine of justification can be accomplished through the motif "union with God." Distinguishing Luther's own theology of salvation from that of the later Lutheran confessions with the help of the recent Finnish Mannermaa school of Luther research,[23] Kärkkäinen suggests that biblical perspectives on salvation read through the early Luther should be understood not only in terms of forensic justification but also in terms of ontological transformation, not just in terms of a spiritual transaction between God and Christ, but also in terms of human participation in the very life of God. Defense of this thesis proceeds through an exposition of the idea of justification in recent New Testament scholarship, an elaboration of deification in the Eastern Orthodox tradition, an explication of justification and deification in Luther's theology and later Protestantism (Anabaptism, Methodism, and evangelical theology), and an overview of recent ecumenical conversations on the doctrine of salvation (Lutheran-Orthodox, Roman Catholic-Lutheran, and Orthodox-pentecostal).

In the final chapter, Kärkkäinen presents a kaleidoscope of supporting perspectives on his soteriological hypothesis. Is not "union" a, if not the, defining motif of Eastern and Western soteriologies? Does not "union" allow for the retrieval of fresh biblical imagery and voices? In what ways does the "union" motif connect justification with sanctification, and recover emphasis on the doctrine of love for the doctrine of salvation? As he weaves his way through these discussions, a substantive pneumatological and Trinitarian theology of salvation emerges, recapturing and extending his earlier work in these theological loci. Kärkkäinen concludes by asking what justification and salvation means in the wider world context of the third millennium, and about how to understand the theological and dialogical implications of deification, justification, and union with God in the Christian encounter with other faiths.

Before we take up in detail aspects of this last question in the next section, it would be helpful to provide some summary remarks on Kärkkäinen as an ecumenical theologian. What is most valuable about Kärkkäinen's introductory surveys is their global awareness, a feature practically absent from most evangelical treatments of these same topics.[24] I gather that this global sensitivity has developed in part not only because of Kärkkäinen's

---

23. Tuomo Mannermaa is a Finnish Lutheran theologian who has led this re-reading of Luther's theology; Kärkkäinen cites Braaten and Jenson, eds., *Union with Christ* as a good introduction to the Mannermaa school.

24. An exception is Spencer and Spencer, eds., *The Global God.*

living, working, and studying on three continents, but in part also because the pentecostalism which nurtures his faith, spirituality, and piety is now truly a worldwide movement. Thinking theologically as a pentecostal (in particular) and as a Christian (in general) today requires just this kind of global vision in order that justice can even begin to be done to the topics under consideration.

But perhaps more importantly, Kärkkäinen is committed not to any parochial theology, but to the development of Christian theology in its full ecumenical breadth and depth. To be sure, the pentecostal perspectives informing Kärkkäinen's early work remain with him (as seen in the inclusion of the pentecostal voice in *One with God*), but the church does not need another theology, pentecostal or otherwise. Rather, what is needed is a Trinitarian theology that is informed by biblical traditions and the many Christian perspectives down through the ages and, now, across the world—in short, a "consensual" and ecumenical theology.[25]

KÄRKKÄINEN AS WORLD THEOLOGIAN

The development of Kärkkäinen as world theologian derives, in large part, from the work of Kärkkäinen the missiologist. Recall not only his missionary work in Thailand but also that his *habilitationsschrift* was a missiology as seen through the Roman Catholic-pentecostal dialogue. Since then, Kärkkäinen has taken out membership in the International Association of Mission Studies (2002–present) and the American Missiological Society (2001–present), and continued publishing on theology of mission in various scholarly periodicals, among other forums.[26] Out of this concern for understanding Christian mission, and confronted with the religiously plural context of such mission in the twenty-first century, Kärkkäinen had already begun to take up in the Trinitarian trilogy some of the theological questions regarding Christian identity in a religiously plural world and the Christian encounter with other faiths. The *Christology* discussed John Hick's universalist view of Christ, and questions concerning religious pluralism were dealt with across the entirety of *The Doctrine of God*.

---

25. Kärkkäinen, "David's Sling," 152.

26. Kärkkäinen's missiological essays have appeared in such publications as the *International Review of Mission, Missiology, Asian Journal of Mission, Mission Studies, Missionalia, International Bulletin of Missionary Research*, and *Exchange: Journal of Missiological and Ecumenical Research*.

In *One with God*, Kärkkäinen queries about the theological potential of the "union with God" motif for interreligious dialogue.[27] Does such an understanding of salvation provide a bridge for dialogue with traditional African notions of "vital participation" (or other ideas from world religions)? Yet Kärkkäinen cautions against a naïve optimism regarding assuming too many commonalities between religious traditions, since surface conceptual similarities often reveal radical differences when the deep structures of the traditions are examined. It is precisely because of these differences, however, that "the common search of humanity to find union with God may teach Christians valuable lessons."[28] In the process, Christians who are made one with God in Christ can manifest to their neighbors in other faiths not only the love of Christ but also, following Luther, even Christ himself.[29] But are there limits to what Christians can learn from those in other faiths? Is there anything genuinely new that can be received from the interreligious encounter that is not already contained within the Christian faith?

It is in part these questions that motivated Kärkkäinen's *An Introduction to the Theology of Religions* (2003) and *Trinity and Religious Pluralism* (2004). The former is an introductory text while the latter is more of an initial attempt to articulate a constructive Christian theology of religions. The breadth of the *Introduction* is typically wide-ranging. Part One presents the "ambiguity and promise" of the various biblical perspectives on the religions, including the tension between the universalism and the particularism of the gospel message, while Part Two follows historical developments from the early church through the consolidation of the "outside the church no salvation" position to the challenges brought by the Enlightenment and our contemporary experience of religious diversity. Part Three provides unique perspectives from ecumenical documents, revealing how different church traditions have attempted to wrestle with the issues, while Part Four presents brief introductions to twenty-one different mostly contemporary theologians of the religions. For this discussion, Kärkkäinen presents a new typology of theologies of religions: ecclesiocentrism, which limits salvation to Christian faith and emphasizes the importance of missionary proclamation in the encounter with religious others; christocentrism, which has Catholic, mainline Protestant, and evangelical manifestations,

---

27. Kärkkäinen, *One with God*, 133–37.

28. Ibid., 136.

29. See the section in the chapter on Luther titled "The Christian as 'Christ' to the Neighbor" (*One with God*, 58–61). I wonder, in light of the parables of the sheep and the goats (Matt 25:31–46) and the Good Samaritan (Luke 10:25–37), whether or not Christians also encounter Christ in their neighbors of other faiths; for explication of this point, see Yong, *Spirit Poured Out*, §6.1.2.

and emphasizes salvation as through Christ, even if God may be at work through Christ (anonymously) by the Spirit in the lives of those in other faiths; and theocentrism, which de-emphasizes the normativeness and absoluteness of Christ for those in other religious traditions.

As with the other introductory textbooks he has written, Kärkkäinen stays primarily with descriptive exposition and rarely ventures to provide critical commentary in this volume. He does note that John Hick's pluralistic theology of religions, which has generated widespread criticism, ultimately denies the absolutistic and particular truth claims of all the religions, an irony which "works against the pluralistic idea."[30] But to Stanley Samartha's similarly pluralistic claim—that with regard to Buddha, Krishna, Rama, and Christ, "Samartha argues that the theory of multiple *avatara* (Hindu, 'incarnated gods or other significant persons') seems to be theologically the most accommodating attitude in a pluralistic setting, one that permits recognition of both the mystery of God and the freedom of people to respond to divine initiatives in different ways at different times"[31]—Kärkkäinen raises nary a counterargument. The *Introduction* does include a concluding chapter of "critical reflections and questions" that queries both the effectiveness of the typology and engages in a critical dialogue with the twenty-one theologians of religions. Here, the questions Kärkkäinen poses to Samartha are metatheological (on the notions of truth and mystery, for example) rather than explicitly theological.

Again, as with his other introductory volumes, Kärkkäinen's tone is conciliatory, and his posture continues to manifest the willingness to learn from his interlocutors, even those who do not adhere to the positions he espouses. The epilogue presents the future tasks for Christian theology of religions: the need for a constructive Trinitarian theology of religions; the need for an empirical engagement with the religions as they exist in reality; and the need for common theological projects emergent from extended and sustained interreligious dialogue between representatives of the various faith traditions.

It is to these tasks that Kärkkäinen turns in *Trinity and Religious Pluralism*. In this volume, he focuses on nine theologians (Barth, Rahner, Dupuis, D'Costa, Pannenberg, Pinnock, Hick, Panikkar, and S. Mark Heim, the only one not discussed in the *Introduction*), and provides a case study of the Roman Catholic Church's engagement with Muslims in France. Kärkkäinen's own theological voice sounds forth much more clearly as he engages in an ongoing critical conversation with his dialogue partners, both with

30. Kärkkäinen, *Theology of Religions*, 293.
31. Ibid., 301.

regard to biblical interpretation and theological formulation. At one level, this volume represents the culmination of Kärkkäinen's work to date insofar as it brings together his systematic orientation, his Trinitarian theological commitments, and his previous work in theology of mission and theology of religions. At another level, however, this book signals the transition of Kärkkäinen as ecumenical theologian to Kärkkäinen as constructive theologian in a worldwide religious context. This development is most clearly seen in the concluding chapter, where a catalog of where we've come from and where we should be headed is presented. In these pages, Trinitarian theology is contrasted with the "normative" pluralism (of Hick and others) insofar as the former provides a basic principle for theology of religions that preserves the particularity of Christian claims about the triune God. Further, a Trinitarian theology of religions must not separate Christ from Spirit, nor Spirit from the triune God, nor the church from the kingdom, and there has to be continuity between the eschatological verification of the truth (here, Kärkkäinen relies on Pannenberg's principle of eschatological verification) and the provisional theological hypotheses that are being tested. Finally, a Trinitarian theology of religions provides an ontological foundation for the one and the many, for communion amidst difference, with the proviso that it affirms only with difficulty Heim's proposal of multiple religious ends.[32]

Kärkkäinen reaffirms his evangelical commitments at the end of *Trinity and Religious Pluralism*: "Christian trinitarian faith, in my understanding, seeks to find outside the human person the grounds for preferring one narrative over another, that is, in the biblical salvation-history which narrates the history of the triune God in sending the Son in the power of the Spirit to save the world and bring it into an eternal communion. If that is foundationalism, so be it."[33] By this, the traditional Christian principle of *fides quaerens intellectum* (faith seeking understanding) is acknowledged to be the starting point for Christian theological reflection, even with regard to the diversity of religions. At the same time, Kärkkäinen also insists (rightly, in my estimation) on a scripturally grounded universalism, described by John the Revelator's "vision of God's people gathered together under one God."[34] But aside from this methodological principle and soteriological affirmation, what exactly does Kärkkäinen believe about the religions? With D'Costa (and Barth), but against Hick and Panikkar (and Rahner and Dupuis, depending on how they are interpreted), Kärkkäinen urges that "other

---

32. As developed in Heim, *Depths of Riches*.

33. Kärkkäinen, *Trinity and Religious Pluralism*, 183 n.5.

34. Ibid., 177; see also ibid., 146, where this eschatological vision is reiterated against Heim's proposal of multiple religious ends.

religions are not salvific as such, but other religions are important for the Christian church in that they help the church to penetrate more deeply into the divine mystery."[35] The question then becomes: what does it mean to "penetrate more deeply into the divine mystery"? It appears that it is Christians who gain access to the depths of God precisely through their encounters with other faiths. But if such deeper understanding is not salvific, then what is it? If according to *One with God*, salvation is participation and union with God, does the interreligious dialogue contribute to such personal and communal transformation? If it does, as the rhetoric of Kärkkäinen seems to imply, then are not other faiths also in some ways conduits of God's gracious and revelatory salvation?

I will return to this matter momentarily. In the meanwhile, however, it is important to recognize that while Kärkkäinen does not shrink back from the speculative aspects of Christian theology of religions, his motivation from the beginning has been more missiological and concerned with Christian self-understanding. In other words, Christian reflection on the religions enables a more self-critical promulgation of the Christian mission and encourages a more dialogical approach to other faiths even as it helps Christians to understand themselves and the diversity of religions within the providential plan of God as enacted in history. In the process of grappling with these matters, Kärkkäinen has come to recognize that religious diversity poses challenging questions to Christian theology today. Inevitably, by taking up these questions Kärkkäinen the evangelical and ecumenical theologian has become Kärkkäinen the world theologian and theologian of the world religions.

CRITICAL QUESTIONS FOR KÄRKKÄINEN

I have two sets of critical questions for Kärkkäinen, one concerning his work as an ecumenical theologian and the other concerning his work as a theologian of the religions. We will take these in order before returning in the last section to the questions relating Kärkkäinen the evangelical theologian to the present and future of evangelical theology.

My first set of questions to Kärkkäinen concerns the overall methodology that underlies his ecumenical theology. In brief, this set of questions can be explicated in terms of three other interrelated questions: 1) Is not all theology contextual? 2) Is not the contextual character of any theology informed, at least in part, both by the questions that it grapples with and by the practices that give it shape? 3) In what ways is Kärkkäinen's own

35. Ibid., 179.

ecumenical theology in this sense contextual, and how can it best proceed as both contextual and ecumenical at the same time? Let me elaborate briefly on each of these questions in order.

First, the question regarding the contextual character of all theology emerges in large part out of Kärkkäinen's own theological categorization. Each volume of the Trinitarian trilogy has a "contextual" section which refers to recently emergent non-Western theologies that "correct and complement the mainly Western approach that has dominated."[36] In the *Christology* and *The Doctrine of God*, Kärkkäinen acknowledges that this does not mean Western theologies are not similarly contextual since no theology is "immune to surrounding philosophical, religious, social, and political influences"[37]; yet the designation "contextual" remains useful and relevant to the extent that any theology is "firmly anchored in a specific context, be it cultural, intellectual, or related to a specific world view,"[38] and to the extent which "theologians *acknowledge* theologies to be contextually shaped."[39]

Any theologian has the prerogative to define his own terms. But what is it that contextualizes any theology? This is a complex question to which no simple answer will suffice. For our purposes, I suggest that a theology is contextually shaped by two interrelated factors: its historical practices and its sociocultural situatedness. By this, I mean that any theology attempts to provide a coherent explanation that makes sense of its practices within the broader social, cultural, religious, and intellectual world. After Tillich, who urged that theology arises in the response of revelation to the questions of the situation, there should be no confusion that what I am calling "sociocultural situatedness" refers precisely to the contemporary world in all its complexity. But the other half of my claim regarding the contextuality of all theology requires further explication.

Following the work of Reinhard Hütter and others, I suggest that theology (Christian belief) is (or should be) shaped as much by the practices of the church as by Scripture or tradition.[40] This is not to deny that Scripture and tradition have played and continue to play important roles in theological reflection. Rather, it is to say that Scripture and tradition are themselves constituted by the practices of the church, among other things. And what are these ecclesial practices? These would be the congregational liturgies (both

---

36. Kärkkäinen, *Pneumatology*, 147.

37. Kärkkäinen, *Christology*, 188.

38. Ibid.

39. Kärkkäinen, *Doctrine of God*, 199; emphasis original.

40. See Hütter, *Suffering Divine Things*; cf. also Volf and Bass, eds., *Practicing Theology*.

structured and unstructured), the devotional life, the symbolic enactments, the economic habits, the political stances, the institutional interactivities, the social organizations and networks, and other concrete manifestations of Christian communities and the individuals that inhabit them. From this perspective, for example, the Christian claim about Jesus Christ as Lord and as God (and, by extension, claims regarding Trinitarian faith) is intricately tied up with the church's adoration and worship of Jesus; the Christian understanding of the Eucharist is inextricably connected with the realization of the presence of Jesus around the communal table; the Christian doctrine of the church is deeply intertwined with the interrelationship between the church's political identity and its social practices; the Christian doctrine of salvation is dependent on which of the biblical metaphors resonate most deeply with the experiences and practices of the church in the various sociohistorical contexts within which it exists, etc.[41] Again, this is not to deny that the Bible is normative and authoritative for shaping Christian practice, but it is to say that the relationship between Scripture and practice is much more complicated than any one-way articulation of such relationship.

For our purposes, the preceding remarks raise the following methodological question about Kärkkäinen's ecumenical theology: insofar as all theology is contextual and thereby informed by the practices of the church (considered both diachronically across the centuries and synchronically around the world today), can Kärkkäinen's ecumenical theology succeed without taking into account the diversity of practices that inform the plurality of voices and perspectives that he has attempted so valiantly to preserve? Kärkkäinen's ecclesiology gives us windows into how the practices of the church contribute to constituting the ecclesiological traditions. But the books published after the ecclesiology are not as helpful in identifying how ecclesial practices shape and inform the teachings of the church(es) and her theologians. In the *Introduction to Theology of Religions*, Kärkkäinen does draw from "official church documents and confessional pronouncements,"[42] but he does not say much about how the liturgical practices of the Latin Church undergird its "no salvation outside the church" stance; or how the sectarian practices of the Free Churches have shaped their more exclusivistic perspectives; or how the sociopolitical practices of the mainline Protestant denominations have similarly shaped the more inclusive attitudes of the ecumenical movement, etc. Granted, Kärkkäinen's intention was to write introductory textbooks about the church's beliefs, not social histories

---

41. E.g., Kärkkäinen, *One with God*, 131–33.
42. Kärkkäinen, *Theology of Religions*, 110.

about the church's practices, so we should not be too hard on him for not doing what he never set out to accomplish.[43]

But the question remains: how viable is an ecumenical theology abstracted from the practices that sustain the beliefs and confessions of the church in all her diversity? In fact, let me put the matter even more strongly: an ecumenical theology is possible only in abstraction; often what continues to divide churches are the practices that inform the diversity of theologies at the ecumenical round table. This was seen in the processes leading up to and following the release and discussion of the ecumenical document *Baptism, Eucharist, and Ministry*,[44] and remains especially problematic when the very different practices of churches in Africa, Asia, and elsewhere are factored into the ecumenical conversation. At the end of the day, how is an ecumenical theology even possible given the radical differences that characterize the practices of the churches around the world?

Here is where I wish to present Kärkkäinen with a suggestion. Rather than attempting to develop an ecumenical theology in the abstract, why not acknowledge that there is no ahistorical ecumenical theology possible, and work toward an ecumenical theology in a confessional perspective? What about acknowledging that theological consensus cannot be achieved through abstract reflection alone, but that a truly ecumenical theology must be informed not only by the diversity of perspectives but also by a diversity of practices? If the "tongues of Pentecost" reflect an ecumenical harmony of different voices declaring the wonders of God (Acts 2:11b),[45] then so too will the diversity of confessions reflect an ecumenical theology of different perspectives into the truth of God. In this case, Kärkkäinen's own pentecostal *habitus* does not inhibit the ecumenical potential of his theological vision. On the contrary, precisely because his pentecostal perspective is rooted in the practices of his churches, the pentecostal contribution is essential rather than marginal to the development of a fully ecumenical theology. This was most clearly seen both in his ecclesiology and in his "decision" to begin his Trinitarian trilogy with pneumatology rather than with the theology proper. The pneumatology was launched first because of the pneumatological orientation nurtured by the pentecostal tradition, while the ecclesiology, as we

43. Yet at one point in his discussion of Pannenberg's theology of religions, Kärkkäinen wonders if the result is a viewpoint that is "one-sidedly rational" (*Trinity and Religious Pluralism*, 93). His question is motivated by what he takes to be the absence of doxology in Pannenberg's quest for truth in the interreligious arena. As such, Kärkkäinen seems to recognize the inseparability of the church's practices from her beliefs.

44. See *Baptism, Eucharist and Ministry* and for commentary, *Baptism, Eucharist and Ministry: Initial Reactions*.

45. I argue this point at length in my "Spirit Gives Utterance."

saw earlier, was shot through with pneumatological motifs and emphases. In fact, as I suggested then, the strength of the ecclesiology was not only in its comprehensiveness (essential for an introductory textbook), but also in its suggestiveness for a systematic reconstruction of the doctrine of the church in pneumatological perspective (a pneumatological or Spirit-ecclesiology). In short, I am simply urging Kärkkäinen to return to and retrieve some of the pentecostal trajectories articulated earlier in his theological career,[46] both to provide more concrete grounding for his ecumenical theology and to reinvigorate the constructive dimension of his future theological work.

This brings me to the second set of questions I have, this time for Kärkkäinen as (an emerging) world theologian. This set of questions can also be explicated in terms of three interrelated questions: 1) What is needed to more fully unfold Kärkkäinen's nascent Trinitarian theology of religions? 2) How does the fact that other religious traditions are similarly constituted by practices provide challenges for contemporary Christian theology of religions? 3) Whither Kärkkäinen as a theologian of world religions in light of these challenges? Again, I will address each briefly in order.

First, Kärkkäinen acknowledges at the end of *Trinity and Religious Pluralism* that he has only taken some first steps toward developing a more comprehensive Trinitarian theology of religions. One of the important principles suggested in that last chapter, however, was to think of the relationship between Christianity and other religions as a kind of "unity in diversity," mirroring the triune communion. In this framework, the Trinity is the structuring principle for Christian faith even as it also "pushes Christians to dialogue with other religions."[47] Yet Kärkkäinen also realizes that this is an idealized model that begs for testing through engagement with the empirical religions. If/when Kärkkäinen moves from ecumenical dialogue to actual interreligious dialogue and from ecumenical theology to a theology informed by the interfaith conversation, he may find himself stretched in one of three directions: a) toward Hick's pluralistic hypothesis, which threatens to collapse the differences between religions; b) toward Heim's Trinitarian theology of religious ends, which threatens to collapse the "unity in duality" of eschatological scenarios deeply embedded in the theological tradition; or c) toward a kind of Hegelian synthesis (syncretism!), which (evangelical) theologians are rightly concerned about. This is because Trinitarian theological reflection sundered from the practices that nurtured it lead to abstract pronunciations regarding the world religions similarly sundered from the practices that nurture these other faiths. The

46. E.g., Kärkkäinen. *Toward Pneumatological Theology*, Part 1.
47. Kärkkäinen, *Trinity and Religious Pluralism*, 163.

interfaith encounter adds increasing levels of theoretical and practical depth that illuminates our basic understanding of other religious traditions, and in that sense, prolonged engagement with the interreligious dialogue will challenge our more abstractly formulated theologies of religions.

What I am saying here, of course, is that other faiths are constituted similarly by a complex web of practices—of liturgies, devotional life, symbols, institutions, commentarial activity, social configurations, economic habits, political stances, etc.—that inform their beliefs and doctrines.[48] Thus, one cannot sustain a theology of religions apart from the religions themselves. In other words, any Christian theology of religions worth its salt will eventually need to deal concretely with the actual beliefs and practices that constitute the world of the religions (just as any theology of science will need to deal with the actual sciences or any theology of culture will need to deal with actual cultures, etc.). When this happens, however, the complexity of the truth question thrown up by the plurality of religions is further exacerbated. Kärkkäinen rightly wishes, following Pannenberg and others, not to discard the question of truth amidst the plurality of religious claims. How to adjudicate these matters in the framework of *fides quaerens intellectum* is one of the foremost challenges for Christian theology in the twenty-first century.

This difficulty can be seen especially in light of the connection between religious beliefs and practices. Christian theological propositions— e.g., about the Trinity and the incarnation—make little sense outside of the larger narrative and practices from which they emerge. Similarly, the truth claims of other faiths are embedded in their narratives (world views) and practices (rituals, etc.). The problem is that truth claims are propositionally formulated, yet their nestedness within wider ways of life and thinking means that theology of religions has to go beyond, beneath, or behind the doctrinal claims of the religions in order to assess their truthfulness. But to do so requires that one enter into that other way of life, so to speak, in order for the sensibility of such claims to emerge within a participatory framework. How can Christian theologians engage in that kind of interreligious encounter without compromising their distinctive religious commitments? Are Christian theologians limited to inviting their dialogue partners from other faiths to enter into the Christian way of life and "taste and see that the Lord is good" (Ps 34:8), while conversely prohibited from accepting the invitation from their dialogue partners to enter into and experience these other religious ways of life? And if Christian theologians cannot proceed in

---

48. As argued forcefully by Lindbeck, *Nature of Doctrine*.

the latter direction, do we lapse into a kind of fideism amidst the multiplicity of truth claims in the world of religions?[49]

My response is that theology has always been an ongoing dialogue between the biblical/theological traditions and the contemporary situation. In the case of theology of religions, the dialogue must now be extended to engage the beliefs and practices of religious others. Hence the importance of further refining the discipline of comparative theology for any Christian theology desiring to take into account the world context. The key to a comparative theology is its dialogical and intersubjective character. Theological and doctrinal statements are compared at various levels, only through a sustained process of dialogue allowing a much deeper sense of familiarity to emerge among the dialogue partners about the wider framework of ideas (world views) and practices within which fundamental religious beliefs are embedded.[50] I suggest that this kind of intersubjectively engaged project in comparative theology is necessary if we want to really honor the beliefs and practices of religious others, if we wish to remain vulnerable to transformative learning, and if we have an authentically eschatological horizon that frames our quest for theological truth.[51]

Against this backdrop, whither Kärkkäinen as a world theologian? Two paths forward suggest themselves. On the one hand, Kärkkäinen could continue in his attempt to develop a Christian theology of other religions for Christians. This would not require that he "get his hands (too) dirty" with actual engagement with those in other faiths. Technically, this move would also limit Kärkkäinen to being a theologian of world Christianity, thus withering his prospects as a world theologian and a theologian of the world religions. Of course, such work—theology by the church and for the church—is necessary, but it is also in some significant senses preliminary to the quest for truth that animates the theological quest. On the other hand, Kärkkäinen could continue his project as a world Christian theologian by engaging with any and all who are interested in the subject matter of theology, including representatives from other faith traditions. This would lead to the kind of intersubjective mode of comparative theology sketched earlier. This move will, of course, allow the project of Kärkkäinen as world theologian to come to fruition, and that precisely because it propels Christian faith

---

49. I expand on these matters elsewhere—e.g., Yong, "Baptist Vision," and "Spirit Bears Witness." [Cf. my discussion of Clooney in ch. 10 of this vol.]

50. For an example of such a venture in comparative theology, see the three volumes of The Comparative Religious Ideas Project: Neville and Wildman, eds., *Ultimate Realities*, *The Human Condition*, and *Religious Truth*.

51. I defend this proposal at much greater length in the concluding chapter of my *Beyond the Impasse*, ch. 7.

seeking understanding to pursue the theological truth question to the ends of the earth.

At this point in Kärkkäinen's theological career, then, my two suggestions are, seemingly, in contrary directions. On the one hand, I have encouraged Kärkkäinen to return to his pentecostal roots, not merely to retrieve a sectarian theological identity (although in certain contexts needing the prophetic truth of the gospel, such a sectarian identity is essential), but also to provide a confessional ground for the particularity of claims which constitute any constructive ecumenical theology. On the other hand, I have also encouraged Kärkkäinen to engage in the interreligious dialogue, not only to further establish his identity as a world theologian, but also because Christian faith presumes a universality to the gospel that cannot (and should not) back down in the face of alternative claims to truth. How to reconcile these two? Perhaps no simplistic reconciliation is possible on this side of the *eschaton,* as theologians are called to live with both the particularity and the universality of the gospel message. Yet in the hands of good theologians, such a tension is not disabling, but rather provides the resources out of which truth is discerned. Kärkkäinen is such a theologian, and I am convinced his celebrating and inhabiting his pentecostal habitus more fully will only stimulate his ecumenical theological program even as it will further ground his comparative theological engagement with the interreligious dialogue.

W(H)ITHER EVANGELICAL THEOLOGY?

While Kärkkäinen is really still only a mid-career theologian with his magnum opus far ahead of him, I have nevertheless been already sufficiently encouraged and challenged by his work to ask about the question concerning the direction that evangelical theology needs to take in the twenty-first century. Allow me to approach this question from three directions: the sociological, the methodological, and the theological. The following remarks are necessarily tentative, attempting to discern the most promising directions for the future of evangelical theology in light of Kärkkäinen's work to date.

From a sociological perspective, the identity of evangelicalism and of evangelical theology is seriously contested. The fundamentalist-evangelical divide has now proliferated into a spectrum that includes neo-evangelicals, postconservative evangelicals, Wesleyan-Arminian evangelicals, ecumenical evangelicals, mainline evangelicals, and pentecostals and charismatics, among other groups and movements. At this level, evangelicalism is too fragmented, and historians will debate endlessly the genealogies of what is "authentic" evangelicalism. Part of the problem is that each of these evangelical identities has been forged in different contexts, protesting different matters.

Yet it is also precisely this situation that illuminates for us the value of Kärkkäinen's work, especially the Trinitarian trilogy and the textbook on ecclesiology. The ecumenical trajectory of these volumes provides us with one example of how to engage with difference: that of understanding it sufficiently so as to be able to describe it on its own terms. Critical engagement cannot proceed through construction of straw positions. Kärkkäinen's ecumenical approach to theology is suggestive for the future of evangelical theology precisely because it protests both against a sectarianism that refuses to take the contemporary context seriously, and against a liberal relativism that refuses to take the question of theological truth seriously.

This raises, of course, the methodological question for evangelical theology. Evangelicals have come to understand the *sola scriptura* of the Reformation not as a literal guideline that limits the sources for theological reflection, but as pointing to the recognition of scripture as authoritative norm for theology.[52] Yet what does this mean and how is this enacted in the practicing of theological reflection? Does Scripture shape theology with its propositions (a la Carl Henry and others) or with its narrative (a la Gabriel Fackre and others)? Alternatively, is the normativeness of scripture connected with the Trinitarian shape of the gospel and the narrative of the Father sending the Son by the power of the Spirit?[53]

I do not intend to address these issues comprehensively. But it is precisely evangelical disputes about theological method that force this question. I suggest, again, that Kärkkäinen's work proposes one way forward for evangelical theological method. We need a spectrum of approaches: biblical, historical, ecumenical, philosophical, cross-cultural, etc. As important is that both ends of any spectrum are important for us to chart an evangelical middle ground. More conservative positions are reminders of the importance of past insights, even while more progressive alternatives would help us explore the acceptable limits of Christian theological discourse. Kärkkäinen's articulation of the pluralism of biblical data on any doctrine also helps us to see the perspectival nature of religious knowing that enriches rather than relativizes the theological task. Hence the diversity of Christian theologies provides a wealth of resources for evangelical theology in our

---

52. For evangelical reconstructions of the doctrine of Scripture, I have found most helpful Abraham, *Canon and Criterion* and Work, *Living and Active*.

53. One example of such a construal of biblical normativeness in terms of the gospel narrative is seen in the Reformed theologian Daniel Migliore, *Faith Seeking Understanding*.

time, so long as, following Kärkkäinen's lead, we adhere to the authority of the scriptural norm, follow closely the consensus gained by the tradition, and engage new ideas and issues with careful discernment. The perennial challenge will be to articulate the unity of the faith in terms of its diversity. Embracing this challenge will invigorate evangelical theology, not to mention ecumenical theology and world theology.

Am I therefore suggesting that any evangelical theology must also be ecumenical and global? At one level, I am actually saying that any evangelical theology concerned as it is with the relevance of the gospel message for the whole world cannot be anything but ecumenical and global in its horizons. Further, from the Pietist perspective, which informs Kärkkäinen's (and my own) pentecostal tradition, to ask about the meaning of Jesus is to ask about the meaning of Jesus for us. Hence, what would Jesus mean to Buddhists, Hindus, Muslims, and Jews, among others? To ask the question about how theology today comprehends the identity of Jesus and the meaning of salvation as formulated through the ecumenical conversation (as Kärkkäinen did in One with God) leads to asking the related question about how a world theology might understand the identity of Jesus and the meaning of salvation as formulated through the interreligious encounter. In this case, does Kärkkäinen's oeuvre to date chart one way forward for evangelical theology as we anticipate the next few years and decades?

I therefore suggest that an authentically biblical, ecumenical, and world theology will be an evangelical theology. Put in other terms, an evangelical theology today will be faithful to the biblical narrative, will be ecumenical in scope according both to Jesus' prayer for the unity of the church and to St. Paul's metaphor about the church being one body constituted by many members, and will anticipate the possibility of the Spirit's speaking through any language, tribe, nation, and even religious tradition, even as this happened on the Day of Pentecost. I have presented Kärkkäinen as modeling one way forward for evangelical theology. Readers who have persevered through this chapter should now turn to Kärkkäinen himself for the details of such a vision for evangelical theology in the twenty-first century.[54]

---

54. My thanks to Veli-Matti Kärkkäinen for looking over this essay to ensure that I have not misrepresented his work; yet I take full responsibility for the ideas in these pages.

CHAPTER 6

Radically Orthodox, Reformed, and Pentecostal

Rethinking the Intersection of Post/Modernity and the Religions in Conversation with James K. A. Smith

As "THE MOST HEAVYWEIGHT theological movement twentieth-century Christianity in England has produced" (*Theology*), Radical Orthodoxy has gained increasing attention and momentum in the North American theological academy. Its most recent spokesperson, James K. A. Smith, has attempted to extend the Radical Orthodoxy vision in dialogue with the Dutch Reformed tradition.[1] Clearly, the central features of "Reformed" Radical Orthodoxy empower a kind of prophetic engagement with the cultural, political, economic, and ideological domains of modern Western society. At another level, however, the globalizing features of our late modern world context mean that the dominant pagan deities are not just secularism, nihilism, or capitalism, but also, arguably, those of other religious traditions. At this level, I suggest that the program of Radical Orthodoxy, especially if accepted in terms of the reforms proposed by Smith, may be vulnerable to an authentic and sustained Christian engagement with the plurality of *mythoi* operative in the public square.

My goal in this chapter is threefold. First, I seek to understand the Reformed Radical Orthodoxy project articulated by Smith. Second, I will raise a set of questions about the viability of this project for engaging the task

---

1. Smith, *Introducing Radical Orthodoxy.* All quotations and references to this book will be made parenthetically in the text with *IRO* followed by the page number(s).

of public theology in a religiously plural context. Finally, however, rather than undermining Smith's theological vision, I hope to provide a "pneumatological assist" to his platform, as I am convinced that a more robust pneumatological theology (actually suggested, but undeveloped by Smith) enables the kind of engagement that is required in our religiously plural late modern world.

RADICALLY ORTHODOX AND REFORMED: MAPPING SMITH'S PROJECT

James K. A. Smith is one of the most promising young theologians on the horizon today. While his graduate training has been in philosophy—a master's degree from the Institute of Christian Studies in Toronto and a PhD in philosophy under John Caputo at Villanova University—his background includes conversion to Christ and Christian discipleship in the North American evangelical and pentecostal movements and teaching experiences at Jesuit and Dutch Reformed institutions of higher education.[2] Over the last decade, including his four years at Villanova, Smith's scholarly output has been nothing short of astonishing. All the more so considering that his scholarship has sought to bring together what may otherwise seem to be four completely unrelated discourses: the evangelical and pentecostal theology nurtured by his ecclesial experiences; the Reformed theological tradition received through the Institute for Christian Studies; the continental philosophy at the heart of his PhD program of study; and the newly emerging Radical Orthodoxy movement.[3]

Many of these themes have also come together in Smith's latest book, *Introducing Radical Orthodoxy* (*IRO*). We are all deeply indebted to him for bringing clarity to authors and texts whose rhetorical obscurity often matches the already overwhelming theoretical density of the subject matter they are addressing. While it is redundant to offer an overview of Smith's

2. Smith began his teaching career at Loyola Marymount University in Los Angeles (1999–2003), and now teaches at Calvin College in Grand Rapids, Michigan. His undergraduate degree was from Emmaus Bible College in Dubuque, Iowa, which remains affiliated with the Plymouth Brethren, and he and his family also spent many years attending and serving in Assemblies of God churches. See his bio, available on his faculty page on the Calvin College website.

3. A revised version of Smith's master's thesis at the Institute for Christian Studies was published as *The Fall of Interpretation*. His doctoral dissertation has also been published as *Speech and Theology*. Smith's engagement with Reformed theology has been refracted through his study of the Dutch Reformed theologian Herman Dooyeweerd; see Dooyeweerd, *Twilight of Western Thought*. Remember, all of these books, including *IRO*, were *published* before Smith's 35th birthday!

own introduction to RO, it is important for me to present my own reading of *IRO* if for no other reason than that my own comments in part two of this chapter can be critically evaluated.

IRO is divided into two parts of equal length. Part I provides a three-chapter "Orientation" that describes RO's project of inhabiting a postsecular world and articulating a postsecular theology. In some ways, RO is merely calling attention to the passing of secularism as the dominant social ideology of our time. If postmodernism has been announcing the death of modernity and postcolonial movements have been successfully shifting discursive perspectives from the North to the South, from the West to the East, does this not signify also the meltdown of what Weber called the "iron cage of rationality" introduced by the Enlightenment? Whereas "the secular city" was heralded just a generation ago, the invasion of the postsecular means that secularism is passe, and secularity may be no more than just another sound bite in the marketplace of ideas.

In other ways, of course, RO's project has taken off precisely because its advocates realize that the arrival of the postsecular will continue to be resisted. Modern secularism is neither easily vanquished nor without its own resources in defending itself against and even defeating the advancing armies of postsecularity. Hence RO mounts a five-pronged offensive meant in part to usher in a postsecular space. First, RO criticizes modernity's individualism, liberalism, and dualism. More specifically, RO deconstructs the allegedly autonomous reason of modernity as flawed, implausible, and nonexistent. Second, and building on the first, if there is no autonomous reason, then there is no purely secular space within which such reason operates. The result is a reconciliation of faith and reason, which modernity had segregated. Within this scheme of things, RO advocates have worked hard to retrieve the illuminationist epistemology of Augustine and the theurgical tradition of Neoplatonism (in the line of Iamblichus, rather than the henological Neoplatonism of Valentinus and Plotinus) (*IRO* 48).

Third, if there is no purely secular space, then the boundaries between the secular and the sacred are also removed. Modernity's dualistic construals—e.g., of nature and spirit, of the material and the spiritual, of transcendence and immanence—are exposed as ideologies designed to prohibit religious engagement with the public spheres of politics, economics, and social life. With this exposé of the totalitarian aspirations of the (allegedly) neutral (i.e., secular) nation-state as an empty ideology comes the possibility of the emergence of a new (and old) kind of Christian socialism. But perhaps even more importantly, it also allows for the reemergence of an ontology of participation wherein the created and material world, rather than being cut off from or existing autonomously over and against the transcendent realm, finds its meaning precisely as it is suspended from that which is transcendent and immaterial. In this way, RO's revised Thomistic notion of analogy postures itself both against Scotus's doctrine of univocity, which collapses the distance between transcendence and immanence, and against any Hellenistic or fundamentalistic dualism that posits an unbridgeable chasm between transcendence and the created world.

From this, fourth, the sacramental life of the church is incarnationally reconceived so that the church's liturgy serves as a particularly intensified iconic indicator of how the material and created order participates in the divine life and work of God. In this case, the worship of the church becomes the means of divine revelation, even while the practices of the church are reconnected to its aesthetic doxologies. Finally, then, it is from this platform of the church as a worshiping community always and already in the world (rather than over and against it) that the church speaks prophetically to the wider culture and acts prophetically in ways directed toward the redemption of all creation.

Part II of *IRO* is a four-chapter "Navigation" wherein Smith further unpacks the Radical Orthodox vision even while he leavens it with critical insights from the Dutch Reformational tradition of Abraham Kuyper and Herman Dooyeweerd. To be sure, Smith stands squarely with RO in terms of its key tenets: the critique of modernity and of the myth of the secular, the participatory ontology, the sacramental view of materiality, the centrality of aesthetics, and the view of the church as an alternative polis. But at various points, a Dutch Reformed dialogue with RO nuances Smith's own views.

To begin, the Reformational theologians have always been suspicious of Neoplatonism, especially in its devaluing of the material world. Smith therefore probes RO's reading of Plato both with regard to the question of the goodness of creation and the material world and with regard to the issue of whether or not Neoplatonic illuminationism can account for the hermeneutical character of the resurrected body's beatific vision. A related issue is the question of whether the Neoplatonic framework of RO's participatory ontology leads to a theological occasionalism such that "God must continually and constantly reach into creation for it to *be* creation" (*IRO* 204, italics original). On each of these issues, Smith is unconvinced that RO can successfully meld its theological vision with Plato's pagan ontology, preferring instead to develop a creational ontology with the help of Leibniz's notion of the created harmony of the world that unfolds according to preestablished structures and forces.[4] The goal is a view of the integrity

4. Interestingly, Smith's attraction to the Leibnizian idea of creation being "frontloaded, so to speak, with all that it requires to function" (*IRO* 214) means that he has to ward off the specter of deism on the one side, even as he is reacting to the threat

of nature that avoids both the Scylla of occasionalism (God does not have to keep intervening in the sustenance of the world) and the Charybdis of materialism (the world is created rather than self-sustaining), even while it preserves all that RO's participatory ontology provides without the liabilities of the Neoplatonic scaffold.[5]

Another Reformational questioning of the RO position concerns the nature of theology itself. RO insists on rescuing theology from its subordination to the secular (whether that be the natural or social sciences), and does so by returning to the medieval view of theology as the queen of the sciences. While the Dutch Reformed theologians would agree with RO's goal, their view of theology as a human activity and therefore also tainted by the fall leads them to see RO's means as bordering on idolatry. Yet Dooyeweerd's own position on this matter views theology as just another special science alongside mathematics, law, ethics, etc., all of which are grounded in the divine revelation informing our lived (pretheoretical) religious life. Now, this way of viewing things seems to "cordon off theology from revelation in any significant sense" (*IRO* 175). Smith proposes instead that we distinguish between our fundamental religious commitments, which include our creeds and confessions (theology$_1$), from our theorized doctrinal and speculative theological statements (theology$_2$) (*IRO* 177). This move preserves both the Dooyeweerdian distinction between our pretheoretical confession and our second-order reflection on the one hand, even as it allows for the RO insistence on the importance of developing specifically Christian accounts (theology$_1$) of other sciences (theology$_2$). What emerges, then, is the possibility of, e.g., "a confessional account of economics that begins from a Christian world view" (*IRO* 177).[6]

This leads, finally (for the purposes of this chapter), to the ecclesiological visions of RO and the Dutch Reformational tradition, especially in terms of how both view the task of cultural engagement. Part of the question concerns whether or not the stance of the church as polis is opposed to a recognition of the state as polis. RO answers affirmatively while those

---

of occasionalism on the other. This is strikingly parallel to the view long defended by Howard van Till, a colleague of Smith's at Calvin, albeit in the physics department. See van Til's essay on "The Fully Gifted Creation."

5. This move allows Smith to further develop his earlier ideas on a creational hermeneutic (see *The Fall of Interpretation* and *Speech and Theology*) in the direction of a creational and incarnational ontology. More on this issue momentarily.

6. Arguably this call to develop a Christian economics, etc., is more plausible when dealing with the social sciences. Is there a distinctively Christian view of the natural sciences, however, or a distinctively Christian mathematics? The issues are much more fuzzy and complex in these cases, as seen in the recent debates over intelligent design. See my essay, "God and the Evangelical Laboratory."

in the Reformed tradition take the opposite position. Smith suggests that while RO will challenge Reformed theology to reconsider the fallenness of the state's direction, Reformed theology in turn should spur RO to develop its ecclesiology along pneumatological, charismatic, and catholic lines (*IRO* 259). Smith seems convinced that this Reformed leaven of RO ecclesiology will only strengthen its platform for cultural engagement. I agree to some extent, but will also suggest some disagreements in the next section.

So where are we at with regard to Smith's own rendition of a Reformed and Radically Orthodox theological vision? A number of central commitments are discernible. First, Smith appears to embrace a kind of ontology of participation, albeit under another label: that of a creational or incarnational ontology. This allows him to emphasize the goodness of the created and material world, insist on its fallen character, and yet participate, by grace, in the redeeming work of God that extends to all creation. The locus of divine redemption, however, is in the church of Jesus Christ, a worshiping and confessing community whose practices are nurtured by the Spirit. In this scheme of things, there is neither an autonomous human reason nor an autonomous secular state, since both human reason and social and political structures are fallen and have been taken captive by sin. Smith therefore affirms a prophetic stance whereby the church engages with the world not apologetically or dialogically, if that means on terms that are allegedly neutral (because there is no such space) or on terms established by the world (because of its fallen character), but confessionally and kerygmatically.[7] Rather, the church attempts to both "out-narrate" other competing *mythoi* and conduct what might be called an "immanent critique" of their plausibility conditions (*IRO* 179–82).[8] Applied to the pretensions of secularism, the church embodies an alternative vision of what a peaceful polis can be and demonstrates (through proclamation, of course) the internal antinomies of secular reason on the one hand and the secular state's perversion of theological reason on the other.

---

7. At least this is the impression I have from reading the text and footnotes of *IRO*. Smith explicitly says that the issues of technical import are discussed in the notes (*IRO* 27), so I will periodically refer to these in dialogue with Smith; for example, Smith does not seem to interrogate RO's insistence that there can be no dialogues as RO "does not recognize other valid points of view outside the theological" (*IRO* 167, quoting from "Radical Orthodoxy: Twenty-Four Theses," thesis 5).

8. There are echoes here of the work of Hauerwas, MacIntyre, and Lindbeck, all of whom are engaged in dialogue in *IRO*; see the index of *IRO*.

RADICAL AND REFORMED: CRITICAL QUESTIONS
IN A RELIGIOUSLY PLURAL WORLD

On one level, I am captivated by Smith's theological and ecclesiological vision. He has not only illuminated the RO project for the rest of us, but has also retrieved the Reformed theological tradition in a way that invigorates the contemporary theological conversation.[9] Yet I am not fully satisfied with the direction I see Smith headed in. I will lay out my concerns by beginning with the point where I think him most vulnerable, and from there interrogate how the remainder of his theological system may add to rather than decrease his vulnerability.[10]

I begin with Smith's affirmation of the RO strategy for cultural engagement: a confessional theological stance that attempts to both "out-narrate" other competing *mythoi* and to conduct an "immanent critique" of their plausibility conditions. The first strategy raises questions not only about how differing theological narratives can compete to begin with, but also about how the differences can be adjudicated if the norms and criteria for such adjudication are tradition specific. This is, of course, the question that has been debated back and forth, especially since the appearance of Lindbeck's cultural-linguistic theory of doctrine.[11] In Lindbeck's (and, by extension, RO's and Smith's) view of "ad hoc apologetics," without any neutral ideological or theological space all "dialogue" can only proceed on tradition-specific terms. If this is so, does that mean that persons who do not share the same presuppositions will only talk past one another? This would dovetail well with the Reformed conviction that only the regenerating work of the Holy Spirit can accomplish what human argumentation can never achieve (e.g., *IRO* 166), but it would also result in a stalemate between Reformed and Wesleyan construals of grace. What, then, if we returned to the previous question, and respond that conversation on tradition-specific terms does not automatically result in the dialogue partners speaking past one another because of a common anthropology or common human con-

---

9. I am especially grateful for Smith's accomplishing the latter, as the Reformed perspective is relatively absent from my work *Spirit Poured Out on All Flesh*. This is ironic, of course, given my insistence in that book on the importance of the diversity of voices in the theological conversation.

10. The following critical comments take off from an initial round of dialogue—see Smith, "Scandalizing Theology," and Yong, "Whither Systematic Theology?"—but should be understood as that which occurs between two colleagues and, more importantly, friends. It is precisely because of my deep respect for Jamie's scholarship and gratefulness for his friendship that I am engaging him further in critical conversation.

11. See, e.g., Marshall, ed., *Theology and Dialogue*, and Phillips and Okholm, eds., *Nature of Confession*.

dition? This response may produce another catch-22: either the problem of how such a common human condition is understood by the dialogue partners if not through their own tradition's rendition of that condition, or the problem of whether or not the common anthropology would vitiate the ad hoc apologetic position that understands the criteria for adjudicating differing theological narratives and claims as themselves tradition specific. In short, I need more help from Smith in seeing how a confessional theological stance can actually out-narrate other competing *mythoi*.

But perhaps Smith's response would be to point to his second strategy of conducting an immanent critique of the other *mythoi's* plausibility conditions. The problem is that this second strategy may not be available to those who stand outside the myth under scrutiny. I suggest RO (and the Kuyperian/Dooyeweerdian tradition within which Smith positions himself) can launch "immanent critiques" of modernity because its representatives stand within the modern experience. We have been sufficiently immersed in modernity to have developed critical insider perspectives on secularism's false ideologies. It is true that insider perspectives can also blind us to certain features of our experience. Yet insider perspectives are absolutely essential for the kinds of *immanent* critiques Smith proposes. One cannot launch an immanent critique from an outsider's position.

If this is true, Smith's strategy may work well for subjecting secularism to immanent criticism and for mapping a postsecular theology, but it may not succeed when we consider the encounter of the diversity of religions in our time. In what ways can we say that Christians also stand within the experiences and practices of other faiths so as to be able to legitimately launch "immanent critiques"? Put in reverse, can Christian faith itself be subjected to immanent critique by those in other faiths? To take up this latter question first, while we may affirm that outsider perspectives often illuminate things that are missed from an insider position, it seems infeasible that an outsider can sustain an immanent critique of Christian faith. The most obvious antinomies of reason in Christian faith—for example, the mysteries of the Trinity, the incarnation, and the compatibility between divine sovereignty and human responsibility—are arguably not only resolved in but actually emergent from Christian praxis and worship.[12] So when outsiders thrust polemical salvos against the alleged incoherence of Christian doctrines, they are rarely convinced that Christian apologies make sense. In turn, Christians eventually figure out that the best response is not to provide further theological arguments but to pray that our critics will be illuminated (re-

12. Thus Smith seems to agree with Milbank and Dooyeweerd in their counter-assertions that the Christian narrative is unencumbered from antinomies like other *mythoi* (IRO 241 n.33).

generated) by the Holy Spirit, to recommend to them adoption of the stance of Christian faith seeking understanding, and to invite them to experience for themselves the goodness of God and the ecclesial life of faith. Precisely because Christian beliefs and practices are intertwined, the Christian tradition is effectively shielded from immanent critiques attempted by outsiders who might recognize our grammar but do not participate in our practices.

But if this is the case, what about the plausibility of Christians conducting immanent critiques of other faiths? Might not similar responses be forthcoming from representatives of other faiths with regard to our pointing out their antinomies? What can Christians say about the antinomies of Buddhist logic if Christians have not engaged in a sustained manner in Buddhist meditative practices? What criticisms can Christians raise about Islamic doctrines that have not already been asked and responded to by Muslims who are committed to living in submission to Allah? How can Christians sustain an interrogation of Hindu views of what is ultimately real if Christians have not traversed the various yogic paths of Jnana (Knowledge), Bhakti (Devotion), and Karma (Service)? The challenge in each instance is not that we cannot raise questions about the antinomies in other faiths from our perspectives, but that the resources for responding that are available to adherents of other traditions who practice their faiths are unavailable to us as outsiders, and that precisely because their availability hinges on our "walking in their shoes" and experiencing (practicing) their faiths from the inside.[13] In short, immanent critiques of other faiths seem to require some sort of (at least initial) conversion to them in order to be sustained.[14]

My concern regarding Smith's apparent adoption of an ad hoc apologetic strategy (he actually uses the language of "the end of apologetics" in *IRO*, 179–82) that engages other *mythoi* through conducting immanent critiques of their antinomies does not stand alone. Smith's strategies seem to me to be intimately tied in with certain epistemological and ontological commitments that seem to perpetuate precisely the kinds of problems I have outlined. Allow me to very briefly identify some of the epistemological and ontological positions that I believe to be problematic in light of my preceding comments.

Epistemologically, let me begin by saying that I think Smith's distinction between theology$_1$ and theology$_2$ is helpful in terms of differentiating

13. As discovered by anthropologists of religion attempting to provide comprehensive accounts of other cultures. For the classic ethnographic study, see Evans-Pritchard, *Witchcraft, Oracles, Magic*. For a classic theoretical restatement of this view, see Geertz, *Interpretation of Cultures*.

14. I develop the line of questioning in this paragraph more completely in my "Spirit Bears Witness."

between what has traditionally been termed first-order religious commitments experiences, beliefs, and practices that underwrite second-order theoretical reflection. At the same time, the lines between the two are not so easily drawn, as when Smith realizes that creedal confessions which function as theology$_1$ are not devoid of second-order theorizing (theology$_2$). Further, such a position does nothing to mitigate the challenges of approaching religious pluralism via the road of ad hoc apologetics. Smith recognizes that other faiths could also be understood in similar terms, but he does not question Dooyeweerd's view that such structures take apostate directions in comparison with Christian faith (*IRO* 177 n.103). Herewith the epistemological question is complexified. For starters, does Dooyeweerd (and by implication, Smith) believe that only Jewish (or Islamic or Buddhist, etc.) theology$_2$ is apostate but not Jewish (etc.) theology$_1$, or are both the theology$_1$ and theology$_2$ of other faiths apostate? If the latter, how can we as Christian outsiders know this? Just as important, we are back to the previous question, how can we even begin to out-narrate religious others so that they can be in a position to convert to Christ? Are we reduced to telling each other our testimonies? Is there nothing at stake in Smith's receiving the testimony of religious others? Is Smith really open to changing his mind (and if so on what grounds, given his confessionalist stance), or is such an exchange of testimonies only for the sake of pleasantries (the kind of Rortyean conversation to which we all say, "yuk!")?

But what if we take the former route that says Jewish (etc.) theology$_1$ is not apostate, only its theology$_2$? Putting to one side for the moment that there is no monolithic Jewish theology$_2$, this approach seems plausible in that it allows for a kind of generous dispensation of what the Reformed tradition calls common grace, which lies at the core of all human encounters with the divine (theology$_1$), but which human beings, because of their fallen state, take in their own apostate directions (theology$_2$). Yet this does not work for Smith for at least two reasons. First, theology$_1$ is not without content, and if so, we cannot simply say that Jewish (etc.) theology$_1$ is either a monolithic whole or that Jewish theology$_1$ is the result of common grace. Second, this move leads in directions that RO seems to be taking, and that Smith is resisting, namely, the blurring of the lines between the church (and it's theology$_1$) and the world (and it's theologies$_1$) insofar as "the human community and the community that constitutes the *ecclesia* would be coextensive" (*IRO* 257).

Yet on what grounds does Smith resist this movement? He does not seem to reject RO's claim that even nihilism (the fundamental religious commitment of secularism) can be "a kind of 'pre-evangelistic' *praeambula fidei* for a participatory creational ontology" (*IRO* 102; cf. *IRO* 193 n.25, in both cases referring to the work of Conor Cunningham). But if this is the case, then why is Jewish, Islamic, or Buddhist, etc., theology$_1$ also not a kind of *praeparatio evangelica*? Isn't this actually what is assumed when we talk about the Judeo-Christian tradition, or is Judaism a special sense such that we can allow only that hyphenated qualification but we cannot grant the possibility of an Islamic or Buddhist, etc., theology$_1$ or talk about a Christo-Islamic or Buddhist-Christian, etc., tradition?[15] In raising these questions, I am merely agreeing with Smith that the relationship between theology$_1$ and theology$_2$ needs to be given much more extensive consideration (*IRO* 176 n.99).

Now of course Smith's epistemological commitments are tied to his increasingly robust ecclesiology. Smith wishes to avoid what he calls a "bastardized notion of common grace" (*IRO* 176 n.101) and hence seems to align himself with RO's emphases on discontinuity rather than continuity (*IRO* 90, 256)—e.g., between church and world, between ecclesial practices and general moral acts, and between the Christian narrative and other *mythoi*. Perhaps such a robust ecclesiology is what sets Smith's Reformed rendition of a creational or incarnational ontology apart from RO's participatory ontology. But can Smith have his cake and eat it too? Let me expound.

Smith likes RO's participatory ontology because of its sacramental principle that values the material world and undergirds a robust theological aesthetics. But he is concerned that RO not be led astray by its embrace of a Thomistic account of the nature/grace distinction (e.g., *IRO* 120–22). Smith fears that going down that road will compromise all that RO has fought for in terms of liberating the church from its captivity to the ideology of the secular (which brings with it various mediating theologies such as Tillich's correlationism, Tracy's analogical imagination, and liberation theology's reliance on social analysis). The question is whether or not Smith's incarnational principle is going to be merely historical and therefore applicable only literally to the incarnation and perhaps metaphorically to the church, or if it is going to be robustly ontological, leading to the sacramental principle and also to a hermeneutical circle that is not only epistemological but also ontological. Alternatively put, is there an irresolvable tension between RO's participatory ontology on the one hand, and its emphases on discontinuity rather than on continuity on the other? On the one hand, if Smith goes down the former path (of participatory or incarnational ontology), does it not bring with it a blurring of the realms of creation-fall-redemption, which

---

15. To deny the latter possibility is to reject the testimonies/confessions of those who affirm some kind of dual- or multiple-religious identity; see Cornille, *Many Mansions?*

he fears because there are no secular realms and all participate in the divine life (*IRO* 189)? On the other hand, if he opts instead for discontinuity rather than continuity, does that not in turn undermine the sacramental principle and the attendant robust theology of the arts to which Smith is committed?

There is, of course, the related epistemo-ontological question: if all knowledge is mediated by our material being in the world—e.g., our confessional and communal practices—can we draw hard and fast lines between divine revelation and pagan knowledge? Put in *IRO*'s terms, does Smith follow Augustine's insistence on there being "only paganism or true worship" (*IRO* 47), or is there more continuity than Augustine lets on? Smith appears to nod in the latter direction when he says that we must "adopt an operative framework of philosophical categories and language that, at the same time, subverts the religious ground-motive that spawned them. Indeed, the New Testament notion of *Logos* may do just that" (*IRO* 154 n.35). But while this rendition of an incarnational ontology allows Smith to embrace the sacramental principle, does it also enable us to draw fairly distinctive lines between church and world, between creaturely realities that can and do act as icons of transcendence and those that do not?

RADICALLY ORTHODOX, REFORMED, AND PENTECOSTAL: A "PNEUMATOLOGICAL ASSIST"

Let me state clearly that my questions to Smith in the preceding section are not at all meant to undermine his project of reforming RO. This is in part because I don't think there is any theological vision that can successfully answer all questions (we are fallen creatures, not omniscient), and in part because (more importantly) I welcome Smith's Reformed RO perspective to the theological conversation. At the same time, I wish to invite Smith to take more seriously the pneumatological suggestions that are interspersed throughout *IRO* because I am convinced that they can fortify his theological position at little or no cost to his investment in reforming RO. Further, as I have previously indicated, Smith's background in the evangelical and pentecostal movements means that his pneumatological intuitions, while still underdeveloped, are nevertheless "grounded" in the liturgies, confessions, and practices of a diverse and global community of faith. In fact, Smith has himself initiated a conversation between RO and pentecostal-charismatic theology informed in large part by his nurturance in the practices of such a community,[16] and suggests even in *IRO* that further discussion is needed

---

16. See Smith, "What Hath Cambridge to Do with Azusa Street?," and Graham Ward's response, "Economy of the Divine."

(*IRO* 151 n.26). For all of these reasons, then, I offer the following very brief suggestions (because of space constraints) as a means of energizing Smith's reforming of RO.

Put succinctly, my thesis is that Smith's incarnational theology needs a "pneumatological assist," both for the purpose of developing a more fully Trinitarian vision (the theological rationale) and in order to ease the tensions of cultural critique and engagement identified in the preceding section (the pragmatic or contextual rationale). I will flesh out this hypothesis at three levels: that of ontology (drawing from the Pentecost narrative of "the Spirit poured out on all flesh"); that of epistemology (drawing from the Johannine claim that the Spirit "leads us into all truth"); and that of ecclesiology or politics (that of the Spirit gifting the many members/communions of the one body of Christ).[17] The goal is to bring the pentecostal perspective more explicitly into the Reformed RO conversation (as already begun by Smith) in order to elaborate on a more cohesive Christian theology of cultural and interreligious engagement for our time.

I begin with the Pentecost narrative of the Spirit's outpouring on "all flesh" (Acts 2:17a).[18] I suggest that this provides us with additional biblical and theological resources for the kind of participatory or creational ontology advocated by Smith. In this case, of course, "nature" is re-envisioned in pneumatological terms so that the chasm between transcendence and creation is overcome theologically rather than philosophically (e.g., through a revised Platonism). Further, the gift of the Spirit to "all flesh" underwrites the ontological participation of all creation in the divine presence and activity that sustains the world, thus providing a "pneumatological assist" to a sacramental principle which revalues the material world. Finally, of course, that the Spirit is given to "all flesh" opens up to a theology of culture that both preserves a point of contact between God and the human realm and provides a theological explanation for a common humanity. However, the gift of the Spirit also preserves human freedom so that only those who respond to the Spirit's gifts (i.e., call on the name of the Lord; Acts 2:21) come into full participation in the community of the redeemed. In other words, there is no temptation to any soteriological universalism in this account. On the contrary, it is precisely the possibility of damnation that demands the proclamation of the gospel by the power of the Spirit, and it is precisely the gift of the Spirit that makes such communication possible to begin with.

---

17. I have defended another form of this thesis at (some might say exhausting) length in my *Spirit-Word-Community*.

18. For details, see my *The Spirit Poured Out on All Flesh*, esp. ch. 4.

This notion of a pneumatologically conceived ontology thus leads to a pneumatological epistemology: the Spirit who is poured out on all flesh is the same Spirit who leads us into all truth. The Johannine rendition of this epistemological Spirit emphasizes Jesus Christ as the way, the truth, and the life. Smith's incarnational ontology goes a long way to putting theoretical flesh on that primordial Christian confession. I suggest that the Lukan rendition of this same insight is exemplified in the many tongues declaring the glory of God (Acts 2:11). The miracle of the Pentecost event consists not so much in the fact that miraculous tongues were spoken as in the fact that there was understanding that took place precisely in, through, and across the diversity of languages.[19]

Pentecost therefore opens up to a pneumatological epistemology that corroborates Smith's creational hermeneutic along at least three lines. First, the revelatory knowledge of God comes mediated through the created order, in this case through human tongues. Second, Luke's narrative provides an alternative means of conceptualizing what Smith calls theology$_1$ and theology$_2$, except that in the Lukan framework this distinction is better understood in terms of the human experience of or encounter with God (the Pentecost event: theology$_1$) leading to discursive reports of that experience (Acts 2: theology$_2$). I am prepared to argue that all religious experience (what Smith calls theology$_1$) can be accessed conceptually and discerned only through language (what Smith calls theology$_2$), and that this includes our reciting (theology$_1$) our creeds (theology$_2$).[20] Finally, testimony to the wondrous works of God can only be received through a multitude of voices, which all provide perspective. In other words, all individual testimonies need to be discerned amidst, by, and through the community of faith. The pneumatological epistemology of the Pentecost narrative thus turns out to be the flip side of pneumatological ontology, one that features mutuality, reciprocity, and intersubjectivity.[21]

What does this mean, then, for our understanding of the church, a topic that may, in the final analysis, lie at the heart of *IRO*? Smith himself acknowledges at the end of his book that any viable ecclesiology must be "deeply pneumatological" (*IRO* 259). This means that the work of the Spirit in forming the community of faith in regeneration and sanctification must

19. This is Michael Welker's argument in *God the Spirit*, ch. 5.

20. I have become more and more convinced about this thesis as I have worked during this past year on my sabbatical project, tentatively titled "Down Syndrome and Human Destiny: Disability Studies and the Renewal of Theology in Late Modernity." [This was published later as *Theology and Down Syndrome*.]

21. Unless I am mistaken, Smith elsewhere argues for exactly such a notion, but calls it "original grace"; see Smith, "Call as Gift," 225.

be central. It is this work that sets the church apart from other communities. At the exact same time, Smith notes that the Spirit constitutes the church as a welcoming and hospitable community, whose doors are ever open to the world. It is this tension that I believe a fully pneumatological ecclesiology is capable of sustaining—again, along three lines.

First, the Spirit maintains the unity of the church precisely in and through its diversity. One Spirit gives many gifts to its many members and, in this way, also confers transcendental value on what may otherwise be despised (cf. 1 Cor 12). In this Pauline perspective, the unity of the church is not found in some ahistorical ideal, but is located mysteriously in the concrete messiness that is the practices of the historical church.

This means, second, that the lines between the church and the world can never be hard and fast in actuality. This is not to say that there are no distinctive communities of faith and no way to discern what is not church. Rather, it means that the historical church is composed of communities and members within communities whose identities are never pure, but always already immersed in the historical world, and therefore also overlapping with many other different communities and identities.[22] In this pneumatological scheme of things, then, there is no absolutely other, since an absolute stranger will always remain unknowable. But any authentic encounter and any dialogical engagement will always be with those who, while far off, have been brought near in some way by the Spirit (cf. Eph 2:13–18).

But then are the lines between church and world completely erased in this pneumatological ecclesiology? Not in the least. As the Orthodox saying goes, "we can only know with some assurance where the Spirit is, rather than where the Spirit is not."[23] Hence, my point is that as Christians we can boldly testify to what we know. But because the church is also in the world, our encounter with otherness is conducted within an eschatological horizon. While what is common or what is different (contrary) are in some respects empirical and can be determined in part through human dialogue, not everything can be so adjudicated. A pneumatological eschatology insists that the church is an end-time fellowship that witnesses to the coming of the Lord and to the implosion of the kingdom in our midst. The arrival of the kingdom will de-absolutize all human claims in the end, even while it accomplishes the redemption of the world testified to by the broken tongues of Pentecost. In this way, a pneumatological ecclesiology actually insists on maintaining the tension between the now and the not yet, between being an

---

22. I elaborate on this in "Spirit Gives Utterance."

23. See Yong, *Beyond the Impasse*, 187 n.27.

established community of faith and yet one that is open to the world and, especially, to the coming kingdom of God.

In the end, then, the "pneumatological assist" I am proposing to Smith's Radically Orthodox and Reformed vision is one that I believe is not only theological through and through (thus resisting being co-opted by other ideologies, narratives, or *mythoi*, as Smith et al. are rightly concerned about), but also essential to the kind of performative theology of culture and theology of religions that enables the church to engage the world. Such engagement is possible, of course, on the terms of the Spirit who is poured out on all flesh and guides us into all truth. And remember that I am suggesting only that my pneumatological theology complements rather than displaces Smith's incarnational ontology and hermeneutic. Expanded in this "deeply pneumatological" direction, a more dialogical space is opened up between the church and the world than is possible on the trajectory of discontinuity that comes through in part of RO's rhetoric and is sometimes accentuated in Smith's own ecclesiology. Further, such a pneumatological approach provides theological reinforcement for the Reformed doctrine of common grace in ways that also help refine our theological anthropology and our distinction between what is common to our human experience of God (theology$_1$) and our varying confessions (theology$_2$). Finally, the pneumatological assist I am commending opens up the possibility of our engaging in immanent critiques of other faith traditions, even as it also makes possible our being transformed by our encounter with those in other faiths.

In each of these ways, perhaps the pentecostal perspective can also contribute something toward the reforming of Radical Orthodoxy.[24]

24. A previous version of this chapter was presented to the Philosophy Section of the 35th Annual Meeting of the Society for Pentecostal Studies, Fuller Theological Seminary, Pasadena, California, 23–25 March 2006. My thanks to Smith for his response at this session, and to my doctoral student and research assistant, Chris Emerick, for correcting my infelicities in a previous draft of this chapter. It was also Chris who pointed out the lacuna in my work mentioned in note 6 above.

PART III

The Postsecular Milieu

Theology Meets Science and Religions

CHAPTER 7

From Quantum Mechanics to the Eucharistic Meal

John Polkinghorne's "Bottom-up" Vision of Science and Theology

REV DR. JOHN POLKINGHORNE, KBE, FRS needs no extended introduction to *Metanexus Online* readers.[1] In brief, he has had two successive careers, first as an elementary particle physicist at Edinburgh and then Cambridge (1956–1979), and then as an Anglican priest (1981–present), during which he has served in a variety of ecclesial positions (as curate, vicar, and chaplain) as well as being president of Queen's College (1989–1996). Since entering the priesthood, Polkinghorne has worked tirelessly at the frontiers of the science and theology conversation, having authored, coauthored, or edited more than twenty-five books on various related topics. His most recent book, *Science and the Trinity: The Christian Encounter with Reality* (2004), serves as the occasion for this review and assessment of his work.[2]

I first met Polkinghorne only last fall [2004], being privileged to work with him at a symposium on pneumatology sponsored by the Templeton Foundation. While I had read some of his books before, I so appreciated the clarity with which he spoke to difficult matters related to science and theology that I was led to revisit his *oeuvre*. I had long been convinced that the

1. Polkinghorne was elected as a Fellow to the Royal Society in 1954, and then appointed Knight Commander of the Order of the British Empire in 1997.

2. Polkinghorne, *Science and the Trinity*. Unless otherwise noted, further references to this volume will be by page numbers inserted parenthetically in the main text, or notes, as the case may be.

major challenges for Christian theology in the twenty-first century remain in two areas: in the engagement with the sciences and in the encounter between religions. Although my own training in the sciences is rather limited (my background and training is in systematic and constructive theology), going back and (re)reading Polkinghorne's work has helped me to refocus the issues much more specifically.

In what follows, I will use *Science and the Trinity* as a springboard to explore Polkinghorne's contributions to the dialogue between science and theology over the last twenty-plus years. My review and assessment will move from considerations of theological method through some of the "thick" details of Polkinghorne's theology to an analysis of his eschatological vision. My objective in this exercise is twofold: to understand and further appreciate Polkinghorne as a scientist-theologian, and to map some of the present trajectories anticipating future conversations between science and theology.

METHODOLOGICAL CONSIDERATIONS: A "BOTTOM-UP, EUCHARISTIC-ASSISTED LOGIC"

Having begun as a scientist and come to theology only later in his career, Polkinghorne has written his fair share of books attempting to integrate theology with the current scientific conception of the world.[3] In *Science and the Trinity*, however, Polkinghorne's goal is to allow theology, rather than science, to shape the agenda. This reversal was already signaled almost a decade ago when Polkinghorne contrasted the more assimilationist strategy of fellow scientist-theologians Ian Barbour and Arthur Peacocke with his own approach to find consonance between science and theology in a way which preserved "the autonomy of theology in its dialogue with scientific culture."[4] In this case, meaning in theology would be governed by Christian praxis and self-understanding rather than imported from the outside. From the perspective of theological method, two features of *Science and the*

---

3. By my count, Polkinghorne has written at least twelve books of this genre over the last twenty-plus years: *The Way the World Is*; *One World*; *Science and Creation*; *Science and Providence*; *Reason and Reality*; *Quarks, Chaos and Christianity*; *Serious Talk*; *Scientists as Theologians*; *Belief in God*; *Science and Theology*; *Traffic in Truth*; and *Faith, Science and Understanding*.

4. Polkinghorne, *Scientists as Theologians*, 85. To be fair, Polkinghorne admitted that Peacocke's "assimilationism" is much more theologically robust than Barbour's process theism, even if not quite manifesting the "theological thickness" of historic Christian orthodoxy.

Trinity are particularly noteworthy with regard to theology setting the stage for the conversation.

First, the terms of the science-and-theology relationship are established via theological categories. In contrast to the now-classic four models approach—conflict, independence, dialogue, integration—that attempts to relate science to religion,[5] Polkinghorne proposes instead four theological frameworks within which theologians may and have sought to engage the sciences. The Deistic model is most akin to traditional natural theology in acknowledging that scientific data point to some sort of creator of the universe, but is theologically "thin" in terms of acknowledging not much more from this same data than did the earlier natural theology: that this creator "wound up" the universe at the beginning and has been absent from it since. The Theistic model goes further than the Deistic one in drawing inspiration from the Bible and even the life of Jesus, but stops short of adopting the dogmatic pronouncements of conciliar Christianity in articulating a theology for a scientific age. The Revisionary model engages with the broad scope of traditional Christian theology, but does so seeking somewhat radical revisions of orthodox theological claims—e.g., the doctrines of the incarnation, virgin birth, and resurrection of Jesus, just to name some christological touchstones—in light of scientific discoveries. Finally, the Developmental model, Polkinghorne's preferred approach, seeks to articulate the science-religion relationship less in terms of radical revision and more in terms of "a continuously unfolding exploration" (26).[6] The emphasis here is on continuity rather than discontinuity between past theological formulations and present affirmations.

How does Polkinghorne seek to ensure such continuity between his own scientifically informed theological reflections and those of historic Christian orthodoxy? This leads to the second feature of *Science and the Trinity,* whereby theology's setting the agenda is clearly seen: a "bottom-up" or abductive theological method, beginning with the basic data of Christian faith experience. As a scientist, Polkinghorne was long ago trained to allow empirical data to give rise to scientific theory. While theory itself certainly shapes what scientists observe to begin with, theories are also revised according to empirical observations. Similarly, then, Polkinghorne has sought

---

5. See Barbour, *Religion in an Age of Science*, ch. 1; Carlson, *Science and Christianity*; and Gregersen and van Huyssteen, *Rethinking Theology and Science.*

6. Not surprisingly, Polkinghorne also suggests that Peacocke represents the revisionary approach, and Barbour the theistic model. Polkinghorne's example of the deistic perspective is the work of physicist Paul Davies; see Davies, *Mind of God.*

to reflect theologically "from the bottom up" by beginning with the empirical data of Christian faith.[7]

What does such a bottom-up approach mean methodologically? Three interlocking methodological movements can be seen in *Science and the Trinity*. Initially, Polkinghorne takes the testimony of Scripture seriously as empirical data for theological reflection. His understanding of Scripture, however, is quite nuanced. While there is an evidential role for Scripture, there are also controlling factors limiting or constraining the interpretation of Scripture, such as its various genres, unedifying material that needs re-valuation based on the developmental character of the Scriptural "database," and theological commitments regarding the divinely inspired (not dictated) character of the biblical text. Hence Polkinghorne acknowledges the polysemous character of the biblical witness, and insists that we need a "flexible hermeneutic" (35). In any case, Christian theology in a scientific age cannot proceed by ignoring the testimony of Scripture.[8]

Secondly, and building on the first point, the experiences and testimonies of the earliest Christians serve as the fundamental empirical data for Christian theological reflection. Of course, these experiences were preserved first in the apostolic tradition and then in the New Testament writings. What Polkinghorne calls "trinitarian thinking" (99–103) is precisely the apostolic witness that "arose primarily as a response to the insistent complexity of human encounter with the reality of God experienced within the growing life of the Church" (99–100). Not without reason, then, Polkinghorne has attempted to take seriously the apostolic portraits of and testimonies to the person and work of Jesus Christ.[9]

Finally, the ongoing experiences of all Christians expand the empirical database for theological reflection. By this, Polkinghorne the Anglican priest is referring to what he calls the "liturgy-assisted logic" of Christian theology, which presumes a sacramental understanding of the human encounter with God in and through the eucharistic experience. While this has been a long-standing motif in Polkinghorne's writings,[10] it finds its most

7. Notice then the subtitle of Polkinghorne's Gifford Lectures given in 1993–1994: Polkinghorne, *Faith of a Physicist: Reflections of a Bottom-Up Thinker.*

8. For more on Polkinghorne's views regarding the nature and interpretation of Scripture, see *Reason and Reality*, ch. 5.

9. Most extensively in his Gifford Lectures, *Faith of a Physicist*, chs. 5–7, on Jesus, the crucifixion and resurrection, and the confession of Jesus' divinity, respectively. Elsewhere, Polkinghorne has suggested that the apostolic experience serves a kind of revelatory function that bears "analogy with the role played by observations and experiments in science" (*Faith, Science, Understanding*, 52).

10. See *One World*, 98; *Science and Providence*, 92–94; and *Faith of a Physicist*, 158–60.

developed expression to date in chapter five of *Science and the Trinity*, titled "The Eucharist: Liturgy-assisted Logic." I am less interested here in the content of Polkinghorne's theology of the Eucharist, than in its methodological implications.[11] On this latter front, the relationship between the eucharistic and liturgical experience and theological reflection is analogous to the relationship between empirical experimentation and scientific theory: "In each case, the cost of illumination is the willingness to have one's everyday habits of thought revised and expanded under the influence of the reality encountered" (141). Hence Polkinghorne's "liturgy-assisted logic" is part and parcel of his "bottom-up" approach to theology that admits "faith seeking understanding receives its impetus from religious experience" (118). His can therefore be rightly understood as a sacramental vision of science and theology: "Sacramental theology is as complex and sophisticated, and ultimately as powerfully insightful, as the considerations that support a fundamental theory in science" (141).[12]

Clearly Polkinghorne's "bottom-up approach" puts him squarely in the Anglican tradition with regard to his theological method. Early on in his theological career he had already affirmed what has historically been affirmed as the "Anglican triad" of reason, tradition, and Scripture as the foundational resources for theological reflection.[13] Reason as a mode of discovery, best represented in scientific inquiry, cannot be rejected, even if its powers have to be recognized as limited. As we shall see momentarily, Polkinghorne's commitment to historic Christian orthodoxy means that he cannot put aside (at least) the creedal confessions handed down by the church's tradition. At the same time, as we have already seen that for Polkinghorne, the church's tradition is not static but fluid, constituted by the ongoing experiences and reflections of her members.[14] This experiential dimension,

11. For the record, some of the central features of Polkinghorne's theology of the Eucharist are that: a) it is celebrated in the context of external threat and internal betrayal—hence it is closed in some respects (not anything goes), but open in others; b) it is a communal experience and activity—the Eucharist conducts the church and her members rather than vice versa; c) through it we commune with one another and with God; d) the bread and wine are not merely natural goods, but "the products of human labor"—hence the Eucharist "unites nature and human culture" (133); and e) it is about the present and future worlds intersecting as we meet the broken and yet resurrected Christ (see *Science and the Trinity*, ch. 5).

12. Polkinghorne's long-standing commitment to these historic sources for theology and to orthodoxy itself have led some to see him (rightly, in my opinion) as an apologist for a scientific age; see Avis, "Apologist from the World of Science."

13. Polkinghorne, *Science and Creation*, 96. For more on the "triad," see Thompson, *Is There an Anglican Way?*

14. I would call this, following Dale Irvin, the church as a "traditioning" reality; Irvin, *Christian Histories, Christian Traditioning.*

however, undergirds not only the church's tradition, but also the reasoning modes of scientific investigation whereby scientists make tacit judgments as they engage personally with the objects of inquiry within a truth-seeking community.[15] In this sense, then, I suggest that Polkinghorne's theological method is actually quite compatible with the approach also known as the Wesleyan "quadrilateral" of Scripture, tradition, reason, and experience.[16]

Before moving on, we need to ask what keeps this experiential, communal, and scriptural approach from lapsing into epistemic subjectivism or relativism. If Polkinghorne grants that scientists and theologians both formulate their theories/theologies from specific vantage points, are not truth claims relative to those perspectives? Certainly Polkinghorne insists that both scientists and theologians need to hold their truth claims in ways that allow for their revisability. At the same time, however, for this scientist-theologian, there is only "one world" (the title of an earlier Polkinghorne volume), not two. Science and theology provide complementary perspectives on this one world. Hence, there is a "unity of knowledge" that emerges over time as scientists and theologians engage this one world both practically and theoretically.[17] The question now becomes this: to what degree does Polkinghorne hold the theological claims of the Christian tradition fallibilistically and, hence, as revisable?

THEOLOGICAL COMMITMENTS: POLKINGHORNE AND THEOLOGICAL THICKNESS

The extent of revision required for theology in a scientific age can be discerned in chapters three and four of *Science and the Trinity* regarding a theology of nature and the nature of divinity. In these chapters, Polkinghorne attempts to accomplish three broad objectives: 1) to rehabilitate, through discussions of the theology of nature and the theology of scripture (chapter two), the ancient Christian conviction regarding the Book of Nature and of Scripture as revelatory of the divine; 2) to correlate our present scientifically informed understanding of the universe with a Trinitarian vision of God on the one hand, and to view the natural world through a Trinitarian theological perspective on the other; and 3) to rearticulate the traditional

15. On this point, Polkinghorne draws on the scientific method of Michael Polanyi; see *Science and the Trinity*, 58; *Reason and Reality*, ch. 4; and *Belief in God*, ch. 5.

16. See Thorsen, *Wesleyan Quadrilateral*, and Gunter et al., *Wesley and Quadrilateral*. My own theological method is both "Anglican" and "Wesleyan"; see Yong, *Spirit-Word-Community*.

17. Polkinghorne, *Traffic in Truth*, 4, and passim.

doctrine of God in light of our current scientific knowledge of the natural world understood as the result of the creative work of God. I will briefly summarize the content of these two chapters, paying special attention to the Trinitarian character of Polkinghorne's theological vision.

There are "seven scientifically disclosed features of our universe" that Polkinghorne sees both as "vestiges of the Trinity" on the one hand, and as illuminated by Trinitarian thinking on the other (61–62).[18] First, the universe is deeply intelligible, rationally transparent, and beautiful; this evidences both the Father's gift of the divine image and of the Holy Spirit of truth to human beings who are thereby enabled to recognize and explore this rational beauty of the universe that we inhabit. Second, the universe manifests an unpredictable evolutionary history that includes many tragic dead ends, even while also seemingly being guided by a so-called "Anthropic Principle" that has allowed for the emergence of complex human life; this reveals not only that the evolutionary course of natural history is an improvisation of God and creation, but also that God is a "fellow-sufferer" (73) who enters into the creation's processes and through death on the cross experiences solidarity with the groanings of the created order. Third, we live in a relational universe (confirmed, for example, through entanglement effects discovered by quantum mechanics); this correlates well with the inner-Trinitarian life of God understood by the ancients in terms of the notion of *perichoresis* (literally, mutual envelopment). Fourth, we have come to realize, through quantum experimentation, for example, that behind the appearances of our everyday experience are hidden realities that belie our commonsense conceptions of the world. Yet on this point, the Trinitarian connection seems rather forced. Polkinghorne suggests that just as we must engage the quantum realm on its own terms (rather than on the terms of the Newtonian physics that govern our everyday engagements with the world), so also must we engage the divine on God's own terms as triune (rather than on our own anthropologically derived preconceptions). In this case, Polkinghorne appears to be drawing an epistemological analogy rather than a Trinitarian correlation.

Fifth, following from point two above, the course of the universe is an open process, given that the unpredictability of quantum events and chaotic systems seems to be a matters of ontological principle rather than of epistemological deficiencies; while Polkinghorne proceeds to reiterate the point about divine action as "an unfolding improvisation and not the performance of an already written score" (81), the Trinitarian conclusion he

18. Much of the scientific material presented in this chapter has appeared in previous Polkinghorne volumes, but the Trinitarian perspective is most succinctly and systematically laid out in this chapter.

draws is that creation is the work of the Word and Spirit as the "two hands of" divine order and contingency. Sixth, and further explicating point two above, we live in an information-generating universe that has allowed and sustained the emergence of complex realities; God is thus understood to be working behind the scenes (so to speak) as the *deus absconditus* and as the "hidden" Spirit who interacts with the world through "the input of information within its open history" (84). Finally, scientific cosmology predicts a universe of eventual futility: either a Big Crunch if the universe begins to collapse back in upon itself, or a gradual whimpering out if the universe continues to expand forever; the Trinitarian response to this anticipation of the end of cosmic history is the promise of the resurrection as seen in the life of Jesus (more on this in the next section).

Polkinghorne then turns from theology of nature to the nature of God. Here, Polkinghorne seeks a "theological thickness" that continues to allow theology (and the theological and dogmatic tradition) to set the agenda, but which at the same time remains open to the insights of contemporary science. The most important claims have to do with the relationship between God and the world articulated in terms of *kenosis*. Rather than adopting the more prevalent (in science and theology circles) panentheistic model to affirm God as both transcendent and immanent to the world, Polkinghorne opts instead to see creaturely "freedom" secured through the divine self-limitation driven by divine love. In particular, God's self-limitation pertains also to the creation of time so that God "exists" in complementary modalities of both eternality and of temporality. This divine kenosis into the temporal process means that, in contrast to classical theism that affirmed God's simple foreknowledge of future events, God possesses what Polkinghorne calls a "current omniscience, temporally indexed" (108).[19] Similarly, in contrast to the medieval doctrine of divine simplicity, God is viewed instead as internally complex, albeit without compromising the divine unity. These theological moves, Polkinghorne suggests, follows from the Trinitarian thinking informed by God's self-revelation in the incarnation: the God revealed as acting in the world in the form of the Son's life being poured out unto death must describe the essential nature of God in Godself.

One might add that a more robust Trinitarian theological vision would be not only incarnational but "Pentecostal," in terms not so much of the modern pentecostal movement (although this may be argued as an expansion of the theme) but of the Spirit's outpouring on all flesh on the fiftieth day after Jesus' ascension (Acts 2). Although it is entitled *Science and the Trinity*, the Spirit receives surprisingly little mention in this volume. Building

---

19. I return to this matter of divine omniscience in the next section.

further on the theology of nature and the doctrine of God articulated in these pages, does not the narrative of the Day of Pentecost (and after) lend itself to our saying more about the Spirit than that the Spirit is the *deus absconditus* who works hiddenly and quietly in the world, or that the Spirit symbolizes the improvisational God who "dances" with the contingencies of a free creation? Let me briefly pursue this line of thinking with regard to Polkinghorne's continually developing theory of divine action.

As a scientist theologian, Polkinghorne has long wrestled with the topic of God's action in the world.[20] The predominant models for conceiving divine action have been unsatisfactory. Interventionism or supernaturalism is dismissed either because God is reduced to being just another actor in the world or because God's action in the world would be inconsistently intermittent; God acting only as creator of the world is too deistic, leaving little if any room for ongoing divine action; the Thomistic doctrine of God as primary cause and creatures as secondary causes results in the bifurcation of one world into two ontological realms, the theological and the scientific; and process thought's doctrine of divine persuasive power is unable to sustain the eschatological promises of God as revealed in Scripture. Polkinghorne's own proposal over the last decade plus has been to advocate a kind of "top-down" or holistic model of divine causality, albeit through God's inputting of "pure" or "active" (as opposed to "energetic") information at the level of nonlinear or chaotic systems that are finely tuned and extremely sensitive to initial conditions and are intrinsically open to the future. Polkinghorne writes:

> The word "information" is being used . . . to represent the influence that brings about the formation of a structured pattern of future dynamical behaviour. This is not the same as the registration or transmission of bits of information in the sense used by telephone engineers or, more formally, by the mathematical theory of communication. A much closer analogue is provided by the "guiding wave" of Bohm's version of quantum theory. The latter encodes information about the whole environment (it is holistic), and it influences the motion of a quantum entity by directional preferences but not by the transfer of energy (it is active in a non-energetic way). For information in the sense of the telephone engineer, there is a necessary cost in energy input, since the signal has to rise above the level of the noise of the background. For the Bohmian guiding wave there is no

---

20. For an introduction to the discussion on divine action in the science-and-religion conversation, see Southgate, *God, Humanity, Cosmos*, ch. 7, and Wildman, "Divine Action Project."

such energy tariff; the wave remains effective however greatly it is attenuated. I believe, therefore, that it is possible to maintain a clear distinction between energetic causality and "informational" causality.[21]

Such input of information does not violate the law of conservation of energy, and also avoids the criticism of "the god of the gaps," since the "gaps" are ontological rather than epistemological.[22] The analogies of other top-down causal inputs of information are the laws of nature, the interaction between the human mind and the processes of the brain, and quantum events. Yet, conceived in this way, divine action would, of course, also be imperceptible to empirical inquiry.

More recently, however, Polkinghorne has reconsidered his claim that God acts in the world only through the input of pure information. Drawing from kenotic theory—that the second person of the Trinity emptied himself in the incarnation (cf. Phil 2:5–8)—Polkinghorne suggests four levels of divine kenosis, the last of which has implications for reconceiving divine action in general and of the causal joint between God and the world in particular.[23] The kenosis of omnipotence, of simple eternity, and of omniscience leads, in part, to the previous claims regarding divine dipolarity and creaturely freedom, both of which combine to suggest the view that God knows the future according to its modal status, rather than as actual. The kenosis of causal status, on the other hand, leads Polkinghorne to suggest that divine action should not be limited to the input of pure information, but would be analogous to creaturely activities which involve "a mixture of energetic and informational causalities"; in this case, God's activity in the world allows for "divine special providence to act as a cause among

21. Polkinghorne, *Belief in God*, 66–67; cf. also *Faith, Science and Understanding*, 124–25. For further details, see Polkinghorne, *Science and Providence*, chs. 2–4; *Quarks, Chaos and Christianity*, ch. 5; *Science and Theology*, ch. 5; "The Metaphysics of Divine Action"; and "The Laws of Nature and the Laws of Physics."

22. At various places, Polkinghorne has argued, against Bohm and others, that "epistemology models ontology"—e.g., *Belief in God in an Age of Science*, 52–53; *Science and Theology*, 30–31; and *Quantum Theory*, 85–86—and that the unpredictability of quantum phenomena has to do with their ontological character rather than with our epistemic ignorance. Yet others—e.g., Arthur Peacocke, "A Response to Polkinghorne," 11—have raised questions precisely about whether or not ontological indeterminism and openness can be legitimately drawn or inferred from epistemological uncertainty. These are issues that require further discussion.

23. Polkinghorne, "Kenotic Creation and Divine Action," 104–5. In dialogue with the work of Jürgen Moltmann, a kenotic theology had already made its way into Polkinghorne's tool kit by the mid-1980s; see *Science and Creation*, ch. 4; cf. also *Faith, Science, and Understanding*, ch. 6.

causes."[24] Polkinghorne's chief (only) example of such divine action is connected to the kenotic framework of thought itself: the incarnation of God in Jesus Christ.

My question concerns whether or not Polkinghorne's present account of divine action is sufficiently Trinitarian. In this new model, the role of the Spirit remains substantially what it was before: associated with the input of pure information and, hence, remaining empirically veiled. But what if we were to take not only the incarnation but also Pentecost seriously? If in the incarnation the Son takes on human flesh, at Pentecost the Spirit is "poured out on all flesh" (Acts 2:17). This more robustly Trinitarian framework would not require abandonment of Polkinghorne's complementary model that includes both "energetic transactions" and "active information" inputs. Rather, it seems to me, divine action explicated pneumatologically could be explored at various levels: that of the indeterminacy of quantum events; that of chaos/dynamical systems which are extremely sensitive to initial conditions; that of "top-down" or whole-part causation of wider (and wider) environments on their subsystems; that of the input of pure information; and that of neurobiological, neuropsychological, and psychosociological processes. My point is that once the possibility of divine action in energetic terms is granted by way of taking the incarnation seriously, then a theologically thick account of divine action must be pneumatologically informed as well.[25]

ESCHATOLOGICAL ANTICIPATIONS: CONTINUITY AND/OR DISCONTINUITY?

Given what we have already seen in Polkinghorne's theology of nature with regard to scientific cosmology's predictions about the end of the world, it should not be surprising that a thick Trinitarian theology would take up the eschatological question. The penultimate chapter of *Science and the Trinity*

24. Polkinghorne, "Kenotic Creation and Divine Action," 101 and 104 respectively.

25. In his fascinating paper, "Divine Action in a World Chaos," Steven D. Crain suggests both that direct divine intervention with regard to saving humans from their sin is theologically and scientifically unobjectionable, and that given God's transcendence, divine action is metaphysical in nature and hence obviates the need for us to find a "causal joint" between God and the world. While recognizing the need to tread carefully with regard to correlating scientific theories with pneumatological theology, I am convinced that any theologically thick account cannot avoid either metaphysical assumptions (if not arguments) or the plausibility conditions of a scientifically informed world view. In this sense, my proposals are not meant to somehow uncover the causal joints for "Pentecostal" phenomena, but rather to take the biblical narratives seriously in the science-and-theology conversation.

turns to this topic. Whereas in previous work Polkinghorne has defended the need for a fairly traditional notion of eschatological hope,[26] here focus is on the nature of life after death. If the universe is to make sense and human experience is to find final fulfillment, then creation must be redeemed from its transience, decay, and brokenness in ways that yet retain some sort of continuity with this present world.

This continuity-in-discontinuity must also exemplify the eschatological experiences of human beings. Polkinghorne suggests characteristic conditions include: embodiment (albeit with transformed spiritual bodies); temporality (albeit no longer subject to death and decay); and processive experience open to the ongoing transformative graciousness of God (even in judgment, surely in purgation, definitely in the dynamical perfection of unending life with God).[27] Perhaps most important is how we account for the continuity of personal selfhood in the afterlife. Polkinghorne retrieves the ancient Aristotelian and Thomistic idea of the soul as the form or pattern of the body, but subjects it to significant revisions insofar as the human soul is an "information-bearing pattern" (161) that is dynamically shaped by its embodiment, social relations, and environmental locatedness. Not intrinsically immortal, the only hope for life after death is the faithfulness of God with regard to the promise of the resurrection from the dead.[28] The final resurrection will be a triple vindication: of God, of Jesus Christ, and of human hopes.[29]

What is at stake for Polkinghorne? Ultimately, eschatology concerns both the credibility of Christian belief and human hope beyond this life. If this is the case, then two other sets of questions arise for Polkinghorne's scientifically informed theological vision: that related to his views regarding

26. See *Faith of a Physicist*, ch. 9, and *Quarks, Chaos and Christianity*, ch. 7.

27. There are indications that Polkinghorne is a hopeful universalist, as in his reading of 1 Corinthians 15:22 (*Science and the Trinity*, 30–31), his denial of traditional (e.g., Dantean) images of hell (46–47), and his view of divine mercy having no limits, even on the other side of death (158–59). Yet Polkinghorne wishes to also take seriously human freedom to reject God, and in that sense, allows for the possibility of hell understood as "the dreary town, lost down a crack in the floor of heaven, of C. S. Lewis's *The Great Divorce*" (159).

28. But it is here at this point of the "intermediate state" where another contemporary Thomistic view of the soul, by Terence Nichols, differs from Polkinghorne's. While also conceiving the soul in terms of "information," Nichols sees no other way to account for biblical data like that of the appearance of Samuel's ghost, or the promises in the Christian Testament that to be absent from the body is to be present with God, than to argue that God graciously endows the soul with immortality, even if such immortality awaits the final resurrection of the body. See Nichols, *The Sacred Cosmos*, ch. 7.

29. See Polkinghorne, *Searching for Truth*, 155.

the omniscience of God, and the world's religious traditions. Let me briefly explicate the implications of each of these topics for Christian eschatology.

I have already introduced (in the preceding section) Polkinghorne's understanding of divine kenosis into time (leading to divine temporality), and divine kenosis of knowledge (leading to a revision of the traditional doctrine of divine omniscience). Put bluntly, "God does not yet know the unformed future, simply because it is not yet there to be known" (54). Unlike process theology, which asserts that God is necessarily limited by temporality, Polkinghorne's kenosis theology insists that God has "*chosen* to possess only a current omniscience, temporally indexed" (108, emphasis original). World history is continuously unfolding, not a "fixed score" (67–68), and biblical prophecy reflects "a consonance of understanding, rather than confirmation of prediction" (53), such that later events are correlated retrospectively with previous writings. God is therefore mutable (107), continuously adjusting his plans in light of developments in the world.[30] It is clear, however, that Polkinghorne has been moved to this view by his work as a physicist: the unpredictability of quantum events and of chaotic systems are ontological features of the world's openness to the future (79–80). Hence, nuancing Polkinghorne's doctrine of divine omniscience, "if God's creation is intrinsically temporal, surely the Creator must know it in its temporality. In other words, God will not simply know that events are successive but God will know them according to their nature, that is to say, *in their succession*" (104, italics original).[31]

While Polkinghorne is driven by scientific and theodicy considerations to revise the classical doctrine of God's exhaustive and definite foreknowledge of future events, a small group of North American evangelical theologians have recently proposed a similar "open theistic" view of divine omniscience largely through a retrieval and reinterpretation of the biblical text.[32] This proposal has generated intense controversy and polemical literature, especially among members of the Evangelical Theological Soci-

30. With regard to relativity theory, God's time is suggested to be that of "the frame that is at rest with respect to the cosmic background radiation" (*Science and the Trinity*, 110). For a similar argument regarding the divine temporal frame after creation as measured according to the cosmic time of the general theory of relativity, see Craig, "God and Real Time."

31. For previous articulations of this view of omniscience, see Polkinghorne, *Quarks, Chaos and Christianity*, 73–78; *Belief in God*, 73–74; and *Faith, Science and Understanding*, 150–51.

32. The chief spokespersons are Clark H. Pinnock, John Sanders, Richard Rice, William Hasker, and Gregory A. Boyd. I summarize the basic issues in the debate in two articles: "Divine Knowledge and Future Contingents," and "Divine Knowledge and Relation to Time."

ety, as open theism is seen to be a plain denial of various biblical claims regarding God's knowledge of the future.[33] Further, the open view is also understood by its detractors to undermine the sovereignty of God, resulting in God being recreated in the image of humankind. Most importantly for our purposes, there is the question about how God's promises regarding eschatological redemption can be accomplished if the historical details are continuously being decided by free creatures, often choosing against the will of God.[34]

Now Polkinghorne has anticipated this question for his own view of divine current knowledge. In response, he asserts that "God will not be caught out by the movements of history into the future, in the way that human beings are so often caught out. . . . This does not negate ultimate divine sovereignty, for we may suppose that God can bring about determinate ends through contingent paths" (108). Here, Polkinghorne's position can actually be further bolstered through the reformulations of the open theistic position by one of its chief North American advocates, Gregory A. Boyd. In response to the criticism that the open view God is incapable of guaranteeing the eschatological promises of Scripture, Boyd has made two key moves that may be of aid to Polkinghorne. First, rather than just saying that God knows future events in their successive nature, Boyd is more specific: God knows past events as past, present events as factual, some future events as necessary (as predetermined by natural law or by God's sovereign decision), and other future events as contingent (due to creaturely freedom). This last class of events is known by God as possibilities or probabilities, rather than as actualities.[35] The important point here is, as Polkinghorne also suggests, the nature of the future as being truly open. Second, Boyd suggests that an infinitely intelligent God is not limited like human beings in terms of the number of possibilities that need to be attended to, and hence can give undivided attention to each possibility that actualizes as though that were the only possibility to which God needed to respond.[36] Put together, might such an account buttress Polkinghorne's eschatological confidence? "If even the omnipotent God cannot act to change the past, it does not seem any more conceivable that the omniscient God can know with certainty the unformed

33. See, e.g., Ware, "Defining Evangelicalism's Boundaries Theologically"; Wilson, *Bound Only Once*; and Piper et al., *Beyond Bounds*.

34. This critical question regarding the impossibility of an open theistic eschatology is raised by Ware, *Their God is Too Small*, esp. ch. 5.

35. For a much clearer articulation of the claim that God knows the future as future and future contingents in terms of possibilities and probabilities, see Boyd, *God of the Possible*, esp. 15–18.

36. See Boyd, "Neo-Molinism."

future"; so even if "God may not fix his will on delivering checkmate by promoting that pawn on that square . . . , he will certainly win the game."[37]

Yet there are at least two further issues here for Polkinghorne. The first is the question raised by North American evangelical critics of open theism: how biblical is Polkinghorne's theological vision given the Scriptural testimony to God's foreknowledge of future contingents? The second has to do with whether or not this reformulation of the classical doctrine of divine omniscience is so radical that Polkinghorne becomes a revisionary rather than developmental theologian, to use Polkinghorne's own terms. If the former, then the lines between Polkinghorne and Peacocke (who is labeled a revisionist by Polkinghorne), for example, become blurred. In this case, for all of Polkinghorne's desire to remain faithful to historical Christian teachings, has his own "bottom-up" thinking led him to cross the line of orthodoxy?[38]

This reference to Polkinghorne's "bottom-up" approach to theology raises the second set of questions relative to his eschatology: that concerning the diversity and plurality of the world's religious traditions. These topics are related because most of the important truth claims made by the religions that appear to be conflicting usually concern either transcendental or eschatological matters.[39] Now Polkinghorne himself has repeatedly acknowledged the difficult theological questions raised by religious pluralism, albeit not usually in the context of discussing eschatology. Throughout, he has consistently maintained a kind of inclusivistic position with regard to the salvation of those in other faiths, even while registering his perplexity with regard to articulating a coherent theology of religions.[40]

In the concluding chapter of *Science and the Trinity*, Polkinghorne defends the particularity of his Christian commitment even while recognizing that, "The problems presented by religious diversity are serious" (175). There are certainly similarities underlying the bewildering diversity of religions, but conflicting concepts such as resurrection, reincarnation, or release from illusion in the religions "do not seem to be culturally different

37. Polkinghorne, *Science and Providence*, 79 and 98.

38. This is no mere speculative question, as theologians the stature of Thomas Oden have called the open view of God "heretical"; see Oden, "Real Reformers are Traditionalists," 45.

39. I argue this point in Yong, "The Spirit Bears Witness."

40. Polkinghorne's inclusivism is best seen in his claim that the monotheistic Semitic faiths "are surely all seeking to speak of the same God, but they do so with very different voices" (*Scientists as Theologians*, 61). For more on Polkinghorne's inclusivism, see his *Faith of a Physicist*, ch. 10, and *Science and Theology*, 124. For his confession of theological perplexity about the diversity of world's religions, see *Science and Providence*, 58, and *Serious Talk*, 16.

ways of expressing the same idea" (175). The way forward is neither to deny truth in other traditions nor to smooth over the differences.[41] Rather, we cannot but "hope that dialogue between the faith traditions, only just beginning to take place with due seriousness and probably needing centuries rather than years for its full development, will help to resolve some of these perplexities" (176).

Besides the value of the interreligious dialogue for dealing with the perennial human questions concerned with life after death, I suggest that it is important for Polkinghorne's theological project for at least three reasons. First, the promise of a "bottom-up" approach to theology remains unfulfilled so long as the challenges raised by the diversity of religions are not confronted head on. To be sure, Polkinghorne attempts to stay true to the Scriptural and dogmatic tradition of Christianity as much as possible. Nevertheless, if Polkinghorne is to truly be a "bottom-up" thinker, then, as Ann Pederson and Lou Ann Trost have suggested, he needs to pay attention not just to the empirical deliverances of the hard sciences but also to the experiences of *all* human beings.[42]

Second, the fully Trinitarian theology Polkinghorne is attempting to articulate will need to emphasize not only the historical particularity of the Word incarnate but also the universal outpouring of the Spirit on all flesh. I have elsewhere argued at length that a pneumatological approach to theology of religions has remained largely unexplored, and should be pursued.[43] Elsewhere, Polkinghorne himself has wondered about the possibility of understanding the testimony of all the world's religious traditions "as a sign of the Spirit's veiled working within the manifold cultural contexts of humanity. Indeed, the concept of the Spirit, immanently present to creation, seems to offer Christian theology its most promising resource for a respectful approach to other faiths. . . . Thus it is possible for the Christian to acknowledge the authenticity of others' experience, without denying those unique aspects of Christian understanding of the divine nature that have to be held as non-negotiable by the believer."[44] Indeed, Polkinghorne is correct to say that we are only at the very beginning of the interreligious dialogue on matters of ultimate concern.

41. So, "I do not believe that progress would come from denying the reality of others' religious experience or of my own Christian convictions" (*Faith, Science and Understanding*, 65).

42. Pederson and Trost, "John Polkinghorne"; Pederson and Trost are concerned primarily with the experiences of women, the marginalized, and the oppressed. I see no reason to exclude the experiences of those in other faiths.

43. See Yong, *Beyond the Impasse*. And beyond even this, there is also the potential for a pneumatological approach to the science-and-theology conversation.

44. Polkinghorne and Welker, *Faith in Living God*, 74.

Finally, however, the interreligious dialogue is important also for invigorating the science-and-theology conversation. Polkinghorne himself has noted that science may serve as a meeting point for the interreligious dialogue.[45] I wholeheartedly agree.[46] More than that, might not the interreligious dialogue also serve to sharpen scientific theorizing about empirical data precisely because of the multiplicity of perspectives that are invited to the science-and-theology discussion? In fact, how might the question regarding the nature of time itself be discussed if representatives from the eastern religious and philosophical traditions were present at the science-and-religion dialogue table?[47] And, of course, to get any clarity at all about the nature of time is to do the same with regard to the nature of eternity—in which case, the results of the science-and-interreligious dialogue may also have something to say about Christian eschatology.

Wherever the conversation goes from here, the work of John Polkinghorne can be seen as a stimulus to the ongoing encounter between science and religion. On the one hand, Polkinghorne's "bottom-up" approach demonstrates how any theology necessarily begins "on the ground" where human beings encounter God. On the other hand, the challenges of theologizing unavoidably from below have made much more explicit the costs involved in theological revision and the dialogue with other faiths. Further, Polkinghorne's insistence on theological thickness is a welcome breath of fresh air in the science-and-theology dialogue, even as his vision of theology reveals how the scientific advances of our time inevitably implicate the kinds of claims that theologians can and should make. Last but not least, Polkinghorne's perennial engagement with eschatological matters not only does not shy away from the most controversial issues for theology in a scientific age, but also points to how religion and theology do indeed have something to say about human hope that cannot be gained through the sciences alone. In all of these matters, theologians who wish to engage the sciences in their work and scientists who are also theologically motivated can do much worse than to follow the lead of John Polkinghorne, FRS. May the conversation continue . . .

45. Polkinghorne, *Science and Theology*, 125–27.

46. See Yong, "Christian and Buddhist Perspectives"; cf. also Yong, "Discerning the Spirit(s) in the Natural World."

47. Polkinghorne himself raises this question in *Scientists as Theologians*, 62.

CHAPTER 8

Mind and Life, Religion and Science

His Holiness the Dalai Lama
and the Buddhist-Christian-Science Trilogue

In this chapter, I explore what happens to the Buddhist-Christian dialogue when another party is introduced into the conversation, in this case, the sciences. My question concerns how the interface between religion and science is related to the Buddhist-Christian encounter and vice versa. I take up this question in four steps, correlating with the four parts of this chapter. First, I sketch a brief overview of the Buddhist-science encounter, and then turn my attention more specifically to the recent exchanges in the Mind and Life Dialogues involving Western scientists and philosophers and Tibetan Buddhist practitioners, including His Holiness the Dalai Lama. Then, in our lengthiest discussion in part three, I focus on three of the most recent books related to the Mind and Life series in order to flesh out some of the details of how Tibetan Buddhists in general and His Holiness more specifically are interacting with the sciences. Finally, I return to the larger implications that the Buddhist-science conversation has not only for the Buddhist-Christian dialogue but also potentially for the religion-science encounter.

The goal of this chapter is to identify the promise and the challenges involved for Buddhists and Christians when the sciences are added into the equation. I am led by a threefold hypothesis. First, the religion side of the "religion and science" dialogue needs to be further specified. Whereas it used to be the case that "religion and science" meant "Christianity and science," no longer can or should this be assumed. Rather, there is an emerging recognition that distinctive shifts occur in the religion and science discussion when Buddhism is factored into the conversation. Second, the interreligious dialogue in general can itself benefit from engaging a third party, in this case, the natural sciences. More specifically, I am convinced that the Buddhist-Christian dialogue has much to gain when the various scientific disciplines are allowed to inform the discussion. To be sure, there will be distinctive challenges that will present themselves, not the least of which are the methodological complexities regarding the interface between religion and science added to the already complicated methodological issues that perennially beset the interreligious encounter. However it is precisely the emergent comparisons and contrasts in dialogical approaches that may contribute to pushing the discussion forward. Finally, if it is the case that religion does indeed have something to contribute to its dialogue with the sciences, so much more is it the case that science may benefit not only from the separate insights of two religious traditions, but also from the cross-fertilization that occurs in the interreligious dialogue.

Two caveats before proceeding with the essay. First, I speak first and foremost as a Christian theologian with academic training in the study of religions, rather than in Buddhist traditions in particular. While my Christian perspectives will inevitably color my understanding of Buddhism, I believe it is possible in this case, given the hypotheses outlined above, that such "biases" can be profitably harnessed to explore what happens when the Buddhist-Christian dialogue is enlarged to become a trilogue between Buddhism, Christianity, and the sciences. In fact, I am convinced that Christian theology for the twenty-first century needs to dialogue both with other faiths and with the sciences, and this chapter is an attempt to bring these essential dialogues together.[1]

Second, I approach the following review essay with a certain degree of fear and trembling given that in a very real sense my primary dialogue partners are Tibetan Buddhist adepts as well as His Holiness the Dalai Lama. I do not in any way intend to be presumptuous about claiming to be able to critically interact with his knowledge of Buddhism or the sciences. On the contrary, I am a mere novice and amateur in these fields of inquiry compared to his lifelong study and practice of the Buddhist tradition, and his decades-long engagement with the sciences. Yet I find encouragement from his own openness to interacting with the Christian tradition, and from his willing to learn from Christians and the Christian faith.[2] Further, while

---

1. I argue the importance of these points in my *Spirit-Word-Community*, 297–305, and *Spirit Poured Out on All Flesh*, chs. 6–7.

2. See Gyatso, *Freedom in Exile*, 189–90, and 201–2.

I began this project with a focus on the Mind and Life Dialogues, I soon came to see that this was an invitation to interact more specifically with and learn from Tibetan Buddhist traditions in general, and, because of the centrality of His Holiness to the entire project, the Dalai Lama himself. Hence my critical questions are designed less to interrogate Buddhist perspectives than they are to open up new lines of investigation for Christian theology. Of course, if in the process Buddhists are also led to new insights, this would be an added benefit to the following reflections.

THE BUDDHISM AND SCIENCE ENCOUNTER: A VERY BRIEF HISTORY

The question of Buddhism and its relationship to modern science can be understood in part against the backdrop of the occidental "discovery of" and fascination with the "exotic" East in the nineteenth century.[3] At the same time that Max Müller and others were beginning to translate Buddhist texts into English (in the Sacred Books of the East series), members of the Theosophical Society were traveling East to explore its wisdom. Insofar as the West itself was wrestling then with what it meant to be both religious and scientific, it was inevitable that similar questions were asked of the Eastern religious and philosophical traditions. At the 1893 Parliament of Religions of the World's Fair in Chicago, Shaku Soyen spoke about the rationality of the "law of cause and effect, as taught by the Buddha," and Anagarika Dharmapala waxed eloquent about Buddhism's "sublime psychology" and its compatibility with evolutionary theory.[4]

Shortly thereafter, one of the first books was published arguing not only for the compatibility of Buddhism with science, but for the former's superiority.[5] Two main theses were presented. First, Western "science" is not as different from (Christian/theistic) faith insofar as it has emerged in the West both as an apologetic strategy in the hands of persons of faith and as having its own "faith" presuppositions; as such, science (understood by the author as "Western science") has served to fill in the gaps of knowledge in faith's striving to know the divine and the realm of the transcendent. Second, and by way of contrast to the first thesis, it is Buddhism alone that

---

3. For an overview of the history of the Buddhism and science encounter, see the two essays in Part I of Wallace, ed., *Buddhism and Science.*

4. Soyen, "Law of Cause and Effect," and Dharmapala, "World's Debt to Buddha." Not surprisingly, of course, Dharmapala's connections with the Theosophists were quite strong; see Bartholomeusz, "Dharmapala at Chicago."

5. Dahlke, *Buddhism and Science.*

provides satisfactory assurance, not by "the creation of any new knowledge [science] *but by bringing to an end a beginningless ignorance.*"[6] As such, Buddhism is the true "science" that provides the most satisfactory world view for our engaging and experiencing reality. The author then proceeds in the attempt to demonstrate the superiority of Buddhism (the Buddha's dharma and teachings) to the sciences of his time—e.g., physics, physiology, biology, cosmology, and epistemology/rationality. In some respects, these early apologetic encounters with science did not consider how their easy division between "true" Buddhism and popular Buddhism was itself the result of the Buddhist encounter with modernity.

Similar efforts at Buddhist apologetics vis-à-vis the claims of science have continued. The rhetoric of these efforts expands on the argument that Buddhism is the true science in large part because it provides not only for a rigorous empirical method, but also because it is more inclusive than science, with its therapeutic and existential dimensions.[7] Now of course there has always been resistance put up against this marriage of Buddhism and science, especially insofar as Buddhism is understood primarily as either a religious and existential philosophy or world view.[8] Yet even in cases like this, what comes to the forefront is the dimension of Buddhism that includes an extensively developed psychology or method of cultivating the mind, thus leading in some ways back toward convergence via this route. Against this background, it is understandable that the need to legitimate Buddhism in a colonialist world dominated by technological (read: scientific) progress led some Buddhist intellectuals to apologetic strategies that engaged with rather than discounted the sciences.[9]

Thus, the twentieth century has seen a spectrum of claims regarding Buddhism not only as superior to science, but also as at least compatible and in harmony with science. In the latter cases, advocates have also urged, in light of the threats of technological advance that were beginning to be realized, that wisdom is needed to handle the deliverances of science and that such wisdom is available in the Eastern traditions. So Buddhist

6. Ibid., 81; italics original.

7. Jayatilleke et al., *Buddhism and Science,* and various essayists in Kirthisinghe, *Buddhism and Science,* make these claims.

8. For example, Wettimuny, *Buddhism and Its Relation to Religion and Science.*

9. A more recent volume in this genre is Weerasinghe, *Origin of Species,* which argues that the Pali canon introduces ideas related to "sensory becoming" that anticipate as well as provide a more comprehensive explanation for the evolutionary processes of Darwinian theory.

mysticism—specifically the kind that produces of wisdom, *not* the super-stitious kind—was important to guide the future progress of science as a whole.[10]

But Buddhism's contribution was not limited, of course, to its wisdom. There were also many who were convinced that the overturning of classical physics and the dawn of quantum mechanics provided evidence for the truth of Buddhist claims concerning ultimate reality through the ages. Those in this camp thought about Buddhism and science not in terms of superiority but in terms of each being complementary or parallel to the other. However, they did not doubt that the central ideas of the Buddhist tradition could contribute to a deeper understanding of the new physics, especially in terms of providing reliable models for imaging, conceptualizing, and articulating the realities engaged in the microworld. Buddhism was, in this case, understood to be at least *parallel* to modern science, both in terms of its methods and approaches to the natural world, and in terms of the content of knowledge delivered. And this was especially the case with explorations in philosophy of mind and quantum physics.[11] As one Buddhist writer put it: the ancient Buddhist "insistence on knowledge as the key for salvation suggests an anticipation of the information age."[12] Not surprisingly, then, this genre of literature has inevitably featured genuine exuberance about the possibilities of a synthesis between Buddhism and science, partly in order to establish the credentials of Buddhism in the modern world, but also in part to salvage and redeem the scientific enterprise for those with religious and spiritual commitments rooted in the traditions of the East.

It is against this general background that we need to understand the emergence and development of the Mind and Life Dialogues as documented in their published volumes.

THE MIND AND LIFE PROJECT: AN OVERVIEW OF THE DIALOGUES AND INITIAL VOLUMES

The Mind and Life Institute (see www.mindandlife.org) was established in the fall of 1985 under the joint leadership of R. Adam Engle, a North

10. E.g., Siu, *Tao of Science*; Yukawa, *Creativity and Intuition*; Jones, *Science and Mysticism*; and Davies, *A Scientist Looks at Buddhism*.

11. The literature is now staggering. For a sampling, see Talbot, *Mysticism and New Physics*; Hayward, *Shifting Worlds, Changing Minds*; Friedman, *Bridging Science and Spirit*; Cooper, *Evolving Mind*; Barrows, *Beyond the Self*; Brissenden, *Zen Buddhism and Modern Physics*; Watson et al., *Psychology of Awakening*; and Dockett et al., *Psychology and Buddhism*.

12. Dow, "Modern Science and Buddhism," 124.

American attorney and businessman who became attracted to Buddhism after spending his first sabbatical in Tibet and the Himalayas, and Francisco J. Varela, a Buddhist practitioner and recognized biologist and cognitive neuroscientist.[13] At the time they met, each was working independently to organize a series of cross-cultural dialogues between His Holiness the Dalai Lama, Tibetan Buddhist practitioner-scholars/scientists, and scientists and philosophers from the West. The first meeting was held in the fall of 1987, and these have continued regularly since.

The Mind and Life Dialogues (henceforth ML) follow a typical format spread out over the course of a few days. Usually formal scientific presentations are given in the mornings, in part to ensure that His Holiness will be informed of the consensus and unresolved debates in particular disciplines. This is followed by open discussion and interaction between participants, during which the morning paper presenter is be free to then enter his or her own personal views where they differed from the scientific mainstream.[14] Two interpreters—a Tibetan, usually Thupten Jinpa, PhD, who has been the personal translator for His Holiness since 1985, and a Western scholar, B. Alan Wallace, with familiarity and training in the sciences and Buddhist traditions[15]—help to facilitate the discussions and prevent miscommunications and misunderstandings. Each of the meetings have been audio- or videotaped for archival and transcription purposes.

Over the last twenty years, fifteen dialogues have been held, mostly private (without press coverage), with the latest on "Mindfulness, Compassion, and the Treatment of Depression" at Emory University in October of 2007 (for a list of all dialogues and their topics, see the appendix). Publication of these dialogues has proceeded at a slower and irregular pace, in

13. Varela's major publications include two books with Humberto R. Maturana, *Autopoiesis and Cognition* and *Tree of Knowledge*; with Eleanor Rosch and Evan Thompson, *Embodied Mind*; with Natalie Depraz and Pierre Vermersch, *A Pragmatics of Experiencing*; his own *Ethical Know-How*; along with numerous other edited volumes. The Mind and Life project has missed his contributions since his death in 2001.

14. However, I should note that all of the scientists invited to the dialogues have been involved in what is more-or-less accurately called "mainstream science." Each one teaches or conducts research at a recognized public university. To the credit of the ML organizers, they have resisted the temptation to engage, so far at least, with the marginal (some would say anomalous, parapsychological, or even pseudo-) sciences, preferring to interact with the scientific consensus. On the other hand, some might respond that the central theme of the science of consciousness is already an effort to explode the categories of the neurological or cognitive sciences "from within"; read on.

15. Wallace has served as the Western interpreter for all except one of the dialogues. He himself has emerged as a central figure in the Buddhism-science encounter, having written a number of important volumes on the science of consciousness. I discuss his work in my "Tibetan Buddhism Going Global?" [the next chapter in this book].

part because they have involved different editorial teams—usually related to the leading organizers of each meeting—as well as different publishers. Nine volumes have appeared to date. In the remainder of this section, I very briefly summarize seven, before devoting more space to interacting with two volumes in the next section.

MLI (October 1987, Dharamsala, India, the home of His Holiness) and II (October 1989, Newport, California) were focused on the science of consciousness, featuring chapters on the cognitive neurosciences, experimental neuropsychology, philosophy of mind, artificial intelligence, evolutionary biology, neurobiology, psychiatry, memory, mental health and illness, and psychopharmacology.[16] While the first meeting was an initial exploration in which the dialogue partners explored the contours of the discussion, including specific attention focused on methodological questions related to scientific research and to the encounter between science and Buddhism in general, and the Tibetan Buddhist tradition in particular,[17] it was nevertheless a success in identifying the possibilities and challenges for the Buddhist-science conversation. If MLI attempted to locate consciousness within the broader bio-evolutionary sciences, MLII focused more specifically on exploring the science of consciousness itself.

One specific area of debate already discernible in these first two ML meetings concerned the relationship of consciousness to the brain. Clearly, the Buddhists did not uncritically accept the dominant neuroscientific reduction of mind to brain. However, His Holiness's explanations of the Tibetan Buddhist view also revealed nuances. In MLI His Holiness seemed to indicate consciousness to be dependent on objects cognized: "a subjective agent . . . has the potential to arise correspondent to an object that appears to it. Through the force of the stimulus of the object, consciousness has the ability to arise in an aspect corresponding to the object."[18] However in MLII, a more genuine interdependence between consciousness and its object is affirmed: "consciousness is understood as a multifaceted matrix of events.

16. See Hayward and Varela, *Gentle Bridge*, and Houshmand et al., *Consciousness at Crossroads*. A related publication, derived from a symposium involving His Holiness and sponsored by the Mind/Body Medical Institute of Harvard Medical School and the New England Deaconess Hospital, in conjunction with the Tibet House of New York is Goleman and Thurman, *MindScience*.

17. For an overview of the Tibetan Buddhist system of thought operative in these dialogues, see Tenzin Gyatso the Fourteenth Dalai Lama, *The World of Tibetan Buddhism*.

18. In Hayward and Varela, *Gentle Bridges*, 194. In a sense, consciousness defines objects retroactively; put alternatively, objects are teleologically determined, and consciousnesses make such determinations. In either case, in the neuroscientific-and-Buddhist dialogue, perceivers and objects arise simultaneously or codependently.

Some of them are utterly dependent on the brain, and, at the other end of the spectrum, some of them are completely independent of the brain. There is no one thing that is the mind or soul."[19] Herein we also see the fundamental Tibetan Buddhist understanding of consciousness at multiple levels: what the Buddhists called "gross consciousness" is now, in the modern context of dialogue with the cognitive sciences, brain and body dependent, while the more subtle levels of consciousness provide a metaphysics or ontology for karmic reincarnation without positing a personal mind or soul that is carried over from life to life.[20] As we shall see, this ontology of consciousness repeatedly surfaces as a contested issue in the ensuing dialogues.

The third ML meeting (November 1990, Dharamsala) carried the discussion forward on mindfulness, emotions, and health, with specific explorations on the interconnectedness between ethics, the virtues, emotions, and health, on the interrelationship between the emotions, the brain, and the body, and on the correlations between mindfulness and behavior as medicinal factors.[21] Central to these interactions were scientific and Tibetan Buddhist clarifications regarding notions such as self-acceptance, self-esteem, and the cultivation of loving-kindness toward oneself, all of which were agreed on as being essential to emotional health. Contrary to the stereotypical Western view that the Buddhist idea of emptiness included the rejection of "selfhood" or ego, there is a distinctively bodhisattvic self-identity that allows for self-sacrifice benefiting other sentient beings.[22] Also reintroduced and further developed were the Tibetan Buddhist notion of various (gross and subtle) levels of consciousness, much of which had previously been ignored by Western science, with the most fascinating comparisons and contrasts being drawn with regard to the how both traditions understand consciousness and bodily energies in relationship to the process of dying.

Not unexpectedly, then, MLIV (October 1992, Dharamsala) was devoted to an inquiry of the consciousness of sleeping, dreaming, and dying.[23] Discussion revolved around the role of the brain in sleep, dreams and the unconscious, lucid dreaming, the various levels of consciousness related to dream yoga, bodily death, and near-death experiences. As expected, further discussion emerged regarding the "subtleties of consciousness." In contrast

---

19. In Houshmand et al., *Consciousness at the Crossroads*, 40.

20. For discussion of karma vis-à-vis biological evolution, see Hayward and Varela, *Gentle Bridges*, 239–43.

21. Goleman, *Healing Emotions*.

22. See ibid., ch. 9, esp. 201.

23. Varela et al., *Sleeping, Dreaming, and Dying*.

to the Western scientific resistance to a dualistic (Cartesian) view of mind and body, His Holiness explained that the body and brain provide the "cooperative conditions" rather than act as a "substantial causes" for mental processes, which includes the various levels of gross and subtle consciousness.[24] However, epistemic access to the "subtle levels of mind" is available only through the kind of introspection practiced by accomplished contemplatives, and then only communicable through analogical rather than clear propositional discourse.

Building on MLIII, the fifth dialogue (in April of 1995 at Dharamsala) further investigated the science of altruism.[25] Topics discussed included the nature of compassion in relation to the cognitive neurosciences, evolutionary biological views on kindness and cruelty, the sciences of empathy and responsibility, and altruism in psychosocial perspective. This volume includes a succinct statement by His Holiness on his view of human nature: that it is fundamentally good, compassionate, and altruistic; that it strives for happiness, truthfulness, and the beautiful; that it is needy of love and affection; and that humans are interdependent and interrelational creations.[26]

The volume produced by MLVIII (March 2000, Dharamsala) carried the discussions of III and V forward, except that it looked instead at the theme of destructive emotions.[27] More specifically, it featured Buddhist and scientific examinations of mental afflictions and emotional imbalance, and discussed how such could be transformed neuroscientifically, socioculturally, and through the practices of meditation, so as to shape kinder, more empathetic, and compassionate lives. The core Buddhist soteriological concerns as identified in the Four Nobel Truths were probably most palpable in the discussions and ensuing volume regarding identifying the cause and prescribing the course of transforming destructive emotions, although this central Buddhist motif also has permeated the entire series to date.[28]

24. See ibid., 164–70.

25. Davidson and Harrington, eds., *Visions of Compassion*.

26. His Holiness the Dalai Lama, "Understanding Our Fundamental Nature." For more on how the idea of happiness is a central feature of the Dalai Lama's view of human nature, see His Holiness the Dalai Lama, *Live in a Better Way*; and His Holiness the Dalai Lama, with Cutler, *Art of Happiness at Work*.

27. Goleman, ed., *Destructive Emotions*. Mind and Life VI and VII were devoted to the discussion of quantum physics; I discuss the volume produced by Mind and Life VI in more detail in the next section.

28. In a real sense, the Four Noble Truths—that there is *dukkha* (suffering); that *dukkha*'s causal factors can be identified; that *dukkha* can be eliminated; and that the elimination of *dukkha* begins with the Eightfold Path—can be said to be the soteriological engine driving Buddhism's engagement with the sciences; for evidence, see Wallace's "Afterword: Buddhist Reflections."

The most recent installment derives from MLXII (October 2004, Dharamsala), and reveals how far the dialogue has come over the years.[29] Although discussion has focused on the sciences of consciousness from the beginning, the technology and experimental research has continued to evolve—in part due to the work of cognitive and neuroscientists involved in the dialogues—so as to include the specific topic of neuroplasticity as related to learning and brain transformation. Questions raised in previous dialogues, such as the possibility and capability of transforming negative emotions into compassion, love, and happiness, are now being experimentally investigated, and the initial findings seem to clearly support the age-old Buddhist conviction that the mind can, over the entire lifetime, exert causal powers over the body and even the patterns of the brain and its functions. Rather than being born with a set supply of brain neurons for life as had been assumed by a previous generation of researchers, sustained meditative practice confirms the capacity of the brain to add neurons to its arsenal (neurogenesis), which in turn aids in memory and other mental functions. The brain's plasticity is also confirmed in its capacity to reorganize itself to make up for the deprivation of any particular sense (i.e., of sight, or of hearing). Last but not least, there now appears to be evidence that human creatures are neurologically "wired" for compassion—as long affirmed by the Tibetan Buddhist tradition—and that it is certainly possible, through the appropriate meditative techniques, to be transformed into being more and more compassionate beings. In short, rather than being simply made up of deterministic properties of the brain, the mind—and the mental practices that constitute it—is not only able to act causally on the brain, but is also capable of transforming the brain itself.[30]

There are a number of unique features to this series of dialogues and their related volumes. In the first place, His Holiness is a vibrant dialogue partner throughout, although by no means the dominant voice. In fact, with two exceptions, there are no chapters authored by His Holiness[31]—which means that those interested in his contributions to the conversation will need to follow the references to the Dalai Lama identified in the indexes.[32]

29. Begley, *Train Your Mind, Change Your Brain*.

30. A massive volume that addresses the topic of brain plasticity from a Zen Buddhist perspective is Austin, *Zen and the Brain*.

31. In addition to his presentation on human nature (see note 17), there is a chapter in Goleman, ed., *Healing Emotions* titled "Medicine and Compassion," which is attributed to the Dalai Lama; however the latter includes a substantive portion involving dialogue participants, unlike the former.

32. In general the indexes are quite detailed, with the unfortunate exception of Houshmand et al., *Consciousness at Crossroads*, which does not include one at all.

This reveals His Holiness's dialogical posture as well as his willingness to listen to and learn from Western scientists (and philosophers) about matters that have been treated at great depth over the centuries by Tibetan Buddhist adepts, scholars, and philosophers.[33] In some instances, His Holiness speaks authoritatively and at some length in order to clarify issues under discussion from a Buddhist point of view. In other cases there are extended interactions in which His Holiness persists in asking for clarification from his scientific interlocutors, all the while probing to discern if mainstream science is compatible with or challenges Tibetan Buddhist understandings. On several specific issues, His Holiness and the Tibetan monks would "push back" against the dominant scientific fronts, e.g., against materialistic theories of mind or consciousness, or reductionist or epiphenomenalist explanations of the emotions, or a bifurcated "two worlds" view of science and ethics. All this means that His Holiness's comments throughout are part of a wider conversation, informed not only by Buddhists monks and Buddhist practitioners (from East and West) who are also scientifically trained, but also by Western scientists and their work.

Perhaps following the lead of His Holiness, then, it is remarkable to observe the genuinely dialogical shape of these interactions. There are minimal signs of defensiveness detectable among the Buddhist parties to the discussions, and little, if any, sense of arrogance among the Western participants. To be sure, the Western scientists and philosophers have been carefully chosen for these dialogues from among those either eager to learn from or open to engaging Buddhist perspectives on common topics. One wonders to what degree the editorial processes behind each volume have smoothed out the difficult moments that in all probability were present in the actual dialogues, and if I were to have written instead a critical review of these volumes, the accent would have been placed instead on the fundamental differences that seem to have been downplayed in the dialogues. Yet a careful reading of these dialogues will be able to identify the various points of contention that emerged over the course of the conversation, including both Western scientific resistance to Tibetan Buddhist interpretations and Tibetan Buddhist challenges to Western assumptions. In almost all instances, both sides recognize the limitations regarding attaining absolute knowledge on the disputed issues, acknowledge more research is needed, and grant that there is space for other perspectives and interpretations. Nevertheless, readers of these books will encounter solid mainstream scientific

---

33. At one point, His Holiness said, "If you find from your own scientific perspective any arguments against a particular issue asserted in Buddhism, I would like you to be very frank, because I will learn and benefit from that" (Houshmand et al., *Consciousness at Crossroads*, 48).

assessments and rich analysis and response from Buddhist perspectives. Those interested in the sciences will find point after point confirmed, extended, or challenged by Buddhist insights, while those interested in the Buddhist side of the conversation will also note repeated acknowledgments by scientists for further research even as they will be motivated to self-critical assessment in light of the scientific data.

THE DALAI LAMA AND THE CONTEMPLATIVE AND PHYSICAL SCIENCES: RECENT MIND AND LIFE VOLUMES AND BACKGROUND

In this part of the essay, I want deepen our interaction with the Buddhist-science dialogue by engaging more deeply with two recent books produced by the ML Dialogues, and with an independently produced set of auto-biographical reflections by His Holiness on the sciences. Along the way, I will provide some justification for focusing on these particular volumes at greater length. My primary objective in this section, however, is to gain further insight into the Dalai Lama's views about science, and how that relates to his life as a Buddhist and as a monk.

I begin with the volume recording the interactions of MLXI, "Investigating the Mind."[34] This was the first meeting that was open to the press and the public (with over 1,200 attendees), and involved limited interaction between the dialogue team and the wider audience. Held at the Massachusetts Institute of Technology in September 2003, the public nature of the dialogue meant that the presentations and discussions were a bit more "staged" than previous encounters. Interactions remained fairly substantive, although less fluid. Reading through this volume, however, the question arises of how dialogues are influenced by their organizational structure. In this case, the presence of the general public may have implicitly shaped the direction of the conversation. In reflecting on the dialogue retrospectively, Arthur Zajonc, a physicist at Amherst College, wrote that the Western Buddhists at the meeting "all focused on the empirical and rational aspects of Buddhism and minimized its more esoteric and explicitly spiritual dimensions."[35] I will return to this issue in my concluding comments below.

The discussions at MIT were focused on the following mental processes: attention and cognitive control, imagery and visualization, and the emotions. In many ways, this dialogue both summarizes and extends the results of the previous dialogues in the series, as might similarly be said of MLXII

---

34. Harrington and Zajonc, *The Dalai Lama at MIT*.

35. Zajonc, "Reflections on 'Investigating the Mind,'" 232.

on neuroplasticity. The major point worth registering with regard to these (two) dialogues is that by this time in the history of the series of meetings, Buddhist practitioners were no longer merely "discussion partners" but "research collaborators," at least at the level of framing experimental designs. When the dialogues first began in the mid-1980s, there were few individuals besides people like Varela who were known to be, simultaneously, engaged in scientific research and in the Buddhist way of life. Over the course of the dialogues, however, not only were more of such scholar-scientist-practitioners identified, but Buddhist contemplative practice had ceased to be just "talked about" and become more and more the object and subject of experimental research. What happened over time was that the Buddhist insistence on the centrality of the role of introspection for the sciences of the mind and of consciousness was gradually heeded. Whereas in previous generations introspection had been considered and rejected for fear of compromising the objectivity of the science of psychology, the dialogues had given further momentum to what was being increasingly recognized in the wider scientific community: that strict objectivity is an illusion and that there is an element of subjectivity related to all scientific experimentation that needs to be controlled, but can nevertheless also be gainfully deployed for the purposeful advance of knowledge and the sciences.

It is precisely the role of introspection that had been cultivated for centuries by Buddhist practitioners and bequeathed to the present generation of monks and nuns that has proven to be invaluable in the contemporary cognitive, neurobiological, neurophysiological, and psychological sciences. Not only were Buddhist adepts skilled in controlling their attention, focusing their mental imagery, and directing their emotions, but they were now willing—with encouragement from His Holiness himself—to participate in neuroscientific research on their practices. Hence it was now possible to document, for example, that loving-kindness meditation activates those portions of the brain that are directed relationally toward other sentient beings. Even better, Buddhists meditators have been collaborating with neuroscientists to devise better neurological and psychological research on their practices. Because of the complexities involved in introspective techniques, research is progressing slowly but definitely steadily as work is being done in the sciences of the mind.

One final point should be noted before moving on: the MIT discussions were readily received by the wider public perhaps because, in my estimation, the Buddhist contingent, including His Holiness, repeatedly emphasized in their presentations and discussion periods the connections between meditative practices and ethics, the cultivation of the virtues, and the goal of seeking to decrease suffering and increase happiness in the world.[36] This "holistic spirituality" resonated with the public (as documented at various points in the book by the applause of certain statements regarding this interrelationship) perhaps in part because the event drew people who were already attracted to Buddhist meditation to begin with, but perhaps also in part because this link meant that the sciences of contemplation and of the mind could not remain completely disengaged from these wider affective, moral, and ethical issues. From a religious point of view, it is noteworthy that the soteriological dimension of Buddhist practice here registers its import: even in a dialogue with the sciences, what is of supreme importance to a religious tradition—its soteriological aims—may be strategically bracketed here and there, but cannot be kept out of the discussion in the long run.

I now turn to a brief discussion of MLVI, which was held in Dharamsala in October 1997, but the volume of which did not appear until 2004.[37] I have reserved comment on this meeting until now because, of the published dialogues, it is uniquely focused on the "harder" natural sciences, especially physics.[38] As has by now been made clearly evident, the distinctive strengths of the Tibetan Buddhist tradition derive from its contemplative traditions, and so it is unsurprising that the vast majority of the dialogues have focused on the intersection of the cognitive and neurosciences, the philosophy and psychology of mind, and contemplative spirituality. MLVI, however, turned to explore how the paradoxes of quantum physics—e.g., wave-particle duality, nonlocality and quantum entanglement, the measurement problem—and the nature of time and space-time relativity, and the cosmological and astrophysical sciences, related especially to Tibetan Buddhist philosophy, logic, and cosmology. Hence the discussions for this meeting were by far the most wide-ranging: from physics to metaphysics, ontology, philosophy, epistemology, and logic.

I want to focus my comments on the question of cosmic origins, partly because it has dominated the Christianity-science dialogue, but also partly because this topic illuminates the seamlessness of the Buddhist world view. The team of physicists involved in the dialogue presented the *status*

36. See His Holiness's closing remarks in Harrington and Zajonc, eds., *The Dalai Lama at MIT*, 214–18; note also Alan Wallace's succinct statement: "in Buddhism . . . the pursuit of knowledge, if it is to go very, very far, is inextricably related to the pursuit of virtue, and the pursuit of virtue is inextricably related to the pursuit of happiness" (ibid., 206).

37. Zajonc, *New Physics and Cosmology*.

38. Mind and Life X (September–October 2002, Dharamsala) covered the spectrum from physics to biology in looking at the nature of matter and of life. However the proceedings of that dialogue have not yet appeared in print.

quaestiones of their fields with regard to various debates in current cosmology, including the notion of a finite but unbounded universe. There has also been increasing discussion of the idea that the moment of creation (the big bang) was a centerless explosion that occurred everywhere at once but yet with infinite velocity (i.e., faster than the speed of light, contrary to the universal constraints of the postinflationary period of the earliest moments in the history of the cosmos), resulting in a temporally finite but perhaps spatially infinite world without a boundary or edge. Others have also suggested the paradox that the expansion of the universe is the same everywhere, but from various frames of reference the galaxies closest to the observer are receding at a slower pace while those farthest away are moving away most rapidly. MLVI provided the occasion for the entire group of Western scientists (and philosophers) and Tibetan Buddhists to wrestle with the implications of these theoretical postulations with regard to fundamental philosophical questions such as causality, the nature of space and time, and the origins and ultimate nature of the world. For example, is either space or time or space-time absolute? Some physicists would say yes to some or all of the above, others similarly no.[39] This in turn raises the Dalai Lama's question of how the notion of "absolute" functions in discussing this set of questions.

At various points in the conversation, His Holiness clarified some of the basic features of Buddhist cosmology. Three in particular are of comparative interest. First, His Holiness was inclined to say that the universe is infinite and without absolute beginning, since to say otherwise requires an uncaused first moment, the notion of which is contrary to Buddhist intuitions. Alternatively, all things arise interdependently from "space particles" (which were catalytically energized by karmic forces so as to produce the big bang and the subsequent evolutionary history of the world), which is postulated especially in the Kalachakra (literally, "wheel of time") school of Tibetan Buddhism, the most complex set of Buddhist teachings presented in the Dalai Lama's tradition. Finally, the boundarylessness of the world implies either what scientists have called an oscillating universe (an innumerable sequence of big bangs followed by universal collapses) or that our "universe," with its beginning at the big bang, is part of an infinite "multiverse" (as implied by the "many universes" theory related to the measurement problem suggested by some quantum cosmologists) with an

---

39. Interestingly, in other Buddhism-and-science conversations that His Holiness has been a part of, the notion of an absolute and irreversible time based on thermodynamics, the generation of electromagnetic radiation, and the expansion of the universe has been defended by Eastern scientists; e.g., Narlikar, "Concept of Time in Science," 109–110.

incalculable number of worlds coming and going, albeit generally physically disconnected from one another.[40]

These are clearly heady and speculative subjects, in some ways a stark contrast with Shakyamuni Buddha's reply when asked about the origins of the world by inquiring disciples, regarding the uselessness of such matters for the purposes of curing human suffering. Yet in the spirit of the Buddha, MLVI closed with a clear affirmation of knowledge, even the knowledge afforded by the natural sciences, as a means to reduce the suffering of sentient beings.

His Holiness has recently published autobiographical work reflecting on his dialogues with ML and other scientists over the last three decades.[41] As the spiritual and temporal leader of the Tibetan people, with the established government in exile in Dharamsala in north India, His Holiness has been tirelessly working for peace and for the freedom of Tibet from Chinese rule since its takeover by the communists in the 1950s.[42] Ironically, the invasion of Tibet, the persecution of Tibetans, and the subsequent Tibetan diaspora have resulted in the flourishing of Tibetan culture and its various Buddhist traditions around the world. The attempted suppression of Tibetan religious culture by the communists and the imposition of the materialistic Marxist and Maoist ideologies on the Tibetan consciousness have generated an exilic Tibetan resistance as well as the intentional effort to preserve and promulgate Tibetan spirituality, piety, and intellectual culture.[43] The life of the Dalai Lama can be understood as representative of the revitalization and internationalization of the Tibetan Buddhist tradition. Born Lhamo Thondup on 6 July 1935, recognized in early childhood as the fourteenth reincarnation of the Dalai Lama, and then enthroned and renamed at the age of six, in its short form, Bstan-'dzin-rgya-mtsho or Tenzin Gyatso (the latter meaning "ocean" in Tibetan),[44] His Holiness has since his teenage years

40. See Laszlo, *Science and the Akashic Field*, esp. 82–93, for an example of how such ideas are being entertained by those working outside of the Western scientific tradition.

41. His Holiness the Dalai Lama, *Universe in a Single Atom*. Note that this volume was then made the subject of the ML XIV meeting at Dharamsala in April 2007. I hope that the presentations and discussions will also see the light of publication at some point.

42. For an overview of the Dalai Lama's life work as Tibetan leader vis-à-vis the Chinese takeover of Tibet, see Goldstein, *Snow Lion and the Dragon*.

43. The Dalai Lama, *Universe in a Single Atom*, 38; cf. Wallace, *Taboo of Subjectivity*, 10, 165–66.

44. "Dalai Lama" literally means "ocean guru," and the holders of this office are considered by Tibetan tradition to be manifestations of Avalokiteshvara (Tibetan: Chenrezig), the Bodhisattva of Compassion. His Holiness's official Tibetan name is Jetsun Jamphel Ngawang Lobsang Yeshe Tenzin Gyatso ("Holy Lord, Gentle Glory,

spearheaded the Tibetan Buddhist opposition not only against the Chinese government but also the communist ideology.[45] And especially since receiving the Nobel Peace Prize in 1989, he is now a worldwide figure, recognized spiritual leader, and accomplished author.[46]

His Holiness's science autobiography begins by reflecting on his own journey with science, beginning at a young age when he encountered mechanical items that he proceeded to take apart and reassemble. Over the course of time, and especially after going into exile in India in 1959, and then traveling the world working for the freedom of Tibet, he became convinced that there was much that Tibet could learn from science in order to take its place in the modern world, even as there were many specific teachings of the Tibetan Buddhist tradition that needed to be revised in light of modern scientific discoveries. At the same time, his widespread travels also persuaded him that Tibetan Buddhist practices, spirituality, and ethics, which were always connected, could also combine with science to transform the world and make it a better and more hospitable place for all people.[47] Hence there is a complementarity between Buddhism and science, each with established traditions, perspectives, and goals, but yet also revisable and focused on better understanding the world.

This complementarity is seen throughout His Holiness's reflections on his life with science. He discusses and presents, in successive chapters, Tibetan Buddhist perspectives on quantum physics, the big bang, the evolution of life, and the nature and science of consciousness. The concluding portions highlight the connections between ethics and the new genetics and the interrelationship of science and spirituality for human life in the twenty-first century. Many of the topics and themes from the ML dialogues reappear in this volume—e.g., on karma as the driving engine of the

Compassionate, Defender of the Faith, Ocean of Wisdom"). For histories of the office of Dalai Lama and Tenzin Gyatso's role in it, see Mullin, *The Fourteen Dalai Lamas*, and Laird, *Story of Tibet*.

45. In his official autobiography (written after receiving the Nobel Peace Prize)— Gyatso, *Freedom in Exile*—His Holiness details traditional Tibetan Buddhist spiritual life and practices, including meditation practices, oracle consultations, and astrological divinations, and devotes one chapter to the discussion of such practices vis-à-vis modern science. For discussion of Buddhism in relationship to such parapsychological phenomena, see Mansfield, *Synchronicity, Science, and Soul-Making*.

46. A volume celebrating the award of the Nobel Peace Prize to His Holiness is Piburn, ed., *The Dalai Lama*. The central themes of His Holiness's life and work focus on the achievement of human happiness, human compassion as interrelational means, and universal responsibility as human ethic. For a sampling of his wide range of publications, see Mehrotra, ed., *The Essential Dalai Lama*.

47. These are themes that His Holiness emphasized early in the Mind and Life dialogues—e.g., Houshmand et al., *Consciousness at Crossroads*, 150–52.

evolutionary history of the world; the reality of downward causation from mind to brain; the notion of brain plasticity—although in some cases, His Holiness indicates how his own mind has changed either as a result of those dialogues or since then, based on further inquiry. One example of the latter is his connecting the Kalachakra theory of space particles with the emerging view of the big bang as deriving from the thermodynamic instabilities that physicists have recently termed the quantum vacuum.[48] Yet throughout the book, rather than only at the end, there is a conscious attempt to show how science and Buddhist spirituality is connected (as indicated by the book's subtitle). More specifically, both science and Buddhism are focused on the formation of a better world, one in which there is less and less suffering, and in which there is more happiness present as a result of our being here.

Before transitioning to the concluding comparative section, I note a tension throughout the ML Dialogues that reappears in this book: that between science as providing a universal perspective and Tibetan Buddhism as providing a particular (religious or philosophical) vision. His Holiness has repeatedly insisted that the claims of the Tibetan Buddhist tradition, if true, are empirically and experientially confirmable quite apart from what Buddhism says. This is in part what has motivated his quest, evident throughout these dialogues, for a universal and secular ethics, one that is not tied down to any one religious or philosophical system. In his view, it is precisely science as a cross-cultural enterprise that is in the best position to identify an ethical posture based on nature itself. Interestingly, while many scientists also think that theirs is the quest for a universally true "viewpoint" (or that the domain of science is distinct from that of ethics—a minority position defended by a smaller number of ML scientists), some of them challenged the idea of a naturalistic ethics shorn of religious or philosophical presuppositions.[49] What is increasingly realized is both that science itself operates according to assumptions derived from elsewhere, and that the fact-value dichotomy is problematic. What is not agreed upon is the precise nature of the relationship between religious and/or philosophical (in this case, Tibetan Buddhist) traditions and science. On the one hand, the Dalai Lama has no interest in promoting Buddhism in any kind of classically understood missionary sense (hence, note, the book is entitled *Science and Spirituality*, not *Science and Buddhism*);[50] on the other hand, as a practicing

48. The Dalai Lama, *Universe in a Single Atom*, 85–87.

49. For extensive accounts of the back-and-forth interactions on this issue, see Goleman, ed., *Healing Emotions*, 17–31 and 243–50; Davidson and Harrington, eds., *Visions of Compassion*, 214–22; and Harrington and Zajonc, eds., *The Dalai Lama at MIT*, 190–94, 206–10, 214–18, 236–41, and passim.

50. Elsewhere in the dialogues, His Holiness explicitly rejected any missionary

Buddhist, there are certain motivating apologetic issues such that scientific legitimation for Buddhist beliefs and practices is embraced whenever such is discerned as present.

I suggest this is unavoidable in cases when world views (or religious or philosophical systems) initially come into contact with science: there is an instinctive reaction to find confirmation from science for apologetic purposes, even while there is the recognition of the parochial and sectarian nature of one's religious or philosophical tradition. It is only natural that the recent emergence of Tibetan Buddhism on the world stage has brought with it these evident tensions. As a Christian theologian interested in the dialogue between religion and science, however, I am pleased to find in His Holiness another viewpoint that links the work of science more closely with ethical considerations. In his case, of course, the ethics of science is understood from the particularity of his own Buddhist tradition. Yet science cannot do without the ethical commitments of the wisdom traditions, and there is much that the ML Dialogues can contribute to the science and religion conversation on this point.

MIND AND LIFE, BUDDHISM AND SCIENCE: CHRISTIAN REFLECTIONS

I want to return to the issue motivating this lengthy review essay: the role of science in the Buddhist-Christian dialogue. In this concluding section, I make some methodological comments, and then propose possible topics for further exploration.

The ML dialogues have provided one model of the religion-and-science conversation.[51] However, when set within the framework of the interreligious dialogue in general and the Buddhist-Christian dialogue more specifically, there are both opportunities and challenges. From a Christian point of view, allow me to elaborate on two issues. First, bringing together the Buddhism-science and the Buddhist-Christian dialogues is not simply like adding a new member into an existing conversation. Rather, it is in some ways like adding two new members, so that the directions of conversations potentially multiply exponentially: the Buddhist now talks not only with the Christian but also with his fellow Buddhist involved in the science discus-

---

motivations with regard to Tibetan Buddhist traditions; see Davidson and Harrington, eds., *Visions of Compassion*, 245.

51. Another that comes to mind is the "Divine Action Project" involving theologians, philosophers, and scientists, most of whom are Christian; for an overview, see Wildman, "The Divine Action Project."

sion, and with the scientist; the scientist now talks with the Buddhist alone, but with a Christian and the Christian's Buddhist dialogue partner; and so on. In other words, the complexity of the discussion increases considerably, and with it, the possibility of misunderstanding.

But, second, complexity is always the precondition for transformation for those who are willing to persevere through the usually steep learning curve. Christians, I submit, can now learn from at least the following three additional lines of inquiry: about science from the Buddhist-science dialogue; about Buddhism from the Buddhist-science dialogue; and about the methodology of interdisciplinary conversation from the Buddhist-science dialogue, and how that compares and contrasts with the methodological complexities of interreligious dialogue. All of the challenges involved in the religion-and-science dialogue and the interreligious dialogue considered separately can now be mutually informing, in part because participants will now be speaking simultaneously as both "outsiders" and as "insiders," albeit with respect to the different hats they are wearing in the Buddhist-Christian-science trilogue. In short, Christians may find resources from the Buddhist-science dialogue to enable a further and deeper comprehension of Buddhism, and to facilitate the transformation of their self-understanding when seen through the lenses with which Buddhists engage the sciences.

Having presented these methodological challenges and opportunities, I now present some concrete proposals for the Buddhist-Christian-science trilogue. Let me suggest three sets of trilogical conversations. First, given the centrality of the science of consciousness in the ML Dialogues and the emerging role that Buddhist adepts and practitioners are playing not only in those discussions but also in the scientific research that is being carried out in those fields, what are the prospects for bringing these Buddhism-and-science perspectives to bear on the monastic interreligious dialogue that has been underway for some time now involving Buddhist and Christian contemplatives? Here, I am referring to the Buddhist-Christian dialogues organized around meditative retreats, usually in monastic settings.[52] I am thinking not only about the possibility of conducting neuroscientific experiments for comparative religious and theological purposes, but about how interreligious reflection on the science of consciousness is related to religious practice, to spiritual piety, and to engagement with the world. How might Buddhist emphases on the techniques of introspection compare and contrast with Ignatian self-reflection, Benedictine spirituality, or Taizé practices? How would the divergent goals of Buddhist and Christian

---

52. E.g., Walker, ed., *Speaking of Silence*; Hardy, *Monastic Quest and Interreligious Dialogue*; Mitchell and Wiseman, eds., *The Gethsemani Encounter*; and Barnhart and Wong, eds., *Purity of Heart and Contemplation*.

contemplation be illuminating? How might scientific perspectives enable further connections or highlight points of tension? Intriguingly, given the Roman Catholic presence at the forefront of the Christian contemplative traditions of the world, a dialogue between the Tibetan Buddhists led by the Dalai Lama and Roman Catholic monks and nuns along with the Holy Father on science and the spiritual quest would surely be mutually enriching conversation that the world would be very interested in.[53]

A second line of conversation for a Buddhist-Christian-science trilogue might revolve around the quest to further understand human nature. More specifically, Christian interests in exploring the philosophy of mind, mind-brain and mind-body relationships, and the nature of the human spirit would be of interest to those involved in the Buddhist-science dialogue, although perhaps for different reasons.[54] There are many trajectories included in this arena, so I will mention only three: (a) the minority of Christian philosophers and theologians who are drawn to more traditional dualistic notions of the mind-brain and mind-body relationship may wish to further explore their position in dialogue with (Tibetan) Buddhist views of the various levels of gross and subtle consciousness;[55] (b) alternatively, the majority who are exploring various forms of physicalist, nonreductionist, emergent, and related models of the human person also would be challenged by the gross-subtle consciousness distinction on the one hand, while being encouraged by the dynamic and interdependent ontology of Buddhist traditions on the other;[56] (c) last but not least, the inseparable relationship in Tibetan Buddhism between epistemology, philosophy of mind, psychology of emotions, and ethics may prove beneficial for Christians involved in the project of a naturalistic and yet theistic ethics.[57] In each of these areas, there are clearly bridges constructed by the ML Dialogues for Christian interlocutors to engage.

53. Note that in this regard His Holiness has already been an active participant in monastic interreligious dialogues involving Roman Catholic contemplatives; see His Holiness the Dalai Lama, *The Good Heart*, and *Spiritual Advice for Buddhists and Christians*.

54. I have begun to work on some of these matters myself, and some preliminary thoughts can be seen in my "Christian and Buddhist Perspectives."

55. E.g., Cooper, *Body, Soul, and Life Everlasting*, and Machuga, *In Defense of the Soul*.

56. E.g., Hasker, *Emergent Self*; Corcoran, *Rethinking Human Nature*; and Green and Palmer, eds., *In Search of the Soul*.

57. As seen, for example, in the work of Nancey Murphy—e.g., Murphy and Ellis, *On Moral Nature of Universe*, and Murphy and Brown, *Did My Neurons Make Me Do It?*

Finally, given my recent work in theology and disability in general and intellectual disability in particular,[58] I cannot but note the implications for this topic of the Buddhist views regarding the interrelatedness of the sciences of mind and the task of alleviating suffering in the world. While the ML Dialogues have focused primarily on dealing with and eliminating mental afflictions (negative emotional mind and bodily states), they have also motivated and guided the recent research on neuroplasticity. The possibility of neurogenesis and the capacity of the brain to transform itself can no doubt inform theories and practices related to people across the spectrum of intellectual disabilities, from mild autism on the one side even to severe mental retardation on the other. In this latter domain dealing with people with minimal or perhaps even no recognizable self-consciousness, Buddhist and Christian soteriologies might indeed overlap and perhaps even be mutually informing while both engage the latest discoveries in brain research. At the same time, disability studies perspectives would challenge both religious traditions as well as the scientific and medical establishment to reconsider the individualistic model of suffering that is located in human bodies (or minds) only, and to adopt a more interrelational and social perspective on how suffering is also conventionally defined and then perpetuated by the "able-bodied" (and "able-minded") through the discriminatory disregard for others who are (physically and/or) intellectually impaired. In this case, the Buddhist-Christian-science trilogue would open up to a Buddhist-Christian-science-disability "quadralogue"!

I have attempted in these pages to reflect on the possibilities of enriching the Buddhist-Christian dialogue through engaging the religion-and-science conversation. In particular, I have explored the Buddhism-and-science exchange, especially as that has occurred over the last twenty years in the Mind and Life Discussions. In the process, His Holiness the Dalai Lama has proven himself as an "engaged Buddhist" with regard to the Buddhism-and-science encounter. He has modeled an approach to the sciences that reveals the vulnerability of his own Buddhist perspective on the one hand, but has at the same time shown how fundamental Buddhist intuitions have over the course of the dialogue been deepened and transformed, rather than compromised. This has also been the burden borne by Christians entering the realms of both the interreligious and the religion-and-science dialogues. For the pursuit of truth, for the alleviation of the suffering of all sentient beings, and for the transformation of the world, may the Buddhist-Christian-science trilogue proceed.[59]

58. See Yong, *Theology and Down Syndrome*.

59. I am grateful to Francis Tiso for allowing me the extra space in *Buddhist-Christian*

APPENDIX: MIND AND LIFE MEETINGS

1. Dialogues between Buddhism and the cognitive sciences, Dharamsala, India, 23–29 October 1987.

2. Dialogues between Buddhism and the neurosciences, Newport Beach, California, 5–6 November 1989.

3. Emotions and health, Dharamsala, India, 5–9 November 1990.

4. Sleeping, dreaming, and dying, Dharamsala, India, 5–9 October 1992.

5. Altruism, ethics, and compassion, Dharamsala, India, 2–6 October 1995.

6. The new physics and cosmology, Dharamsala, India, 27–31 October 1997.

7. Epistemological Questions in Quantum Physics and Eastern Contemplative Sciences, Innsbruck, Austria, 15–22 June 1998.

8. Destructive emotions, Dharamsala, India, 20–24 March 2000.

9. Transformations of Mind, Brain & Emotion, Madison, Wisconsin, 21–22 March 2001.

10. The Nature of Matter, The Nature of Life, Dharamsala, India, 30 September—4 October 2002.

11. Investigating the Mind: Exchanges between Buddhism & Biobehavioral Science with His Holiness the XIVth Dalai Lama, Cambridge, Massachusetts, 13–14 September 2003.

12. Neuroplasticity: The Neuronal Substrates of Learning and Transformation, Dharamsala, India, 18–22 October 2004.

13. The Science and Clinical Applications of Meditation, Washington, DC, 8–10 November 2005.

14. A Dialogue on *The Universe in a Single Atom*, Dharamsala, India, 9–13 April 2007.

Studies for this review essay. Thanks to my student, Bradford McCall, for his critical reading of this manuscript, and to two anonymous referees for their many suggestions that have helped improve the argument. The infelicities that remain are my own fault.

CHAPTER 9

Tibetan Buddhism Going Global?

A Case Study of a Contemporary Buddhist Encounter with Science

THERE IS A GROWING awareness of Tibetan Buddhism as one viable representative of the Buddhist tradition in global context.[1] In this chapter, I want to add to the case for viewing Tibetan Buddhism as a global Buddhist tradition by focusing on its contemporary encounter with science. More specifically, I suggest that the recent Tibetan Buddhist dialogue with the sciences provides one avenue to understand the dynamic character of this tradition as an emerging global presence.

Elsewhere, I have argued a similar thesis by analyzing the dialogues between His Holiness the Dalai Lama and Western scientists.[2] Here I want to focus on the work of B. Alan Wallace as a case study of the globalization of the Tibetan Buddhist tradition. I will show not only that Wallace's work has complemented that of His Holiness, but also that he has done yeoman's labor in bridging the Tibetan tradition and the modern world.[3] We will

1. See, e.g., Cabezón, "Tibetan Buddhist Society"; cf. the more extensive discussion by Zablocki, "The Global Mandala."

2. See Yong, "Mind and Life, Religion and Science" [the preceding chapter of this volume].

3. Although Wallace's Buddhist training, as we shall see, is rather eclectic, it is also fair to say that his most formative influences have derived primarily from the Gelug tradition and then secondarily from the Nyingma school. However, Wallace himself usually refers to "Tibetan Buddhism" rather than focusing specifically on these lineages when discussing his own work. Hence I will follow Wallace in this regard, although readers should be attentive to the contextual clues that may further specify the

proceed in three steps: a) a brief overview of Wallace's life against the back-drop of globalization processes; b) a focused review of four of his books devoted to Buddhism and science; and c) a brief assessment of his work from the perspective of two global conversations: that of religion and science, and that of Buddhism and Christianity.

Three caveats need to be registered before proceeding. First, I am suggesting neither that Wallace is the only or best representative of contemporary Tibetan Buddhism in its encounter with the modern world nor that his work is the foremost exemplar of the globalization of Tibetan Buddhism; rather, I want to look at Wallace's bridging of Tibetan traditions with modern science as but one aspect of the encounter between ancient Buddhism and the contemporary global context. Second, I am not seeking to reduce the globalization of Tibetan Buddhism to its encounter with the sciences; rather, I think the Buddhism-science dialogue provides a window into the processes of globalization with which Tibetan Buddhists are engaged. Finally, I approach this chapter as a Christian theologian interested in the religion and science encounter rather than as either a Tibetologist or a scholar of Buddhist studies. My scholarly training lies in comparative theology, interreligious dialogue, and the exploration of how ancient religious self-understandings are being transformed in our new global context, and these interests will be reflected especially in my comments in the final section.

B. ALAN WALLACE AS "GLOBE-TROTTER": A BIOGRAPHICAL APPROACH TO TIBETAN GLOBALIZATION

Born in southern California in 1950 to a biblical scholar, David H. Wallace (1924–present), B. Alan came into adulthood during the tumultuous 1960s, with the civil rights movement, feminism, and the war in Vietnam all in full swing.[4] His college journey took him from studies in biology and ecology at the University of California, San Diego, for the first two years, during which his interests expanded to include the philosophy of religion, to the University of Göttingen, West Germany, in 1970. He would not complete his undergraduate degree for another 16 years (more on that momentarily), since his studies pushed him even further east (relative to his southern California roots) at that time, taking him from Göttingen to India. From 1971–1975 Wallace immersed himself in Indo-Tibetan Buddhist philoso-

---

references to "Tibetan Buddhism" in the remainder of this chapter.

    4. For some brief autobiographical remarks, see the Preface to Wallace, *Attention Revolution*, esp. xiii–xv.

phy, psychology, and meditation in Dharamsala, India, home since 1960 to His Holiness the Dalai Lama and the Tibetan "government in exile." Wallace received oral transmission in 1973 from Ku-ngo Barshi, a lay teacher of the "mind training" tradition traced back to Atīśa (982–1054 CE), one of the major founding figures of what later came to be known as the Gelug school of Tibetan Buddhism.[5] He was thereafter also fully ordained by His Holiness himself in 1975.

From 1975–1979, under advisement from His Holiness, Wallace moved to Switzerland to study further at the Tibet Institute under the renowned Buddhist contemplative Geshé Rabten (1920–1986). While there, he began teaching at the Center for Higher Tibetan Studies in Mt. Pelerin, Switzerland. Toward the end of this period, Wallace produced a book on the life and teachings of Geshé Rabten, focused particularly on the topics of renunciation, awakening mind, mental quiescence, and penetrating insight.[6] This would be the first of many volumes from the hand of Wallace, translating Tibetan Buddhism to a Western audience.

After this period and for the next four years, Wallace began serving as an interpreter for His Holiness in India, Sri Lanka, and the United States, while also conducting meditative retreats, sometimes for up to sixteen hours a day, under the guidance of Gen Lamrimpa (1934–2003), an experienced recluse. From 1987–1989, Wallace would interpret for Lamrimpa in the United States on several occasions, out of which he translated and published three books of Lamrimpa's exposition of the Dzogchen ("Great Perfection") teaching (from the Tibetan Nyingma school), of the Kālacakra form of Vajrayāna practice, and of the work of major Buddhist figures like Tsongkhapa (1357–1419) and Asanga (4th century CE).[7]

Throughout this period of time, however, Wallace's early fascination with science did not leave him. In 1984 he returned to the US and enrolled in Sanskrit, physics, and philosophy of science courses at Amherst College. He completed his undergraduate degree summa cum laude in 1987 with an honors thesis subsequently published in two volumes: *Choosing Reality: A Buddhist View of Physics and the Mind* (which we will discuss below) and *Transcendent Wisdom: A Commentary on the Ninth Chapter of Shantideva's Guide to the Bodhisattva Way of Life*.[8] The first of the Mind and Life Dia-

---

5. Wallace has since written two commentaries on the "mind training" teaching, which he also considers as valuable for "heart training"; see Wallace, *A Passage from Solitude,* and, from a set of 1997–1998 lectures, Wallace, *Buddhism with an Attitude.*

6. Wallace, ed. and trans., *Life and Teaching of Geshé Rabten.*

7. See Lamrimpa, Śamantha *Meditation* (2nd ed., *Calming the Mind*); Lamrimpa, *Realizing Emptiness*; and Lamrimpa, *Transcending Time.*

8. Wallace, *Transcendent Wisdom.* Shantideva was an eighth-century Indian

logues between His Holiness and western scientists and philosophers also occurred in 1987 (see www.mindandlife.org); Wallace helped organized many of these dialogues. He has also participated in them, at first primarily as one of two main translators for His Holiness, but increasingly in more recent dialogues as one of the team members representing the Tibetan tradition.[9]

Also in 1987, with the blessing of His Holiness, Wallace returned to lay life. Over the next two years he led two extended meditative retreats in the high desert of California and in the rural area of southwestern Washington. The latter, conducted with Gen Lamrimpa, produced a set of Wallace lectures published as *Tibetan Buddhism from the Ground Up*.[10] In 1989, Wallace married Vesna Acimovic. Both embarked on PhD studies in Asian religions, Wallace at Stanford University and his wife at the University of California at Berkeley. Vesna began lecturing at the University of California at Santa Barbara in 1997 and assumed a tenure-track position there in 2001, where she remains to the present.[11]

Wallace spent his time at Stanford focused on the interface between Buddhism and science. After passing his comprehensive examinations, he undertook a five-month meditation retreat employing the Dzogchen approach, as a kind of "lab assessment" of his work on consciousness theory. Wallace conducted much of his research for his book *The Taboo of Subjectivity* (more on it in the next section) during this period of study at Stanford, but focused his dissertation instead on shamantha meditation.[12] After completing his PhD in 1995, he worked as a visiting scholar in the religious studies and psychology departments at Stanford University. He was then invited to a position with the faculty in the Department of Religious Studies at the University of California, Santa Barbara, in 1997, where, over the next few years, he taught courses in Tibetan languages, culture, and religion, and on religion and science. Throughout much of the 1990s, Wallace served intermittently also as an interpreter for and translator of (four books or

---

Buddhist teacher of the Prasangika Madhyamaka philosophy.

9. Wallace also coedited, with Zara Houshmand and Robert B. Livingston, Mind and Life II: *Consciousness at the Crossroads.*

10. See Wallace, with Wilhelm, *Tibetan Buddhism from the Ground Up.*

11. Together, the Wallaces produced a full translation of Shantideva's *Guide to the Bodhisattva Way of Life.* Vesna Wallace's own scholarship has focused on the Tibetan *Kālacakratantra* tantra; see Wallace, *The Inner Kālacakratantra,* and Wallace, *The Kālacakratantra.*

12. A revised version of the dissertation is Wallace, *Bridge of Quiescence,* reprinted as *Balancing the Mind.* Wallace, *Boundless Heart,* which derives from Wallace's lectures in 1992 on shamantha meditation, is based on Buddhaghosa's *Visuddhimagga.*

commentaries by) Ven. Gyatrul Rinpoche (1924–present), a high-ranking lama in the Nyingma Order who had been appointed as dharma teacher to the West by His Holiness.[13]

In 2001, Wallace left his university position and retreated (again) to the high desert of California for six months of solitary meditation. Returning with a renewed vision, he established the Santa Barbara Institute for Consciousness Studies (SBICS) in 2003, a nonprofit institution devoted to exploring and synthesizing science, contemplative traditions and practices, and consciousness studies (see http://www.sbinstitute.com/). The central focus of the SBICS remains the "Shamantha Project," a one-year residential retreat involving the evaluation of the cognitive sciences. From his base in Santa Barbara, Wallace remains active as an academic and popular writer—both *Contemplative Science* and *Hidden Dimensions*, which will be reviewed below, were written in the last few years—and keeps a busy schedule as a lecturer and speaker on the international scene.[14]

Before we shift to a more detailed examination of Wallace's work at the interface of Buddhism and science, a number of summary comments are apropos regarding this biographical overview. First, while the globalization of the Tibetan Buddhist tradition cannot be understood apart from the political developments in Sino-Tibetan relations in the second half of the twentieth century, the other side of the story concerns Western fascination with the East, which bloomed after the relaxation of immigration laws in 1965. Wallace's initial visit to and stay in India and his globe-trotting ventures since then have been enabled by globalization processes in the last generation and are representative of the treks of many Westerners seeking a deeper encounter with Asian religious traditions. In a sense, his experience is not unique; what is exceptionally noteworthy, however, are the results of his journey.

---

13. See Rinpoche, *Ancient Wisdom* (2nd ed., *Meditation, Transformation, and Dream Yoga*); Rinpoche, *Natural Liberation*; Chagmé, *A Spacious Path to Freedom*; and Chagmé, *Naked Awareness*.
  Padmasambhava (lit: "born from a lotus") was an eighth-century Indian Buddhist tantric master who some consider the founder of Buddhism in Tibet; his book was titled *The Profound Dharma of the Natural Liberation through Contemplating the Peaceful and the Wrathful: State of Completion Instructions on the Six Bardos*, and Gyatrul Rinpoche's commentary was based on the text preserved through fourteenth-century Tibetan master Karma Lingpa. Karma Chagmé (1613–1678) produced an introductory meditation manual for the Karma Kagyu tradition and the Payül Nyingma order of the Tibetan Buddhism, thus combining the two great meditative traditions in Tibet.

14. Wallace has a gift for taking difficult ideas in the Tibetan tradition and translating them into modern idiom accessible to laypeople in the west; see, e.g., a revised set of lectures, Wallace, *Genuine Happiness*.

This leads, second, to the observation of Wallace as a tireless interpreter and translator of the Tibetan Buddhist tradition to the modern West. The preceding account is a selective rather than exhaustive catalogue of his work in this area. Whatever else will finally be said of Wallace's legacy, his contribution of making available ancient Buddhist and Tibetan texts for scholarly and lay use will need to be acknowledged. Further, however, his work as an interpreter cannot be overlooked. His Holiness, Geshé Rabten, Gen Lamrimpa, and Gyatrul Rinpoche are only the most well-known among the many Tibetan teachers that Wallace has served. In this unassuming way, then, Wallace has been a vehicle of the globalization of the Tibetan Buddhist tradition.

Finally, I see that the globalization of the Tibetan Buddhist tradition has paralleled the intensification of the encounter between Buddhism and modern science.[15] In one sense, it might be thought that the attention paid to science by His Holiness, Wallace, and other Tibetan scholars is motivated by apologetic purposes related to translating and validating ancient Buddhist teachings in the modern world. While this rationale should not be minimized, I would suggest an alternative perspective that sees the global expansion of the Tibetan tradition as leading to its own distinctive engagement with the sciences. In this view, globalization produces less a Tibetan Buddhist apologetic than it does a creative and constructive Tibetan Buddhist encounter with science. Wallace's work provides a case study of this type of globalization dynamic. I suggest that his distinctive approach to science cannot be understood apart from his work as a retriever and translator of ancient Buddhist teachings and meditation practices.

BUDDHISM AND SCIENCE:
A REVIEW OF THE WORK OF B. ALAN WALLACE

While the sciences have been of interest to Wallace since he was a teenager, he has been productive as a Buddhist philosopher of science especially in the last decade. Long convinced that the way of dialogue is best suited to chart a *via media* between scientistic materialism on the one hand and postmodern relativism on the other,[16] his published books on Buddhism and science have attempted to demonstrate the fruitfulness of such collaboration. In this section, I will briefly summarize four of his books on the topic. Our goal here is to achieve understanding rather than to provide critical

15. See my "Trinh Thuan."

16. Wallace, "Introduction: Buddhism and Science"; see also my review of this book—Yong, "Review of *Buddhism and Science*."

assessment. Some comparative analysis will be presented in part three of this chapter.

We begin with Wallace's Amherst College thesis, written under the guidance of Professors Arthur Zajonc (a physicist) and Robert Thurman (a scholar-practitioner of Tibetan Buddhism), and published as *Choosing Reality: A Buddhist View of Physics and the Mind*.[17] Remember, however, that this BA thesis was written after extensive "boots-on-the-ground" training and research on the Tibetan Buddhist tradition in India and around the world. Wallace's quest in this volume was to seek out a "middle way" between realism and instrumentalism in science. Neither realism nor instrumentalism remain as viable options given the emergence of quantum physics (where physics bleeds into metaphysics and religion, where objectivism breaks down on the wave/particle duality, where the role of the observer seems essential to the results of quantum experimentation, and where there is widespread agreement, following Heisenberg and others, that we observe not nature itself but nature that is open to our questioning, etc.); given the "conclusions" handed on by the history of science (e.g., that Newton's *Principia* was more a mathematical predicting device than an explanatory tool regarding "reality"); given developments in mathematics (from Euclidean geometry to Gödelian conventionalism); and given a critical rereading of the ancients (e.g., the implausible legacies of Ptolemaic astronomy, which saved the appearances, and of Platonic philosophy, which idealized empirical reality). In the late-twentieth-century context, we can no longer think we have an "objective" view of reality in the sense that science provides us with the one true view of the world—Wallace's major contribution in *Choosing Reality* may be the sustained (almost 100-page) argument he provides in the first half of the book against the realist position—but neither can we depend only on an instrumentalist view of science, since that requires an untenable agnosticism regarding the world and our engagements with it.

What then might be a way forward? Drawing from and applying a Madhyamaka Buddhist viewpoint, Wallace presents in the second half of the volume a participatory universe that avoids dichotomizing experience into objective or subjective, and that opens up to a contemplative and introspective approach to the mind, to embodiment, and to the world. A participatory and nondualist approach rejects the Kantian bifurcation between noumena and phenomena, and hence allows for what Wallace calls a participatory centrism: our conceptions bring the world that we know into existence. Wallace reminds us that the word *conception* means not only "derived from cognition," but also suggests *origination*: "The anthropic

17. Wallace, *Choosing Reality*.

principle . . . suggests that the world that we experience can be grasped by thought because it owes its very existence to our concepts. The two are mutually interdependent. The universe that we observe is then a human-oriented world, and it would not exist apart from our presence in it."[18] Human interdependence with the world therefore opens up multiple interpretations of reality, which in turn endow human subjects with the responsibility to "choose" their realities in interdependence with others.

If *Choosing Reality* provides the basic metaphysic and epistemology for a Buddhist encounter with modern science, Wallace's next book on the topic, *The Taboo of Subjectivity: Toward a New Science of Consciousness*,[19] further expands on two topics: a critical assessment of the ideology of scientific materialism (Part I), and a consciousness-based approach to science (Parts II and III). The former must be explicitly undertaken because otherwise the stronghold of a positivistic approach to science—scientism, in the pejorative sense—will continue to block the emergence of any science of consciousness. Wallace's goal, informed by decades of meditation practice devoted to engaging, exploring, and transforming the mind, is to register consciousness on the scientific agenda.

What is consciousness? In brief, consciousness is, for Wallace, "the sheer events of sensory and mental awareness by which we perceive colors and shapes, sounds, smells, tastes, tactile sensations, and mental events such as feelings, thoughts, and mental imagery."[20] Wallace's argument for a new science of consciousness to replace the objectivism, monism, and reductionism of scientism unfolds in three basic steps. First, building on the basic thrust of *Choosing Reality*, after the quantum revolution in twentieth-century science, consciousness can no longer be ignored in scientific endeavors. Second, we need to take another serious look at the work of William James (1842–1910), one of the founding fathers of the science of psychology, especially his proposals for a science of introspection. James's ideas were discarded by behaviorist approaches, and the materialist ontology of behaviorist psychology continues to dominate brain science even to the present day. While the cognitive neurosciences privilege the use of mechanical instruments in brain study (e.g., those related to the new technologies that enable studies of brain states correlated with mental functions), these so-called "hard sciences" of the brain are nowhere close to resolving the Cartesian problem of the mind-brain relationship, or to understanding the intricate and complex workings of the mind. What they are attempting

18. Ibid., 109.

19. Wallace, *Taboo of Subjectivity.*

20. Ibid., 5–6.

to do—a study *of* consciousness from the outside—will leave us seriously deficient in our understanding of the mind. Instead, the sciences of introspection may be our only hope of probing mental phenomena more deeply and directly.

Third, Wallace recommends the methods for refining attention that are essential for developing introspection as a viable scientific inquiry. Here he draws from the meditative practices of the wide range of Theravādan and Mahāyāna traditions, especially the Tibetan traditions with which he is most familiar. These millennia-old approaches have been cultivated by contemplative adepts, and their usefulness for understanding the wide range of consciousness—including that of conceptually unstructured awareness as taught by Padmasambhava, the eighth-century founder of Tantric Buddhism in Tibet, who was introduced to Wallace by Gyatrul Rinpoche[21]—has been repeatedly confirmed through multiple testimonies. So yes, the new science of consciousness will involve personal introspection, but the results are not merely subjective when assessed against the findings of the long history of Buddhist praxis.

The title of the third volume under review, *Contemplative Science: Where Buddhism and Neuroscience Converge*, implies that Wallace seeks to carry the investigation forward via a more sustained interaction with the cognitive neurosciences.[22] Some of this does happen in the volume, but not in any way that substantially advances his previous discussions. The shift of language from "science of consciousness" to "contemplative science," however, signals the emergence of a more mature Wallace, one less concerned with appeasing scientists and more concerned with championing the cause of contemplation for both scientific inquiry and religious practice. Wallace's goal is still to argue for a more-or-less intersubjective account of consciousness, but the major developments in this volume have to do, I suggest, with his taking seriously the religious traditions that sustain the contemplative practices being proposed.

Hence *Contemplative Science* is just as much about religion as it is about science. Wallace is attentive to the religious character of Buddhist meditation practice, as well as sensitive to the charge that religion just as often collides rather than cooperates with science. He hypothesizes that while the emergence of Western science was motivated (at least in part) by a theology of creation, this same set of theological convictions eventually hindered the flourishing of a science of introspection.[23] Yet these divergent

21. Ibid., 109–12 and 115–18.

22. Wallace, *Contemplative Science*.

23. Ibid., ch. 4, esp. 66–67.

trajectories between Buddhist traditions and Western monotheistic ones do not ultimately mean that no common ground is to be found. Instead, any honest survey of Buddhist traditions will reveal a wide range of attitudes, ranging from the quasi-agnosticism of most Theravādan traditions to the quasi-monotheism, even polytheism, of Mahāyāna traditions, and even a kind of robust monotheism in Vajrayāna sources.[24] This discussion is directed toward making the case that contemplation not only fuels the convergence between Buddhism and science, but also provides a possible bridge for dialogue between East and West.

A major thread running throughout *Contemplative Science* concerns the spiritual, moral, and transformative goals of contemplative practice. As Wallace learned from his teachers in the Tibetan tradition, contemplation is not an end in itself, but serves the purposes of making possible a meaningful life, the essential features of which include clarifying the truth, nurturing health and wholeness, cultivating virtue, and bringing about psychological flourishing and happiness.[25] Buddhist meditation—shamatha practice—"begins with the premise that the mind is the primary source of human joy and misery and is central to understanding the natural world as a whole," and the "central goals of its cultivation are the development of attentional stability and acuity."[26] Western science, as traditionally understood, of course, could not and did not factor these teleological realities into its equations as these lay in the domain of religion. Wallace therefore works hard to show that the highest religious aspirations of East and West—of monotheistic faiths and Buddhist traditions—not only converge on these ideals but also could potentially agree about the value of contemplative practice for the purpose of attaining these objectives.[27] To be sure, meditative practices could lead to the idolization of the self, just as monotheistic faith may lead to the idolization of the deity.[28] However, the best in both traditions, especially the guidelines developed by Buddhist adepts to keep meditation focused, provide safeguards against the seductions that would otherwise hinder the goals of the practice from being achieved.

---

24. Ibid., ch. 5.

25. Ibid., 2–6. Hence Wallace has also translated Yeshi Dhonden's *Healing from the Sources*.

26. Wallace, *Contemplative Science*, 136 and 137.

27. Wallace briefly mentions the perennial philosophy as one possible explanation of this convergence, not necessarily endorsing it, but suggesting that deployment of the empirical science of introspection may help us further understand the issues; see *Contemplative Science*, 107–8.

28. Ibid., 149–52.

His most recent book (as of the time of this writing, and the last we will review), *Hidden Dimensions: The Unification of Physics and Consciousness*,[29] in some ways brings us back full circle to the metaphysical explorations of *Choosing Reality*. Wallace, however, advances the discussion by presenting what he calls a special and a general theory of ontological relativity. The special theory advocates that our perceived realities, both physical and mental phenomena, "emerge from and exist only relative to a subtle dimension of existence of pure forms, or archetypal symbols."[30] This is a metaphysical theory that expands on the participatory universe idea, but does so in dialogue with Spinoza's *causa sui*, Jung's archetypal domain, and Bohm's "implicate order," among other proposals regarding mind and matter as being in effect emergent from two sides of one underlying reality.

The general theory of ontological relativity is more an epistemological theory that, drawing from Einstein's theory of general relativity regarding the invariant speed of light vis-à-vis all frames of reference, states "there is no theory or mode of observation—no infallible method of inquiry, scientific or otherwise—that provides an absolute frame of reference within which to test all other perceptions or ideas";[31] this is because although "there is one truth that is invariant across all cognitive frames of reference: *everything that we apprehend, whether perceptually or conceptually* [as opposed to Wallace's special theory of ontological relativity that concerns perceptual phenomena only], *is devoid of its own inherent nature, or identity, independent of the means by which it is known.* Perceived objects, or observable entities, exist relative to the sensory faculties or systems of measurement by which they are detected."[32] Hence what we need is a science of intersubjectivity, albeit one that is not limited to individual claims but critically interacts with those which have withstood the test of time across a variety of contemplative traditions. This would be a science of introspection that is unabashedly anthropomorphic in recognizing the central role of the mind in our knowledge of the world, but that results neither in a Kantian dualism (because knowers participate, however perspectively, in and with reality) nor a nihilistic relativism (since there are norms for truth, goodness, and even beauty based on the community of knowers).

Combined, Wallace's special and general theories of ontological relativity suggest that at the ontological level of human consciousness, the extinction of our (human) consciousness will result also in the extinction of

---

29. Wallace, *Hidden Dimensions*.

30. Ibid., 70.

31. Ibid., 71.

32. Ibid., 72; italics original.

the world as we know it, although that does not mean that the world will cease to exist in relationship to other conscious beings or creatures.[33] At the same time, this also means that no one theory will suffice to explain or enable understanding of the richness of the world as we experience it. Thus we need both "top-down" (e.g., mathematical or Platonic) and "bottom-up" (e.g., empirical, introspective, and even physicalist) approaches that complement each other.[34]

However, given the interdependent and participatory universe as articulated in the special theory, the introspective sciences of mind and of consciousness provide indispensable empirical modes of inquiry for illuminating all other fields of knowledge, including philosophy, mathematics, religion, and even the sciences. Entry into what Buddhists call the "Great Perfection"—literally, "Dzogchen," the tradition of which Wallace had learned, at least in part, from Gen Lamrimpa—would confirm, both perceptually and conceptually, this "unification of physics and consciousness" (the subtitle of *Hidden Dimensions*).[35] But sustained interaction with the textual legacy of a cumulative contemplative tradition *and* extensive and substantive meditative practices refined over the course of thousands of hours of individual practice are both necessary for this task. Almost forty years after embarking on the study of science and religion, these two "topics" have fused in the translator, practitioner, and theorist B. Alan Wallace.

TIBETAN BUDDHISM AS A GLOBAL PRESENCE: B. ALAN WALLACE IN GLOBAL "TRILOGUE"

A subtext of this review essay concerns the globalization of the Tibetan Buddhist tradition. I have presented a case study of B. Alan Wallace to suggest how his work illuminates the processes of globalization along at least three trajectories. First, in Wallace, we see the meeting of ancient texts and the modern sciences. Not only are the reading, translating, and interpreting of Tibetan classics now a global activity, but the legacies of the tradition are being seen as pertinent to the scientific endeavor considered as a global enterprise. Second, ancient Buddhist convictions about the nonduality of beliefs and practices, of sitting and doing, of meditation and action—these

---

33. Wallace writes: "all possible worlds vanish simultaneously with the disappearance of the cognitive frames of reference within which they are apprehended. The worlds experienced by other conscious beings will continue to exist relative to them. In this sense, conscious observers cocreate the worlds in which they dwell" (ibid.; 80).

34. Ibid., 56–57.

35. Wallace discusses the Great Perfection in the final chapter of *Hidden Dimensions*.

are all being brought into dialogue with the sciences. The practices of the lamas are not only said to be convergent with the new (quantum mechanical) sciences, but also provide platforms from which to launch additional critiques against the objectivism, positivism, and materialism of modern scientism. This leads, finally, to the possibility of a convergence between a global Tibetan Buddhism and a postmodern science of consciousness. In other words, the dialogue between Tibetan Buddhist traditions and modern science may shape new discoveries in the physical, psychological, and cognitive sciences, as well as chart new paths of inquiry for the philosophy of mind, the philosophy of religion, and even in theology. It is precisely the nature of global traditions to potentially have such wide-ranging impact.[36]

In conclusion, I want to raise two sets of questions related to the global conversation that Wallace's work invites us into. The first concerns matters at the intersection of science and the philosophy of mind. Wallace's new contemplative science views consciousness as arising interdependently with matter from the primordial (nondual) archetypal domain (his special theory). This widely held Buddhist position could gain, however, from further precision, especially in dialogue with the physical and biological sciences. Two claims by Robin Cooper will help raise the issue more pointedly: a) that the evolutionary trail of life depends on "behavior-led" selection that is related to and informed by consciousness ("top-down" influences of how behaviors shape environments/niches which in turn revise selection pressures at the genetic level), and b) that, "In Buddhism, while body and mind mutually condition one another, it is consciousness that is said to be primary."[37] Would Wallace say that Cooper is simply mistaken about the primacy of consciousness (b) in light of the interdependence thesis, or that (b) explains (a) in light of his (Wallace's) general theory of ontological relativity? On the one hand, the Buddhist doctrine of dependent origination would seem to invite an agnosticism about (or, put positively, faith in) the primordial archetypal domain from which consciousness and matter arise; on the other hand, the energies with which Buddhist traditions, and Wallace in these four books, have put into developing and cultivating the science of introspection suggest that consciousness is primary in more than just an epistemological manner. I suspect that Tibetan Buddhism going global will continue to wrestle with these issues.

This leads to my second set of questions, which concern matters related to the interreligious dialogue in general and the Buddhist-Christian

---

36. Others who are also exploring these matters include Hayward, *Shifting Worlds, Changing Minds*, and Varela and Shear, eds., *View from Within*.

37. Cooper, *Evolving Mind*, 69.

encounter more specifically (remember, my background and training is in Christian and comparative theology). Questions regarding the philosophy of mind such as those just articulated have long been the concern of Christian philosophers and theologians.[38] In contemporary discussions, there are at least four views of the mind-body relation: the traditional (Thomist and Cartesian) dualist account; an emergentist relation that embraces an evolutionary explanation for the development of the mind but rejects a monistic or materialist ontology of mentality; a nonreductive physicalist view in which the soul or mind is constituted by the brain (and body) but is irreducible to its material parts; and a constitutive-materialism that holds that human persons are constituted by but not identical with their material bodies, that bodies are necessary although insufficient causes of human personhood, and that human beings possess unified consciousnesses that are nevertheless not immaterial souls.[39] In view of Wallace's convictions both that Buddhist traditions are not necessarily non- or atheistic, and that there may be an underlying common ground discernible between Buddhist and monotheistic traditions, especially when approached through the practices of their contemplative traditions, there are potentially fruitful lines of dialogue between Buddhists and Christians that can center around such discussions in the philosophy of mind. Even after rejecting the more obvious dualistic explanations of the mind-body relation, there is still much that Buddhists and Christians can learn from one another regarding the interdependence and mutuality of mind and body. In fact, wrestling with such issues in dialogue with Christian interlocutors may well help to sharpen Wallace's own response to the first set of questions regarding the nature of consciousness in light of the biological and evolutionary sciences. Perhaps in future work, Wallace will contribute to the Buddhist-science-Christianity trilogue in ways that may also make it possible for him to re-engage the religious tradition of his childhood and upbringing.

In this case, the globalization of the Tibetan Buddhist tradition means neither just a dialogue between Tibetan and Western science, nor just a dialogue between Eastern Buddhists and Western Christians, but perhaps a trilogue between Buddhists, Christians, and scientists—including scientists who are Buddhist and scientists who are Christian—East and West.[40] For me as a Christian theologian, Wallace is a thought-provoking ally against all forms of ontological materialism and distorted scientism. He is a partner

---

38. E.g., MacDonald, *History of the Concept of Mind*.

39. See discussion in Green and Palmer, eds., *In Search of the Soul*.

40. See Yong, "Christian and Buddhist Perspectives." [Cf. also Yong, *Cosmic Breath*, and *Pneumatology and the Buddhist-Christian Dialogue*, Parts I and II.]

in the search for a fully aesthetic, affective, embodied, and social spirituality that defines what it means to be human so that we are not just using scientifically developed drugs for temporary pacification, but seeking the healing of our minds and hearts via reconnecting ourselves to our bodies, others, and the rest of the world. Tibetan Buddhism going global means that there are now additional resources and alliances for Western Christians and others in monotheistic traditions who have been working to restore spirituality to our scientific endeavors, and perhaps also in the longer run, to our politics, education, and our lives.[41] In the process, of course, both "us" and "them" will be transformed—and hopefully, the processes of globalization will be rendered more humane.[42]

---

41. See Wallace, *Taboo of Subjectivity*, ch. 8.

42. My thanks to Franz Metcalf for being open to my suggestion for this review essay on the work of Wallace, and for his editorial suggestions that have improved the first draft. Thanks also to my graduate assistant Bradford McCall for proofreading the earlier version of this essay. All other errors of fact or interpretation remain my responsibility.

PART IV

The Postmodern Situation:
Pluralism and Theology in Global
Context

CHAPTER 10

The True Believers?

Francis X. Clooney and "Dual Religious Belonging" in the Comparative Theological Enterprise

IN THE LAST TWENTY-PLUS years, Francis X. Clooney, SJ, has emerged as perhaps one of the most important theologians in our contemporary global Christian context through his work on reading Hindu and Christian texts side by side. Yet despite his remarkable output, Clooney's work has received little attention from evangelical thinkers or theologians. I would urge, however, that evangelicals neglect interacting with Clooney's work to their loss; rather, Clooney's project is important precisely because of his concerns about maintaining confessional integrity as a Christian theologian (in his case as a lifelong Roman Catholic priest) while crossing over into and taking other religions (in his case, Hindu traditions) seriously.[1] I believe that evangelicals have much to learn from Clooney's resolutely Christian foray into the Hindu faith tradition even if such a sojourn may raise more questions for us than the state of his work presently answers.[2]

This review unfolds in three parts. The first locates Clooney's work, at least his earlier efforts, within the broader field of comparative theology,

[1]. The classic discussion of "passing over" into other religions and yet remaining and returning to a Christian standpoint is Cobb Jr., *Beyond Dialogue*, chs. 4–5.

[2]. I consider myself an evangelical theologian, if that is understood broadly enough to include my pentecostal commitments, and so consider the challenges inherent to Clooney's project with deep personal interest. My reading of Clooney's work is informed by a long and extensive engagement with the field of theology of religions, since I have published three books—e.g., *Discerning the Spirit(s)*; *Beyond the Impasse*; and *Hospitality and the Other*—and many articles on the topic.

especially as that has unfolded in the last generation; within the compass of this sweeping overview, we will observe the emergence of the phenomenon of what some call "dual religious belonging" as a theme that is pertinent in reflecting on the issues raised by considering the theological methodology of our Jesuit protagonist. Part two delves more deeply into three of Clooney's recent books, excavating their theological depth as emerging out of the tensions of inhabiting what might be considered a dual religious (Christian and Hindu) identity. We conclude with a brief assessment of Clooney's work from an evangelical perspective, raising especially methodological questions about his proposals while querying about the nature of religious belief and assent in general and about Christian faith in a pluralistic world in particular. My thesis is that this Jesuit theologian provides us with one model for how to be *in the world* (with dual religious commitments of a sort on the one hand) and yet not *of the world* (in unapologetic Christian confession on the other hand), and this is something that evangelicals need to ponder even if in the end they may opt to develop their own models for missional engagement with other faiths in a pluralistic world.[3]

One caveat before proceeding. There are certainly many other ways to read Clooney, and obviously many other topics and issues on which to engage him in discussion. I focus, however, on the issue of dual religious belonging both because I think this is one area that evangelicals will be most concerned about and also because I think there is much to learn about this very important and complicated matter from Clooney's project and example. Thus, my evangelical concerns will dictate my fairly selective reading of Clooney even if I hope he (if he ever reads this) and others familiar with his writings will feel I have attempted to fairly represent his work.

---

3. I will be quoting Clooney a great deal in what follows for various reasons, chief of which is that the controversial nature of his project (at least for evangelicals) urges us to take special care in representing him as accurately as possible and to avoid caricaturing or creating "straw men" arguments in response. Further, as we shall see, a great deal of what he hopes to achieve hinges on the claim that texts are important not only for theological reflection but for religious life, so we should pay attention to the textuality of Clooney's own arguments. Last but not least, my own background, research, and publications have been in the Buddhist-Christian rather than Hindu-Christian dialogue, so here I am treading on somewhat foreign territory in engaging with Clooney's expertise on the Hindu scriptural and commentary traditions. My hope ultimately is that evangelicals read and engage with Clooney's work for themselves. Other evangelicals will surely interact with his work in very different ways than I, and that in itself is important for the evangelical theological enterprise.

COMPARATIVE THEOLOGY: POSSIBILITIES AND CHALLENGES

There is a new kind of comparative theological project afoot that is quite different from the comparative religion initiatives launched in the nineteenth century and perpetuated to some extent through the middle of the last century in the work of scholars of religion such as Mircea Eliade. The older comparative paradigm was quick to zero in on similarities on the surface, whereas the new paradigm seeks to understand religious traditions "thickly," so that initial resemblances are understood as being deeply informed by long histories of beliefs, practices, and entire ways of life before associations and, especially, contrasts are made.[4] Part of the problem was the assumption that there are universal notions like "religion" or "salvation" without either the realization that these are very problematic abstractions,[5] or the lack of realization about how comparative categories function and why they need to be carefully chosen in order to facilitate meaningful judgments about parallels and contrasts across religious lines.[6] Last for our purposes, the classical approaches were firmly rooted in the Western academic paradigm of "objective scholarship" and thus generally were insensitive to how Christian commitments "objectivized" the living faith of other religious traditions, whereas the new comparativism eschews the "detached scholar"

---

4. The multiple volumes by Keith Ward are good examples of this approach, with chapters in each book devoted to unpacking other religious views of whatever he is discussing: e.g., *Religion and Revelation*; *Religion and Creation*; *Religion and Human Nature*; *Concepts of God*; *Religion and Community*; and *Religion and Human Fulfillment*. Ward's readers have always complained that his own constructive discussions of each theological idea or doctrine are too "Christian" and do not take into sufficient account the contributions of other faiths unfolded in his books, and his response inevitably has been that we need to move carefully before presuming that surface similarities allow us to combine religious ideas that are birthed within and nurtured by very different sets of practices.

5. As brilliantly argued by Smith, whose book *Meaning and End of Religion* urged abandonment of the word "religion" because it was more misleading than helpful, and recommended replacement of this notion instead with the "faith" and "cumulative tradition" to describe, respectively, the subjective and objective aspects of religious experience and phenomena. While Smith's proposals have not garnered universal adherence, there is much more sensitivity today to being presumptuous about how "religion" functions as a noun, particularly in the field of religious studies.

6. Leading our way in thinking methodologically about the importance of developing adequate comparative categories has been Neville, esp. the three volumes of The Comparative Religious Ideas Project: Neville and Wildman, eds., *Ultimate Realities*, *The Human Condition*, and *Religious Truth*.

mentality and urges instead both an immersion in other religious worlds and an embrace of an identity that is in solidarity with religious others.[7]

In the last twenty-plus years, Jesuit scholar and theologian Francis X. Clooney has published at least ten books that have contributed to the emergence of this new comparative theological project. Clooney's own journey began in the early 1970s when he taught high school students in Nepal. This eventually led to his ordination to the Catholic priesthood in 1978, graduate study in the Hindu tradition, long periods of time residing in India, and the completion of a history of religions PhD dissertation from the University of Chicago in 1984 on ancient Indian thought focused on the emergence and development of the Mīmāmsā School of Brahmanic ritual analysis.[8] While this initial venture into Vedic India was not explicitly comparative in nature, it set the stage for all of Clooney's work, not only by providing an in-depth and thick understanding of the intellectual history of the Mīmāmsā exegetical tradition (which unfolded from around 200 BCE with Jaimini's *Pūrva Mīmāmsā* and continued to expand and morph into the more philosophically oriented Vedanta tradition at the end of the first century CE), but also by enabling comprehension of the logic of Mīmāmsā ritual and sacrificial practices, and their practical and religious significance. From here on, Clooney has been steeped in the foundations of the Hindu religious tradition, adept in navigating its contours and alert to the internal debates that have propelled the discussion forward over the centuries.

In hindsight, after years of work in the field, Clooney has come to describe comparative theology as follows:

> *Comparative theology—comparative* and *theological* beginning to end—marks acts of faith seeking understanding which are rooted in a particular faith tradition but which, from that foundation, venture into learning from one or more other faith traditions. This learning is sought for the sake of fresh theological insights that are indebted to the newly encountered tradition/s as well as the home tradition.[9]

A brief overview of four major books he published from the early 1990s to 2001 will help me better illustrate the three important features of this definition.

First, note that in Clooney's understanding, comparative theology is neither a marginal nor aberrant theological enterprise; rather, it is part and parcel of the venerable task of *fides quaerens intellectum* that has long been

---

7. E.g., Fredericks, *Buddhists and Christians*.

8. His PhD was eventually published as Clooney, *Thinking Ritually*.

9. Clooney, ed., *Comparative Theology*, 10.

central to the Christian tradition. In our own time of globalization and a continuously shrinking global village, faith seeking understanding has to be a universal achievement—not just presumed to apply to all people at all times and everywhere, as it was for prior centuries of Christian reflection—so that the theologian has to work not just confessionally but also comparatively, dialogically, and interreligiously to engage with outsiders in order to make the case that what Christians believe is applicable beyond the "in-group."[10] Fideism is no longer acceptable: "If a theologian merely ignores other theologians or merely talks about them rather than to them, those other theologians will not be persuaded, and one's own theology will appear even weaker than before."[11] Thus Christian faith now seeking self-understanding in a pluralistic world cannot but be aware only of the home tradition's sacred texts, practices, and traditions. Instead, the quest for understanding in a post-Western, post-Enlightenment, and postcolonial context cannot but be particularistic, sensitive to and aware of others on their terms, and proficient in the various textual traditions that constitute the world faiths as vibrant and dynamic ways of life.

Second, then, all of Clooney's books since his doctoral dissertation have ventured into comparative territory from the standpoint of his Catholic faith. The following are the major comparative exercises written mostly during the 1990s:

- Reading the *Uttara Mīmāṃsā* sūtras (related to Jaimini's *Pūrva Mīmāṃsā*) of Bādarāyana, a key theologian for the formation of the Advaita Vedānta tradition in the fourth/fifth century CE, with Thomas Aquinas's *Summa Theologica*;[12]

- Juxtaposing the *Tiruvāymoli* (a long poem devoted to Lord Viṣṇu/ Krishna) of Śatakōpan, a ninth-century-CE theologian, with various Christian texts of divine ascent (the Song of Solomon; John's Gospel; St. Bonaventure's *The Journey of the Mind of God*; St. Ignatius of Loyola's *Spiritual Exercises*; and Hans Urs von Balthasar's early but now classic book, *Prayer*);[13]

- Reasoning with Hindu and Christian traditions about specific philosophical and theological topics—the existence of God, God's identity, divine embodiment, and divine revelation—by thinking with and through Richard Swinburne, von Balthasar, Karl Rahner, and Karl

10. Clooney, *Hindu God, Christian God*, 7–12.

11. Ibid., 176.

12. Clooney, *Theology after Vedanta*.

13. Clooney, *Seeing through Texts*.

Barth (representative of positions on the aforementioned topics) on the Christian side and various theological traditions and systems of thought on the Hindu side, and coming to a realization about how, in the process of comparison, we might find ourselves siding with those in other faiths against disputants in our own tradition (e.g., Barth and Kumārila, a seventh-century Mīmāṃsā theologian, would agree about not allowing for cross-religious inquiry, which would terminate interreligious dialogue, but we would find this out only through the rigorous and careful process of interreligious reading).[14]

In each of these works, Clooney the Jesuit Christian spends much more time expositing and exegeting the other tradition and its sacred texts, and much less space and effort on explicating the Christian sources. This is in part because he is writing primarily as a Christian for other Christians and thus assumes his readers have knowledge of the Christian side of things. So while some might say that the similarities Clooney finds on the topics he chooses are there only because they remain at a high enough level of abstraction so that the major comparative categories can be specified in both Christian and Hindu traditions (and perhaps in others as well), we do well to remember that Clooney's effort is a self-conscious project of faith seeking understanding in a pluralistic world; hence his venturing into Hindu texts and traditions is intentional and sustained.

This leads us to the third aspect of Clooney's definition, that comparative theology is ultimately about obtaining "fresh theological insights" for both traditions. Evangelicals might be comfortable introducing fresh theological insights into other traditions (in the hopes that other religionists will eventually convert to Christian faith), but will be much less comfortable in thinking that there is anything substantially new to be gleaned for their own faith from engaging with religious others. Or, evangelicals might be happy to register the differences that inevitably emerge in comparative theological reflection rather than to accentuate the similarities that Clooney finds. I only note here that Clooney is cautious about assuming what others have to learn from the comparative enterprise; that is for them to say.[15] For himself as a Christian, a dialectical process of learning is initiated so that Christian faith now looks different when mirrored in the other even as the other also looks different when approached from the standpoint of Christian commitment.

14. Clooney, *Hindu God, Christian God*, ch. 5, on revelation in Barth and in Vedic and Mīmāṃsā theology.

15. Thus, e.g., the conclusion of *Hindu God, Christian God* includes "A Hindu Theologian's Response" by Parimal G. Patil of Emory University.

How is Clooney able to sustain not only his incursion into the world of Hinduism but also his comparative theological edge? In the midst of the preceding comparative studies, Clooney published a little book, *Hindu Wisdom for All God's Children*, where he recommended facets of Hindu ideas for Christian theological consideration if not appropriation.[16] While discussing many of the themes that had already appeared in the other volumes—e.g., the nature of the one true self and of human freedom; Krishna as mediating a vision of the divine; Shiva as facilitating access to the divine mystery; the goddess Devi/Kali as opening up venues into the female dimension of the universe—what is noteworthy here is Clooney's invitation to experience the other tradition, in this case the Hindu way of life: "To understand another tradition, to learn from Hindu wisdom, we need to practice it—in some deliberate way, with some selected text or image or practice—until we realize what Hinduism is not, what it is, how it matters for us, and who we have become in light of it."[17] This is because Hindu texts are not meant to be read silently, individually, discursively, and merely cognitively; rather, Hindu texts invite affective practice so that we begin to realize the deities "in sound, sight, and action."[18] Hence, he writes in his discussion of Devi/Kali two passages that deserve to be reproduced more extensively:

> We need to spend time listening to the sounds along with the verses, to repeat them aloud and to hear them, before we think about which meanings they might best have. If we can hear them, they may impress on us that the Goddess is not abstract or distant, that she is as close as sense experience, as every sound we hear. If we do not actually understand *hrim* or *srim*, we might try uttering them slowly, over and over for a period of time, as one might recite a rhythmic prayer. . . .[19] Verses, contemplations, chakras, pure sounds, yantras, rituals: by all these factors taken together, the *Ocean of Beauty* [a one-thousand-year-old Sanskrit poem] invites the worshiper to participate in a very complete encounter with the Goddess. It offers a way to maximize participation—in doing, hearing, seeing—for the sake of a heightened sense awareness that opens into an awareness of the total, all-encompassing presence of the Goddess in relation to the world and human self.[20]

16. Clooney, *Hindu Wisdom for All God's Children*.

17. Ibid., 27.

18. Ibid., 99.

19. For further discussion of the centrality of sound to Hindu religiosity, not to mention to goddess spirituality, see Beck, *Sonic Theology*.

20. Clooney, *Hindu Wisdom for All God's Children*, 102 and 106.

These are challenging invitations, especially for evangelicals, in light of the performative dimension of the Hindu sacred texts.[21]

This leads us into the heart of the analytical lens with which I wish to read Clooney as an evangelical: the possibility of dual religious belonging for the Christian theological enterprise. What exactly does *dual religious belonging* mean? Descriptively, there are many dimensions to this phenomenon. While at one level we may argue that human beings have had dual or multiple religious identities for as long as they have been around, at another level contemporary globalization and immigration trends have precipitated much more exposure to the world religious traditions and made them live options for citizens in the contemporary global village. For various reasons, people may not want to leave their home faith before trying out other faith practices, or they may find themselves being guests of their neighbors and work colleagues in other faiths. More intensely, there are now interreligious marriages so that at least in some areas, even if the parents remain in distinct faith traditions, children are oftentimes brought up in both religious worlds. Last but not least, there are all sorts of sociopolitical and environmental projects that draw people from diverse faith traditions together in engaging the task of the common good, and even in these contexts there is exposure to the diversity of faiths to the point that some people begin to take on another religious identity overlaid upon the home faith.[22]

When we shift from describing what dual religious belonging is to thinking about what ought to be from an explicitly theological point of view, of course, many questions emerge.[23] Are dual or multiple religious identities a reflection of the varied nature of religious, mystical, or spiritual experiences of the divine? Do not the apophatic traditions of the world's religions invite multiple expressions of religious truth and ways of life? Given the fulfillment thesis that is held by some theologians in almost all other world religions—the idea that one's home faith most inclusively explains or fulfills the highest or noblest aspirations of other faiths—is it possible that the religions do not actually contradict one another at a fundamental level and hence can be practiced alongside one another or simultaneously? What about the unfinished (eschatological) nature of Christian identity; how does that facilitate, if at all, the possibility of multiple religious identities

---

21. This is precisely because Hindu sacred texts are no more or less performative than the scriptures of other religious traditions, including those of monotheistic faiths like Christianity. It is the transformative power of scripture that marks its sacrality, regardless of tradition. For further discussion, see Flood, "Phenomenology of Scripture," and Smith, *What is Scripture?*.

22. Each of these aspects is discussed in Berthrong, *Divine Deli*.

23. The following are discussed in Cornille, *Many Mansions?*.

on this side of the eschaton? Is it possible that there is a complementarity of religions in practice, even if not in belief structures? Are religions not static entities but dynamic ways of life, and does this not suggest that their appropriation is always fluid, partial, and functional, by various people for many reasons in different contexts?[24]

Now Clooney himself acknowledges that he has "had to cultivate a double identity, as a Christian writer . . . , and as gaining something of the insight and docility of a Srivaisnava [a Hindu devotee from the southeast Indian region and theological tradition]."[25] Thus the course of his many years of living in India and of studying Hindu traditions has produced a "cultivated hybridity,"[26] one that has allowed him to acquire Hindu wisdom especially for God's Christian children. Is Clooney's dual religious identity an anomaly or should it be exemplary?

MULTIPLE RELIGIOUS IDENTITIES AND THE COMPARATIVE ENTERPRISE: CLOONEY'S RECENT VOLUMES

I wish to delve into these issues by probing more deeply Clooney's recent work for clues about what is involved and what is at stake. Three books that represent, arguably, his more seasoned and mature reflections will occupy our attention in this section. Each also provides us a window into important aspects of his Catholic Christian identity: Marian piety, spiritual practice, and ultimate commitment. I suggest that evangelicals can learn from, even if they choose not to imitate, Clooney's handling of the complicated theological issues that converge where Catholic Christianity meets (in his case) Srivaisnava Hinduism.

We begin with Clooney's *Divine Mother, Blessed Mother: Hindu Goddesses and the Virgin Mary*, published in 2005.[27] To be clear from the beginning: Clooney is resolutely orthodox in insisting repeatedly that Mary is *not* divine, even if the lines between her role as *Theotokos* (mother of God)

24. This last point regarding the piecemeal appropriation of various traditions under a primary Christianity commitment that is and has long been occurring in the Christian tradition is made by Vietnamese American Catholic theologian Peter C. Phan, leading him to conclude that multiple religious belonging "is not only possible but also desirable" for enriching Christian faith, assuming these other religious practices and beliefs "are not patently contradictory to Christian faith and morals"; see Phan, *Being Religious Interreligiously*, ch. 4, esp. 67–68.

25. Clooney, *Comparative Theology*, 159.

26. Ibid., 160.

27. Clooney, *Divine Mother, Blessed Mother*.

and deity are sometimes blurred in popular Roman Catholic piety.[28] But it is also clearly the case that as a faithful Catholic, Clooney sees bridges to Hinduism from the Catholic veneration of Mary and bridges back from Hinduism in the role and function of goddesses in the South Indian theological traditions. This book reads together, compares, and contrasts six hymns: three devoted to Hindu goddesses (the eighth–tenth century *Ocean of Beauty—Soundarya Lahari*—attributed to the major theologian Śhankara; the twelfth-century *Śrī Guna Rana Kośa*—"Auspicious Treasury of the Jewels that are Śriā's Qualities"—of Parāśara Bhattar; and the eighteenth-century *Apirāmi Antāti*—"Linked Verses for Apirāmi, the Beautiful One"—by Apirāmi Bhattar) and three drawn from the cult and theology of Marian piety (a sixth-century Orthodox Christian song, *Akathistos*; the thirteenth-century *Stabat Mater*, with Mary at the foot of the cross of her song; and *Mātaracammaṇ Antāti*, a nineteenth-century Tamil hymn of praise to Mary as mother of Mylapore, a central South Indian religious site). Together these cross-readings invite reconsideration of pertinent issues in the contemporary theological landscape: theology of gender, the path of union with God(s or goddesses), and the experience of divinity as female presence in the heart.

Space constraints prohibit extensive commentary on Clooney's arguments in this or the other books. But evangelical theological interests will no doubt be piqued by Clooney's observations of Śrī, the consort to Visnu. From an anthropomorphic perspective, Śrī is to her divine husband as women/wives are to males/husbands: the latter are sovereign and the former are, in patriarchal societies, certainly subservient. Yet, as Clooney notes, the authoritative males are nevertheless fully motivated to do all things for their wives and to please them; hence, in that sense, it is not a stretch to say that these goddesses, by prompting and inducing almost every facet of their husband's activities, rule the world as well. So although

> the Lord [Visnu] is the cause of the world's arising, and so on, [yet] Śrī's glance of pleasure is what gives it meaning. . . . Her gaze continually motivates His activity, and it is the same gaze by which She graciously accepts those who come to Her,

28. Evangelical readers may wonder why we ought to spend time thinking about Clooney's Mariology when Mary is quite far removed from much of evangelical spirituality and piety. I would urge only that Mary has been emerging more recently in evangelical theological reflection so that heeding what Clooney says in this regard will be helpful for next steps in the evangelical-Catholic dialogue. For recent contributions to the discussion in evangelical circles, see Oberman, *Virgin Mary in Evangelical Perspective*; Wright, *Chosen by God*; Longenecker and Gustafson, *Mary*; Braaten and Jenson, *Mary, Mother of God*; Perry, *Mary for Evangelicals*; and McKnight, *Real Mary*.

the Lord included. In a striking sense, Visnu is the exemplary recipient of Her favor, rather than Her master and patron. He models how the devotee is to feel and act, while Her gracious reciprocation fills out the picture of the ideal relationship of devotee and deity.[29]

Paradoxically, then, Visnu is supreme but dependent on the goddess. It is Śrī "who permits Him to be independent. . . . Because She gives unfailingly, His independence can be counted as of His essence."[30] Similarly, Śrī "is not judged secondary, since Her deference is a free choice on her part, and since in their mutual delight Visnu surrenders to Her as well."[31] As Clooney thus observes: "ultimately it is She who is the source and finality of His desire and desirability, right there amid the community of gods, goddesses, and humans who love them both."[32] To be sure evangelicals will be troubled by the polytheistic implications of this portrayal, but it could just as well be said that there are all sorts of implications in the preceding for a Christian theology of Trinitarian love. These will have to be postponed, however, in order for us to move to the major issues at stake in our consideration of Clooney's dual religious identity.

Here it is important to first note that hymns are not merely locutions that describe the world. They are certainly that, but they are also illocutionary and performative speech-acts:

> [T]hese are hymns meant to be sung in acts of worship. . . . Hymns speak not simply about but also to the one who is praised and loved. . . . Even first-time readers are invited to participate and enjoy these acts of praise. . . . If the hymns are listened to thoughtfully, readers are drawn by words of praise into acts of praise and into encounter with the deity who is praised. . . . If we begin to understand, we may end up praying or doing something very much like praying; at least, we become able to choose whether or not to address Śrī, Devī, and Apirāmi directly by the words of these hymns.[33]

In other words, to merely read these hymns at a cognitive level is to fail to engage or understand them. Rather, one is urged to sing them, or, if one cannot hold a tune (like myself!), then one is invited to go beyond the cognitional to the affective level of entering the world of the hymn. "What

29. Clooney, *Divine Mother, Blessed Mother*, 116–17.

30. Ibid., 125.

31. Ibid., 141.

32. Ibid., 163.

33. Ibid., 24–25.

matters for the reader is that the hymn produces the fruits of experience rather than simply offering information about experience."[34] So if readers were to become singers—metaphorically if not literally—then they would know the goddess in their hearts as well: "To know Apirāmi is to experience bliss, and to know Mary is similarly a way to bliss."[35] In the end, then, Clooney suggests: "The goddesses and Mary serve as mirrors in which humans see their own potential for divinization and its possible fulfillment, and are thus guided toward their fulfillment as complete human and even divinized persons. The Hindu hymns tell us that by grace or inner potential, humans are invited to participate in Her divine bounty and perhaps even to dwell within the divine reality."[36]

Here of course Clooney is presuming the Orthodox and Roman Catholic soteriology of deification. While evangelicals rarely think about the doctrine of salvation in these classical terms, there is no a priori reason why the preceding cannot be transposed into terms amenable with evangelical soteriologies.[37] My point, however, is not to engage with these specifically theological issues but to underscore the underlying methodological and experiential dynamics of Clooney's comparative work. To gain theological enrichment from other faiths, one must first understand them in terms of their own particularity and distinctiveness; and for Hindu goddess traditions, that may involve being touched, in some respect, by their transformative (salvific?) power. Is there an alternative? As Clooney notes: "The hymns invite us more urgently to participation, and if we do not want to participate, we may first have to protect ourselves by refusing to engage in the reading, thinking, and understanding that open the way to participation."[38] Would this be a retreat to an unsustainable fideism in a pluralistic world? This is not a marginal issue to the comparative theological enterprise, as we shall see in the next two books under review.

The Truth, the Way, the Life (2008)[39] invites readers to appropriate three holy mantras at the heart of Śrīvaisnava Hindu faith in a Christian way:

Tiru Mantra: Aum, obeisance to Nārāyana [to know the truth].

---

34. Ibid., 193.

35. Ibid., 216.

36. Ibid., 230.

37. As clearly articulated by evangelical and pentecostal theologian, Kärkkäinen, *One with God.*

38. Clooney, *Divine Mother, Blessed Mother,* 234.

39. Clooney, *The Truth, the Way, the Life.*

Dvaya Mantra: I approach for refuge the feet of Nārāyana with Śrī; obeisance to Nārāyana with Śrī [the way of radical faith]

Carama Śloka: Having completely given up all *dharmas,* to Me alone come for refuge. From all sins I will make you free. Do not grieve [a divine invitation, to live in freedom].[40]

The entire volume consists, as the title indicates, of a Christian commentary on the three mantras. At one level, some may object that such Christian readings of the mantras for Christian purposes are illegitimate; they are imperialistic raids on other religious traditions for Christian purposes. This possibility cannot be easily set aside in light of Clooney's repeated reminders of his primary Christian commitments and how these shape his readings of and engagements with other texts.[41] The only thing to be said here in defense of Clooney's objectives—aside from the preceding rationales and the substance of this chapter taken as a whole—is that this task explores both the universal reach and translatability of the Christian faith on the one hand, and the relevance of South Indian culture and religion for Christian faith on the other hand. More precisely, Clooney is guardedly nonimperialistic since he urges us not to deny to the mantras "their power in encompassing an entire religious world, [one that impinges] deeply on our Christian religious world."[42]

More important for me is the question driving this inquiry: can a Christian commentary on Hindu mantras succeed apart from chanting or even praying them, and if so what would that mean or look like? Can Clooney open himself up to these mantras without denying his Christian commitment, or does this just involve some kind of bracketing of the latter in order to engage in the task of the former? These are not idle questions, since exclusivism belongs not only to Christianity but also to Hindu traditions. More specifically, as Clooney notes: "The Tiru Mantra's exclusive focus on Nārāyana enables the ālvār [the theologian as devotee] to break free of other gods, their cult, and to distance himself from the communities worshipping such deities."[43] So let us press the dilemma before the Christian

40. Ibid., 15; the brackets at the end of each mantra are the titles of the major chapters 1–4, which are of course meant to parallel Jesus' saying, "I am the way, and the truth, and the life" (John 14:6, NRSV).

41. Most recently reiterated by Clooney in his *Comparative Theology,* 139.

42. Clooney, *The Truth, the Way, the Life,* 185; see also *Theology after Vedanta,* 7. There is now an emerging interreligious conversation about this approach of reading the world through Scripture, especially among the monotheistic traditions—e.g., Ford and Pecknold, *Promise of Scriptural Reasoning.*

43. Clooney, *The Truth, the Way, the Life,* 21.

interpreter or commentator: if she or he were to enter into the world of the mantra, does that not mean turning from all other allegiances toward Nārāyana? That does not appear to have happened with Clooney—or has it? From some evangelical perspectives, Clooney's view of Christ is now compromised even if he were to understand making obeisance to Nārāyana as declaring loyalty to Christ. The particularity of adherence to Nārāyana suggests the impossibility of anonymously saluting Christ via another name.[44] As Clooney recognizes, the commentary, much less the mantras, are occasions for abandonment to the invoked deities: "total surrender to God, in a moment of realization and choice, becomes a real possibility, daunting yet simple."[45]

Let us press into this question of the possibility of dual religious commitments with Clooney's help. The Tiru Mantra, for instance, can never be merely an intellectual exercise; rather, the mantra "is an act of potent, transformative praise: to study it is already a grace."[46] In addition, the Dvaya Mantra "is not a statement about taking refuge: it is rather a performative word that, when uttered [read?], brings about the reality of which it speaks."[47] In Clooney's exposition, Nārāyana and Śrī are both the means and the goal, according to these mantras, so that chanting (reading?) them is both an invocations of these deities and an entrustment of the hearts and lives of devotees to their salvific powers.

Now Clooney is not blind to the religious dynamics of what is happening in engaging (reading) these mantras, clearly recognizing that the fundamental question concerns "how to understand these other deities respectfully and yet with fidelity to Christian faith."[48] After all, the "God" of Christianity should not be uncritically assimilated to Nārāyana and Śrī.[49] In fact, if the particularities of this tradition should be respected, one appropriate response is that a "respectful Christian reader might honor the Carama Śloka by deciding that it is *not* addressed to Christians, because Christian faith does not enable us to hear this as a Word addressed to us."[50] Perhaps this is the only valid response, as Nārāyana is specific to this Hindu tradition: "We must therefore ask not whether to respect and take the Mantra

44. These same evangelicals would also object to the by now classic thesis captured in the title of Panikkar, *Unknown Christ of Hinduism*, insisting that Christ cannot be known by the names of any of the Hindu deities.

45. Clooney, *The Truth, the Way, the Life*, 23.

46. Ibid, 35.

47. Ibid., 126.

48. Ibid., 13.

49. Ibid., 16 n.18.

50. Ibid., 105; italics original.

seriously—that seems almost a necessity, once we understand it—but rather when we must stop affirming and uttering it as our own truth, a truth in harmony with Christian truth."[51] If Clooney is right, "we will find ourselves on a difficult middle ground: it is an inclusive Mantra, yet by its power and tradition, it is exclusive too; and for us, finding where to stand is the key factor"[52]

It is this quest for standing on the terrain where Christianity meets Hinduism that urges Clooney onward. Toward this end, he suggests instead that when Nārāyana is explicated according to the Hindu tradition—Clooney documents Nārāyana's 108 qualities along with an additional sixty-eight qualities of the devotee who take refuge in the Lord and fifty-seven additional erroneous views that such devotion protects people from[53]—the result is quite relevant to Christian faith: "There is almost nothing . . . that could not be accepted by the Christian."[54] In fact, there are multiple interpretations of the mantra, and it is precisely this plurivocity that constitutes a more effective bulwark against erroneous interpretations.[55] In short, if Nārāyana is universal and true, then according to the logic of monotheism it must refer to what Christians also consider to be the universally true God, and we can then engage the divine in and through either name. Yet the end is neither a syncretism nor a relativism: "Indeed, a relativistic outcome would be ironic, given the highly confessional and focused perspective of both Christian and Śrīvaisnava prayer. Rather, my hope is that a richer, gracious, reflective reality of and in faith is now seen in the perspective of Christ, heard through the prayerful exchanges that constitute the Mantras."[56]

51. Ibid., 65.

52. Ibid., 73.

53. Ibid., 46–57.

54. Ibid., 50. What Clooney does here is similar to what is undertaken in Miroslav Volf's *Allah*; Volf painstaking argues that the Allah submitted to by Muslims can be understood to refer to the Yahweh of Judaism and to the God of Jesus Christ worshipped by Christians. I have elsewhere reviewed Volf's book—Yong, "Review of *Allah*"—so here will not weigh in the validity of his argument, which will be contested among evangelicals. My only point here is methodological: if we grant that there is a mode of argumentation that succeeds at least in suggesting that the fundamental characteristics of the Muslim Allah do not contradict the fundamental features of the Christian God of Jesus Christ (Volf), then we ought to be open to the similar argument that the fundamental characteristics of the Śrīvaisnava Nārāyana also may turn out to not contradict the fundamental features of the Christian God of Jesus Christ (Clooney).

55. Clooney, *The Truth, the Way, the Life*, 59–60, as opposed to a singular authorial intent of any text, including sacred ones, which wards off other possible understandings.

56. Ibid., 191.

Still, in order to arrive at such a destination, the fact is that Clooney has at least opened up to a kind of personal encounter of and interaction with Nārāyana. As he grants, there is a "potency of the name *Nārāyana* by itself," and the mantra itself reflects "the speaker's most essential and intimate relationship to Nārāyana."[57] As with the hymns to the Hindu goddesses, the three holy mantras are not merely intended as descriptive locutions about what Śrīvaisnavas do, although that may well be the case. But to truly understand these mantras, and to embark on a viable commentary on them, requires a kind of experience of their power. Arguably this witness comes forth from, in, and through *The Truth, the Way, the Life*, suggesting that Clooney is here mediating not merely on intellectual curiosities about Nārāyana and Śrī but affective, imaginative, and living renditions of their salvific potency.

If the reader of *The Truth, the Way, the Life* has managed to put off making obeisance, at least in any conscious manner, to Nārāyana and Śrī, this question is called out in the final book we now discuss, Clooney's *Beyond Compare: St. Francis de Sales and Śrī Vedānta Deśika on Loving Surrender to God* (2008).[58] Here the focus is on two major spiritual classics: the *Treatise on the Love of God* by St. Francis de Sales, an early seventeenth-century Roman Catholic bishop, teacher, preacher, and spiritual director, and the *Essence of the Three Auspicious Mysteries* by Śrī Vedānta Deśika, a thirteenth-fourteenth-century Śrīvaisnava and one of the leading theologians of the Hindu tradition. Both classics are about "finding a path to loving surrender," directed toward "awakening: reading and learning on the way to God," and on the intensity of "loving surrender" and self-abandonment to God (the quoted material consists of titles or subtitles of the central chapters of the book). Clooney reads both texts with each other, against each other, and through each other.

My interest in this chapter is on whether or not authentic readings and engagements with the sacred texts and spiritual classics of other traditions require or lead to a kind of dual religious commitment. Clooney's description of what his spiritual masters are up to focus the point:

> The fundamental life change that both Deśika and de Sales aim to inspire cannot be fully apprehended or assessed conceptually, even if the reader's analysis proceeds by lucid and logical arguments. . . . This exercise requires that we move from reading at a distance, with professional control that correctly and necessarily prizes detachment, toward a submission to these texts,

57. Ibid., 33.
58. Clooney, *Beyond Compare*.

immersion finally in a double reading that makes us vulnerable
to the realities of God and self as imagined by the authors. . . .
Our best practice, then, is to attend to the *Treatise* and the *Essence* as the effective communicative acts they were intended to
be . . . .⁵⁹

In other words, neither the *Treatise* nor the *Essence* are meant to be merely
cognitive texts for intellectual consumption; rather, "Both are deeply concerned with communicating a practical message that will bear practical
implications in their readers' lives—and for this they write highly original
and effectives treatises that promise to transform all who would read them
carefully."⁶⁰ After all, these texts are about self-abandonment to the deities
they extol. Hence, they have become "normative (and canonical) because
over time [they] remain capable of helping readers to reimagine their
own life choices in accord with imaginative and affective energies that are
deeper and more enduring than overt reasons that might be given to justify
behavior."⁶¹ To truly read and understand these texts is to move from "a
theology *about* God [to] a theology in encounter *with* God."⁶²

What Clooney is describing through encountering these texts is the
possibility of religious conversion and commitment. Conversion is "the
event of spiritual awakening and self-appropriation in which a person comes
to see that her life must be lived very differently."⁶³ For both Deśika and de
Sales, this is possible because "The divine persons are not simply described;
they are invoked and made present for the sake of the contemplation that
leads toward loving surrender to them."⁶⁴ Thus, for example, "De Sales' hope
is that no one who can imagine this scenario—Christ dying on the cross
thinking of *me*—will casually put aside the text and return to ordinary business with the same feelings and habits as before."⁶⁵ Similarly, for Deśika,
"conversion" follows clear insight, so he speaks about this surrendering to
the deity in less affective terms than de Sales (who emphasizes contrition,
remorse, and repentance).⁶⁶ But does this then mean that Clooney has been
lead to the brink of conversion to both de Sales's beatific vision of the Triune

59. Ibid., 22.
60. Ibid., 21.
61. Ibid., 134.
62. Ibid., 43; italics original.
63. Ibid., 56.
64. Ibid., 107.
65. Ibid., 121; italics original.
66. Ibid., 224 n.70.

God and also to Deśika's clear insights regarding Nārāyana and Śrī? How might such a dual conversion be possible?

Now we should also restate that Clooney works as a comparative theologian who seeks to understand his faith. The difference is that his primary dialogue partners are not those at the fount of the Western tradition like Plato and Aristotle but are Hindu interlocutors. Further, however, as these are not merely philosophic but also religious texts, Christians are admonished to engage them religiously and theologically—not merely to write *about* them, but to think *with* them. As Clooney writes:

> In the end, then, these Śrīvaisnava resources cannot simply be treated as objects for Christian theological reflection, as if only we have achieved self-conscious, multi-dimensional reflection on matters of faith. Rather, this will be a theology of religions that moves away from judgments-about-religions to an understanding that is profoundly dialogical, self-critical as well as critical, and enacted in actual peer theological conversation with the Śrīvaisnava tradition and its contemporary proponents.[67]

After almost forty years of living with these resources, then, what Clooney wrote toward the end of his doctoral dissertation (completed in the early to mid-1980s) remains apropos: "through our understanding we become in a sense members of that tradition—commentators of [a] sort. . . . To understand the Mīmāmsā we must also try to make sense of the transition from the world view of Jaimini to that of his commentators; we must enter their world too."[68]

EVANGELICALS AND THE COMPARATIVE THEOLOGICAL PROJECT: QUESTIONS AND CONCERNS

Has Clooney gone too far? Has he crossed over into the other religious tradition beyond the point of being able to return as an authentic Christian? As already noted, there are very few evangelical readers of Clooney.[69] Con-

---

67. Clooney, *The Truth, the Way, the Life*, 184. Thus Clooney is not oblivious to the fact that even the comparative theological exercise presumes some kind of theology of religions—e.g., as argued by Beise Kiblinger, "Relating Theology of Religions and Comparative Theology"—but his response is that the persistent work of specific comparisons will in turn also inform, shape, and even revise whatever is believed theologically about the religions.

68. Clooney, *Thinking Ritually*, 222.

69. Robinson, *Christians Meeting Hindus*, 346, briefly discusses Clooney's *Theology after Vedanta* and commends it as an exemplary model for allowing, if not inviting,

servative evangelicals familiar with his work might be concerned about the status of his Christian identity. For them, Clooney provides what would be a reassuring confession at the end of his book *Hindu God, Christian God*, published in 2001:

> As a Christian believer—who also happens to be a theologian—
> I willingly profess my faith in the God of our Lord Jesus Christ,
> who was born as the child of Mary, who died on the cross for
> our sins, rose into glory, and sent forth the Spirit upon us. . . .
> I confess that Jesus is Lord, but I cannot now assert that Śiva is
> not Lord nor that Nārāyana did not graciously undergo embodi-
> ment in order to enable humans to encounter their God.[70]

But has this confession changed in the last decade? Has it been compromised by his envisioning the Hindu goddesses, reading (chanting?) the three holy mantras, or being spiritually directed by Śrī Vedānta Deśika's calls to self-abandonment? Anticipating our more specifically evangelical assessment momentarily, let us take stock of Clooney's dual religious location from his own perspective. A number of points are worth mentioning.

First, it is difficult to identify Clooney according to the usual theology of religions categories. According to the above profession of faith, he can be understood as a soft exclusivist: with exclusive devotion to Christ but yet not one that denies the reality of Hindu deities. (*Hard exclusivists*, of course, would deny the coherence of Clooney's *soft* stance as a legitimate variation of exclusivism.) More recently he has indicated that his own theological views are "in harmony with" the inclusivist theologies of Karl Rahner and Jacques Dupuis, other Jesuit theologians who "balance claims to Christian uniqueness with a necessary openness to leaning from other religions."[71] Yet he is also a pluralist, not of the type perpetuated by John Hick and his colleagues, but as one who sees pluralism "as an opportunity for an intensification of previous truths, revered spiritual paths, and ultimate religious acts as known and written in multiple traditions."[72] It appears then that Clooney is somewhat agnostic about the ultimate soteriological efficacy of other faiths, at least when measured according to Christian understandings, although he

---

the Hindu context "to reshape Christian theology," but concludes saying, "whether it is possible to offer a critical restatement of Christian beliefs in the context of a nonreductionist reading of the Hindu traditions is not yet clear."

70. Clooney, *Hindu God, Christian God*, 180–81.

71. Clooney, *Comparative Theology*, 16. And let us recall that other evangelicals have also urged an openness to other faiths—e.g., Pinnock, *Wideness in God's Mercy*; Sanders, *No Other Name*; and McDermott, *Can Evangelicals Learn from World Religions?*.

72. Clooney, *Beyond Compare*, 218 n.46.

seems to be fully convinced about their power in historical and existential life to add meaning to the human quest. One wonders, however, what keeps him from affirming a full blown pluralistic soteriology in light of the present experiential and explanatory power he appears to have encountered in the Hindu tradition.

Second, Clooney has put his finger on an important point: that at least now, if not previously, diversity is "within us."[73] In our time, all of us are now "'intertexted' in our spiritual practice," linked to and informed by the wisdom traditions of the world in more ways than we can consciously recognize.[74] Through the explicit and intentional task of comparative theology, however, each of us becomes "an 'insider-outsider' several times over."[75]

Yet, third, this internally diverse, intertextual, and insider-outsider identity is not and can never be neutral in a religiously plural world. Even for contemporary Vedantins, "There is no extra-textual common ground for conversation or argument."[76] Rather, there are only borderline or marginal existences, even and perhaps especially in the world of academia where "detached objectivity" remains an ideal.[77] Yet as an academic, Clooney also seeks an approach where "neither text is to be allowed to dominate the other, neither tradition's mode of reading is to be given absolute priority, and no higher academic perspective is to be permitted to decide what counts in the reading."[78] So even though neutrality is impossible across these textual fields, methodologically, "impartiality is a virtue, but only as preparatory to a more intense engagement. . . . My ambition here is to write in accord with the power of both texts, in deference to both of them, for readers willing to read intelligently, religiously, and without complete certainty about where the reading will lead them."[79] Still the question persists: can there be complete uncertainty on the way of Christ?

This leads, fourth, to Clooney's ever-dynamic reconception of his Christian identity, which some might interpret as a kind of perpetual falling away. Clooney describes how this process of interreligious reading produces an interpreter who "becomes distant from the totalizing power of both texts, precisely because she or he knows both, cannot dismiss either, and does not

---

73. Clooney, *Comparative Theology*, 6.

74. Ibid., 148–49.

75. Ibid., 161.

76. Ibid., 84.

77. Clooney acknowledges that his life's work has involved "crossing religious borders"; see Clooney, "Response," 200.

78. Clooney, *Beyond Compare*, 30.

79. Ibid., 79.

submit entirely to either."[80] Put another way, the kind of interreligious readings he advocates produces "the (ideally) irreversibly changed situation of the reader who, through interreligious study, becomes intensely involved in both traditions and yet at the same time detached from both because each is so vividly and insistently nearby to the other. Consequently, the reader is intellectually and spiritually enriched and yet too distanced from her or his own home tradition."[81] This distancing and detaching will be seen, at least by some, as a type of loosening of Christian commitment.

Alternatively, fifth, Clooney is also convincing when he argues that it is only by exposure to the depths of another religious tradition that true believing in the home faith is possible. Without thorough knowledge of other religious options and their similarities to and differences from one's primary faith, no genuine freedom of choice exists. Hence it's not that we have to choose from Devi or Mary, for example, but that our thinking about both "is diffused and transformed into a wider array of smaller and more specific theological possibilities that can be taken up one at a time."[82] As important, "it is not that the reader now lives inside the world of the novel or drama and responds to its situation in a kind of fiction, but rather that by the reading she or he is able to imagine, feel, and choose differently."[83] Only after crossing over into another religious path are we able to truly claim our original faith as our own since now we can decide to surrender in love (not just intellectually but affectively, with our hearts!), as de Sales or Deśika want us to do, or choose to withhold our former allegiances. All of these now become intentional possibilities for the interreligious sojourner. In that sense, then, Clooney confesses also to "knowing too much and believing too much to be received with great ease in either the religious or academic setting."[84] If Clooney is right, then the *true believer* in any faith tradition cannot be less than the interreligious reader, singer, and chanter that Clooney invites us to be.

80. Ibid., 209.

81. Ibid., 217 n.45.

82. Clooney, *Divine Mother, Blessed Mother*, 236.

83. Clooney, *Beyond Compare*, 136. That is, after all, the nature of religious texts, produced (not just written) not only for the sake of consumers but for those committed to the religious quest and life in order that they may be "read (heard), reread, memorized, pondered upon, excerpted, commented upon, chewed over, smelled, and incorporated" (Griffiths, *Religious Reading*, 147). While Griffiths is here discussing Indian Buddhist texts, these are applicable also to the writings that Clooney discusses; thus Clooney (*Beyond Compare*, 77–79) views his own work as a natural extension of Griffiths's views about the specifically religious (not merely intellectual or cognitive) character of reading these sacred canons.

84. Clooney, *Comparative Theology*, 159.

Still, while all of this seems theoretically sound, Clooney also grants: "what is theologically plausible may not be religiously acceptable."[85] In other words, what Clooney does as a comparative theologian may work within the halls of academia, but find no place in the real spaces of religious life, at least not in confessional traditions like Roman Catholicism or the broad spectrum of evangelical Christianity. Some Roman Catholic theologians may think it is possible for Catholics to inhabit multiple religious worlds since such a posture or spiritual path presumes God's universal salvific will, does not need to deny salvation through Christ, and could even affirm the church as necessary for salvation (if the church were defined spiritually rather than institutionally or visibly).[86] How would evangelical theologians respond?

One theologian who has done so is Steven Tsoukalas.[87] His published dissertation comparing Krishna and Christ reflects an awareness of Clooney's work, often quoting, in some instances extensively, from him. Tsoukalas does not provide any substantive critical comment on Clooney's work, but readers of his book who are also knowledgeable of Clooney's *oeuvre* will recognize the underlying differences. If Clooney highlights the similarities between the traditions (even without identifying them), Tsoukalas concludes toward disagreements between the two traditions. For him, ultimately, the historicity of incarnation is contrasted with the lack of such for Hindu theologies. To be sure, Tsoukalas is willing to emphasize the structural similarities in the doctrines of incarnation across the two faiths, but only for the sake of establishing common ground for evangelical mission and evangelism.[88] If Tsoukalas correctly represents the overall thrust of evangelical commitments, then Clooney's project will be understood as fundamentally misdirected. At best, our Jesuit theologian is misguided in his priorities. Even given the benefit of the doubt, he is deluded about the value of inhabiting these two religious worlds and he is not only wasting his time but in danger of misleading others who are not so informed. At worst, he is stubborn in his persistent devotion to studying the Hindu tradition, and is truly in danger of apostasy from faith in Christ. None of these appear to me to be charitable readings of Clooney's work given the preceding exposition.

In this final part of our review essay, then, I would like to essay my own interpretive assessment of Clooney's project. The following raises especially methodological questions across three trajectories: biblical/textual studies,

85. Clooney, *Divine Mother, Blessed Mother*, 234.

86. Tilley, *Religious Diversity and the American Experience*, esp. chs. 3 and 10, the latter of which is coauthored by Louis T. Albarran and titled, "Multiple Religious Belonging: Can a Christian Belong to Other Traditions Too?"

87. Tsoukalas, *Krsna and Christ*.

88. Ibid., 259–61.

missions/praxis, and theology/truth. The critical questions should be read in light of an overall appreciation for Clooney's contributions.

First, evangelicals who have long been known as people of the book should at least respect the care with which Clooney approaches, reads, and interprets Hindu texts. In fact, the sophistication with which Clooney interprets Hindu texts is exemplary for the modern study of Hinduism. If evangelicals are concerned about higher critical approaches to their own Scriptures, they will rightly also be dismissive of similar readings of other traditions' sacred texts; but if evangelicals have now seen the value of modern Scripture studies, why would they think that such hermeneutical tools are inapplicable to the sacred canons of other faiths?

On the other side, evangelicals may be reminded about, if not actually learn from, how their Bible effectively informs and transforms their personal piety and spirituality. Clooney's handling of Hindu texts reflects a sensitivity to the affective power of Scriptural and commentarial traditions that in turn illuminates evangelical convictions about their Word of God being "living and active" (Heb 4:12). After all, as Clooney observes, authentic reading of Hindu texts is a process that involves "a (ritual) transformation of the reader."[89] Thus there is no "fast-food" version of "digesting" Scripture; instead, we must "spend time with . . . key verses. Study them, leave aside what seems too mysterious or obscure, imagine them as [we] are able, and see what meanings and images come to [us]."[90] Evangelicals can be reminded by Clooney that these religious texts invite not just intellectual acknowledgement but participatory and experiential engagement. Perhaps evangelicals can now approach their own devotional practices with a fresh sensitivity to the affective and imaginative dimensions of biblical reading.

But even if so, the nub of the problem comes with how Clooney appears to inhabit the Hindu tradition. Beyond this is the challenge, specified in this chapter, that authentic understanding of other faiths involves a kind of affective and imaginative conversion toward the other, and a commitment to comprehend it experientially and even existentially from within, as it were.[91] Evangelicals might tolerate, even encourage, such crossover to varying degrees, all the while assuming that down the line one returns to the home faith more fully informed about the other so that one's witness to those in other faiths will be more effective. This is an instrumental and missional justification for the contextualization, indigenization, or enculturation of the gospel in other religious environments. But having said this,

89. Clooney, *Theology after Vedanta*, 35 and 55.

90. Clooney, *Hindu Wisdom for All God's Children*, 95.

91. As I recently summarize in my "Guests of Religious Others."

we must also recognize that our every invitation to the religious other to embrace our commitments is preceded and followed by invitations from others to embrace their own. Can we expect others to open their hearts to us without us opening our hearts to them? From this perspective, Clooney becomes a model missionary, one who has invested deeply enough in engaging religious others to the point of risking his own security in an uncharted exploration of their religious world. He who confesses Christ now does so almost literally as a lone voice crying in the wilderness, surely as a stranger in a very strange land. Clooney might not be holding altar calls in the traditional sense, but surely his testimony points to Christ's own vulnerability, so that those to whom he is bearing witness cannot say that Clooney's life invites them to something that he himself has not experienced.

Yet even if we were to pause at this notion that mission is a two-way street going in as many directions as there are religious traditions, recall that the goals of comparative theology, at least as outlined by Clooney, are not first and foremost missional. Rather, the comparative theologian is in search of understanding, except that his or her quest occurs in a world of many faiths. Thus, if evangelicals were to say that a pluralistic world is a place where we can introduce God, Clooney says that "religious diversity is already a place where we can meet God."[92] Whereas evangelicals seek to evangelize the religious other, Clooney himself is evangelized through encountering the other.

Evangelicals are rightly concerned here that, to use a marital metaphor, we are introducing other lovers into our existing love affair with Jesus. After all, if encountering the other is not merely an intellectual exercise but also an affective one, and if loving God involves not just our minds but also our hearts and our souls,[93] then how can we genuinely open up our hearts to other deities without defiling the intimacy of our love relationship with the God of Jesus Christ? Clooney is, of course, fully aware of the classical admonitions on this issue, even as he also observes similar warnings about flirting with other deities in the Hindu texts.[94]

So what can evangelicals say in the end? Is it possible for us to "merely" read other religious texts but not sing, chant, or pray them? Joseph Molleur, one of Clooney's students, confesses he has been "unable, perhaps even unwilling, to 'really pray' to Visnu and Krishna as [he prays] to Yahweh and Jesus," but yet also confesses that he has "read the songs of *Tiruvaymoli*

---

92. Clooney, *Comparative Theology*, 152.

93. I explicate, from a Christian perspective on the affective aspects of loving God and receiving the love of God in my *Spirit of Love*, esp. ch. 5 and passim.

94. E.g., Clooney, *Seeing through Texts*, 309, and *Beyond Compare*, 51–52.

with the eyes of a devotee because, on a number of occasions when reading and meditating on them . . . [he has] been deeply moved by their beauty and profoundly convinced of their religious value"; so he acknowledges: "Since I have repeatedly found my own Christian life has been deeply edified by reading and meditating on the songs of *Tiruvaymoli*, I can only conclude that these songs *do* share a great deal in common with 'the idea of Christianity.'"[95] So even if Molleur stops short of "asserting that Srivaisnava *arul* and Christian grace are identical notions," he can "wholeheartedly affirm a complementarity between the two."[96] Can evangelicals take a similar approach? Is it not possible, in other words, to be touched deeply and affectively in our hearts by other faiths, even while remaining faithfully in love with Jesus?

Interestingly, perhaps Clooney himself is much more ambivalent, and maybe even not as radical, as the preceding has portrayed him to be. At one point, in reflecting on his writing of *The Truth, the Way, the Life*, Clooney admitted either his inability or lack of desire to pray with the texts he had been trying to understand: "I wanted to do this [the comparative work] while still knowing the value of exclusive commitment, balancing the impropriety of praying in another tradition with the cost of trying to understand a tradition, without *allowing understanding to open into prayer*."[97] Clearly, Clooney is embracing this tension rather than ignoring or collapsing it. Perhaps it is precisely in this posture that Clooney the marginal figure (to both Christian and Hindu traditions, not to mention to both religious and academic communities) now appears at the vanguard of next steps in the task of thinking theologically in global context.

In the end, then, perhaps evangelicals need such a context within which to understand their Christian commitments. After all, the central message of the gospel is the incarnation of the Son and the Pentecostal outpouring of the Spirit. These involved the travelling of the Son of God to a far country (to use Barth's metaphor),[98] and (this is my contribution as a pneumatological theologian) the Holy Spirit's being poured out upon all flesh (Acts 2:17) in ways that preserved, rather than annulled, the many tongues and languages of a diverse humanity.[99] In either case, God did not

95. Molleur, *Divergent Traditions, Converging Faiths*, 159; emphases Molleur's.

96. Ibid., 160.

97. Clooney, *Comparative Theology*, 160; emphasis added.

98. See Karl Barth's famous articulation of the incarnational journey of the Son of God into the "far country" of human life in his *Church Dogmatics*, Vol. IV/1, §59.1.

99. This pneumatological emphasis has of course been a staple of my work as a Christian theologian of religious pluralism; see my book, *Spirit Poured Out on All Flesh*, esp. chs. 4 and 6.

see a problem with entering fully into the strange and alien world of human cultures. To be sure, these are redemptive activities of the Triune God, but I see them as salvaging, reappropriating, and renewing rather than negating the human condition.

It took the early Christians a few hundred years to discern how to go about doing the same with the pagan traditions of their time—salvaging, reappropriating, and renewing Plato and Aristotle, for example—rather than merely rejecting what these had to offer. So also today, Clooney repeatedly urges our patience.[100] In a real sense we are still only in the very beginning stages of coming to grips with the legacy of the world's great religious traditions, and the comparative theological communities in our time are still small and fragile.[101] Might evangelical theologians also begin to undertake the task of comparative theology in order that their own commitments, perspectives, and sensibilities might also be registered in the discussion?

In at least one respect Clooney has it right: the theological task has always been one of faith seeking understanding. What he has now also suggested to us is that in a pluralistic world, this task of loving God with our minds cannot ignore loving God with our hearts and souls as well, and this invitation is surely now much more complicated in a world of many faiths than we had previously realized.[102]

100. E.g., Clooney, *Theology after Vedanta*, 187–88, and *Hindu Wisdom for All God's Children*, ch. 8.

101. Clooney, *Beyond Compare*, 209–10; *Comparative Theology*, 160–62.

102. Thanks to Roger Hedlund for giving me the space for this review article and for extending for me the time needed to write it. Thanks also to my graduate assistant Timothy Lim for his reading a previous draft. Terry Muck also commented on an earlier version of this essay; I remain most appreciative of his work, exemplary leadership in this area of evangelical scholarship, and collegial friendship. The opinions represented in the preceding, however, are my own.

CHAPTER 11

Observation-Participation-Subjunctivation

Methodological Play and Meaning-Making in the Study of Religion and Theology[1]

DISCUSSION ABOUT THE INSIDER-OUTSIDER "problem" continues to unfold in the academic study of religion.[2] This chapter sketches a threefold taxonomy of methodological options—methodological atheism or naturalism, methodological agnosticism, and methodological theism—prevalent in this field, and then explores whether anthropologist André Droogers's methodological ludism provides for a posture that allows for simultaneous embrace of all three types, as he suggests it might. The concluding section will reflect on these methodological alternatives from a theological perspective.

In anticipation of the specifically theological discussion at the end of this chapter, some authorial self-disclosure is warranted. Although I have been trained in the scholarly study of religion,[3] much of my work and writing has been as a theologian. So, while alert to many of the issues as they have been contested within the academic study of religion, my motivation to enter into this foray is distinctively theological. I am particularly

1. "Subjunctivation" in my title is a neologism whose meaning will become clear in the course of this chapter.

2. McCutcheon, ed., *Insider/Outsider Problem in Study of Religion*; Arweck and Stringer, *Theorizing Faith*.

3. I did my PhD in the Department of Religion at Boston University where I had coursework under Buddhologist M. David Eckel, Sinologist John H. Berthrong, anthropologist Inus Daneel, and philosophers Robert Cummings Neville and Ray L. Hart, among others.

interested in the theological implications of these methodological disputes in the field of religious studies, especially the ramifications for theological understandings of religious pluralism, interfaith encounter/dialogue, and comparative theology, arenas within which I have long been at work. I hope, however, that scholars across the broad spectrum of this field of inquiry—from nonconfessional scholars of religion, on the one side, to theologians on the other—will at least benefit from the mapping I provide. I believe that the discussion to come is relevant to all scholars of religion who are self-conscious about methodological issues, although my nontheological readers may be less enthused by the article's distinctively theological turn at the end.

One final caveat needs to be registered. Some scholars might consider a theologian incapable of handling adequately the methodological issues related to the study of religion due to the conviction, in some religious studies circles, that theology belongs in seminaries and divinity schools, but not in the university, and by definition, then, that theologians who work in a confessional framework are ill equipped to understand or to appreciate how the nonconfessional study of religion ought to be undertaken. Of course, it will be beyond the scope of this chapter for me to argue fully otherwise, although the essay as a whole provides one set of counter-considerations to this objection.[4] Suffice for me to say here that it is also impossible for academics to refrain from rendering judgment, whether implicit or explicit, about the beliefs of the subjects they study, who are religious people (such beliefs being undeniably part of the data that constitutes the study of religion), and if that is the case, then at that level there is little difference between a scholar of religion and a theologian.[5] It is precisely from this vantage point that I think the following discussion is relevant to those working across the broad spectrum of the study of religion since it provides not just theologians but also scholars and researchers options for negotiating their engagement with the religious ideas and beliefs of their subjects.

---

4. Those interested can consult the literature this debate has generated. I am partial to the arguments for including theology in the twenty-first-century university. See, for example Cady and Brown, *Religious Studies, Theology, and University*, and Brittain and Murphy, *Theology, University, Humanities*.

5. Similar motivation from the anthropological side can be seen in Salamone and Adams, *Explorations in Anthropology and Theology*, although their call to their fellow anthropologists to cross to the theological side appears not to have fallen upon fertile ground. The challenges to be overcome, however, involve the long history of anthropological self-understanding being defined over and against Christianity, especially Christian theological ideas, as Cannell eloquently details in "Introduction: The Anthropology of Christianity." My hopes are that this chapter will provide one more plank for the bridge between these two disciplines.

METHODOLOGICAL OPTIONS
IN THE STUDY OF RELIGION

A taxonomy of the dominant approaches concerning methodology in the study of religion can be summarized under three headings: methodological atheism or naturalism, methodological agnosticism, and methodological theism. In what follows I sketch the state of the question, while in the process engaging discussions in the sociology and anthropology of religion. This interdisciplinary inquiry not only sets in relief the contested matters that cut across contemporary research and scholarship in religious studies, but also will be crucial to considering the theological implications later. To be sure, the methodological arguments in the study of religion are far more involved than the following suggests.[6] My focus is limited to the disputes that arise specifically with regard to the relationship of the researcher or scholar to the religious phenomenon being studied. My motivation is that this is an important but undertheorized aspect of theological work, and approaching the issues within this broader landscape will invite the kind of interdisciplinary conversation that needs to occur.

What Peter Berger labeled *methodological atheism* needs to be understood in its wider context. Writing at the height of the "death of God" controversy, when secularization theories were predicting the imminent disappearance of religion in the modern world, and motivated as a sociologist by the conviction that human beings construct their social—and religious—lives in some very fundamental ways, Berger urged that at least for the purposes of an empirical sociology of religion, sociologists ought to proceed in what might be called a naturalistic mode, as if God, even if God existed (which Berger, himself a Christian, did not deny), should not be a factor in the analysis. As he put it:

> Within this frame of reference, the religious projections can be dealt with only as such, as products of human activity and human consciousness, and rigorous brackets have to be placed around the question as to whether these projections may not *also* be something else than that (or, more accurately, *refer to* something else than the human world in which they empirically originate). In other words, every inquiry into religious matters that limits itself to the empirically available must necessarily be based on a "*methodological* atheism."[7]

6. For an introduction to the broad scope of religious studies theory and method, see Pals, *Eight Theories of Religion*.

7. Berger, *Sacred Canopy*, 100; emphasis original.

There are of course metaphysical naturalists for whom all such bracketing is unnecessary, although most other sociologists (or other scholars of religion) recognize such a metaphysically naturalistic position to be an extra-sociological (or scholarly) presupposition that goes beyond what can be assumed within their disciplinary field. But after distinguishing such metaphysical atheism (or naturalism) from Berger's methodological atheism, his point still is that sociologists *qua* sociologists ought to be examining social, not transcendental (or theological) phenomena. So if sociology concerns social realities and even the sociology of religion studies but the social dimensions of human religiosity, then, as religion scholar Kurt Rudolph quipped: "Either one engages in scholarship (*Wissenschaft*) or in worship."[8]

Contemporary scholars of religion working in this vein more often advocate versions of methodological naturalism rather than Berger's methodological atheism. In part in order to defend the scientific character of the field of religious studies, such scholars (in the spirit represented by Berger's dictum) are insistent upon an objective or value-free approach to the phenomenon of religion, rather than one that advocates on behalf of religious doctrines, practices, or communities.[9] Even the theological or doctrinal ideas of religious traditions are human data to be studied, understood, and explained.[10] Enthusiasm about the possibility of a more scientific approach to the study of religion persists within these circles. A stance of metaphysical naturalism (atheism) enables the scholar or researcher to stand apart from the subject of her gaze, in order to get a more objective perspective.

Interestingly, it was almost immediately after he wrote about methodological atheism that Berger himself appeared to backpedal, at least a bit. Putting on at least an amateur theologian's hat, he not only defended the possibility of theological thinking but also buttressed his argument sociologically, drawing from, as he labeled it, "signals of transcendence"—e.g., hope, humor, pity/compassion, morality, play, courage, love, injustice, and the demands of justice—detectable through social scientific research.[11] At least for himself as a person of faith, it was clear that a watertight compartmentalization of his sociological and Christian identity was difficult to maintain. Beyond this perhaps more existential challenge, however, critics of methodological atheism have also pointed out that it is both too strong, requiring a self-assured judgment about what is and what is not possible

8. Rudolph, "Some Reflections on Approaches."

9. See, prominently, McCutcheon, *Critics Not Caretakers.*

10. Wiebe, *Religion and Truth.*

11. Berger, *Rumor of Angels*, ch. 3; cf. Yong, "'Tongues', Theology, and Social Sciences."

methodologically, and that a thoroughgoing practice of such an attitude bleeds over into a metaphysical atheism (or naturalism), which further confuses issues.[12]

In the wake of Berger's proposal, a more restrained *methodological agnosticism* has been on the table.[13] If Berger is to be able to genuinely salvage theology's claims to identify "signals of transcendence" (i.e., perceive and engage with the real world of religious life), then sociology is either inferior to theology (in never attaining more than the sociologist's construction about social reality) or it ought to at least be open to such signals from its own sociological vantage point, as Porpora argues against the early Berger.[14] Thus the sociology of religion ought to be at least open to the fact that the phenomenon under study provides a window into the transcendent domain that religious people claim to experience and interact with. Such a methodologically agnostic position would be more consistently empirical in suspending judgment long enough to explore purported realities from the viewpoint of religious people.

Historians have long developed a historiographic method that allows them to report the perspectives of their subjects rather than explaining them away. Thus it is appropriate to report of religious folk that they believed God acted or intervened in their lives, regardless of what the historian herself thinks is the case. Similarly, sociologists of religion like Margaret Poloma and Matthew Lee have adopted such a methodologically agnostic approach in their research on religion.[15] This posture allows for the viewpoints of their religious subjects—accessed through ethnographic and qualitative methods—to be registered in their work. Beyond this, however, they suggest that such a methodological agnosticism invites a further level of inquiry related to the effects that perceived experiences of the divine have on their research subjects. Whatever the nature of the experiences, perceptions have real effects, and such effects can be sociologically researched, measured, and even evaluated.[16]

Such methodological agnosticism promises to open up space not only for sociologists but also anthropologists to suspend judgment about the beliefs and practices of those who they are studying. It appears to provide a neutral space, one neither for nor against the views and convictions of

12. See Garrett, "Troublesome Transcendence," and Dawes, "In Defense of Naturalism."

13. See, e.g., Smart, *Science of Religion and Sociology of Knowledge*, 147–148; Bellah, "Religious Studies as 'New Religion,'" 106.

14. Porpora, "Methodological Atheism."

15. Lee and Poloma, *Sociological Study of Great Commandment*.

16. See also chapters in Part II of Lee and Yong, *Science and Theology of Godly Love*.

their subjects. But there remain real questions about the viability of such an agnostic neutral space, with some claiming that this supposed neutrality is "more ideal than real."[17] In order to understand such pessimism, consider that observer neutrality is practically impossible given observer bias, observer epistemic limitations, and observer effect (on those who are being observed).[18] In practice, then, methodological agnosticism may be a goal rather than any reality, although this is perhaps more the case in anthropology than sociology.

The third (not necessarily last) option, then, might be a kind of methodological theism, as a counterpart to methodological atheism or agnosticism. What this means, however, has been difficult to define. As unfolded in Berger's own case, his theistic commitments were part of his private (religious) life; his sociological methods, however, were putatively "atheistic." Certainly, Berger the (amateur) theologian operated according to a kind of methodological theism, but few of his sociological colleagues would have granted that such convictions should have had any implications for his work as a social scientist. In order for us to delve deeper into the logic of such methodological theism and its implications for the human sciences, then, we need to turn more explicitly to developments in the field of anthropology.

Over the last almost century, although perhaps less in the last generation, anthropologists have debated amongst themselves about the viability of "going native."[19] In its best sense, "going native" refers to the process of cultural adaptation that anthropologists undergo during their fieldwork so that they learn to empathize with and see the world from the perspective of their informants, members of the host culture.[20] What is disputed is whether those who have become immersed into the host culture's way of life, even to the point of undergoing a process of identity transformation, can remain objective in their analysis, evaluation, and scholarship as anthropologists. The latter sense of going native is certainly taboo in anthropological circles,[21] even if there is a wide spectrum of positions, from mere empathy to thoroughgoing acculturation.

---

17. Poewe, "Introduction: Nature, Globality, History," 15.

18. Donovan, "Neutrality in Religious Studies," 104.

19. Geertz, "'From the Native's Point of View,'" is cited along with E. E. Evans-Pritchard (1902–1973), as "two excellent examples of superior fieldworkers and innovative theorists who abandoned the attempt to establish scientific rigor and universal laws in anthropology as a direct result of their adherence to a too literal-minded empiricism in the face of fieldwork" (Salamone, "Epistemological Implications of Fieldwork," 51).

20. Smart, Concept and Empathy.

21. Ewing, "Dreams from a Saint."

The contemporary postmodern climate has certainly contributed to the growing sense among anthropologists that even if none ever went native, all need to acknowledge that the days of ethnographic fieldwork resulting in "objective" representations of native "subjects" are long over.[22] Increasingly prominent among ethnographic studies are reflections on the intersubjective implications of fieldwork, and how this recognition has impacted the discipline. This is a move beyond reflectiveness to self-reflexivity—"In ordinary 'reflectiveness,' one is conscious of oneself as an Other, but in 'reflexivity,' one is conscious of *being self-conscious* of oneself as an Other"[23]—so that the lines are blurred between representations of others as subjects of study and representations of the self as a studying subject. So even if anthropologists do not claim to have gone native, they are also calling for a kind of "reciprocal ethnography" wherein the representation of others involves self-representation and vice versa.[24] More radically conceived is a kind of decentered notion of the anthropological self, understood ethnographically in terms of "multiple definitions of selves in specific situations . . . 'selves' as potential sites for the play of multiple discourses and shifting, multiple subject-positions."[25] All of this has combined to open up space for anthropologists to study their own religious tradition. In these cases, however, unlike when Berger had to switch disciplinary hats almost a generation ago—to that of an (amateur) theologian to talk theologically—anthropologists are suggesting it is possible to not only "go" native, but to "be" native in ways that not only retain a form of recognizable scholarly objectivity, including both emic and etic points of view, but also provide distinctive perspectives on both the work of ethnography and anthropological theory.[26]

While few would expect that such a "believer's approach" will disappear anytime soon in anthropological studies, this is not to say that no difficult questions remain. Anthropologists remain concerned about at least two tendencies. On the one hand, in the contemporary postmodern milieu, some are anxious that the "going native" trend results in a form of identity

22. See especially Tyler, "Post-Modern Ethnography." By using the rhetoric of postmodernism, I am only following what I am finding in the literature. My own predilections are to talk about "late modernity" rather than about postmodernity.

23. Tedlock, "From Participant Observation to Observation of Participation," 85 n.16.

24. Lawless, *Holy Women, Wholly Women*, esp. 14.

25. Kondo, *Crafting Selves*, 44.

26. See Howell, "The Anthropology of Christianity," 361, who discusses in these terms the work of evangelical African American anthropologist Frederick, *Between Sundays*. See also Howell, "The Repugnant Cultural Other Speaks Back," and Jacobs-Huey, "Natives Are Gazing and Talking Back."

politics that inhibits serious engagement with the methodological issues. In this case, simply speaking from a particular perspective "is an attempt to resolve the epistemological problem of disciplinary knowledge production through the assertion of an inappropriate ontological privilege."[27] So, I agree that arguments will still need to be produced about the relevance of a scholar's identity for scholarship. On the other hand, and more worrisome epistemologically, philosophically, and methodologically, are the implications of "going native." Here the questions involve what it means to understand the religious point of view. While some might say that such understanding is achieved if one can explain the *why* of a religious belief or practice in ways that are recognizable by an insider, the argument might also be made that unless one were convinced of such from that emic perspective, one has not really grasped the insider's viewpoint. Against this, of course, the methodological naturalist (or atheist) might respond that true explanation in the study of religion needs to focus on horizontal rather than transcendental causes,[28] the latter at least lying beyond the ken of scientific inquiry if not altogether meaningless.

The preceding no doubt covers too much too fast, and its interdisciplinary analyses and generalizations are surely open to contestation from multiple angles. My goal, however, is neither to provide a scientifically rigorous taxonomy nor to delineate exhaustively the issues under adjudication. Instead, we have explored the ferment in the study of religion through a multidisciplinary assessment of its major methodological currents. No definitive way forward is in sight, despite the fact that this or that theoretical voice presumes to have made a final pronouncement. What seems undeniable, however, is that the contemporary methodological dis-ease, which the main lines of have been here demarcated, begs for a fresh reconsideration. Beyond the fact that our present era is seeing the abandonment of the facts-values distinction, "[t]he hollowness of empiricism, the perplexing plurality of perspectives, the urgency of contemporary social problems, all catalyze the quest for an outlook which offers authentically 'human' alternatives."[29]

ANDRÉ DROOGERS'S METHODOLOGICAL LUDISM AND MEANING-MAKING

How then to proceed? Although distinct from the natural sciences in important respects (i.e., related to experimental replicability, for instance),

27. Ritchie, "Contesting Secularism," 452.

28. Prozesky, "Explanations of Religion."

29. Lyon, "Idea of a Christian Sociology," 240.

the human sciences are no less scientific enterprises in involving data observation, interpretive understanding, and evaluative judgment. Appropriate forms of the latter (that require some degree of objective separation) presume substantial achievements in the former arena (which depend on some degree of subjective participation). It might seem as if the study of religion ought to include moments for both methodological atheism and methodological theism. While some might then conclude that this is what a methodologically agnostic approach provides, I think there is a difference. The latter's suspension of judgment may theoretically never be lifted; the former two postures, however, are sustained by some degree of normative reasoning. My sense, however, is that both are needed, at least at different moments, for the study of religion.

Into the fray, then, comes the proposal of André Droogers. In brief, Droogers invites us to consider what he calls a methodological ludism, a playful mode of studying the religions that promises a path forward beyond either reductionism (our methodological atheism) and religionism (our methodological theism),[30] but yet—and here is the key—leaves neither behind. In what follows, I provide some biographical perspective, outline his ludic perspective, and provide a brief application to the anthropology of pentecostal-charismatic Christianity (which Droogers has studied and the form of religiosity with which I, as a theologian, identify).

Since 2006 Droogers has been Emeritus Professor of Cultural Anthropology in the Department of Social and Cultural Anthropology at the Vrije Universiteit, Amsterdam.[31] Raised in and long affiliated with the Dutch Reformed Church (with associations with the *Gereformeerde* and the *Hervormde* sides of the divide), Droogers earned his PhD in cultural anthropology in 1974 with a study of the initiation rituals among the Wagenia of Kisangani, Zaire.[32] After numerous stints of fieldwork in Africa in the 1970s, he spent the first half of the 1980s in Brazil studying Afro-Brazilian religions and pentecostalism (with four more months later in 1987 traveling throughout South America). Since 1985 he has been at the Vrije Universiteit, promoted to full professor in 1988, and engaged with various research projects in that position since.

Droogers tells us that he initially made the connection between play and religion under the mentorship of Jan van Baal (1909–1992), the first

30. Thus the title of chapter 14, "Methodological Ludism: Beyond Religionism and Reductionism," in Droogers, *Play and Power in Religion*.

31. The following biographical remarks derive in large part from the introductory chapter to Droogers' recent *Play and Power in Religion* (2012), which includes seventeen previously published articles that summarize the major thrusts of his life's work.

32. See Droogers, *Dangerous Journey*.

chair holder in anthropology of religion in the Netherlands. This perspective, informed by additional theoretical studies such as those of the ritual anthropologist Victor Turner (1920–1983) and the Dutch historian Johan Huizinga (1872–1945), alerted him to the playful character of ritual during his fieldwork experiences in both Africa and South America. Huizinga's *Homo Ludens* by this time, of course, had become somewhat of a classic.[33] Human beings are inherently players; play itself is both fun and serious (seriously fun, even); is enacted freely and voluntarily; is bracketed out of life's other routines (thus being scheduled in time and limited in space), but yet is an inherent part of life itself; is rule governed yet is full of uncertainty, chance, and tension (not to mention intensity); can be instrumentally understood in some senses (i.e., to the degree that the ludic releases human stress) but yet also serves nothing but its own purposes in other fundamental senses. Religious rites and rituals are also forms of play through which human beings make meaning and construct their lives, Huizinga urged: "the unity and indivisibility of belief and unbelief, the indissoluble connection between sacred earnest and 'make-believe' or 'fun', are best understood in the concept of play itself."[34] Thus did Huizinga conclude the initial, foundational chapter of his work: "Primitive, or let us say, archaic ritual is thus sacred play, indispensable for the well-being of the community, fecund of cosmic insight and social development but always play in the sense Plato [Huizinga references and discusses Plato's conception in *The Laws*] gave to it—an action accomplishing itself outside and above the necessities and seriousness of everyday life. In this sphere of sacred play the child and the poet are at home with the savage."[35]

Droogers has not only been a keen observer of the deep ludic dimension of religion—noticing, for instance, that believers also assume the "as if" mode across the spectrum from existential doubt to sincere "certain" belief no less than anthropological fieldworkers—but he has also suggested that the ludic posture might provide methodological insights for students of religion. His working definition of the ludic, fairly consistently articulated and elaborated since 1996 when he first formulated it, suggests that "the ludic is the capacity to deal simultaneously and subjunctively with two or more ways of classifying reality."[36] There are two elements of this definition that need to be unpacked.

---

33. Huizinga, *Homo Ludens*.
34. Ibid., 24.
35. Ibid., 25–26.
36. Droogers, *Play and Power in Religion*, 321.

First, the ludic stance enables, invites, and even requires human beings to live in two forms of reality simultaneously. Human play involves such multireality inhabitation. In a real sense, when human beings enter into play, they step out of their ordinary time and space into another agreed upon mode of engagement with others. At one level, ordinary life is put on hold. Yet the seriousness with which we attend to our playing suggests that it would be inappropriate to think of playful reality in merely fictive terms. Yes, the world of play is a world of make-believe, but it is no less real or serious for all that. Skillful players are those very adept at applying real world skills in their playful activities—living and performing simultaneously in both worlds. Droogers calls this the capacity for a "double awareness," following Paul Proyser.[37] So while ending or leaving play involves a return to conventional reality, in effect, playing itself can be understood also as a form of conventional reality. Applied to religion, "[b]elievers play with the possibility of two realities, one natural and one supernatural. Their play can become so engaged that the two realities merge into one or at least position themselves on the same spectrum."[38]

This observation opens up to Droogers's emphasis on the subjunctive nature of the ludic mode. The subjective mood—and here Droogers has consistently followed Turner—involves the "domain of the 'as if,' to be distinguished from the indicative 'as is.'"[39] There are at least two senses in which play proceeds subjunctively. First, players imagine the possibilities before them in entering and executing play; second, players imagine the possibilities before those who they are playing with in order to anticipate and react to how play transpires. Play thus activates the human capacity of entering into another "as if" realm, one pregnant with possibilities, engaging the imagination, inviting improvisation, and requiring innovation. Again, applied to religion, Droogers writes: "That which is specifically religious in play is the hunch—and often the experience—that there is another dimension, beyond the differentiating and restricting limits of time and space, that transforms fragmentedness into wholeness."[40]

What are the methodological implications of ludism not only for anthropology but also, as Droogers is keenly aware, for religious studies and theology? If play involves "the human capacity to articulate, in a subjunctive, connectionist manner,[41] dissimilar ways of classifying reality, thus pre-

37. See ibid., 75, 106, 137, 333, and Proyser, *Dynamic Psychology of Religion.*

38. Droogers, *Play and Power in Religion*, 396.

39. Ibid., 106.

40. Ibid., 351.

41. Throughout, Droogers draws on recent connectionist developments in the

senting alternatives to dominant views,"[42] what are its broader applications? Because such subjunctivity is "stereophonic,"[43] allowing us "to listen to two channels at the same time,"[44] and playing out "an inner dialogue of contrasting views,"[45] the ludic aspect of human potential enables people to simultaneously and subjunctively deal with, classify, and respond to contrasting phenomena and possibilities. More, a ludic approach makes possible "the simultaneous adoption of two or more perspectives" and thus "opens up the scholar's eyes to the believer's 'constellation' view."[46]

Methodologically speaking, Droogers suggests that ludism both accomplishes all that the atheistic, theistic, and agnostic points of view offer, yet goes beyond them. This is because, first, a methodological ludism "offers the extra of a simultaneous view. This is not necessarily a synthesis, but much more an overview of the total constellation of possibilities. It is also more than empathy, since the subjunctive 'make-believe' guarantees a sympathy that is honest and absolute as long as it lasts."[47] In this sense, a ludic approach goes beyond religionist (which seeks only to believe) and reductionist (which seeks only to be critical) perspectives. With regard to methodological agnosticism, on the other hand, a ludic approach "is not the same as abstention, but rather the—albeit temporary—acceptance, through empathic participation, of a particular religious or scientific claim to truth."[48] Hence, "[t]he difference is that in methodological ludism the claim to truth is—temporarily but seriously—accepted and not just considered unverifiable in a vaguely tolerant or politically correct way."[49] Ludism underwrites in a subjunctive attitude, then, both the observational methods of the critic and the participative presence of the believer.

To be sure, the ludic posture is eclectic, but it is not relativistic. Rather, "[i]t is the condition of simultaneity, instead of coexistence, that prevents relativism. In that manner the ludic also points to a way beyond a choice

---

cognitive and neurological sciences that are uncovering how the two halves and various spheres of the brain continuously function simultaneously, engaged in "parallel processing," as it were, in sorting, evaluating, and directing human perception, experience, and activity.

42. Droogers, *Play and Power in Religion*, 381.

43. Ibid., 75.

44. Ibid., 380.

45. Ibid., 346.

46. Ibid., 331.

47. Ibid., 332.

48. Ibid., 358.

49. Ibid., 383.

between objectivity and subjectivity."[50] This is because it both simultaneously and separately enables emic (insider, methodologically theistic) and etic (outsider, methodologically atheistic and agnostic) perspectives,[51] and hence can render judgment where necessary from one or both of these perspectives. Thus methodological ludism honors the anthropological value of cultural relativism, but does not fall into a moral relativism.[52]

Before transitioning to more explicitly theological considerations, I want to provide some more autobiographical considerations for why I find Droogers's methodological ludism so provocative even while raising a tangential question. As I have already indicated, much of Droogers's research, especially in South America, was conducted among pentecostal communities and churches.[53] While Droogers certainly recognizes the element of play in pentecostal ritual, he has more consistently interpreted pentecostalism according to the category of power.[54] While I am not challenging Droogers's understanding of pentecostalism,[55] there is a deep ludic dimension to pentecostal spirituality that leads me, as a pentecostal theologian, to resonate with the preceding analysis. Here I am referring not only to the spontaneity and improvisational modality of pentecostal spirituality and praxis, but also what might be called its subjunctive imagination.[56] The pentecostal spirit, I suggest, is a posture of faith that is open to new possibilities (one form of what Berger calls signals of transcendence), even possibly beyond what has

50. Ibid., 334.

51. Ibid., 342–43.

52. Ibid., 358. Another way anthropologists defend moral judgment is via "methodological relativism," in which judgment is permissible in stages, following research leading to understanding of a culture on its terms. See Rynkiewich, *Soul, Self, and Society*, 29. For further, albeit succinct, discussion of why cultural relativism need not fall into moral relativism, see Howell and Paris, *Introducing Cultural Anthropology*, 31–32.

53. This research has been published in numerous articles (some of which are gathered in Droogers, *Play and Power in Religion*) and at least three English-language volumes: Boudewijnse and Droogers, eds., *More Than Opium*; Corten and Marshall, eds., *Between Babel and Pentecost*; and Droogers and van der Laan, eds., *Fruitful in This Land*. Interestingly, even in a book titled *Playful Religion*, edited by van Harskamp et al., to which Droogers contributed four essays, the three on pentecostalism did not accentuate the playful character of pentecostal spirituality. That task was left up to another contributor to the volume, Clarke, in his "Playful Religion?"

54. Droogers, *Play and Power in Religion*, chs. 4, 8, 12, 13.

55. He has become one of the most respected anthropological theorists of pentecostalism, e.g., Anderson et al., *Studying Global Pentecostalism*; Droogers, "Cultural Dimension of Pentecostalism."

56. Vondey, *Beyond Pentecostalism*, ch. 1; Wariboko, *Pentecostal Principle*; Suurmond, *Word and Spirit at Play*.

been previously thought or even imagined.[57] Here I digress into a phenomenological, if not quasi-theological, mode prematurely. My critical point (if it can indeed be called such amidst my broad appreciation for Droogers's proposals) is that an understanding of religion as play provides windows into understanding pentecostalism that Droogers may have inadvertently downplayed (pun intended) in his focus on pentecostal power. This leads then to my theological point: is the methodological ludism Droogers suggests applicable for the scholar of religion and student of theological studies, broadly conceived, and if so, what are the implications?

A LUDIC APPROACH TO RELIGIOUS STUDIES AND THEOLOGY?

I now want to reflect on the deliverances of Droogers's methodological ludism for the study and especially teaching of religion and for certain aspects of the contemporary theological task.[58] As we shall see, I think we need something like a ludic approach that includes, but does not leave behind, the atheistic, theistic, and even agnostic modes of engagement. I am going to focus, however, on cases in which scholars of religion or theologians study and engage a religious tradition other than their own, since that raises the more interesting questions for discussion. To be sure, it is possible to apply our discussion in these disciplines to cases of engaging the home tradition, which will predominate when talking about theologians. In such cases, I still think that a ludic model suffices: the scholar of religion or theologian will operate primarily in a theistic or believer's perspective, albeit ludically (not ludicrously, as some might suggest!) entertaining an agnostic or skeptical posture when genuine questions emerge and even on occasion adopting an atheistic—by which I mean critical—stance when warranted (i.e., when needing to challenge emic conventions within the tradition). Droogers himself displays these characteristics in his research in the Dutch context, which he studies comparatively vis-à-vis new immigrant religious movements (primarily pentecostalism) that are emerging as transnational communities. Consider the following extensions and elaborations from a religious studies and theological perspective of Droogers's own reflections about comparative theology and interreligious dialogue (see these terms in the index of Droogers, *Play and Power in Religion: Collected Essays*), although I will also

57. Smith, "Is There Room for Surprise in the Natural World?"

58. Droogers has himself already begun to address those working in religious studies (e.g., Droogers, "Towards the Concerned Study of Religion"); consider the following as complementary proposals from a more specifically theological perspective.

conclude with some critical reflections on a ludic methodology vis-à-vis the possibility of "going native" for scholars of religion and theologians, something Droogers is understandably silent about.

Does the ludic approach suggest that scholars of religion, in their studying of traditions other than their own, no longer need to adopt only one of the three dominant methodological stances in their work but can, even simultaneously, adopt two or even all three? The advantages of a ludic orientation would be at least the following. First, the scholar of religion would be able with integrity (seriousness) to enter subjunctively into the world she is studying and attempt to understand it from the inside. Second, concurrently, the scholar can maintain her critical objectivity, perhaps shifting emic and etic perspectives, or perhaps considering emic in light of etic view points and vice versa. Third, a ludic form of research and reflection could subjunctively consider hitherto unrecognizable alternatives now possible through various emic and etic combinations, both for her scholarship but also possibly even for her life of faith (if she has one).[59] Thus, the scholar embraces the otherness of the religious tradition as her own, in effect bracketing, but never completely suspending, her scholarly identity. A believer's perspective is inculcated, while the vantage point of the scholarly critic remains in the background. On this or that perception, the scholar can adopt an agnostic response, albeit one that is subject to the ebb and flow of ongoing inquiry and consideration.

Such a ludic model is even more important in the religious studies classroom. Especially in liberal arts college and university environments (even amidst institutions with confessional affiliations), teachers can model the advantages of methodological ludism for their students.[60] Such playful yet intensely serious study allows students to engage in the ultimate form of evaluation by asking what is at stake, even normatively, for them as students. Whereas the older model emphasizing scholarly objectivity would have separated the *facts* of the study of religions from the *values* of religious life, a ludic comportment invites students to consider how, if at all, the values of the other faith translate into their own lives. Yet along the way, methodological ludism admonishes against any naïve nativism. Students of other

59. Joel Robbins, in his article, "Anthropology and Theology," asks what, if anything, is at stake for anthropologists in light of the discipline of theology and the deliverances of the theologians. As he is probing to identify how taking theology seriously makes a difference to anthropologists, I am led to ask how taking the religious way of life of others seriously potentially makes a kind of double difference—for scholarship and for religious life—for scholars of religion.

60. Jaffee, "Fessing Up in Theory," does not deploy Droogers's model, but his urging about the importance of both *professing* (the responsibility of the scholar) and *confessing* (the response of the believer) in the classroom invites a ludic interpolation.

religions remain outsiders, and this does not need to be either denied or apologized for. Yet such an "objective" viewpoint functions simultaneously with an empathic, even playful, subjective entering into another world.

I turn now to ask about the implications of methodological ludism for theology. Space limitations prohibit any extensive discussion, but I will take up the nexus of theological work at the interface where the theologian meets other religious traditions in a pluralistic world. At this intersection, the theological tasks involve thinking theologically about religious plurality in general and about other faith traditions in particular, the form of inter-faith or interreligious engagement along with its methods and goals, and the rethinking of the theological task as a whole in light of the interfaith encounter.[61] Certainly theological work proceeds in many guises, some of which are outside of confessional frameworks, but the same methodological options are available, generally speaking. An atheistic approach would be to view the other religious way of life (including its beliefs and practices) objec-tively, usually serving polemical or apologetic goals. A theistic or believer's mode of exploration would be willing, at least, to enter empathetically into the other faith and try to comprehend its logic from the inside. The method-ological ludist would neither have to compromise her faith commitments, if any, nor be disingenuous about her empathetic openness to the other faith.

There are two interrelated dimensions of theological work that are afforded by a ludic stance. First, understanding religious traditions is ir-reducible to a cognitive register. Religious ways of life resist reduction to their doctrinal or propositional constructs.[62] A ludic theologian thus will recognize that the subjunctive capacity to adopt multiple intellectual frameworks will be enhanced by a more holistic, playful immersion into the world of the religious other. Second, and building on the former, un-derstanding leads to theological (re)construction. Theological work in the third millennium will be increasingly dialogical and such conversations will cross religious lines. Theological reflection in a religiously pluralistic world will be reflexive in the anthropological sense, self-consciously aware of the methodological challenges involved in confessional commitments on the one hand but also open to insights from outside on the other hand. As such, theological projects will be ludically interreligious: those who are able to cross over into other faiths in deeper ways will return to construct more

61. See further Yong, *Beyond the Impasse*, *Hospitality and the Other*, and *Pneumatol-ogy and the Christian-Buddhist Dialogue*.

62. Thus, for instance, religious life in Aquinas and Calvin involves faith, affective reorientation, and the witness of the Spirit respectively, as shown by Dawes, "Religious Studies, Faith."

plausible theological hypotheses that will have greater explanatory power in a new global context.[63]

Interreligious crossover and return is inherently ludic, as Droogers understands it. Adapting Droogers's methodological ludism within the framework of a Lakatosian scientific research program for constructive theologians,[64] the Lakatosian "hard core" is the confessional faith commitments of the theologian, while the Lakatosian "auxiliary belt" is the data from other faith traditions whose truths, goodness, and beauty will need to be factored into the theological world- and life view of the home tradition. The one difference may be that the theologian's faith commitments may be less falsifiable, at least existentially speaking, than the Lakatosian "hard core" by the "auxiliary belt" that constitutes the data of other faiths.

But is that the case? Perhaps falsifiable is too strong of a word in the case of theology,[65] but surely theologians can also change their minds, even radically. That should certainly be the case if they are truly open to following the evidence where it may lead. In the extreme case, the collapse of the theological "hard core" may invite disaffiliation of theologians from their religious community, and maybe even an entering into that of another faith tradition. Such a turn of events would be considered apostasy in theological terms and framed in terms of religious conversion. In the case of students of religion, the collapse of their "hard core" may simply result in having to completely rethink their explanatory hypotheses about religion. In some cases, the other faith may prove to be more convincing as an overall personal construct, leading to what anthropologists call "going native." People convert from being of no faith to being of faith, or from one faith to another faith, and then grow in faith also—all by entering into, subjunctively, the way of life represented by that otherness. Insofar as anthropologists, scholars of religion, and theologians are people, they are also susceptible to following out the implications of such subjunctive excursions. This is one aspect of the ludism that has more than the methodological implications recognized in Droogers's earlier work.[66]

63. Cobb Jr., *Beyond Dialogue*.

64. See Lakatos, *Methodology of Scientific Research Programmes*, more succinctly in the 1978 publication, 91–195.

65. For Christians, presumably, finding the dead body of Jesus would qualify to falsify its truth claims and, in Lakatosian terms, undermine the Christian theological task as a research program. Yet I am not sure how feasible such a criterion of falsification is, even as I am unsure that theology can provide adequate falsification criterion. Some would therefore conclude that theology in this sense differs from science in its incapacity to specify the conditions under which it is falsifiable.

66. More recently, Droogers has been wrestling with the existential risks involved in the ludic mode—e.g., André F. Droogers, "Playing with Perspectives." My thanks to

This raises a set of questions about the viability of Droogers's ludic model, whether or not it has the capacity to address instances of going native. By and large, I think there are resources within the model for adaptation to the variety these cases constitute. In the case of the scholar of religion, it is possible that such "conversion" results in giving up the scholarly identity. That would certainly be the default expectation from the methodological atheists who think that scholars cannot give up on their objective stance toward the subjects of their study. Yet why can't the scholar of religion simply switch ludic frames so her now-native perspective is negotiated afresh vis-à-vis her scholarly identity? Methodological ludism makes no prescriptions about faith commitments; it only asserts that the ludic character of life, religion, and scholarship enables simultaneous and subjunctive participation in multiple settings and positions.

The more complicated cases involve the missionary anthropologist or missionary scholar of religion engaging with other religions, and even committing to at least a form of going native. While there has been a great deal of tension in the relationship of especially the discipline of Christian missiology with that of anthropology,[67] there are as many similarities between these undertakings in terms of both missionaries and anthropologists as outsiders seeking emic perspectives and, in the case of the latter, insider recognition.[68] The theological challenge involves identifying when the missionary efforts to contextualize, accommodate, and enculturate her faith into the other culture becomes an assimilation into that culture and its religious ways of life. The former ways of "going native" are acceptable,[69] but not the latter. One might even say, in light of this discussion, that what anthropologists and scholars of religion fear is not the kind of empathy that allows them to get inside the world view and way of life that they are studying, but the kind of "going native" that leads to the loss of the objective stance and turns the scholar into a mere apologist. Still, there is a fine, maybe indiscernible, line between apologetics and an ethnography that leads readers to empathize with the "other" that is being described.

As with missiologists, theologians have similar concerns about going native in relationship to their study and embrace of other faiths. To do so would be to have one's identity transformed in a fundamental way. There is no *a priori* reason why a ludic approach to the study of religions,

---

Professor Droogers for sharing an earlier version of this chapter with me.

67. For some discussion of the perennial friction, see Berg, "More Than You Think."

68. Cf. the astute discussion by van der Geest, "Anthropologists and Missionaries," and "Shifting Positions Between Anthropology, Religion, Development."

69. Keidel, *Career-Defining Crises in Mission.*

or the interfaith encounter, should prohibit such developments. Empathic consideration of other realities will certainly infuse human beings with an expanded range of values, and occasionally, when the "as if" mode leads to a genuine "as is" reality, bring about different commitments. This applies no less to anthropologists and scholars of religion than it does to theologians and even missiologists (although perhaps less often in the latter case). When this happens, however, the ludic stance simply switches with regard to the person's primary and secondary identities.[70]

But what about the perhaps special case of dual- or multiple-religious belonging? Here I am referring to a kind of going native that does not necessarily leave behind one's prior commitments. I suggest that a ludic perspective can make sense of the nature of double-belonging across a broad spectrum.[71] Some double-belongers adopt sequential moments in which they practice their faith, alternating between practices in order to maintain the authenticity and integrity of each while yet attempting to live faithfully to both; other double-belongers either still have a primary identity that provides the overarching framework for understanding the secondary identity or attempt to synthesize—scholars of religion would say "syncretize," albeit without its pejorative overtones—their faith commitments.[72] Presuming for the moment the validity of these double-religious identities, a ludic account would be open to the simultaneous operation of three perspectives—that of the scholarly discipline plus that of the two religious tradition. As scholars or theologians, such double-belongers will engage subjunctively with the triad of possible viewpoints at any given juncture.[73]

In this last part of the chapter I have explored the fecundity of Droogers's anthropologically informed methodological ludism for religious studies and theology respectively. Given the perspectival character of all human knowing and meaning-making, I think, as a scholar of religion and

70. Or, as is more often the case, one's primary identity expands in order to account for perspectives afforded by the ludic stance regarding the "natives' point of view"; see, for instance, the perceptively self-reflexive analysis by Kim Knibbe about how the "play" of the fieldworker is similar to that of an earnest "seeker" (Knibbe and Droogers, "Methodological Ludism").

71. One form of double-belonging ought not to be technically called such, but it involves the kind of deep crossover immersion into another religious-cultural tradition so that the other tradition becomes a resource for the theologian's craft (see Yong, "Francis X. Clooney's 'Dual Religious Belonging'" [ch. 10 in this volume]).

72. Drew, *Buddhist and Christian?*, suggests that Roger Corless can be understood as a "sequential" double-belonger, while the rest of the Buddhist-Christians she studied either have one primary identity or attempt synthetic lives—all with greater or lesser degrees of success (at least according to Drew's criteria).

73. I attempt something of such a triadic constructive theology in my *Cosmic Breath*.

especially as a comparative and constructive theologian, that some kind of subjunctive engagement across religious lines is imperative for contemporary scholarship in these arenas. The comparative, interreligious, and constructive theological ludist will be able to, with integrity, entertain more than one religious world view and way of life without giving up on her primary theological and religious commitments. This enables the persistence of both the etic scholarly posture—as represented by both the discipline of inquiry and the faith commitments, if any—and yet also makes possible emic sensitivities (to the insiders' viewpoints and values). Methodological ludism in the study of religion allows, as Droogers suggests, atheistic, theistic, and even agnostic perspectives, simultaneously, sequentially, and dynamically. Applied to the theological laboratory, the same outsider-insider-agnostic variables pertain, with different theologians navigating with and between these differently. In the process, imaginative possibilities open up from the ludic stance that suggests that none of these—reductionism, religionism, or agnosticism—need have the final word.[74]

74. Research for this chapter was generously funded by the Biola University Center for Christian Thought. Thanks to Naomi Haynes for her help in arranging presentation of a previous draft to members (especially faculty Joel Robbins and Jon Bialecki and graduate students) of the Department of Anthropology at the University of California at San Diego on 1 May, 2012. The feedback from the audience on this occasion has helped improve the article. I am grateful also to André Droogers, Christopher Stephenson, Tony Richie, and my graduate assistants, Evan Rosa and Vincent Le, for their help with various aspects of this chapter.

CHAPTER 12

Toward a Relational Apologetics in Global Context

A Review Essay of Benno van den Toren's *Christian Apologetics as Cross-Cultural Dialogue*

LET ME SAY UP front that van den Toren's book takes the discussion of apologetics to a whole new level.[1] In the distant background is a Kampen Theological University (Dutch-language) PhD thesis on Barth and apologetics,[2] from which the central ideas have been leavened by eight years of living and teaching in the Central African Republic. The work of at least four or five other books later, many of these interfacing with the theme of apologetics as well as with a broad spectrum of approaches to apologetics, informs the present contribution by this current dean of the faculty at Wycliffe Hall, Oxford.

The argument of the eight chapters is wide ranging. The first chapter lays out the two challenges for Christian apologetics in our time: that of postmodernist relativism and skepticism and of multicultural pluralism. The next two chapters both detail the valid postmodern criticisms of modern Western apologetics (i.e., its foundationalism, the linguistic turn, and individualism) and articulate a specifically theological understanding and critique of the modern and postmodern Western theological enterprises (as complicit with the modernist emphasis on freedom and autonomy and as presuming the subject-object dualism bequeathed by modernity). Chapters

1. van den Toren, *Christian Apologetics as Cross-Cultural Dialogue*.
2. van den Toren, *Breuk en brug*.

four and five then begin the constructive argument, initially by presenting a Christian anthropology of relationality (with God, the creation, and others), and a Christian theology of creation in sophisticated dialogue with modern, late modern, and postmodern developments in philosophy of science that argue toward a critical realist and yet hermeneutical epistemology (the metaphor used is that knowing works like reading books: we begin with some knowledge but this can be adjusted depending on what we find). The final three chapters constitute the sketch of how Christian apologetics can proceed in a postmodern and multicultural world as cross-cultural dialogue. This involves a contextual approach to apologetics (chapter six); suggests a goal of cross-cultural *persuasion*—as opposed to polemical debate focused on winning and avoiding losing—that identifies barriers, communicates Christ contextually as the illuminating power of the whole, exploits bridge-heads (connection points), utilizes antinomies (or tensions and anomalies), and emerges out of a church that presents itself as a counter-cultural and alternative plausibility structure (chapter seven); and focuses on reaching the reasons of the heart via being attentive to the desires and will of people and trusting in the power of the cross of Christ (chapter eight). Van den Toren believes that "effective apologetics is person- and culture-relative and contextual" (55), and his book is an extended argument for such a vision.

There is much that the preceding overview does not capture. The author sympathetically but not uncritically engages a host of apologetic strategies, whether that of Lindbeck (van den Toren's views are consistent with postliberal ad hoc apologetic practices but he questions their theoretical premises), Barth (there is acceptance of Barth's critique of liberalism but severe qualification of at least the early *Nein!*, which is shown to be too beholden to the modernist subject-object cleavage), Van Til (his presuppositionalism rightly identifies our situatedness as knowing creatures, but his idealism, among other commitments, is inconsistent with central aspects of Christian praxis), or evangelical rationalism and evidentialism (which presume universal reason or access to non-culturally relative criteria), among others. He takes seriously the tradition-dependent character of all knowing, while mounting a convincing argument about how this ought to shape, but not impede, the apologetic enterprise. Part of the implication, repeatedly stressed, is that Christian claims do have universal application, but such has to be argued for a posteriorly rather than presumed in an a priori sense. Yet the proposal is appropriately and even fundamentally theological throughout, as in the argument that situates cultural diversity within a theology of creation rather than fall (e.g., 103–105). But the theological commitments undergirding the book also do not inhibit—perhaps they even motivate—the robustly dialogical and helpfully practical aspects of the discussion. The constructive moves operate at multiple levels, recognizing the intellectual character of the apologetic task on the one hand while also aware that people are not floating heads but embodied, affective, and communal creatures.

I would like to pay tribute to the achievement that is this volume by entering into a conversation with the author along five interconnecting and overlapping trajectories: epistemology, the dialogical encounter, ecclesiology, eschatology, and Christology. The following is meant not to critically dismantle the argument—after all, I confess to be largely sympathetic to the basic thrust of the book—but to engage with some of the hopefully productive tensions that may be noticeable even within its ranks. Perhaps these will be illuminating regarding the ongoing challenges confronting Christian apologetics in a postmodern and multicultural world.

Epistemological issues: I have in mind a few observations and questions here, pertaining both to Christians and to non-Christians. For the former, very few Christians, especially evangelicals of the sort that I hang around (and arguably also who reside in van den Toren's circles), would quibble with the theological claim that while God's self-revelation is most clearly presented and preserved in the Bible, fallen human beings are in need of the illumination of the Holy Spirit in order not only to comprehend but to accept its claims. At a fundamental level, as Barth also suggests, and as it appears van den Toren would agree (83), even Christians remain impacted by the noetic effects of sin. So if "completely contrasting cultures can all be an outworking of the tensions that make up the human being as a sinner" (168), "Christian culture"—however we might understand such—is also not exempt from this characterization. What is epistemologically salvific for Christians is that the person and work of the Holy Spirit ameliorate the effects of the fall and thus enable us to be transformed by the gospel message found in Scripture.

But of course the question then arises about how non-Christians can come to see, much less be convinced about, the biblical message. Are human beings in need of the regenerating work of the Holy Spirit in order that the noetic effects of sin on our embodied and affective reason is restored (204–205)? Or perhaps full regeneration follows from the presalvific work of the Spirit that convicts the world "about sin and righteousness and judgement" (John 16:8)? Does such conviction only follow the (dialogical) proclamation of the biblical message? But would not others then also claim epistemic privileges, such as Buddhists insisting that unless non-Buddhist were to experience awakening they would not truly see things as they really are? Stepping back from the fray, however, van den Toren rightly notes that experiences on their own, even those of a spiritual sort, are unreliable—everyone has them but few are led to Christian conversion on that account.

Even religiously "self-authenticating experiences" (204) are ambiguous and have to be adjudicated within communities and traditions of discourse.

The epistemological question, however, is exacerbated when we consider how individuals are situated within such communities and traditions of reasoning. While those interested in engaging in cross-cultural apologetics can gain much from van den Toren's book with regard to how to approach and engage non-Christian persons, his entire argument recognizes that individuals are never isolated but are part of larger communities and even cultures. Cognition is thus constituted not only of the intellect but also our embodiment, affectivity, and the social and communal matrices that give shape to human lives. Christian apologetics thus is addressed to whole persons (34), but more precisely, to whole persons in communities. Hence, the nature of Christian apologetics is not only personally contextual, but also communally contextual. But in that case, dialogue, conversation, and even proclamation are directed to groups as well. If so, our rhetoric will be more abstract (than concrete) and our discourse more general (than particular).

But is that so? Perhaps the particularity of the gospel account (140) is as powerful as it is precisely because it is so generalizable (and hence universalizable)?! How might this be? The pentecostal side of me is tempted to suggest this happens perhaps by the Holy Spirit. While I will return to the pneumatological aspect later, perhaps at this point it is better to emphasize more the framework of common grace (that van den Toren and many of his Reformed interlocutors will affirm in some or another respect) that enables the work of the Spirit before, during, and after the presentation of the gospel. Or, for those who are more Wesleyan in their theological sensibilities, perhaps the common- and saving-grace distinctions are still too dualistic, and the notion of prevenient grace less so. Within this Wesleyan approach, the prevenient workings of the Spirit, enabled by the cross of Christ, provides for those "bridgeheads" wherein those in Christ meet those not yet in Christ.

This leads us to a discussion of the dialogical encounter. I appreciate van den Toren's urging Christian apologists to approach non-Christians not seeking to win arguments, but looking to be persuasive. The former drives up defenses and confirms for others why they ought to be suspicious of Christians to begin with. Persuasive reason, however, is less defensively minded and more invitational. Its narrative and testimonial approach invites others to share their own stories as well. Through such mutual interaction, people inevitably begin to enter into our world—van den Toren implies that others come to find themselves, perhaps unknowingly, "with one foot already within the Christian circle" (184)—and they begin to engage us as whole persons, not just as talking heads. For this reason, successful apologetics "is not *based* on . . . an abstract comparison, but rather on an encounter with Christ" (209, italics original). Arguments and reasons, while indispensable, can only take most people so far. Much more effective is to invite others "to open [themselves] to God and to reality as it is" (219), and to "taste and see that the Lord is good" (Ps 34:8). In this way, Christian apologetics engages not only the head but also the will, not only the mind but also the heart, not only the intellect but also human hopes, fears, loves, and desires.

I wonder, however, if for van den Toren the dialogical encounter runs in both directions. Of course, I as a Christian desire that others try out the way of Christ. Will I be open to doing the same in response to similar invitations of others? To what degree is my willingness to do so defining of what authentic dialogue looks like? I completely agree with van den Toren that effective cross-cultural apologetics involves engaging with the "reasons of the heart" shaped by other traditions. I want others to long for and pursue after what I love; does authentic dialogue require that I also be open to the affective reason of others, what others long for, hope in, and pursue? The force of this question is intensified when we turn to ecclesiological matters.

Van den Toren recognizes, and rightly so, that the plausibility of the Christian message hinges on what is manifest in and through the Christian community (202 ff.). In effect, people are drawn to Christ through members of his body, and knowledge about Christianity slowly (sometimes more quickly) leads to participation in the Christian community. All of this, of course, involves the establishing and building of relationships. To the degree that local churches and congregations embody the biblical message, to the same degree Christian apologetic efforts will be more plausible. "That God's self-revelation is particular implies . . . that it is entrusted to a *community*" (141, italics original), and others learn to trust in God in part through "trusting the community that is shaped by [God's] revelation" (32). Conversely, to the degree that those who are called after the name of Christ do not live out the gospel message, to that same degree the Christian apologetic will seem less plausible. A number of questions emerge from here.

First, retrieving the previous line of thinking about how cross-cultural dialogue might involve Christian willingness to enter into the way of life of others, to what degree does authentic dialogical interaction involve Christian openness to entering into other religious communities? Of course, as a Christian, I want my non-Christian friends to visit my church, and I hope that my Christian friends will be on their best, and have the most loving behavior while visitors are present. I wonder also how I might respond to the aspirations of my non-Christian friends that I also attend their places of worship or participate in their religious communities—have one of my feet in their circles, as it were—despite their apprehension of how their friends might behave while I am present. What would it mean for me as a Christian interested in dialogical apologetics to be open to the other's reasons of the heart? To what degree is any of this mutual visitation and entering into other religious spaces and times—the willingness to walk in one another's shoes, so to speak—central to a truly dialogical apologetics?

Second, however, I note that while van den Toren does discuss the church variously in his book, "church" is itself absent from the index. If the plausibility of the Christian gospel is intertwined to some degree with how it is lived out among the people of God, then it seems to me the divergences within the Christian tradition loom increasingly large as we consider what it takes to present a convincing Christian apologetic. What I mean is that if the church of Christ is as divided as it in fact is, does this not undermine cross-cultural and interfaith apologetic endeavors? If van den Toren is correct that there are two sides of the apologetic enterprise—the dogmatics side and the engagement side (163 ff.)—then the fact that the former is irredeemably ecclesial highlights the challenges confronting the apologetic task. Not only is there the problem of the degree to which the dogmatic tradition is a convergence of the culturally relative message of the Bible and the culturally conditioned recipients of those faith communities that articulated the church's various dogmas in its different times and places, but there is also the fact that there is not one but numerous dogmatic traditions, some more but others less aligned with the orthodox theological tradition. (With regard to the last point, for instance, I am thinking about Oneness pentecostals who are very mission and apologetic minded but who have a heterodox doctrine of the unity of God when compared to the Nicene confession; this is just one example among many others that we can consider both historically and in the contemporary scene.) As a Protestant myself, I resonate with much of what is presented in *Christian Apologetics as Cross-Cultural Dialogue*, but I wonder if our Roman Catholic and Orthodox friends and colleagues might consider the arguments herein too individualistic in their presuppositions and not sufficiently ecclesially shaped. With all of these differences, some vigorously argued about and contested, how is the plausibility, much less credibility, of the Christian world view not impacted?

Last but not least, ecclesiological questions continue to persist in a pluralistic world. The emergence of Messianic Judaism, for instance, begs the ecclesiological definition at its very roots. Beyond this particular set of discussions (and debates!) related to Jewish-Christians, there are also growing numbers of Muslim-Christians, Buddhist-Christians, Hindu-Christians, and Confucian-Christians, among others, with conversations (and debates) amidst each spectrum about what Christian commitment entails. Some might be inclined to dismiss many of these developments as aberrations, as marginal, or as involving numerically miniscule numbers of people to devote much attention to. However, I think van den Toren is correct to stress that cross-cultural apologetics is and ought to be attentive to the particularities that mark the lives of those with whom we might come into dialogue. In this case, each particularity is important in its own way, with its distinctive challenges. My larger point, however, is that each of these communities of faith press the ecclesiological question that in turn impinges upon the plausibility structures for effective cross-cultural apologetics. Perhaps cross-cultural apologetics is difficult in part because of the fragmentation of the apologizing church.

The preceding consideration alerts us not only to the pluralism within the Christian tradition but also to the diversity that exists within and across other world views' positions, communities, cultures, and religions. Just as Christianity is not monolithic, neither are any of these others. Perhaps such diversity in part explains why rationally and intellectually, there are few universally commanding defeaters. As van den Toren says: "The way world views function makes them relatively immune from criticism" (181). So it ought not to be surprising that just as Christians can always explain potential defeaters from within their own understanding of the gospel, those who hold to other world views, in particular those that are religiously informed, can also, potentially, absorb Christian explanations (188–89).

It is here that I wonder if van den Toren ought to consider a more eschatologically oriented posture, particularly with regard to how he envisions the unfolding of the cross-cultural dialogue. I think, for instance, that in a genuine dialogue, both sides take something away, and are even transformed. The non-Christian may come to experience Christian conversion, but I as a Christian may also come to see things in a different light—and be converted in some sense—even if I maintain my commitments to Christ. In my reading of van den Toren, I sense that he also wants to adopt an appropriately humble posture that sees through a glass dimly (1 Cor 13:12, which he cites on 226) but yet rightly insists that such a view also informs a courageous and bold attitude. So on the one hand, van den Toren wants to avoid Barth's either/or—i.e., either human understanding or divine revelation (86)—yet with regard to other matters, he appears to insist such demarcations are important: alternative world views ought to be seen "as either vehicles of spiritual oppression or freedom" (180). On the third hand, however, he also admits to overlap between Christian and non-Christian world views (189) since "all truth that can be recognized elsewhere is God's truth" (192).

I am not sure any of us can do much better in terms of articulating a humble approach willing to learn from and be transformed by our dialogue partners on the one hand, but yet also be bold and courageous enough to persuasively engage our interlocutors on the other hand. Still, perhaps there are also theological and other reasons why we can never be humble enough. For instance, in his discussion of theological anthropology, van den Toren states: "the Christian understanding of the human being and condition proves more respectful of reality and more coherent in its consideration of our relationship to the world around us" (118). Perhaps this "more than" is vis-à-vis only postmodernist skepticism (perhaps a la figures such a Paul Feyerabend, who is not mentioned in this regard), but implicitly, it would appear that this premise is held also vis-à-vis all rival anthropologies. If that is so, isn't such a claim overreaching? Does it not allow for consideration of the possibility that other world views might have something to contribute, if not now, then in the future, even to Christian anthropological reflection? Any claims about the superiority of the Christian view are always eschatological. This is due in part to our epistemic limitations and in part to the dynamic and dialogical modalities of cross-cultural and interreligious interaction. To say that *all* other schemes are less adequate than our Christian one presupposes almost a practically infinite amount of knowledge, a practically infinite number of dialogues, and a practically infinite number of interactions that explore all the issues from every possible interpretive angle, many of which have not yet even emerged in the historical scheme of things. In a postfoundationalist world, then, it would seem that even our Christian commitments ought to be open not necessarily to abandonment but to revision—indeed, open to being eschatologically surprised by reality, as intimated in the title of the fifth chapter of the book under review.

Isn't this what happens when we engage in cross-cultural dialogue? Van den Toren says that we can place our perspective "alongside others, sometimes as a complementary perspective, sometimes as a contradictory and alternative one" (68). I take the latter for granted. From an evangelical point of view, however, many get worried about the former. For some, complementarity is fine, so long as what is found to be parallel or correlative are more minor or incidental matters. But if somehow it is possible for Christians to learn something new and important from dialogue with others, then all of a sudden Christian faith is threatened and potentially undermined. Might it be possible that the goodness, truth, and beauty of other faiths "may find [their] accomplishment and true meaning under Christ as the true head of creation" (193), but yet the result could still be epistemologically new for Christians?

This leads then to the final set of reflections: that revolving around Christology. At one point, van den Toren likens the hermeneutical circle to reading a book (137–38). While the analogy is helpful in highlighting how a non-foundationalist approach can be secured in an identity while yet being open to learning something new, why not liken this process to meeting and learning more about a person instead? Books are still closed, bound, and finite, even when we have fourteen volumes like Barth's *Church Dogmatics*! But persons are in the image of God, or more precisely, Christ who is the "image of the invisible God" (Col 1:15) and in whom "the whole fullness of deity dwells bodily" (Col 2:9)—Christ is inexhaustible indeed! So on the one hand, the Christian confession of Christ is secure by the Holy Spirit. But on the other hand, our knowledge of Christ remains finite and limited: "when he is revealed, we will be like him, for we will see him as he is" (1 John 3:2). In fact, there may even be many who know and confess his name to whom he will say, "I never knew you; go away from me, you evildoers" (Matt 7:23).

Is it to too much of a stretch to say that Christian apologetics involves on the one hand an introduction of Christ to others but also, on the other hand, the ongoing reception of the fullness of Christ in unexpected ways from others? Van den Toren is correct that "all non-Christian—and all non-orthodox Christian—views of Christ break down on the reality of Jesus Christ Himself as He meets us in the Gospel" (200); but he is also correct when he states: "If the finality of this faith is thus bound up with Jesus Christ, Christians cannot claim finality for *their* particular understanding of Christ or for their understanding of what a Christian world view should look like" (207). Herein is the eschatological reserve that allows us to chart a middle way between humility and confidence (226–28), and that invites us Christians to engage in the cross-cultural dialogue fully with boldness and also with humility. The dialogue is now genuinely mutual and reciprocal since we speak not from some universal epistemological foundation but from the gospel revealed in Christ; simultaneously, we also realize that the Christ of the gospel will repeatedly correct our ideas about him—perhaps even through our apologetic interlocutors!—precisely because he is not just a book but a person, indeed the second person of the Triune God.

Good books prompt thinking; the preceding are only some of the thoughts I had when reading through *Christian Apologetics as Cross-Cultural Dialogue*. More importantly, noteworthy books empower the Christian witness in a more effective and faithful manner. Our author herein inspires Christian evangelism, mission, and apologetics across cultural lines precisely by highlighting the dialogical nature of the church's witness to Christ, even as his ideas might be considered an invitation to consider how the living Christ can reveal himself to us through our dialogical and apologetic encounters. Herein may be the "foundations" for the relational apologetics desperately needed in our twenty-first century postmodern, post-Western, and even post-Christian world. I hope this volume gets a wide reading; evangelical theologians, philosophers, missiologists, and apologists in particular are in Benno van den Toren's debt.[3]

---

3. Thanks to Joe Gorra of *Philosophia Christi* for inviting my review of this volume and then giving me the space to write what turned out to be an extended review essay rather than a more regular-sized book review.

Christian Theological Method

Toward a Pneumatological Imagination for the Third Millennium

IT IS NOW TIME to quickly review where we have come from in order to situate where we have arrived and anticipate next steps. The preceding has attempted to do theology dialogically, with twelve conversation partners, in order to exemplify an effective model of Christian theological inquiry at the beginning of the third millennium. I have also shown that such a dialogical approach is theologically funded by a pneumatological imagination as manifest particularly in the Acts narrative. Further, such a pneumatologically inspired dialogical method may be uniquely suited to enable navigation of our postfoundationalist, post-Christendom, postsecular, postmodern, and pluralistic landscape. This is not to say that other approaches are impotent in this era; it is to say that for those wondering if Christian reason is up to the task of the present time, a pneumatological and dialogical imagination is certainly one candidate charting the path forward.

In these last few pages, however, I want to attend more systematically to such a pneumatological and dialogical methodology. If before I have elaborated at length on the ontological, epistemological, and hermeneutical aspects of the pneumatological imagination,[1] here I want to lift up specifically its dialogical character, make explicit the pneumatological correlates, and then provide a summary methodological sketch. The following remarks build on but also clarify the preceding discussion. In many respects they

---

1. See Yong, *Spirit-Word-Community*.

make explicit what the dialogical efforts of this book presume, while in some respects they will also illuminate the lacunae in these pages.

THE *DIALOGICAL* SPIRIT

We begin with some remarks on the nature of dialogue going forward. This volume has suggested that Christian theological method is empowered by dialogical activity. The dialogical undertakings modeled here are those with other individuals: philosophers, theologians, theologian-scientists, scholars of other faiths, comparativists, anthropologists, missiologists—the list could be expanded if this were a longer book. To be sure, the question of why these twelve specific discussion partners and not another twelve (or however many) is a bit arbitrary. In some ways, we choose our friends (or interlocutors), but in other ways, our friends choose us. I have given some reasons (in the Introduction) for how my thinking with these "friends" emerged, but I will never be able to exhaustively rationalize how they arrived or why they remain (or not) within my conversation orbit. As a Christian theologian, I would thank God for these blessings, yes, even for my Buddhist conversation partners. What each one has taught me is that to appreciate and understand (to the extent that has happened at all) requires respectful and patient listening. To the degree that these have challenged and informed my own thinking, that is because they themselves have wrestled deeply with the difficult questions of theological (or philosophical, or religious) methodology in our complex postfoundationalist, et al., domain. If I am going to disagree with them, I cannot do so apart from prolonged and sustained accompaniment with their ideas and even ways of life. More often than not, I feel less motivated to critically oppose their views; rather, I see many opportunities to expand my own thinking in conversation with them. This reflects my sense that Christian theologians like me aspire to make universal truth claims, but realize that in our contemporary public square, such proceeds best as an a posteriori achievement rather than an a priori assumption.

Of course, there will be some who will balk at the kinds of conversation partners I have chosen, or perhaps counter-suggest that there are limits to who ought to be around the discussion table. I agree: in some instances, when greeted by the devil for example, the dialogical approach ought to be replaced expeditiously by an exorcistic strategy.[2] Part of the difficulty here, of course, is that the Satan, however "he" may be understood, comes as an angel of light (2 Cor 11:14) so as to be somewhat unrecognizable, even as, on the other side, we might believe we are encountering the Satan when we

---

2. I discuss the challenges involved in my *Hospitality and the Other*, 118–25.

are not. Without minimizing the import for proper discernment, I would clarify that theological dialogue proceeds both contextually (within specific situations) and teleologically (for specific purposes), among other criteria.

The present discussion has been lifted up under four overarching contexts: an epistemological environment after the demise of early modern foundationalism; a cultural period after the passing of Christianity as a politically dominant reality; an information age beyond the sacred-secular divide that brings science and the religions together in the public square in new ways; and a late if not postmodern era within which the meeting of the religions portends either a clash of civilizations or a debilitating subjectivism and relativism. Together, these contexts emphatically announce that ours is an exceedingly pluralistic world, one in which a multitude of voices are both clamoring to be heard as well as attempting to resound over those of others. To be sure, who the appropriate dialogue partners are for any conversations will need to be discerned on a case-by-case basis. But it also may well be that any discussions will be attended by many others. Even any more narrowly circumscribed dialogue will be conducted in the presence of others, some more, others less interested. Hence the dialogical spirit is always already polyphonic and multivocal, both in fact and potentially.

None of this is to say that any case will not be contested; such disputes can derive from arguing variously about the appropriateness of potential discussants while others might result in disagreement either about the nature of the context/s or the prioritization of the various issues. In any case, although Christian proclamation will always be carried out in the public square and will proceed at least where there are democratic governments and religious freedom, Christian theological reflection only goes as far as making the case for such succeeds. So if in the twenty-first century Christian claims to universality cannot be presumed amidst the many voices, then arguments will have to be made on at least the four fronts that I have identified in this book, if not more. Some might want to argue that the universality of Christian truth can be asserted regardless of the contexts—that by nature is what Christian truth consists of, however scandalous such may sound to politically correct ears. Even if such scandal were presumed theologically, declaration without argumentation—the rhetorical scandal—will not convince, not to mention also will not be heard by, those who otherwise exist amidst at least these four contexts I have identified.

But even if we agreed on the horizons toward which global Christian theology traverses, what is the goal of such navigation? Why dialogue at all? What are the ends in view? There are at least three reasons for the Christian theological tasks in the present global context. First, Christian self-understanding is contextually situated; hence, mature Christian identities, for individual persons or groups of persons (congregations), or collections of faith communities (networks, denominations, church traditions, etc.) will need to be articulated at least in part vis-à-vis the identities of others, both within (ecumenically) and without (interreligiously) the Christian faith. Hence dialogue accomplishes the important purpose of getting to know others in order that we can understand ourselves better, how we are distinct from others, and what commonalities we may or may not share.

Second, dialogue that leads to the understanding of others enables more faithful, appropriate, and relevant Christian witness in relationship to and with the other, especially those of other or no faith, although also ecumenically. Such witness might be relational, ethical, social, activistic, or kerygmatic (involving Christian proclamation of the gospel). In any case, such witness unfolds more effectively—as measured not necessarily by conversions (although that may be one criterion) but by the full scope of the Scriptural witness concerning the Christian testimony—when informed by dialogical interchange. At the very least, we are better prevented from bearing false witness against our neighbor because authentic dialogue exposes our prejudices and replaces them with a more truthful portrait. At its best, the Christian witness brings about repentance and the expansion of the gospel message.

Last but not least, dialogue with others, Christians and religious or unreligious others, informs faithful Christian praxis. How then do we live faithfully in the complicated postfoundationalist, post-Christendom, postsecular, postmodern, and pluralist context of our present situation? Faithful living means, in part, being able to flourish with others, and such flourishing requires that we know our neighbors in order that we can develop common cause toward a more just and humane world. Dialogue enables such vital praxis to emerge. The Christian theological endeavor contributes to such an important objective when it proceeds dialogically in and with the company of others.[3]

THE DIALOGICAL *SPIRIT*

So far, my comments in this concluding chapter have unpacked the dialogical aspect of theological work in terms of its nature, context, and aims. In this section, however, we have to make an explicitly theological turn. More particularly, our pivot will be pneumatological, in light of this major thrust over the course of this book. The argument throughout is that only

---

3. See Jensen, *In the Company of Others*; see also my review essay, "Globalizing Christology."

a pneumatologically inspired and empowered imagination is capable of both listening to the many voices but also critically discerning their contributions. Put alternatively, only a pneumatological imagination is able to sustain the dialogical task in a pluralistic world. However, although the pneumatological imagination proposed is informed specifically by pentecostal-charismatic spirituality and perspective, in theological terms, the Holy Spirit is still no less than the Spirit of Jesus and the Spirit of God. How then might we further understand the dialogical character of theological reflection and formulation in light of these pneumatological themes?

First and foremost, the dialogue enabled by the Holy Spirit will ultimately point to Jesus Christ. This means that Christians who are dialogically engaged will inevitably, even if also incessantly, revolve around Christ. Here the life of Christ, his teachings, and his selfless and atoning death are the normative shape of the Spirit's presence and activity. Voices, behaviors, and phenomena that are contrary to this Christic and cruciform character are those of the antichrist and hence opposed also to the spirit of Jesus. Those that manifest the fruits of the spirit of Christ (Gal 5:22–24) and are consistent with the values of the *shalom* Jesus, proclaimed and embodied, can be said to at least anticipate, if not also participate in, the coming reign of God.

At the same time, because Christ is the one who is also yet to come and we see through a glass dimly (1 Cor 13:12), it may well be that this testimony to Christ proceeds without the awareness of those who are witnessing, at least for the moment. Furthermore, our reception of the testimony of others may also lead us to deeper awareness and new appreciation of the living Christ, even if we are initially unable to communicate why. We may find ourselves transformed into greater Christlike-ness only in hindsight, even as others come into more consciously thematized knowledge of Christ only eschatologically. On the other hand, if we gradually or otherwise cease to bear the fruits of the spirit of Christ in the course of our dialogical encounter, then the conversation will be animated by other spirits—at least our own, certainly—rather than the spirit of Jesus. Similarly, others who bear fruits opposed to those of the Holy Spirit are animated also by forces other than Christ. And when moved by the spirit of Jesus, there may come moments when dialogue ceases and other activities commence. Christians will often disagree about if and when such moments arrive. Arguably, the more christomorphic the pneumatological imagination, the more sensitivity exists about whether to press ahead dialogically versus shifting the *modus operandi*.

Christian Trinitarianism also insists that however else the doctrine of the triune deity is understood, the spirit of Jesus is also the spirit of God and these aspects of the Spirit's identity are both related and distinct. Certainly, this distinction-in-relationship cannot involve internal contradictions so that to be the Spirit of one disallows being the Spirit of the other. Simultaneously, this relationship-in-distinction can open up to complementarity so that the light of the spirit of God can illuminate the person of Christ while the sending of the spirit of Jesus can unveil or reveal the image of God. Hence that the spirit of Jesus is the spirit of God accentuates the eschatological horizon of the dialogical journey. In the end, those who of are of the spirit of Jesus will also be subordinate to the living God "so that God may be all in all" (1 Cor 15:28), even as those who are of the spirit of God will bend their knee at the name of Jesus and confess Christ's lordship "to the glory of God the Father" (Phil 2:12). In some cases in this time before the end, we may not recognize the one from the other; in other cases, there will be harmony and rejoicing when we come to see the other in the light of our commitments. If the disagreements obstruct the manifestation of the Spirit's fruits, then the spirit of God and of Christ has been grieved. On the other side, the appearance of the fruits of the Spirit is no guarantee. Somehow, "no one can say 'Jesus is Lord' except by the Holy Spirit" (1 Cor. 12:3), even as some will say "Lord, Lord" but Jesus will respond: "I never knew you; go away from me, you evildoers" (Matt 7:21, 23). The point for Christians is both not to be overly confident that their confession always reflects the spirit of Jesus and to realize that others who do not (yet) have the spirit of Christ, at least epistemologically, may nevertheless have the spirit of God, at least provisionally even if partially. But in the latter case the proper response should always be Christian witness, and this engages, again, the dialogical Spirit.

Last but not least, the spirit of Christ is also the Spirit of Pentecost, the Spirit of the church understood as the body of Christ, the people of God, and the fellowship of the Holy Spirit. This means that the church plays a distinctive role in bearing witness to Jesus by the power of his Holy Spirit. Simultaneously, the Spirit has been poured out eschatologically on all flesh (Acts 2:17) so as to make possible the witness to Jesus through the many tongues of the human condition. Hence the church boldly declares the name of Jesus even while it receives the testimony of others "about God's deeds of power" (Acts 2:11). This is the nature of the dialogical Spirit, to empower the witness of all to all, albeit in different respects. Those of the gathering of God—the *ekklesia* or congregation—are filled with the spirit of Jesus to lift up his name so that not only will Israel "know with certainty that God has made him both Lord and Messiah, this Jesus whom you crucified" (Acts 2:36), but that "all the families of the earth shall be blessed" (Acts 3:25). Simultaneously, those with the spirit of God will encounter dreams and visions, not to mention "portents in the heaven above and signs on the earth below" (Acts 2:19) so that "everyone who calls on the name of the Lord shall be saved" (Acts 2:21) according to his salvific power achieved through the spirit of Jesus. The scriptural reference to the eschatological outpouring of the Spirit "on all flesh" (Acts 2:17) would in this case involve also a perlocutionary invitation to those filled with the Spirit to bear witness to Christ to the ends of the earth (Acts 1:8).

The dialogical Spirit hence resolutely lifts up the person of Christ through his body; simultaneously, the dialogical Spirit builds up the body of Christ through the testimony of others, precisely so that the fellowship of the Spirit can bear more and more adequate witness to the God of Jesus Christ, as delineated above. Hence the spirit of Christ is present and at work in and through dialogue even as the spirit of God makes dialogue with others possible at all.

THE PNEUMATOLOGICAL IMAGINATION AND THEOLOGICAL METHOD FOR THE TWENTY-FIRST CENTURY

We are now on the final stretch and I need to sketch some responses to one final set of questions before we conclude this discussion. Treatises on theological method classically deal both with the sources for theological reflection and their operational procedures.[4] This volume has argued that a pneumatological imagination inspires and enables dialogical relationality that furthers the thinking and doing of theology. Yet we have said little about how to bring Scripture and tradition into the conversation. In this final section I briefly and quickly outline three models of such dialogical integration—one scripturally oriented, another communally shaped, and a third systematically construed—from my own work in order to illustrate the pneumatological imagination's capacity for bringing the past into the present and future.

First, one approach to Scripture and tradition attempts to foreground especially Scripture's own horizons of understanding. Classically, such a hermeneutical model emphasizes exegesis or a biblical-theological methodology that privileges Scripture's own categories and discursive rationality. My book, *Who Is the Holy Spirit?: A Walk with the Apostles*,[5] is the closest I come to such a scripturally framed argument, beginning and working

---

4. The Anglican "triad" of Scripture, tradition, and reason, and the Wesleyan "quadrilateral" that added experience, focus on theological sources; the classical operational "manual," as it were, is Lonergan's *Method in Theology*.

5. Yong, *Who Is the Holy Spirit?*

through the book of Acts and then, every other chapter, returning to the Gospel of Luke to reflect on the life and teachings of Jesus as may have been pertinent to whatever it was the apostolic community was encountering and having to resolve. Even in this sense, however, the Acts narrative provides the framework for reading the third Gospel and some exegetes might complain that this reversal does not honor Luke's own ordered sequence (in the sense that the Gospel was written before the Acts narrative). Beyond this important point, *Who Is the Holy Spirit?* presents a reading of the Acts-Luke material framed by the quest to understand the public rather than only the ecclesial work of the Holy Spirit. Yet although I argue in the book that such an approach is consistent with Luke's own insistence that the outpouring of the Spirit is to the ends of the earth and upon all flesh, and thus has explicitly public scope, others might disagree that my justification is warranted.[6] In my own defense, I can only say that any reading of Scripture that tries only to stay with the Scriptural horizon will be of little interest to third millennium, much less twenty-first century, concerns. And once the latter is factored into the equation, then what often emerges is a conflict of interpretations (as Paul Ricoeur put it)[7] for many reasons, including how dialogical (or not) the intersection is between the scriptural and contemporary vistas.

Who Is the Holy Spirit?, while not being a work of pentecostal hermeneutics per se, reflects my own quest as a pentecostal Christian to understand the Holy Spirit's wider work in the world. In that respect, I would insist that the Scriptures, including Luke-Acts, do not stand alone but are what they are as the authoritative word of God precisely as and through belonging to the church, the people of God. Hence, every faithful reading of scripture is ecclesial or traditioned in some respect. My own is specifically pentecostal in overall hermeneutical sensibilities,[8] although as should be apparent from this book, such a pentecostal orientation is not set off from evangelical, ecumenical, and even broader cultural and interfaith concerns. The point is that Scripture is mediated in part by tradition and hence has a communal or ecclesial dimension. The dialogical imagination thus involves scripture, tradition, and the church, along with contemporary voices.

My book *In the Days of Caesar: Pentecostalism and Political Theology*[9] reflects both how Scripture (again Luke-Acts, which predominates here) is carried ecclesially and how specific ecclesial perspective's (in this case pentecostal communities) reading and retrieving Scripture combine to enable

6. Most vociferous here is Stronstad, "A Review Essay on Amos Yong."

7. Ricoeur, *Conflict of Interpretations*.

8. Which I summarize briefly in an article, "Reading Scripture and Nature."

9. Yong, *In the Days of Caesar*.

engagement with important matters of the present time (in this case related to the political arena of Christian life). What emerges out of this book are five sustained interfaces with the Lukan material in the five constructive chapters of the book (Part II), informed by the pentecostal "five-fold gospel" (of Jesus as savior, sanctifier, Spirit-baptizer, healer, and coming king), and applied to matters of public and political importance. Scripture is here read as informing contemporary issues, although care is taken to ensure that the biblical authors' commitments are not taken in directions that they would have opposed. The point is that communal concerns and motivations (pentecostal ones here) shape, at least in part, how the scriptural message is reappropriated from age to age. The dialogical imagination is thus mediated by the opportunities and challenges confronted by ecclesial communities in attempting to remain faithful to the apostolic witness in the present global political context.

As first and foremost a systematic theologian,[10] however, the genre and its traditional manifestations could also shape my reading of Scripture and engagement with the tradition. How then might the dialogical and pneumatological imagination developed in this volume structure systematic theological reflection in the twenty-first century global context? I am glad you asked, as one of my newest books, *Renewing Christian Theology: Systematics for a Global Christianity*, presents precisely such a model.[11] Three interconnected aspects of *Renewing Christian Theology*'s methodology concretely unfold the claims of the present volume. First, starting with the Spirit means we begin with pneumatology and eschatology, the Spirit being the triune person of the present and coming age who reconciles creation back to the Father in and through the Son. Our systematic theology thus proceeds from eschatology (where we are going) to the doctrine of Scripture so that the foundations of Scripture are illuminated within an ecclesial and theological framework rather than the other way around. Second, the focus is on the renewal movement that is at the vanguard of contemporary global Christianity, so each doctrinal locus is discussed not only historically in light of the church's traditional teachings but also with regard to the dogmatic commitments of a specific renewal movement (the classical Pentecostal Assemblies of God church) and vis-à-vis the global theological ferment. Third, then, the third section of each chapter focuses on reading a specific book of the New Testament in light of the historical, ecclesial, and contextual issues and directed toward reconsidering how to understand the doctrinal theme that chapter addresses in the present time.

10. One of my earliest essays was "Whither Systematic Theology?"
11. See Yong, with Jonathan A. Anderson, *Renewing Christian Theology*.

I have opted for such a methodological approach to the scriptural traditions in order to weave two kinds of dialogical commitments into the systematic theological task. First, rather than a proof-text approach, the various theological and doctrinal considerations will benefit from sustained interactions with whole scriptural texts (i.e., Gospels, letters). Thus we will be able to develop a deeper scriptural treatment when we unveil what the biblical author has to say about any particular topic in light of the whole of that writing. Second, of course, what is proposed within the scope of a limited volume, as long as it might be, is still only a model for reading Scripture, and readers are invited to continue their reflection by adding other scriptural books, eventually even consulting the entirety of the scriptural canon, for a more thorough set of authoritative perspectives. In other words, the dialogue with Scripture is fluid and dynamic, always ever unfolding, ebbing and flowing as those motivated to theological reflection continue to mine the wellsprings of the Christian tradition and revision new and faithful responses in ever-changing contemporary contexts. The result is, as the book's title aspires to achieve, the renewal of Christian theology.

Much more can be said about reading Scripture and tradition in dialogue with present circumstances and realities. I can only suggest that all of my monographs attempt such a dialogical approach and each is informed by the authority of Scripture, albeit in its own way (related to the topic, audience, purposes, etc.). Any dialogical theology will feature multiple modalities of not only thinking with Scripture but also of engaging the tradition with current opportunities and challenges. The pneumatological imagination that we have presented in this book thus can be seen to not only invite such an expansive dialogical vision but also in many ways to mandate that any theology desiring to speak boldly and faithfully will need to listen to and interact with the many voices and engage with, even enter practically into, the many ways of life present in the third millennium.

Bibliography

Abraham, William J. *Canon and Criterion in Christian Theology: From the Fathers to Feminism*. New ed. Oxford: Oxford University Press, 2002.

Almeder, Robert. *The Philosophy of Charles S. Peirce: A Critical Introduction*. Totowa, NJ: Rowman and Littlefield, 1980.

————. "Peirce's Thirteen Theories of Truth." *Transactions of the Charles S. Peirce Society* 21, no. 1 (1985) 77–94.

Alston, William. *Epistemic Justification: Essays in the Theory of Knowledge*. Ithaca, NY: Cornell University Press, 1989.

————. *Perceiving God: The Epistemology of Religious Experience*. Ithaca, NY: Cornell University Press, 1991.

Altizer, T. J. J. "The Primordial, Godhead, and Apocalyptic Christianity." In *Theology in Global Context: Essays in Honor of Robert Cummings Neville*, edited by Amos Yong and Peter G. Heltzel, 265–76. New York: T & T Clark, 2004.

Altshuler, Bruce. "Peirce's Theory of Truth and the Revolt Against Realism." *Transactions of the Charles S. Peirce Society* 18, no. 1 (1982) 34–56.

Anderson, Allan, Michael Bergunder, André F. Droogers, and Cornelis van der Laan, eds. *Studying Global Pentecostalism: Theories and Methods*. Berkeley, CA: University of California Press, 2010.

Anderson, Victor. *Pragmatic Theology: Negotiating the Intersections of an American Philosophy of Religion and Public Theology*. Albany, NY: State University of New York Press, 1998.

Apel, Karl-Otto. *Charles S. Peirce: From Pragmatism to Pragmaticism*. Translated by John Michael Kroi. Amherst, MA: University of Massachusetts Press, 1981.

Arweck, Elisabeth, and Martin D. Stringer. *Theorizing Faith: The Insider/Outsider Problem in the Study of Ritual*. Birmingham, UK: University of Birmingham Press, 2002.

Austin, D. Brian. *The End of Certainty and the Beginning of Faith: Religion and Science for the 21st Century*. Macon, GA: Smyth and Helwys, 2000.

Austin, James H. *Zen and the Brain: Toward an Understanding of Meditation and Consciousness*. Cambridge, MA: MIT Press, 1999.

Auxier, Randall. "The Decline of Evolutionary Naturalism in Later Pragmatism." In *Pragmatism: From Progressivism to Postmodernism*, edited by Robert Hollinger and David Depew, 180–207. Westport, CT: Praeger, 1995.

Avery, Jon. "Three Types of American Neo-Pragmatism." *Journal of Philosophical Research* 18 (1993) 1–13.

Avis, Paul. "Apologist from the World of Science: John Polkinghorne FRS." *Scottish Journal of Theology* 43 (1990) 485–502.

Ayers, Robert H. "C. S. Peirce on Miracles." *Transactions of the Charles S. Peirce Society* 16 (1980) 242–54.

Barbour, Ian G. *Religion in an Age of Science*. San Francisco: Harper & Row, 1990.

Barnhart, Bruno, and Joseph Wong, eds. *Purity of Heart and Contemplation: A Monastic Dialogue between Christians and Asian Traditions*. New York: Continuum, 2001.

Barrows, Paul. *Beyond the Self: Consciousness, Mysticism and the New Physics*. London: Janus, 1998.

Barth, Karl. *Church Dogmatics*. Vol. IV/1. Translated by G. W. Bromiley. London: T and T Clark, 1956.

Bartholomeusz, Tessa. "Dharmapala at Chicago: Mahayana Buddhist or Sinhala Chauvinist?" In *A Museum of Faiths: Histories and Legacies of the 1893 World Parliament of Religions*. Classics in Religious Studies 9, edited by Eric J. Ziolkowski, 235–50. Atlanta: Scholars, 1993.

Beck, Guy L. *Sonic Theology*. Columbia, SC: University of South Carolina Press, 1993.

Begley, Sharon. *Train Your Mind, Change Your Brain: How a New Science Reveals Our Extraordinary Potential to Transform Ourselves*. New York: Ballantine, 2007.

Beise Kiblinger, Kristin. "Relating Theology of Religions and Comparative Theology." In *The New Comparative Theology: Interreligious Insights from the Next Generation*, edited by Francis X. Clooney, SJ, 21–42. New York: T & T Clark, 2010.

Bellah, Robert. "Religious Studies as 'New Religion.'" In *Understanding the New Religions*, edited by Jacob Needleman and George Baker, 106–12. New York: Seabury 1978.

Berg, Todd Vanden. "More Than You Think, But Still Not Enough: Christian Anthropologists." *Perspectives on Science and Christian Faith* 61, no. 4 (2009) 211–19.

Berger, Peter L. *A Rumor of Angels: Modern Society and the Rediscovery of the Supernatural*. Garden City, NY: Doubleday, 1970.

———. *The Sacred Canopy: Elements of a Sociological Theory of Religion*. Garden City, NY: Doubleday, 1967.

Bernstein, Richard. *Beyond Objectivism and Relativism: Science, Hermeneutics, and Praxis*. Philadelphia: University of Pennsylvania Press, 1983.

Berthrong, John H. *The Divine Deli: Religious Identity in the North American Cultural Mosaic*. Maryknoll, NY: Orbis, 1999.

Boudewijnse, Barbara, and André F. Droogers, eds. *More Than Opium: An Anthropological Approach to Latin American and Caribbean Pentecostal Praxis*. Lanham, MD: Scarecrow, 1998.

Boyd, Gregory A. *God of the Possible: A Biblical Introduction to the Open View of God*. Grand Rapids: Baker, 2000.

———. "Neo-Molinism and the Infinite Intelligence of God." *Philosophia Christi* Series 2, Vol. 5, no. 1 (2003) 187–204.

Braaten, Carl E., and Robert W. Jenson, eds. *Mary, Mother of God*. Grand Rapids: Eerdmans, 2004.

———. *Union with Christ: The New Finnish Interpretation of Luther*. Grand Rapids: Eerdmans, 1998.

Brandom, Robert B., ed. *Rorty and His Critics*. Oxford: Blackwell, 2000.

Brent, Joseph. *Charles Sanders Peirce: A Life*. Bloomington, IN: Indiana University Press, 1993.

Brissenden, R. J. *Zen Buddhism and Modern Physics: Morality and Religion in the New Millennium*. Atlanta: Minerva, 1999.

Brittain, Christopher Craig, and Francesca Aran Murphy, eds. *Theology, University, Humanities: Initium Sapientiae Timor Domini*. Eugene, OR: Cascade, 2011.

Buckley, James J., and David S. Yeago, eds. *Knowing the Triune God: The Work of the Spirit in the Practices of the Church*. Grand Rapids: Eerdmans, 2001.

Cabezón, José Ignacio. "Tibetan Buddhist Society." In *The Oxford Handbook of Global Religions*, edited by Mark Juergensmeyer, 91–109. Oxford: Oxford University Press, 2006.

Cady, Linell, and Delwin Brown, eds. *Religious Studies, Theology, and the University: Conflicting Maps, Changing Terrain*. Albany, NY: State University of New York Press, 2002.

Callen, Barry L. *Radical Christianity: The Believers Church Tradition in Christianity's History and Future*. Nappanee, IN: Evangel, 1999.

Camp, Lee C. *Mere Discipleship: Radical Christianity in a Rebellious World*. Grand Rapids: Brazos, 2003.

Cannell, Fenella. "Introduction: The Anthropology of Christianity." In *The Anthropology of Christianity*, edited by Fenella Cannell, 1–49. Durham, NC: Duke University Press, 2006.

Carlson, Richard F., ed. *Science and Christianity: Four Views*. Downers Grove, IL: InterVarsity, 2000.

Cartledge, Mark J. *Charismatic Glossolalia: An Empirical-Theological Study*. Aldershot, UK: Ashgate, 2001.

———. *Testimony in the Spirit: Rescripting Ordinary Pentecostal Theology*. Burlington, VT: Ashgate, 2013.

Chagmé, Karma. *A Spacious Path to Freedom: Practical Instructions on The Union of Mahāmudrā and Atiyoga*. Commentary by Gyatrul Rinpoche. Translated by B. Alan Wallace. Ithaca, NY: Snow Lion, 1998.

———. *Naked Awareness: Practical Instructions on The Union of Mahāmudrā and Dzogchen*. Commentary by Gyatrul Rinpoche. Translated by B. Alan Wallace. Edited by Lindy Steele and B. Alan Wallace. Ithaca, NY: Snow Lion, 2000.

Chan, Simon. *Pentecostal Theology and the Christian Spiritual Tradition*. Journal of Pentecostal Theology Supplemental Series 21. Sheffield, UK: Sheffield Academic Press, 2000.

Clapp, Rodney. "How Firm a Foundation: Can Evangelicals Be Nonfoundationalists?" In *The Nature of Confession: Evangelicals and Postliberals in Conversation*, edited by Timothy R. Phillips and Dennis L. Okholm, 81–92. Downers Grove, IL: InterVarsity, 1996.

Clark, David K. *To Know and Love God: Method for Theology*. Wheaton, IL: Crossway, 2003.

Clarke, Bowman L. "Peirce's Neglected Argument." *Transactions of the Charles S. Peirce Society* 13, no. 4 (1977) 277–87.

Clarke, Peter B. "Playful Religion? Experience, Meaning and the Ludic Approach." In *Playful Religion Challenges for the Study of Religion*, edited by Anton van Harskamp, 97–108. Delft, the Netherlands: Eburon Academic, 2006.

Clooney, Francis X., SJ. *Beyond Compare: St. Francis de Sales and Śrī Vedānta Deśika on Loving Surrender to God*. Washington, DC: Georgetown University Press, 2008.

———. *Comparative Theology: Deep Learning Across Religious Borders.* Malden, MA: Wiley-Blackwell, 2010.

———. *Divine Mother, Blessed Mother: Hindu Goddesses and the Virgin Mary.* Oxford: Oxford University Press, 2005.

———. *Hindu God, Christian God: How Reason Helps Break Down the Boundaries between Religions.* Oxford: Oxford University Press, 2001.

———. *Hindu Wisdom for All God's Children.* Maryknoll, NY: Orbis Books, 1998. Reprint, Eugene, OR: Wipf & Stock, 2005.

———. "Response." In *The New Comparative Theology: Interreligious Insights from the Next Generation,* edited by Francis X. Clooney, SJ, 191–200. New York: T & T Clark, 2010.

———. *Seeing through Texts: Doing Theology among the Śrīvaisnavas of South India.* Albany, NY: State University of New York Press, 1996.

———. *Theology after Vedānta: An Experiment in Comparative Theology.* Albany, NY: State University of New York Press, 1993.

———. *Thinking Ritually: Rediscovering the Pūrva Mīmāmsā of Jaimini.* Publications of the De Nobili Research Library 17. Vienna: Sammlung De Nobili Institut für Indologie der Universität Wien, 1990.

———. *The Truth, the Way, the Life: Christian Commentary on the Three Holy Mantras of the Śrīvaisnava Hindus.* Christian Commentaries on Non-Christian Sacred Texts. Grand Rapids: Eerdmans, 2008.

Clooney, Francis X., ed. *The New Comparative Theology: Interreligious Insights from the Next Generation.* New York: T & T Clark, 2010.

Cobb, John B., Jr. *Beyond Dialogue: Toward a Mutual Transformation of Christianity and Buddhism.* Philadelphia: Fortress, 1982.

———. *Grace and Responsibility: A Wesleyan Theology Today.* Nashville: Abingdon, 1995.

Comay, Rebecca. "Interrupting the Conversation: Notes on Rorty." In *Anti-Foundationalism and Practical Reasoning: Conversations between Hermeneutics and Analysis,* edited by Evan Simpson, 83–98. Edmonton: Academic Printing and Publishing, 1987.

Comstock, Gary. "Two Types of Narrative Theology." *Journal of the American Academy of Religion* 55 (1987) 687–717.

Cooper, John. *Body, Soul, and Life Everlasting: Biblical Anthropology and the Monism-Dualism Debate.* 2nd ed. Grand Rapids: Eerdmans, 2000.

Cooper, Robin. *The Evolving Mind: Buddhism, Biology, and Consciousness.* Birmingham, UK: Windhorse, 1996.

Corcoran, Kevin. *Rethinking Human Nature: A Christian Materialist Alternative to the Soul.* Grand Rapids: Baker Academic, 2006.

Corduan, Winfried. *Reasonable Faith: Basic Christian Apologetics.* Nashville: Broadman & Holman, 1993.

Cornille, Catherine, ed. *Many Mansions?: Multiple Religious Belonging and Christian Identity.* Maryknoll, NY: Orbis, 2002.

Corrington, Robert. *An Introduction to C. S. Peirce: Philosopher, Semiotician, and Ecstatic Naturalist.* Lanham, MD: Rowman & Littlefield, 1993.

———. *The Community of Interpreters: On the Hermeneutics of Nature and the Bible in the American Philosophical Tradition.* 2nd ed. Macon, GA: Mercer University Press, 1995.

Corten, André, and Ruth Marshall-Fratani, eds. *Between Babel and Pentecost: Transnational Pentecostalism in Africa and Latin America*. Bloomington, IN: Indiana University Press, 2001.

Cox, Harvey. *Fire from Heaven: The Rise of Pentecostal Spirituality and the Reshaping of Religion in the 21st Century*. Reading, MA: Addison-Wesley, 1995.

———. "Response to Professor Nimi Wariboko." *Pneuma: The Journal of the Society for Pentecostal Studies* 33, no. 3 (2011) 409–16.

———. *The Secular City*. New York: Macmillan, 1996.

Craig, William Lane. "God and Real Time." *Religious Studies* 26 (1990) 335–47.

Crain, Steven D. "Divine Action in a World Chaos: An Evaluation of John Polkinghorne's Model of Special Divine Action." *Faith and Philosophy* 14, no. 1 (1997) 41–61.

Cross, Terry L. "The Rich Feast of Theology: Can Pentecostals Bring the Main Course or Only the Relish?" *Journal of Pentecostal Theology* 16 (2000) 27–47.

———. "Can There Be a Pentecostal Systematic Theology? An Essay on Theological Method in a Postmodern World." Unpublished paper presented to the Society for Pentecostal Studies, Oral Roberts University, Tulsa, OK, March 2001.

Cunningham, Floyd T. "Interreligious Dialogue: A Wesleyan Holiness Perspective." In *Grounds for Understanding: Ecumenical Resources for Responses to Religious Pluralism*, edited by S. Mark Heim, 188–207. Grand Rapids: Eerdmans, 1998.

Dabney, D. Lyle. "Otherwise Engaged in the Spirit: A First Theology for the Twenty-first Century." In *The Future of Theology: Essays in Honor of Jürgen Moltmann*, edited by Miroslav Volf, Carmen Krieg, and Thomas Kucharz, 154–63. Grand Rapids: Eerdmans, 1996.

Dahlke, Paul. *Buddhism and Science*. Translated by Bhikkhu Sîlâcâra. London: Macmillan, 1913.

Dalai Lama. *The Good Heart: A Buddhist Perspective on the Teachings of Jesus*. Translated by Geshe Thupten Jinpa. Edited by Robert Kiely. Boston: Wisdom, 1996.

———. *Live in a Better Way: Reflections on Truth, Love and Happiness*. Edited by Renuka Singh. New York: Penguin Viking Compass, 2001.

———. "Medicine and Compassion." In *Healing Emotions: Conversations with the Dalai Lama on Mindfulness, Emotions, and Health*, edited by Daniel Goleman, 243–50. Boston: Shambhala, 1997.

———. *Spiritual Advice for Buddhists and Christians*. Edited by Donald W. Mitchell. New York: Continuum, 1998.

———. "Understanding Our Fundamental Nature." In *Visions of Compassion: Western Scientists and Tibetan Buddhists Examine Human Nature*, edited by Richard J. Davidson and Anne Harrington, 66–80. Oxford: Oxford University Press, 2002.

———. *The Universe in a Single Atom: The Convergence of Science and Spirituality*. New York: Morgan Road, 2005.

Dalai Lama, with Howard C. Cutler. *The Art of Happiness at Work*. New York: Riverhead, 2003.

Davaney, Sheila Greeve. *Pragmatic Historicism: A Theology for the Twenty-First Century*. Albany, NY: State University of New York Press, 2000.

Davidson, Richard J., and Anne Harrington, eds. *Visions of Compassion: Western Scientists and Tibetan Buddhists Examine Human Nature*. Oxford: Oxford University Press, 2002.

Davies, Mansel. *A Scientist Looks at Buddhism*. Sussex, UK: The Book Guild, 1990.

Davies, Paul. *The Mind of God*. New York: Simon and Schuster, 1992.

Davis, William. *Peirce's Epistemology*. The Hague: Martinus Nijhoff, 1972.

Dawes, Gregory W. "Religious Studies, Faith, and the Presumption of Naturalism." *Journal of Religion & Society* 5 (2003) 1–19.

———. "In Defense of Naturalism." *International Journal of Philosophy of Religion* 70 (2011) 3–25.

Debrock, Guy, and Menno Hulswit, eds. *Living Doubt: Essays Concerning the Epistemology of Charles Sanders Peirce*. Dordrecht: Kluwer Academic, 1994.

Dewey, John. "The Development of American Pragmatism." In *Pragmatism: The Classic Writings*, edited by H. S. Thayer, 23–40. New York: New American Library, 1970.

Dharmapala, Anagarika. "The World's Debt to Buddha." In *The Dawn of Religious Pluralism: Voices from the World's Parliament of Religion, 1893*, edited by Richard Hughes Seager, 410–19. LaSalle, IL: Open Court, 1993.

Dhonden, Yeshi. *Healing from the Sources: The Science and Lore of Tibetan Medicine*. Translated by B. Alan Wallace. Ithaca, NY: Snow Lion, 2000.

Diggins, John Patrick. *The Promise of Pragmatism: Modernism and the Crisis of Knowledge and Authority*. Chicago: University of Chicago Press, 1994.

Dockett, Kathleen H., G. Rita Dudley-Grant, and C. Peter Bankart, eds. *Psychology and Buddhism: From Individual to Global Community*. New York: Kluwer Academic/ Plenum, 2003.

Donovan, Peter. "Neutrality in Religious Studies." *Religious Studies* 26 (1990): 103–15.

Dooyeweerd, Herman. *In the Twilight of Western Thought: Studies in the Pretended Autonomy of Philosophical Thought*. Collected Works. Vol. B/4. Edited by James K. A. Smith. Lewiston, NY: Edwin Mellen, 1999.

Dow, Tsung-I. "Modern Science and the Rediscovery of Buddhism." In *Buddhism and the Emerging World Civilization: Essays in Honor of Nolan Pliny Jacobson*, edited by Ramakrishna Puligandla and David Lee Miller, 113–24. Carbondale, IL: Southern Illinois University Press, 1996.

Drew, Rose. *Buddhist and Christian? An Exploration of Dual Belonging*. New York: Routledge, 2011.

Droogers, André F. "The Cultural Dimension of Pentecostalism." In *The Cambridge Companion to Pentecostalism*, edited by Cecil M. Robeck Jr. and Amos Yong, 195–214. Cambridge: Cambridge University Press, 2014.

———. *The Dangerous Journey: Symbolic Aspects of Boys Initiation Among the Wagenia of Kisangani, Zaire*. The Hague: Mouton, 1980.

———. *Play and Power in Religion: Collected Essays*. Reason and Religion 50. Berlin: Walter de Gruyter, 2012.

———. "Playing with Perspectives." In *Methods for the Study of Religious Change: From Religious Studies to Worldview Studies*, edited by André F. Droogers and Anton van Herskemp. London: Equinox, 2013.

———. "Towards the Concerned Study of Religion: Exploring the Double Power-Play Disparity." *Religion* 40 (2010) 227–38.

Droogers, André F., and Cornelis van der Laan, eds. *Fruitful in This Land: Pluralism, Dialogue and Healing in Migrant Pentecostalism*. Geneva: WCC Publications, 2006.

Droogers, André F., Peter B. Clarke, Grace Davie, Sidney M. Greenfield, and Peter Versteeg. *Playful Religion: Challenges for the Study of Religion*. Edited by Anton van Harskamp. Delft, the Netherlands: Eburon Academic, 2006.

Dulles, Avery, S. J. *The Craft of Theology: From Symbol to System.* New York: Crossroad, 1992.

Dyrness, William A., and Veli-Matti Kärkkäinen, eds. *Global Dictionary of Theology: A Resource for the Worldwide Church.* Downers Grove, IL: IVP Academic, 2008.

Echeverria, Eduardo J. "Do Human Rights Spring from Our Nature as Human Beings? Reflections on Richard Rorty." *Philosophia Christi* 20, no. 1 (1997) 41–53.

———. "Revelation and Foundationalism: Towards a Historically Conscious Foundationalism." *Josephinum Journal of Theology* 19, no. 2 (2012) 1–39.

Eco, Umberto. "Unlimited Semeiosis and Drift: Pragmaticism vs. 'Pragmatism.'" In *Peirce and Contemporary Thought: Philosophical Inquiries,* edited by Kenneth Laine Ketner, 205–21. New York: Fordham University Press, 1995.

Erickson, Millard J. *Christian Theology.* 3 vols. Grand Rapids: Baker, 1983.

Ewing, Katherine. "Dreams from a Saint: Anthropological Atheism and the Temptation to Believe." *American Anthropologist* 96 (1994) 571–83.

Evans-Pritchard, E. E. *Witchcraft, Oracles, and Magic among the Azande.* Oxford: Clarendon, 1937.

Fackre, Gabriel. *Restoring the Center: Essays Evangelical and Ecumenical.* Downers Grove, IL: InterVarsity, 1998.

Farrell, Frank B. *Subjectivity, Realism, and Postmodernism: The Recovery of the World.* Cambridge: Cambridge University Press, 1994.

Faupel, D. William. *The Everlasting Gospel: The Significance of Eschatology in the Development of Pentecostal Thought.* Journal of Pentecostal Theology Supplement series 10. Sheffield, UK: Sheffield Academic Press, 1996.

Flood, Gavin D. "The Phenomenology of Scripture: Patterns of Reception and Discovery behind Scriptural Reasoning." *Modern Theology* 22, no. 3 (2006): 503–14.

Ford, David F., and C. C. Pecknold, eds. *The Promise of Scriptural Reasoning.* Malden, MA: Blackwell, 2006.

Frederick, Marla F. *Between Sundays: Black Women and Everyday Struggles of Faith.* Berkeley, CA: University of California Press, 2003.

Fredericks, James L. *Buddhists and Christians: Through Comparative Theology to Solidarity.* Maryknoll, NY: Orbis, 2004.

Frei, Hans W. *The Eclipse of Biblical Narrative: A Study in Eighteenth and Nineteenth Century Hermeneutics.* New Haven, CT: Yale University Press, 1974.

———. *Theology and Narrative: Selected Essays.* Edited by George Hunsinger and William C. Placher. New York: Oxford University Press, 1993.

Friedman, Norman. *Bridging Science and Spirit: Common Elements in David Bohm's Physics, the Perennial Philosophy and Seth.* Reprint, St. Louis: Living Lake Books, 1994. First published 1990.

Gallie, W. B. *Peirce and Pragmatism.* 2nd ed. New York: Dover, 1966.

Galloway, Glenn. "The Efficacy of Propositionalism: The Challenge of Philosophical Linguistics and Literary Theory to Evangelical Theology." PhD diss., Southern Baptist Theological Seminary, 1996.

———. "Peirce and Postmodern Evangelical Hermeneutics: Reading Between the Lines." Paper presented to the American Academy of Religion, November 1997.

Garrett, William R. "Troublesome Transcendence: The Supernatural in the Scientific Study of Religion." *Sociological Analysis* 35, no. 3 (1974) 167–80.

Geertz, Clifford. "'From the Native's Point of View': On the Nature of Anthropological Understanding." In *The Insider/Outsider Problem in the Study of Religion: A Reader*, edited by Russell T. McCutcheon, 50–63. London: Cassell, 1999.

———. *The Interpretation of Cultures: Selected Essays*. New York: Basic Books, 1973.

Gelpi. Donald L. *Charism and Sacrament: A Theology of Christian Conversion*. New York: Paulist, 1976.

———. *Committed Worship: A Sacramental Theology for Converting Christians*. 2 vols. Collegeville, MN: Liturgical, 1993.

———. *The Conversion Experience: A Reflective Process for RCIA Participants and Others*. New York: Paulist, 1998.

———. "Conversion: The Challenge of Contemporary Charismatic Piety." *Theological Studies* 42 (1983) 606–28.

———. *Discerning the Spirit: Foundations and Futures of Religious Life*. New York: Sheed and Ward, 1970.

———. *The Divine Mother: A Trinitarian Theology of the Holy Spirit*. Lanham, MD: University Press of America, 1984.

———. *Endless Seeker: The Religious Quest of Ralph Waldo Emerson*. Lanham, MD: University Press of America, 1991.

———. *Experiencing God: A Theology of Human Experience*. New York: Paulist, 1978.

———. *The Firstborn of Many: A Christology for Converting Christians*. 3 vols. Marquette Studies in Theology 20–22. Milwaukee: Marquette University Press, 2001.

———. "The Foundational Phoenix: Regrounding Theology in a Postmodern Age." In *Continuity and Plurality in Catholic Theology: Essays in Honor of Gerald A. McCool, SJ*, edited by Anthony J. Cernera, 35–51. Fairfield, CT: Sacred Heart University Press, 1998.

———. *Functional Asceticism: A Guideline for American Religious*. New York: Sheed and Ward, 1966.

———. *God Breathes the Spirit in the World*. Wilmington, DE: Michael Glazier, 1988.

———. *Grace as Transmuted Experience and Social Process and Other Essays in North American Theology*. Lanham, MD: University Press of America, 1988.

———. *The Gracing of Human Experience: Rethinking the Relationship between Nature and Grace*. Collegeville, MN: Liturgical/Michael Glazier, 2001.

———. "'Incarnate Excellence': Jonathan Edwards and an American Theological Aesthetic." *Religion and the Arts* 2, no. 4 (1998) 443–66.

———. *Inculturating North American Theology: An Experiment in Foundational Method*. Atlanta: Scholars, 1988.

———. *Life and Light: A Guide to the Theology of Karl Rahner*. New York: Sheed and Ward, 1966.

———. *Peirce and Theology: Essays in the Authentication of Doctrine*. Lanham, MD: University Press of America, 2001.

———. *Pentecostal Piety*. New York: Paulist, 1972.

———. *Pentecostalism: A Theological Viewpoint*. New York: Paulist, 1971.

———. *The Turn to Experience in Contemporary Theology*. New York: Paulist, 1994.

———. *Varieties of Transcendental Experience: A Study in Constructive Postmodernism*. Collegeville, MN: Liturgical/Michael Glazier, 2000.

Gelpi, Donald L., ed. *Beyond Individualism: Toward a Retrieval of Moral Discourse in America*. Notre Dame, IN: University of Notre Dame Press, 1989.

Geras, Norman. *Solidarity in the Conversation of Humankind: The Ungroundable Liberalism of Richard Rorty.* London: Verso, 1995.

Goldberg, Michael. *Theology and Narrative: A Critical Introduction.* Nashville: Abingdon, 1982.

Goldstein, Melvyn C. *The Snow Lion and the Dragon: China, Tibet, and the Dalai Lama.* Berkeley, CA: University of California Press, 1997.

Goleman, Daniel, ed. *Healing Emotions: Conversations with the Dalai Lama on Mindfulness, Emotions, and Health.* Boston: Shambhala, 1997.

————. *Destructive Emotions: How Can We Overcome Them?* New York: Bantam, 2003.

Goleman, Daniel, and Robert A. F. Thurman, eds. *MindScience: An East-West Dialogue.* Boston: Wisdom, 1991.

Goodman, Russell B., ed. *Pragmatism: A Contemporary Reader.* New York: Routledge, 1995.

Gouinlock, James. "What is the Legacy of Instrumentalism? Rorty's Interpretation of Dewey." In *Rorty and Pragmatism: The Philosopher Responds to His Critics*, edited by Herman J. Saatkamp Jr., 72–90. Nashville: Vanderbilt University Press, 1995.

Green, Joel B. and Stuart L. Palmer, eds. *In Search of the Soul: Four Views of the Mind-Body Problem.* Downers Grove, IL: InterVarsity, 2005.

Grenz, Stanley J. *Renewing the Center: Evangelical Theology in a Post-Theological Era.* Grand Rapids: Baker Academic, 2000.

————. *The Social God and the Relational Self: A Trinitarian Theology of the Imago Dei.* Louisville: Westminster John Knox, 2001.

Greenway, William N. A., Jr. "Richard Rorty's Revised Pragmatism: Promise for and Challenge to Christian Theology (With Special Reference to the Philosophy of Charles Taylor)." PhD diss., Princeton Theological Seminary. Ann Arbor, MI: University Microfilms International, 1997.

Gregersen, Niels Henrik, and J. Wentzel van Huyssteen, eds. *Rethinking Theology and Science: Six Models for the Current Dialogue.* Grand Rapids: Eerdmans, 1998.

Griffiths, Paul J. *Religious Reading: The Place of Reading in the Practice of Religion.* New York: Oxford University Press, 1999.

Groothuis, Douglas. "Postmodernism and Truth." *Philosophia Christi*, series 2, vol. 2, no. 2 (2000) 271–81.

Guignon, Charles B. "Pragmatism or Hermeneutics? Epistemology after Foundationalism." In *The Interpretive Turn: Philosophy, Science, Culture*, edited by David R. Hiley, James F. Bohman, and Richard Shusterman, 81–101. Ithaca, NY: Cornell University Press, 1991.

Gunn, Giles. *Thinking across the American Grain: Ideology, Intellect, and the New Pragmatism.* Chicago: University of Chicago Press, 1992.

————. "Pragmatism, Democracy, and the Imagination: Rethinking the Deweyan Legacy." In *Pragmatism: From Progressivism to Pstmodernism*, edited by Robert Hollinger and David J. Depew, 298–313. Westport, CT: Praeger, 1995.

Gunter, W. Stephen, Scott J. Jones, Ted. A. Campbell, Rebekah L. Miles, and Randy L. Maddox. *Wesley and the Quadrilateral: Renewing the Conversation.* Nashville: Abingdon, 1997.

Gyatso, Tenzin. *Freedom in Exile: Autobiography of the Dalai Lama.* New York: HarperCollins, 1990.

————. *The World of Tibetan Buddhism: An Overview of Its Philosophy and Practice.* Translated by Geshe Thupten Jinpa. Boston: Wisdom, 1995.

Haack, Susan. "Descartes, Peirce and the Cognitive Community." In *The Relevance of Charles Peirce*, edited by Eugene Freeman, 238–63. La Salle, IL: The Hegeler Institute/Monist Library of Philosophy, 1983.

Hackett, Stuart. *The Reconstruction of the Christian Revelation Claim: A Philosophical and Critical Apologetic*. Grand Rapids: Baker, 1984.

Hall, David L. *Richard Rorty: Prophet and Poet of the New Pragmatism*. Albany, NY: State University of New York Press, 1994.

Hall, Douglas John. *Christian Theology in the North American Context*. 3 vols. Minneapolis: Augsburg, 1996.

Hardwick, Charley D., ed. *Semiotic and Significs: The Correspondence between Charles S. Peirce and Victoria Lady Welby*. Bloomington, IN: Indiana University Press, 1977.

Hardwick, Charley D., and Donald A. Crosby, eds. *Pragmatism, Neo-Pragmatism, and Religion: Conversations with Richard Rorty*. New York: Peter Lang, 1997.

Hardy, Gilbert G. *Monastic Quest and Interreligious Dialogue*. New York: Peter Lang, 1990.

Harrington, Anne, and Arthur Zajonc, eds. *The Dalai Lama at MIT*. Cambridge, MA: Harvard University Press, 2006.

Harris, James F. *Against Relativism: A Philosophical Defense of Method*. La Salle, IL: Open Court, 1992.

Hasker, William. *The Emergent Self*. Ithaca, NY: Cornell University Press, 1999.

Hauerwas, Stanley. "Reading McClendon Takes Practice: Lessons in the Craft of Theology." *The Conrad Grebel Review* 15, no. 3 (1997) 235–50.

Hauerwas, Stanley, and L. Gregory Jones, eds. *Why Narrative? Readings in Narrative Theology*. Grand Rapids: Eerdmans, 1989.

Hauerwas, Stanley, Nancey Murphy, and Mark Nation, eds. *Theology Without Foundations: Religious Practice and the Future of Theological Truth*. Nashville: Abingdon, 1994.

Hayward, Jeremy W. *Shifting Worlds, Changing Minds: Where the Sciences and Buddhism Meet*. Boston: Shambhala, 1987.

Hayward, Jeremy W., and Francisco J. Varela, eds. *Gentle Bridges: Conversations with the Dalai Lama on the Sciences of Mind*. Boston: Shambhala, 1992.

Heim, S. Mark. *The Depths of the Riches: A Trinitarian Theology of Religious Ends*. Grand Rapids: Eerdmans, 2001.

Henry, Carl F. H. *God, Revelation and Authority*, 6 vols. Waco, TX: Word, 1976–83.

Hitchen, John M. "What It Means to Be an Evangelical Today—An Antipodean Perspective." *Evangelical Quarterly*, part I, 76, no. 1 (2004) 47–64, and part II, 76, no. 2 (2004) 99–115.

Hocking, William Ernest. *The Meaning of God in Human Experience*. New Haven, CT: Yale University Press, 1963.

Hollenweger, Walter. *Pentecostalism: Origins and Developments Worldwide*. Peabody, MA: Hendrickson, 1997.

Hookway, Christopher. *Peirce*. Reprint, London: Routledge, 1992. First published 1985.

House, D. Vaden. *Without God or His Doubles: Realism, Relativism and Rorty*. Philosophy of History and Culture 14. Leiden: E. J. Brill, 1994.

Houshmand, Zara, Robert B. Livingston, and B. Alan Wallace, eds. *Consciousness at the Crossroads: Conversations with the Dalai Lama on Brain Science and Buddhism*. Ithaca, NY: Snow Lion, 1999.

Howard, Evan B. *Affirming the Touch of God: A Psychological and Philosophical Exploration of Christian Discernment.* Lanham, MD: University Press of America, 2000.

Howell, Brian M. "The Anthropology of Christianity: Beyond Missions and Conversion—A Review Essay." *Christian Scholar's Review* 34 (2005) 353–362.

———. "The Repugnant Cultural Other Speaks Back: Christian Identity as Ethnographic 'Standpoint.'" *Anthropological Theory* 7 (2007) 371–91.

Howell, Brian M., and Jenell Williams Paris. *Introducing Cultural Anthropology: A Christian Perspective.* Grand Rapids: Baker Academic, 2011.

Huizinga, Johan. *Homo Ludens: A Study of the Play Element in Culture.* Reprint, Boston: Beacon, 1955. First published 1950.

Hütter, Reinhard. *Suffering Divine Things: Theology as Church Practice.* Translated by Doug Scott. Grand Rapids: Eerdmans, 2000.

Irvin, Dale T. *Christian Histories, Christian Traditioning: Rendering Accounts.* Maryknoll, NY: Orbis, 1998.

Jacobs-Huey, Lanita. "The Natives Are Gazing and Talking Back: Reviewing the Problematics of Positionality, Voice, and Accountability Among 'Native' Anthropologists." *American Anthropologist*: NS 104 (2002) 791–804.

Jaffee, Martin S. "Fessing Up in Theory: On Professing and Confessing in the Religious Studies Classroom." In *The Insider/Outsider Problem in the Study of Religion: A Reader*, edited by Russell T. McCutcheon, 274–86. London: Cassell, 1999.

James, William. *The Meaning of Truth: A Sequel to "Pragmatism."* London: Longmans, Green, and Co., 1909.

———. "Pragmatism's Conception of Truth." In *Essays in Pragmatism*, edited by Alburey Castell, 159–76. New York: Hafner, 1948.

Jansen, Henry. *Relationality and the Concept of God.* Grand Rapids: Eerdmans, 1995.

Jayatilleke, K. N., Robert F. Spencer, and Wu Shu. *Buddhism and Science: Collected Essays.* Kandy, Sri Lanka: Buddhist Publication Society, 1958.

Jenkins, Philip. *The Next Christendom: The Coming of Global Christianity.* Oxford: Oxford University Press, 2002.

Jennings, Willie James. "Recovering the Radical Reformation for Baptist Theology: An Assessment of James Wm. McClendon Jr.'s *Doctrine* (A Review Article)." *Perspectives in Religious Studies* 24, no. 2 (1997) 181–93.

Jensen, David H. *In the Company of Others: A Dialogical Christology.* Cleveland: Pilgrim, 2001.

Johns, Cheryl Bridges. *Pentecostal Formation: A Pedagogy among the Oppressed.* Journal of Pentecostal Theology Supplemental Series 2. Sheffield, UK: Sheffield Academic Press, 1993.

Johnson, Todd M., and Kenneth R. Ross, eds. *Atlas of Global Christianity 1910–2010.* Edinburgh: Edinburgh University Press, 2009.

Jones, Kelvin. "The Formal Foundation: Toward an Evangelical Epistemology in the Postmodern Context." In *The Challenge of Postmodernism: An Evangelical Engagement*, edited by David S. Dockery, 344–58. Wheaton, IL: Victor, 1995.

Jones, Richard H. *Science and Mysticism: A Comparative Study of Western Natural Science, Theravada Buddhism, and Advaita Vedanta.* Lewisburg, PA: Bucknell University Press, 1986.

Kärkkäinen, Veli-Matti. *Ad ultimum terrae: Evangelization, Proselytism, and Common Witness in the Roman Catholic-Pentecostal Dialogue (1990–1997).* Studies in the Intercultural History of Christianity 117. Frankfurt am Main: Lang, 1999.

———. "Christianity and Other Religions." In *Karl Barth and Evangelical Theology,* edited by Sung Wook Chung, 236–57. Grand Rapids: Baker, 2005.

———. *Christology: A Global Introduction.* Grand Rapids: Baker Academic, 2003.

———. *A Constructive Christian Theology for a Pluralistic World.* 5 vols. Grand Rapids: Eerdmans, 2013–.

———. "David's Sling: The Promise and the Problem of Pentecostal Theology Today: A Response to D. Lyle Dabney." *Pneuma: The Journal of the Society for Pentecostal Studies* 23, no. 1 (2001) 147–52.

———. *The Doctrine of God: A Global Introduction.* Grand Rapids: Baker Academic, 2004.

———. "Evangelical Theology and Religions." In *Cambridge Companion to Evangelical Theology,* edited by Timothy Larsen and Daniel J. Treier, 199–212. Cambridge: Cambridge University Press, 2005.

———. *The Holy Spirit and Salvation: The Sources of Christian Theology.* Louisville: Westminster John Knox, 2010.

———. *The Holy Spirit: A Guide to Christian Theology.* Louisville: Westminster John Knox, 2012.

———. *An Introduction to Ecclesiology: Ecumenical, Historical and Global Perspectives.* Downers Grove, IL: InterVarsity, 2002.

———. *An Introduction to the Theology of Religions: Biblical, Historical, and Contemporary Perspectives.* Downers Grove, IL: InterVarsity, 2003.

———. *One with God: Salvation as Deification and Justification.* Collegeville, MN: Liturgical, 2004.

———. *Pneumatology: The Holy Spirit in Ecumenical, International, and Contextual Perspective.* Grand Rapids: Baker Academic, 2002.

———. "Spiritual Power and Spiritual Presence: The Contemporary Renaissance in Pneumatology in Light of a Dialogue between Pentecostal Theology and Tillich." In *Spiritual Presence and Spiritual Power: Pentecostal Readings of and Engagements with the Legacy of Paul Tillich,* edited by Amos Yong and Nimi Wariboko. Bloomington, IN: Indiana University Press, forthcoming.

———. *Spiritus ubi vult spirat: Pneumatology in Roman Catholic-Pentecostal Dialogue (1972–1989).* Schriften der Luther-Agricola-Gesellschaft 42. Helsinki: Luther-Agricola-Society, 1998.

———. "Theology of the Cross: A Stumbling Block to Pentecostal/Charismatic Spirituality?" In *The Spirit and Spirituality: Essays in Honour of Russell Spittler,* edited by Wonsuk Ma and Robert Menzies, 150–63. London: T & T Clark, 2004.

———. *Toward a Pneumatological Theology: Pentecostal and Ecumenical Perspectives on Ecclesiology, Soteriology, and Theology of Mission.* Edited by Amos Yong. Lanham, MD: University Press of America, 2002.

———. *Trinity and Religious Pluralism: The Doctrine of the Trinity in Christian Theology of Religions.* Aldershot, UK: Ashgate, 2004.

———. *The Trinity: Global Perspectives.* Louisville: Westminster John Knox, 2007.

———. "The Uniqueness of Christ and Trinitarian Faith." In *Christ the One and Only: A Global Affirmation of the Uniqueness of Jesus Christ,* edited by Sung Wook Chung, 111–35. Grand Rapids: Baker, 2005.

Keidel, Paul. *Career-Defining Crises in Mission: Navigating the Major Decisions of Cross-Cultural Service.* Pasadena, CA: William Carey Library, 2005.

Kermode, Frank. "The Argument about Canons." In *The Bible and the Narrative Tradition,* edited by Frank McConnell, 78–96. New York: Oxford University Press, 1986.

Kessler, Gary E. "A Neglected Argument." Paper presented at the Twentieth World Congress of Philosophy, Boston, MA, 10–16 August 1998. http://www.bu.edu/wcp/Papers/Reli/ReliKess.htm.

Kinast, Robert L. *What Are They Saying about Theological Reflection?* New York: Paulist, 2000.

King, Rebekka. "Notes on a North American Anthropology of Christianity." *Bulletin for the Study of Religion* 39 (2010) 12–17.

Kirthisinghe, Buddhadasa, ed. *Buddhism and Science.* Delhi: Motilal Banarsidass, 1984.

Knibbe, Kim, and André F. Droogers. "Methodological Ludism and the Academic Study of Religion." *Method and Theory in the Study of Religion* 23 (2011) 283–303.

Knight, Henry H., III. *A Future for Truth: Evangelical Theology in a Postmodern World.* Nashville: Abingdon, 1997.

Knight, Thomas S. *Charles Peirce.* New York: Washington Square, 1965.

Kolenda, Konstantin. *Rorty's Humanistic Pragmatism: Philosophy Democratized.* Tampa, FL: University of South Florida Press, 1990.

Kondo, Dorinne K. *Crafting Selves: Power, Gender, and Discourses of Identity in a Japanese Workplace.* Chicago: University of Chicago Press, 1990.

Kuklick, Bruce. *The Rise of American Philosophy: Cambridge, Massachusetts, 1860–1930.* New Haven, CT: Yale University Press, 1977.

Laird, Thomas. *The Story of Tibet: Conversations with the Dalai Lama.* New York: Grove, 2006.

Lakatos, Imre. *The Methodology of Scientific Research Programmes: Philosophical Papers.* Edited by John Worrall and Gregory Currie. Vol. 1. Reprint, Cambridge: Cambridge University Press, 1999. First published 1978.

Lamb, Christopher, and M. Darrol Bryant, eds. *Religious Conversion: Contemporary Practices and Controversies.* London: Cassell, 1999.

Lamrimpa, Gen (Ven. Jampal Tenzin). *Realizing Emptiness: The Madhyamaka Cultivation of Insight.* Translated by B. Alan Wallace. Edited by Ellen Posman. Ithaca, NY: Snow Lion, 1999.

———. *Samantha Meditation: Tibetan Buddhist Teachings on Cultivating Meditative Quiescence.* Translated by B. Alan Wallace. Edited by Hart Springer. Ithaca, NY: Snow Lion, 1992. Revised as *Calming the Mind: Tibetan Buddhist Teachings on Cultivating Meditative Quiescence.* 2nd ed. Translated by B. Alan Wallace. Edited by Hart Springer. Ithaca, NY: Snow Lion, 1995.

———. *Transcending Time: An Explanation of the Kālacakra Six-Session Guru Yoga.* Translated by B. Alan Wallace. Edited by Pauly B. Fitze. Somerville, MA: Wisdom, 1999.

Land, Stephen. *Pentecostal Spirituality: A Passion for the Kingdom.* Journal of Pentecostal Theology Supplemental Series 1. Sheffield, UK: Sheffield Academic Press, 1993.

Langsdorf, Lenore, and Andrew R. Smith, eds. *Recovering Pragmatism's Voice: The Classical Tradition, Rorty, and the Philosophy of Communication.* Albany, NY: State University of New York Press, 1995.

Laszlo, Ervin. *Science and the Akashic Field: An Integral Theory of Everything.* 2nd ed. Rosemont, VT: Inner Traditions, 2007.

Lawless, Elaine. *Holy Women, Wholly Women: Sharing Ministries through Life Stories and Reciprocal Ethnography.* Philadelphia: University of Pennsylvania Press, 1995.

Lederle, Henry I. *Treasures Old and New: Interpretation of "Spirit Baptism" in the Charismatic Renewal Movement.* Peabody, MA: Hendrickson, 1988.

Lee, Matthew T., and Amos Yong, eds. *The Science and Theology of Godly Love.* DeKalb, IL: Northern Illinois University Press, 2012.

Lee, Matthew T., and Margaret M. Poloma. *A Sociological Study of the Great Commandment in Pentecostalism: The Practice of Godly Love as Benevolent Service.* Lewiston, NY: Edwin Mellen, 2009.

Levinson, Henry Samuel. *Santayana, Pragmatism, and the Spiritual Life.* Chapel Hill, NC: The University of North Carolina Press, 1992.

Lindbeck, George. *The Nature of Doctrine: Religion and Theology in a Postliberal Age.* Philadelphia: Westminster, 1984.

Lints, Richard. "The Postpositivist Choice: Tracy or Lindbeck?" *Journal of the American Academy of Religion* 61 (1993) 655–77.

Lodahl, Michael. *The Story of God: Wesleyan Theology and Biblical Narrative.* Kansas City, MO: Beacon Hill, 1994.

Loder, James E., and W. Jim Neidhardt. *The Knight's Move: The Relational Logic of the Spirit in Theology and Science.* Colorado Springs: Helmers & Howard, 1992.

Lonergan, Bernard. *Method in Theology.* New York: Seabury, 1979.

Longenecker, Dwight, and David Gustafson. *Mary: A Catholic-Evangelical Debate.* Grand Rapids: Brazos, 2003.

Lundin, Roger. "Deconstructive Therapy." *The Reformed Journal* 36, no. 1 (1986): 15–20.

Lyon, David. "The Idea of a Christian Sociology: Some Historical Precedents and Current Concerns." *Sociological Analysis* 44 (1983) 227–242.

Macchia, Frank. "Tongues as a Sign: Toward a Sacramental Understanding of Pentecostal Experience." *Pneuma: The Journal of the Society for Pentecostal Studies* 15 (1993) 61–76.

————. *Justified in the Spirit: Creation, Redemption and the Triune God.* Grand Rapids: Eerdmans, 2010.

MacDonald, Paul S. *History of the Concept of Mind: Speculations about Soul, Mind, and Spirit from Homer to Hume.* Aldershot, UK: Ashgate, 2003.

Machuga, Ric. *In Defense of the Soul: What It Means to Be Human.* Grand Rapids: Brazos, 2002.

Maffie, James. "Recent Work on Naturalized Epistemology." *American Philosophical Quarterly* 27 (1990) 281–93.

Malachowski, Alan R., ed. *Reading Rorty: Critical Responses to Philosophy and the Mirror of Nature (and Beyond).* Oxford: Blackwell, 1990.

Mansfield, Victor. *Synchronicity, Science, and Soul-Making: Understanding Jungian Synchronicity through Physics, Buddhism, and Philosophy.* La Salle, IL: Open Court, 1995.

Margolis, Joseph. *Pragmatism without Foundations: Reconciling Realism and Relativism.* Oxford: Basil Blackwell, 1986.

Marsden, George. *Reforming Fundamentalism: Fuller Seminary and the New Evangelicalism.* Grand Rapids: Eerdmans, 1995.

Marshall, Bruce D., ed. *Theology and Dialogue: Essays in Conversation with George Lindbeck*. Notre Dame, IN: University of Notre Dame Press, 1990.

McClendon, James Wm., Jr. *Biography as Theology: How Life Stories Can Remake Today's Theology*. Nashville: Abingdon, 1974.

———. *Systematic Theology*. 3 vols. Nashville: Abingdon, 1986–1994.

McClendon, James Wm., Jr., and James M. Smith. *Convictions: Defusing Religious Relativism*. Valley Forge, PA: Trinity Press International, 1994.

McCutcheon, Russell T. *Critics Not Caretakers: Redescribing the Public Study of Religion*. Albany: State University of New York Press, 2001.

McCutcheon, Russell T., ed. *The Insider/Outsider Problem in the Study of Religion: A Reader*. London: Cassell, 1999.

McDermott, Gerald R. *Can Evangelicals Learn from World Religions? Jesus, Revelation and Religious Traditions*. Downers Grove, IL: InterVarsity, 2000.

McKnight, Scot. *The Real Mary: Why Evangelical Christians Can Embrace the Mother of Jesus*. Brewster, MA: Paraclete, 2007.

McQueen, Larry R. *Joel and the Spirit: The Cry of a Prophetic Hermeneutic*. Journal of Pentecostal Theology Supplement Series 8. Sheffield, UK: Sheffield Academic Press, 1995.

Meadows, Philip R. "'Candidates for Heaven': Wesleyan Resources for a Theology of Religions." *Wesleyan Theological Journal* 35, no. 1 (2000) 41–66.

Mehrotra, Rajiv. ed. *The Essential Dalai Lama: His Important Teachings*. New York: Viking, 2005.

Menzies, William W. "Synoptic Theology: An Essay in Pentecostal Hermeneutics." *Paraclete: A Journal Concerning the Person and Work of the Holy Spirit* 13, no. 1 (1979) 14–21.

Migliore, Daniel L. *Faith Seeking Understanding: An Introduction to Christian Theology*. Grand Rapids: Eerdmans, 2004.

Miller, Keith B. "Theological Implications of an Evolving Creation." *Perspectives on Science and Christian Faith: Journal of the American Scientific Affiliation* 45 (1993) 150–60.

Misak, C. J. *Truth and the End of Inquiry: A Peircean Account of Truth*. Oxford: Clarendon, 1991.

Mitchell, Donald W., and James Wiseman, eds. *The Gethsemani Encounter: A Dialogue on the Spiritual Life by Buddhist and Christian Monastics*. New York: Continuum, 1999.

Molleur, Joseph. *Divergent Traditions, Converging Faiths: Troeltsch, Comparative Theology, and the Conversation with Hinduism*. American University Studies Series VII Theology and Religion 213. New York: Peter Lang, 2000.

Moore, Edward C. *American Pragmatism: Peirce, James, and Dewey*. New York: Columbia University Press, 1961.

Moser, Paul K. "Does Foundationalism Rest on a Mistake?" *Philosophical Studies (Ireland)* 31 (1987) 183–96.

Mouffe, Chantal. "Deconstruction, Pragmatism and the Politics of Democracy." In *Deconstruction and Pragmatism*, edited by Chantal Mouffe, 1–12. London: Routledge, 1996.

Mounce, H. O. *The Two Pragmatisms: From Peirce to Rorty*. London: Routledge, 1997.

Mouw, Richard J. "Ethics and Story: A Review Article." *The Reformed Journal* 37, no. 8 (1987) 22–27.

Mullin, Glenn H. *The Fourteen Dalai Lamas: A Sacred Legacy of Reincarnation.* Edited by Valerie Shepherd. Santa Fe, NM: Clear Light, 2001.

Munz, Peter. "Philosophy and the Mirror of Rorty." In *Evolutionary Epistemology, Rationality, and the Sociology of Knowledge,* edited by Gerard Radnitzky and W. W. Bartley III, 343–98. La Salle, IL: Open Court, 1987.

Murphy, John. *Pragmatism: From Peirce to Davidson.* Boulder, CO: Westview, 1990.

Murphy, Nancey. "Textual Relativism, Philosophy of Language, and the Baptist Vision." In *Theology Without Foundations: Religious Practice and the Future of Theological Truth,* edited by Stanley Hauerwas, Nancey Murphy, and Mark Nation, 245–72. Nashville: Abingdon, 1994.

Murphy, Nancey C., and George F. R. Ellis. *On the Moral Nature of the Universe: Theology, Cosmology, and Ethics.* Minneapolis: Fortress, 1996.

Murphy, Nancey C., and Warren S. Brown. *Did My Neurons Make Me Do It? Philosophical and Neurobiological Perspectives on Moral Responsibility and Free Will.* Oxford: Oxford University Press, 2007.

Nañez, Rick. *Full Gospel, Fractured Minds? A Call to Use God's Gift of the Intellect.* Grand Rapids: Zondervan, 2005.

Narlikar, Jayant V. "Concept of Time in Science." In *Science, Spirituality and the Future: A Vision for the Twenty-First Century—Essays in Honour of His Holiness The Fourteenth Dalai Lama, Tenzin Gyatso,* edited by L. L. Mehrotra, 103–12. New Delhi: Mudrit, 1999.

National Association of Diocesan Ecumenical Officers. *Baptism, Eucharist and Ministry: Initial Reactions from Roman Catholic Dioceses in the United States.* N.p.: National Association of Diocesan Ecumenical Officers, 1986.

Netland, Harold A. *Dissonant Voices: Religious Pluralism and the Question of Truth.* Grand Rapids: Eerdmans, 1991.

Neville, Robert Cummings. "American Philosophy's Way around Modernism (and Postmodernism)." In *The Recovery of Philosophy in America: Essays in Honor of John Edwin Smith,* edited by Thomas Kasulis and Robert Cummings Neville, 251–68. Albany, NY: State University of New York Press, 1997.

———. *The Highroad Around Modernism.* Albany, NY: State University of New York Press 1992.

———. *Recovery of the Measure: Interpretation and Nature.* Albany, NY: State University of New York Press, 1989.

———. *Religion in Late Modernity.* Albany, NY: State University of New York Press, 2002.

Neville, Robert Cummings, and Wesley J. Wildman, eds. *The Human Condition.* Albany, NY: State University of New York Press, 2002.

———. *Religious Truth.* Albany, NY: State University of New York Press, 2002.

———. *Ultimate Realities.* Albany, NY: State University of New York Press, 2002.

Newbigin, Lesslie. *The Household of God: Lectures on the Nature of the Church.* New York: Friendship, 1954.

———. *Truth to Tell: The Gospel as Public Truth.* Grand Rapids: Eerdmans, 1991.

Nichols, Terence L. *The Sacred Cosmos: Christian Faith and the Challenge of Naturalism.* Grand Rapids: Brazos, 2003.

Nielsen, Kai. *After the Demise of Tradition: Rorty, Critical Theory, and the Fate of Philosophy.* Boulder, CO: Westview, 1991.

Oberman, Heiko Augustinus. *The Virgin Mary in Evangelical Perspective*. Philadelphia: Fortress 1971.

Ochs, Peter. "The Sentiment of Pragmatism: From the Pragmatic Maxim to a Pragmatic Faith." *The Monist* 75, no. 4 (1992) 551–68.

———. "Charles Sanders Peirce." In *Founders of Constructive Postmodern Philosophy: Peirce, James, Bergson, Whitehead, and Hartshorne*, edited by David Ray Griffin, 43–88. Albany, NY: State University of New York Press, 1993.

Oden, Thomas C. "The Real Reformers are Traditionalists." *Christianity Today*, February 9, 1998, 45.

Okrent, Mark. "The Metaphilosophical Consequences of Pragmatism." In *The Institution of Philosophy: A Discipline in Crisis?*, edited by Avner Cohen and Marcelo Dascal, 177–98. La Salle, IL.: Open Court, 1989.

Oliver, Harold H. *A Relational Metaphysic*. The Hague: Martinus Nijhoff, 1981.

Olshewsky, Thomas. "Realism and Antifoundationalism." In *Living Doubt: Essays Concerning the Epistemology of Charles Sanders Peirce*, edited by Guy Debrock and Menno Hulswit, 25–31. Dordrecht: Kluwer Academic, 1994.

Orange, Donna. *Peirce's Conception of God: A Development Study*. Lubbock, TX: Institute for Studies in Pragmatism, 1984.

Outler, Albert. "The Wesleyan Quadrilateral—In John Wesley." *Wesleyan Theological Journal* 20 (1985) 7–18.

Pals, Daniel L. *Eight Theories of Religion*. Oxford: Oxford University Press, 2006.

Panikkar, Raimundo. *The Unknown Christ of Hinduism*. London: Darton, Longman, & Todd, 1964.

Parker, Stephen. *Led By the Spirit: Toward a Practical Theology of Pentecostal Discernment and Decision Making*. Journal of Pentecostal Theology Supplement Series 7. Sheffield, UK: Sheffield Academic Press, 1996.

Patil, Parimal G. "Conclusion: A Hindu Theologian's Response." In *Hindu God, Christian God*, by Francis X. Clooney, 185–96. Oxford: Oxford University Press, 2001.

Peacocke, Arthur. "A Response to Polkinghorne." *Science and Christian Belief* 7 (1995) 109–15.

Pederson, Ann, and Lou Ann Trost, "John Polkinghorne and the Task of Addressing a 'Messy' World." *Zygon: Journal of Religion and Science* 35, no. 4 (2000) 977–83.

Peirce, Charles Sanders. *Collected Papers of Charles Sanders Peirce*, Vols. I–VI, edited by Charles Hartshorne and Paul Weiss; Vols. VII–VIII, edited by Arthur W. Burks. Cambridge, MA: Belknap, 1931–58.

Perry, Ralph Barton. *The Thought and Character of William James*. Briefer version. New York: George Braziller, 1954.

Perry, Tim S. *Mary for Evangelicals: Toward an Understanding of the Mother of Our Lord*. Downers Grove, IL: IVP Academic, 2006.

Peters, Ted. *God as Trinity: Relationality and Temporality in Divine Life*. Louisville: Westminster John Knox, 1993.

Pettegrew, John, ed. *A Pragmatist's Progress? Richard Rorty and American Intellectual History*. Lanham, MD: Rowman & Littlefield, 2000.

Phan, Peter C. *Being Religious Interreligiously: Asian Perspectives on Interfaith Dialogue*. Maryknoll, NY: Orbis, 2004.

Phillips, D. Z. *Faith After Foundationalism: Plantinga-Rorty-Lindbeck-Berger—Critiques and Alternatives*. Boulder, CO: Westview, 1988.

Phillips, Timothy R., and Dennis L. Okholm, eds. *The Nature of Confession: Evangelicals and Postliberals in Conversation.* Downers Grove, IL: InterVarsity, 1996.

Piburn, Sidney, ed. *The Dalai Lama: A Policy of Kindness.* Ithaca, NY: Snow Lion, 1990.

Pinnock, Clark H. *A Wideness in God's Mercy: The Finality of Jesus Christ in a World of Religions.* Grand Rapids: Zondervan, 1992.

Piper, John, Justin Taylor, and Paul Kjoss Helseth, eds. *Beyond the Bounds: Open Theism and the Undermining of Biblical Christianity.* Wheaton, IL: Crossway, 2003.

Plantinga, Alvin. "Reason and Belief in God." In *Faith and Rationality: Reason and Belief in God,* edited by Alvin Plantinga and Nicholas Wolsterstoff, 16–93. Notre Dame, IN: University of Notre Dame Press, 1983.

———. *Warrant and Proper Function.* New York: Oxford University Press, 1993.

———. *Warranted Christian Belief.* New York: Oxford University Press, 2000.

Poewe, Karla. "Introduction: The Nature, Globality, and History of Charismatic Christianity." In *Charismatic Christianity as a Global Culture,* edited by Karla Poewe, 1–47. Columbia, SC: University of South Carolina Press, 1994.

Polkinghorne, John. *Belief in God in an Age of Science.* New Haven, CT: Yale University Press, 1998.

———. *The Faith of a Physicist: Reflections of a Bottom-Up Thinker.* Princeton, NJ: Princeton University Press, 1994.

———. *Faith, Science and Understanding.* New Haven, CT: Yale University Press, 2000.

———. "Kenotic Creation and Divine Action." In *The Work of Love: Creation as Kenosis,* edited by John Polkinghorne, 90–106. Grand Rapids: Eerdmans, and London: SPCK, 2001.

———. "The Laws of Nature and the Laws of Physics." In *Quantum Cosmology and the Laws of Nature: Scientific Perspectives on Divine Action,* edited by Robert John Russell, Nancey Murphy, and C. J. Isham, 429–40. Vatican City State: Vatican Observatory, and Berkeley, CA: The Center for Theology and the Natural Sciences, 1996.

———. "The Metaphysics of Divine Action." In *Chaos and Complexity: Scientific Perspectives on Divine Action,* edited by Robert John Russell, Nancey Murphy, and Arthur R. Peacocke, 147–56. Vatican City State: Vatican Observatory, and Berkeley, CA: The Center for Theology and the Natural Sciences, 1995.

———. *One World: The Interaction of Science and Theology.* Reprint, Princeton, NJ: Princeton University Press, 1987. First published 1986 by SPCK.

———. *Quantum Theory: A Very Short Introduction.* Oxford: Oxford University Press, 2002.

———. *Quarks, Chaos and Christianity: Questions to Science and Religion.* Reprint, New York: Crossroad, 1998. First published 1994 by SPCK.

———. *Reason and Reality: The Relationship between Science and Theology.* Philadelphia: Trinity Press International, 1991.

———. *Science and Creation: The Search for Understanding.* Boston: Shambhala/New Science Library, 1989.

———. *Science and Providence: God's Interaction with the World.* Boston: Shambhala/New Science Library, 1989.

———. *Science and Theology: An Introduction.* London: SPCK, and Minneapolis: Fortress, 1998.

———. *Science and the Trinity: The Christian Encounter with Reality.* New Haven, CT: Yale University Press, 2004.

————. *Scientists as Theologians: A Comparison of the Writings of Ian Barbour, Arthur Peacocke and John Polkinghorne*. London: SPCK, 1996.

————. *Searching for Truth: Lenten Meditations on Science and Faith*. New York: Crossroad, 1996/

————. *Serious Talk: Science and Religion in Dialogue*. Valley Forge, PA: Trinity Press International, 1995.

————. *Traffic in Truth: Exchanges between Science and Theology*. Reprint, Minneapolis: Fortress, 2002. First published 2000 by Canterbury Press.

————. *The Way the World Is: The Christian Perspective of a Scientist*. Grand Rapids: Eerdmans, 1983.

Polkinghorne, John, and Michael Welker. *Faith in the Living God: A Dialogue*. Minneapolis: Fortress, 2001.

Porpora, Douglas V. "Methodological Atheism, Methodological Agnosticism and Religious Experience." *Journal for the Theory of Social Behavior* 36 (2006) 57–75.

Potter, Vincent G. "'Vaguely Like a Man: The Theism of Charles S. Peirce." In *God Knowable and Unknowable*, edited by Robert J. Roth, 241–53l. New York: Fordham University Press, 1973.

Prado, C. G. *The Limits of Pragmatism*. Atlantic Highlands, NJ: Humanities Press International, 1987.

Proyser, Paul. *A Dynamic Psychology of Religion*. New York: Harper and Row, 1976.

Prozesky, Martin. "Explanations of Religion as Part of and Problem for Religious Studies." *Religious Studies* 24 (1988) 303–10.

Rambo, Lewis R. *Understanding Religious Conversion*. New Haven, CT: Yale University Press, 1993.

Raposa, Michael. *Peirce's Philosophy of Religion*. Bloomington, IN: Indiana University Press, 1989.

————. "Peirce and Modern Religious Thought." *Transactions of the Charles S. Peirce Society* 27, no. 3 (1991)341–69.

Rescher, Nicholas. *Methodological Pragmatism: A Systems-Theoretic Approach to the Theory of Knowledge*. New York: New York University Press, 1977.

————. *Realistic Pragmatism: An Introduction to Pragmatic Philosophy*. Albany, NY: State University of New York Press, 2000.

Ricoeur, Paul. *The Conflict of Interpretations*. Edited by Don Ihde. Evanston, IL: Northwestern University Press, 1974.

Ring, Nancy C. *Doctrine within the Dialectic of Subjectivity and Objectivity: A Critical Study of the Positions of Paul Tillich and Bernard Lonergan*. Distinguished Dissertation Series 6. San Francisco: Mellen Research University Press, 1991.

Rinpoche, Gyatrul. *Ancient Wisdom: Nyingma Teachings on Dream Yoga, Meditation and Transformation*. Translated by B. Alan Wallace and Sangye Khandro. Ithaca, NY: Snow Lion, 1993. Reprinted as *Meditation, Transformation, and Dream Yoga*. 2nd ed. Translated by Sangye Khandro and B. Alan Wallace. Ithaca, NY: Snow Lion, 2002.

————. *Natural Liberation: Padmasambhava's Teaching on the Six Bardos*. Translated by B. Alan Wallace. Boston: Wisdom, 1998.

Ritchie, Susan J. "Contesting Secularism: Reflexive Methodology, Belief Studies, and Disciplined Knowledge." *Journal of American Folklore* 115 (2002) 443–56.

Robbins, J. Wesley. "Does Belief in God Need Proof?" *Faith and Philosophy* 2, no. 3 (1985) 272–86.

Robbins, Joel. "Anthropology and Theology: An Awkward Relationship." *Anthropological Quarterly* 79 (2006) 285–94.

Robin, Richard. "Peirce on the Foundations of Knowledge." In *Proceedings of the C. S. Peirce Bicentennial International Congress*, edited by Kenneth L. Ketner, et al., 293–99. Lubbock, TX: Texas Tech Press, 1981.

Robinson, Bob. *Christians Meeting Hindus: An Analysis and Theological Critique of the Hindu-Christian Encounter in India*. Carlisle, UK: Paternoster, 2004.

Rorty, Richard. *Consequences of Pragmatism: Essays 1972–1980*. Minneapolis: University of Minnesota Press, 1982.

———. *Contingency, Irony, and Solidarity*. Cambridge: Cambridge University Press, 1989.

———. *Essays on Heidegger and Others: Philosophical Papers*. Vol. 2. Cambridge: Cambridge University Press, 1991.

———. "Metaphilosophical Difficulties of Linguistic Philosophy." In *The Linguistic Turn: Recent Essays in Philosophical Method*, edited by Richard Rorty, 1–39. Chicago: The University of Chicago Press, 1967.

———. *Objectivity, Relativism, and Truth: Philosophical Papers*. Vol. 1. Cambridge: Cambridge University Press, 1991.

———. *Philosophy and the Mirror of Nature*. Princeton, NJ: Princeton University Press, 1979.

———. *Philosophy and Social Hope*. New York: Penguin Books, 1999.

———. "Philosophy without Principles." In *Against Theory: Literary Studies and the New Pragmatism*, edited by W. J. T. Mitchell, 132–38. Chicago: University of Chicago Press, 1985.

———. "Pragmatism as Romantic Polytheism," In *The Revival of Pragmatism: New Essays on Social Thought, Law, and Culture*, edited by Morris Dickstein, 21–36. Durham: Duke University Press, 1998.

———. "Pragmatism, Categories, and Language." *The Philosophical Review* 70 (1961) 197–223.

———. "Response to Charles Hartshorne." In *Rorty and Pragmatism: The Philosopher Responds to His Critics*, edited by Herman J. Saatkamp Jr., 29–36. Nashville: Vanderbilt University Press, 1995.

———. *Truth and Progress: Philosophical Papers*. Vol. 3. Cambridge: Cambridge University Press, 1998.

———. "Universality and Truth." In *Rorty and His Critics*, edited by Robert Brandom, 1–30. Oxford: Blackwell, 2000.

Rosenthal, Sandra. *Speculative Pragmatism*. Amherst, MA: University of Massachusetts Press, 1986.

———. *Charles Peirce's Pragmatic Pluralism*. Albany, NY: State University of New York Press, 1994.

Rucker, Darnell. *The Chicago Pragmatists*. Minneapolis: University of Minnesota Press, 1969.

Rudolph, Kurt. "Some Reflections on Approaches and Methodologies in the Study of Religions." Translated by Gregory D. Alles. In *Secular Theories on Religion: Current Perspectives*, edited by Tim Jensen and Mikael Rothstein, 231–47. Copenhagen: Museum Tusculanum, 2000.

Rynkiewich, Michael A. *Soul, Self, and Society: A Postmodern Anthropology for Mission in a Postcolonial World*. Eugene, OR: Cascade, 2011.

Saatkamp, Herman J., Jr., ed. *Rorty and Pragmatism: The Philosopher Responds to His Critics*. Nashville: Vanderbilt University Press, 1995.

Salamone, Frank A. "Epistemological Implications of Fieldwork for Their Consequences." *American Anthropologist* 81 (1979) 46–60.

Salamone, Frank A., and Walter Randolph Adams, eds. *Explorations in Anthropology and Theology*. Lanham, MD: University Press of America, 1997.

Sanders, John. *No Other Name: An Investigation into the Destiny of the Unevangelized*. Grand Rapids: Eerdmans, 1992.

Schreiter, Robert. *Constructing Local Theologies*. Maryknoll, NY: Orbis, 1985.

Shantideva, *Guide to the Bodhisattva Way of Life*. Translated by B. Alan Wallace and Vesna Wallace. Ithaca, NY: Snow Lion, 1997.

Short, T. L. *Peirce's Theory of Signs*. Cambridge: Cambridge University Press, 2007.

Shults, F. LeRon. *Reforming Theological Anthropology: After the Philosophical Turn to Relationality*. Grand Rapids: Eerdmans, 2003.

Singer, Beth J. "Pragmatism and Pluralism." *The Monist* 75, no. 4 (1992) 477–91.

Siu, R. G. H. *The Tao of Science: An Essay on Western Knowledge and Eastern Wisdom*. Cambridge, MA: MIT Press, 1957.

Sleeper, Ralph W. "Rorty's Pragmatism: Afloat in Neurath's Boat, But Why Adrift?" *Transactions of the Charles S. Peirce Society* 21 (1985) 9–20.

———. "The Pragmatics of Deconstruction and the End of Metaphysics." In *Philosophy and the Reconstruction of Culture: Pragmatic Essays after Dewey*, edited by John J. Stuhr, 241–56. Albany, NY: State University of New York Press, 1993.

Smart, Ninian. *The Science of Religion and the Sociology of Knowledge: Some Methodological Questions*. Princeton, NJ: Princeton University Press, 1973.

———. *Concept and Empathy: Essays in the Study of Religion*. Edited by Donald Wiebe. New York: New York University Press, 1986.

Smith, James K. A. "The Call as Gift: The Subject's Donation in Marion and Levinas." In *The Hermeneutics of Charity: Interpretation, Selfhood, and Postmodern Faith*, edited by James K. A. Smith and Henry Isaac Venema, 217–27. Grand Rapids: Brazos, 2004.

———. *The Fall of Interpretation: Philosophical Foundations for a Creational Hermeneutic*. Downers Grove, IL: InterVarsity, 2000.

———. *Introducing Radical Orthodoxy: Mapping a Post-secular Theology*. Grand Rapids: Baker Academic, 2004.

———. "Is There Room for Surprise in the Natural World? Naturalism, the Supernatural, and Pentecostal Spirituality." In *Science and the Spirit: A Pentecostal Engagement with the Sciences*, edited by James K. A. Smith and Amos Yong, 34–49. Bloomington, IN: Indiana University Press, 2010.

———. "A Little Story About Metanarratives: Lyotard, Religion, and Postmodernism Revisited." *Faith and Philosophy* 18 (2001) 261–76.

———. "Scandalizing Theology: A Pentecostal Response to Noll's *Scandal*." *Pneuma: The Journal of the Society for Pentecostal Studies* 19, no. 2 (1997) 225–38.

———. *Speech and Theology: Language and the Logic of Incarnation*. New York: Routledge, 2002.

———. "The Spirit, Religions, and the World as Sacrament: A Response to Amos Yong's Pneumatological Assist." *Journal of Pentecostal Theology* 15, no. 2 (2007) 251–61.

———. *Thinking in Tongues: Pentecostal Contributions to Christian Philosophy*. Grand Rapids: Eerdmans, 2010.

————. "What Hath Cambridge to Do with Azusa Street? Radical Orthodoxy and Pentecostal Theology in Conversation." *Pneuma: The Journal of the Society for Pentecostal Studies* 25, no. 1 (2003) 97–114.

Smith, James K. A., and Amos Yong, eds. *Science and the Spirit: A Pentecostal Engagement with the Sciences*. Bloomington, IN: Indiana University Press, 2010.

Smith, John Clark. "Peirce's Religious Metaphysics." *International Philosophical Quarterly* 19, no. 4 (1979) 407–25.

Smith, John E. "Community and Reality." In *Perspectives on Peirce: Critical Essays on Charles Sanders Peirce*, edited by Richard Bernstein, 92–119. New Haven, CT: Yale University Press, 1965.

————. *Purpose and Thought: The Meaning of Pragmatism*. New Haven, CT: Yale University Press, 1978.

Smith, Wilfred Cantwell. *The Meaning and End of Religion: A New Approach to the Religious Traditions of Mankind*. New York: Macmillan, 1963.

————. *What is Scripture? A Comparative Approach*. Minneapolis: Fortress, 1993.

Solivan, Samuel. *The Spirit, Pathos and Liberation: Toward an Hispanic Pentecostal Theology*. Journal of Pentecostal Theology Supplemental Series 14. Sheffield, UK: Sheffield Academic Press, 1998.

Southgate, Christopher. *God, Humanity, and the Cosmos: A Textbook in Science and Religion*. Harrisburg, PA: Trinity Press International, 1999.

Soyen, Shaku. "The Law of Cause and Effect, as Taught by Buddha." In *The Dawn of Religious Pluralism: Voices from the World's Parliament of Religion, 1893*, edited by Richard Hughes Seager, 406–9. LaSalle, IL: Open Court, 1993.

Spencer, Aida Besancon, and William David Spencer, eds. *The Global God: Multicultural Evangelical Views of God*. Grand Rapids: Baker, 1998.

Stoeger, W. R., and G. F. R. Ellis. "A Response to Tipler's Omega-Point Theory." *Science and Christian Belief* 7 (1995) 163–72.

Stone, Jon R. *On the Boundaries of American Evangelicalism: The Postwar Evangelical Coalition*. New York: St. Martin's, 1999.

Stronstad, Roger. *Spirit, Scripture and Theology: A Pentecostal Perspective*. Baguio City, Philippines: Asia Pacific Theological Seminary Press, 1995.

————. "A Review Essay on Amos Yong, *Who is the Holy Spirit?: A Walk with the Apostles*." *Journal of Pentecostal Theology* 22, no. 2 (2013) 295–300.

Suurmond, Jean-Jacques. *Word and Spirit at Play: Towards a Charismatic Theology*. Translated by John Bowden. Reprint, Grand Rapids: Eerdmans, 1995. First published 1994.

Sykes, Stephen W. *The Identity of Christianity: Theologians and the Essence of Christianity from Schleiermacher to Barth*. Philadelphia: Fortress, 1984.

Talbot, Michael. *Mysticism and the New Physics*. New York: Bantam, 1981.

Tedlock, Barbara. "From Participant Observation to the Observation of Participation: The Emergence of Narrative Ethnography." *Journal of Anthropological Research* 47, no. 1 (1991) 69–94.

Thayer, H. S. *Meaning and Action: A Critical History of Pragmatism*. Indianapolis: Bobbs-Merrill, 1968.

————. "Peirce and Truth: Some Reflections." *Transactions of the Charles S. Peirce Society* 32 (1996) 1–10.

————. "Peirce on Truth." In *Pragmatism and Purpose: Essays Presented to Thomas A. Goudge*, edited by L. W. Sumner, John G. Slater, and Fred Wilson, 121–32. Toronto: University of Toronto Press, 1981.

———. "Pragmatism: A Reinterpretation of Its Origins and Consequences." In *Pragmatism: Its Sources and Prospects*, edited by Robert J. Mulvaney and Philip M. Zeltner, 1–20. Columbia, SC: University of South Carolina Press, 1981.

Thiel, John. *Nonfoundationalism*. Minneapolis: Fortress, 1994.

Thiemann, Ronald F. *Revelation and Theology: The Gospel as Narrated Promise*. Notre Dame, IN: University of Notre Dame Press, 1987.

Thorsen, Donald A. D. *The Wesleyan Quadrilateral: Scripture, Tradition, Reason and Experience as a Model of Evangelical Theology*. Grand Rapids: Zondervan, 1990.

Thompson, Ross. *Is There an Anglican Way? Scripture, Church, and Reason: New Approaches to an Old Triad*. London: Darton, Longman, and Todd, 1997.

Tilley, Terrence W. "Reformed Epistemology and Religious Fundamentalism: How Basic are Our Basic Beliefs?" *Modern Theology* 6 (1990) 237–55.

———. *Religious Diversity and the American Experience: A Theological Approach*. New York: Continuum, 2007.

Tilley, Terrence W., with Louis T. Albarran. "Multiple Religious Belonging: Can a Christian Belong to Other Traditions Too?" In *Religious Diversity and the American Experience: A Theological Approach*, by Terrence W. Tilley, 160–74. New York: Continuum, 2007.

Tipler, Frank J. *The Physics of Immortality: Modern Cosmology, God, and the Resurrection from the Dead*. New York: Doubleday, 1994.

Topping, Richard R. "The Anti-Foundationalist Challenge to Evangelical Apologetics." *Evangelical Quarterly* 63 (1991) 45–60.

Triplett, Timm. "Rorty's Critique of Foundationalism." *Philosophical Studies* 52 (1987): 115–29.

———. "Recent Work on Foundationalism." *American Philosophical Quarterly* 27 (1990) 93–116.

Turrisi, Patricia Ann, ed. *Pragmatism as a Principle and Method of Right Thinking: The 1903 Harvard Lectures on Pragmatism by Charles Sanders Peirce*. Albany, NY: State University of New York Press, 1997.

Tsoukalas, Steven. *Krsna and Christ: Body-Divine Relation in the Thought of Śankara, Rāmānuja, and Classical Christian Orthodoxy*. Milton Keynes, UK: Paternoster, 2006.

Tyler, Stephen A. "Post-Modern Ethnography: From Document of the Occult to Occult Document." In *Writing Culture: The Poetics and Politics of Ethnography*, edited by James Clifford and George E. Marcus, 122–40. Berkeley, CA: University of California Press, 1986.

van den Toren, Benno. *Christian Apologetics as Cross-Cultural Dialogue*. London: T & T Clark International, 2011.

———. *Breuk en brug: in gersprek met Karl Barth en postmoderne theologie over geloofsverantwoording*. Zoetermeet, the Netherlands: Boekencentrum, 1995.

van der Geest, Sjaak. "Anthropologists and Missionaries: Brothers Under the Sun." *Man* NS 25 (1990) 588–601.

———. "Shifting Positions Between Anthropology, Religion, and Development: The Case of Christianity." *Exchange* 40 (2011) 257–73.

Van Till, Howard J. "The Fully Gifted Creation." In *Three Views on Creation and Evolution*, edited by J. P. Moreland and John Mark Reynolds, 159–218. Grand Rapids: Zondervan, 1999.

Varela, Francisco J., and Humberto R. Maturana. *Autopoiesis and Cognition: The Realization of Living*. Holland: Dordrecht, and Boston: D. Reidel, 1980.

———. *Ethical Know-How: Action, Wisdom, and Cognition*. Stanford, CA: Stanford University Press, 1999.

———. *The Tree of Knowledge: The Biological Roots of Human Understanding*. Boston: New Science Library, 1987.

Varela, Francisco J., Eleanor Rosch, and Evan Thompson. *The Embodied Mind: Cognitive Science and Human Experience*. Cambridge, MA: MIT Press, 1991.

Varela, Francisco J., Natalie Depraz, and Pierre Vermersch. *A Pragmatics of Experiencing*. Advances in Consciousness Research 43. Amsterdam: J. Benjamins, 2003.

Varela, Francisco J., and Humberto R. Maturana, eds. *Sleeping, Dreaming, and Dying: An Exploration of Consciousness with the Dalai Lama*. Boston: Wisdom, 1997.

Varela, Francisco, and Jonathan Shear, eds. *The View from Within: First-Person Approaches to the Study of Consciousness*. Thorverton, UK: Imprint Academic, 1999.

Volf, Miroslav. *Allah: A Christian Response*. San Francisco: HarperOne, 2011.

Volf, Miroslav, and Dorothy C. Bass, eds. *Practicing Theology: Beliefs and Practices in Christian Life*. Grand Rapids: Eerdmans, 2002.

Vondey, Wolfgang. *Beyond Pentecostalism: The Crisis of Global Christianity and the Renewal of the Theological Agenda*. Grand Rapids: Eerdmans, 2010.

Vondey, Wolfgang, and Martin W. Mittelstadt, eds. *The Theology of Amos Yong and the New Face of Pentecostal Scholarship: Passion for the Spirit*. Global Pentecostal and Charismatic Studies 14. Leiden: Brill, 2013.

Wacker, Grant. *Heaven Below: Early Pentecostals and American Culture*. Cambridge, MA: Harvard University Press, 2003.

Walker, Susan, ed. *Speaking of Silence: Christians and Buddhists on the Contemplative Way*. New York: Paulist, 1987.

Wallace, B. Alan. "Afterword: Buddhist Reflections." In *Consciousness at Crossroads: Conversations with the Dalai Lama on Brain Science and Buddhism*, edited by B. Alan Wallace, Zara Houshmand, and Robert B. Livingston. Mind and Life II. Ithaca, NY: Snow Lion, 1999.

———. *The Attention Revolution: Unlocking the Power of the Focused Mind*. Boston: Wisdom, 2006.

———. *The Bridge of Quiescence: Experiencing Tibetan Buddhist Meditation*. La Salle, IL: Open Court, 1998. Reprinted as *Balancing the Mind: A Tibetan Buddhist approach to Refining Attention*. Ithaca, NY: Snow Lion, 2005.

———. *Boundless Heart: The Four Immeasurables*. Edited by Zara Houshmand. Ithaca, NY: Snow Lion, 1999.

———. *Buddhism with an Attitude: The Tibetan Seven-Point Mind-Training*. Edited by Lynn Quirolo. Ithaca, NY: Snow Lion, 2001.

———. *Choosing Reality: A Buddhist View of Physics and the Mind*. Ithaca, NY: Snow Lion, 1996.

———. *Contemplative Science: Where Buddhism and Neuroscience Meet*. New York: Columbia University Press, 2007.

———. *Genuine Happiness: Meditation as the Path of Fulfillment*. New York: Wiley, 2005.

———. *Hidden Dimensions: The Unification of Physics and Consciousness*. New York: Columbia University Press, 2007.

————. "Introduction: Buddhism and Science—Breaking Down the Barriers." In *Buddhism and Science: Breaking New Ground*, edited by B. Alan Wallace, 1–30. New York: Columbia University Press, 2003.

————. *A Passage from Solitude: Training the Mind in a Life Embracing the World—A Modern Commentary on Tibetan Buddhist Mind Training*. Edited by Zara Houshmand. Ithaca, NY: Snow Lion, 1992. Reprinted as *The Seven-Point Mind Training*. Edited by Zara Houshmand. Ithaca, NY: Snow Lion, 2004.

————. *The Taboo of Subjectivity: Toward a New Science of Consciousness*. Oxford: Oxford University Press, 2000.

————. *Transcendent Wisdom: A Commentary on the Ninth Chapter of Shantideva's Guide to the Bodhisattva Way of Life*. Ithaca, NY: Snow Lion, 1988.

Wallace, B. Alan, and Steven Wilhelm, *Tibetan Buddhism from the Ground Up: A Practical Approach for Modern Life*. Boston: Wisdom, 1993.

Wallace, B. Alan, ed. *Buddhism and Science: Breaking New Ground*. New York: Columbia University Press, 2003.

Wallace, B. Alan (Gelong Jhampa Kelsang), ed. and trans. *The Life and Teaching of Geshé Rabten: A Tibetan Lama's Search for Truth*. London: George Allen & Unwin, 1980.

Wallace, B. Alan, Zara Houshmand, and Robert B. Livingston, eds.. *Consciousness at Crossroads: Conversations with the Dalai Lama on Brain Science and Buddhism*. Mind and Life II. Ithaca, NY: Snow Lion, 1999.

Wallace, Vesna A. *The Inner Kālacakratantra: A Buddhist Tantric View of the Individual*. Oxford: Oxford University Press, 2001.

Wallace, Vesna A., trans. *The Kālacakratantra: The Chapter on the Individual Together with the Vimalaprabhā*. Treasury of the Buddhist Sciences series. New York: American Institute of Buddhist Studies, Center for Buddhist Studies, and Columbia University Press, 2004.

Ward, Graham. "In the Economy of the Divine: A Response to James K. A. Smith." *Pneuma: The Journal of the Society for Pentecostal Studies* 25, no. 1 (2003) 115–20.

Ward, Keith. *Concepts of God: Images of the Divine in Five Religious Traditions*. Oxford: Oneworld, 1998.

————. *Religion and Community*. Oxford: Clarendon; New York: Oxford University Press, 2000.

————. *Religion and Creation*. Oxford: Clarendon, and New York: Oxford University Press, 1996.

————. *Religion and Human Fulfillment*. London: SCM, 2008.

————. *Religion and Human Nature*. Oxford: Clarendon, and New York: Oxford University Press, 1998.

————. *Religion and Revelation: A Theology of Revelation in the World's Religions*. Oxford: Clarendon, and New York: Oxford University Press, 1994.

Ware, Bruce A. "Defining Evangelicalism's Boundaries Theologically: Is Open Theism Evangelical?" *Journal of the Evangelical Theological Society* 45, no. 2 (2002) 193–212.

————. *Their God is Too Small: Open Theism and the Undermining of Confidence in God*. Wheaton, IL: Crossway, 2003.

Wariboko, Nimi. "Fire from Heaven: Pentecostals in the Secular City." *Pneuma: The Journal of the Society for Pentecostal Studies* 33, no. 3 (2011) 391–408.

————. *The Pentecostal Principle: Ethical Methodology in New Spirit*. Grand Rapids: Eerdmans, 2011.

Watson, Gay, Stephen Batchelor, and Guy Claxton, eds. *The Psychology of Awakening: Buddhism, Science, and Our Day-to-Day Lives.* York Beach, ME: Samuel Weiser, 2000.

Weerasinghe, Mahinda. *The Origin of Species According to the Buddha.* Colombo, Sri Lanka: Stamford Lake, 2002.

Welker, Michael. *God the Spirit.* Translated by John F. Hoffmeyer. Minneapolis: Fortress, 1994.

Welker, Michael, ed. *The Work of the Spirit: Pneumatology and Pentecostalism.* Grand Rapids: Eerdmans, 2006.

Wenk, Matthias. *Community-Forming Power: The Socio-Ethical Role of the Spirit in Luke-Acts.* Journal of Pentecostal Theology Supplemental Series 19. Sheffield, UK: Sheffield Academic Press, 2000.

Wettimuny, R. G. de S. *Buddhism and Its Relation to Religion and Science.* Colombo, Sri Lanka: M. D. Gunasena and Co. Ltd., 1962.

Wiebe, Donald. *Religion and Truth: Towards an Alternative Paradigm for the Study of Religion.* Religion and Reason 23. The Hague: Mouton, 1981.

Wildman, Wesley J. "The Divine Action Project, 1988–2003." *Theology and Science* 2, no. 1 (2004) 31–75.

Wilson, Douglas, ed. *Bound Only Once: The Failure of Open Theism.* Moscow, ID: Canon, 2001.

Wood, Mark David. *Cornel West and the Politics of Prophetic Pragmatism.* Urbana, IL: University of Illinois Press, 2000.

Wood, Ralph C. "James Wm. McClendon, Jr.'s *Doctrine*: An Appreciation." *Perspectives in Religious Studies* 24, no. 2 (1997) 195–99.

Work, Telford. *Living and Active: Scripture in the Economy of Salvation.* Grand Rapids: Eerdmans, 2001.

World Council of Churches. "Baptism, Eucharist and Ministry." *Faith and Order Paper,* no. 111, 1982.

Wright, David F. *Chosen by God: Mary in Evangelical Perspective.* London: Marshall Pickering, 1989.

Yandell, Keith. "Modernism, Postmodernism, and the Minimalist Canons of Common Grace." *Christian Scholar's Review* 27 (1997) 15–26.

Yong, Amos. "'As the Spirit Gives Utterance . . .': Pentecost, Intra-Christian Ecumenism, and the Wider *Oekumene.*" *International Review of Mission* 92, no. 366 (2003) 299–314.

———. "The 'Baptist Vision' of James William McClendon, Jr.: A Wesleyan-Pentecostal Response." *Wesleyan Theological Journal* 37, no. 2 (2002) 32–57.

———. *Beyond the Impasse: Toward a Pneumatological Theology of Religions.* Grand Rapids: Baker Academic, 2002.

———. "A Catholic Commitment to Process Cosmology: An Appreciation of Joseph Bracken's Latest Works." Metanexus Website, February 12, 2010, http://www.metanexus.net/book-review/catholic-commitment-process-cosmology.

———. "Christian and Buddhist Perspectives on Neuropsychology and the Human Person: *Pneuma* and *Pratityasamutpada.*" *Zygon: Journal of Religion and Science* 40, no. 1 (2005) 143–65.

———. "Conclusion: The Missiology of Jamestown: 1607–2007 and Beyond—Toward a Postcolonial Theology of Mission in North America." In *Remembering Jamestown: Hard Questions about Christian Mission,* edited by Amos Yong and Barbara Brown Zikmund, 157–67. Maryknoll: Orbis Books, 2010.

———. *The Cosmic Breath: Spirit and Nature in the Christianity-Buddhism-Science Trialogue*. Philosophical Studies in Science & Religion 4. Leiden: Brill, 2012.

———. "The Demise of Foundationalism and the Retention of Truth: What Evangelicals Can Learn from C. S. Peirce." *Christian Scholar's Review* 29, no. 3 (2000) 563–88.

———. *Discerning the Spirit(s): A Pentecostal-Charismatic Contribution to Christian Theology of Religions*. Journal of Pentecostal Theology Supplement Series 20. Sheffield, UK: Sheffield Academic Press, 2000.

———. "Discerning the Spirit(s) in the Natural World: Toward a Typology of 'Spirit' in the Theology and Science Conversation." *Theology & Science* 3, no. 3 (2005) 315–29.

———. "Divine Knowledge and Future Contingents: Weighing the Presuppositional Issues in the Contemporary Debate." *Evangelical Review of Theology* 26, no. 3 (2002) 240–64.

———. "Divine Knowledge and Relation to Time." In *Philosophy of Religion: Introductory Essays*, edited by Thomas Jay Oord, 136–52. Kansas City, MO: Beacon Hill/Nazarene, 2003.

———. "Francis X. Clooney's 'Dual Religious Belonging' and the Comparative Theological Enterprise: Engaging Hindu Traditions." *Dharma Deepika: A South Asian Journal of Missiological Research* 16, no. 1 (2012) 6–26.

———. "Globalizing Christology: Anglo-American Perspectives in World Religious Context." *Religious Studies Review* 30, no. 4 (2004) 259–66.

———. "God and the Evangelical Laboratory: Recent Conservative Protestant Thinking about Theology and Science." *Theology and Science* 5, no. 2 (2007) 203–21.

———. "Guests of Religious Others: Theological Education in the Pluralistic World." *Theological Education* 47, no. 1 (2012) 75–83.

———. *Hospitality and the Other: Pentecost, Christian Practices, and the Neighbor*. Faith Meets Faith series. Maryknoll, NY: Orbis, 2008.

———. *In the Days of Caesar: Pentecostalism and Political Theology—The Cadbury Lectures 2009*. Sacra Doctrina: Christian Theology for a Postmodern Age series. Grand Rapids: Eerdmans, 2010.

———. "Mind and Life, Religion and Science: The Dalai Lama and the Buddhist-Christian-Science Trilogue." *Buddhist-Christian Studies* 28 (2008) 43–63.

———. *The Missiological Spirit: Christian Mission Theology for the Third Millenium Global Context*. Eugene, OR: Cascade, 2014.

———. *Pneumatology and the Christian-Buddhist Dialogue: Does the Spirit Blow through the Middle Way?* Studies in Systematic Theology 11. Leiden: Brill, 2012.

———. "Reading Scripture and Nature: Pentecostal Hermeneutics and Their Implications for the Contemporary Evangelical Theology and Science Conversation." *Perspectives on Science and Christian Faith* 53, no. 1 (2011) 1–13.

———. Review of *Allah: A Christian Response*, by Miroslav Volf. *The Pneuma Review* 14, no. 4 (2011) 59–63.

———. "Review of *Buddhism and Science: Breaking New Ground*, by B. Alan Wallace." *Buddhist-Christian Studies* 25 (2005): 176–80.

———. "Review of *No Place for Truth, or Whatever Happened to Evangelical Theology?* and *God in the Wasteland: The Reality of Truth in a World of Fading Dreams*, by David Wells." *Pneuma: The Journal of the Society for Pentecostal Studies* 18 (1996) 239–43.

———. "In Search of Foundations: The *Oeuvre* of Donald L. Gelpi, S.J., and Its Significance for Pentecostal Theology and Philosophy." *Journal of Pentecostal Theology* 11, no. 1 (2002) 3–26.

———. "The Spirit Bears Witness: Pneumatology, Truth and the Religions." *Scottish Journal of Theology* 57, no. 1 (2004) 1–25.

———. *Spirit of Love: A Trinitarian Theology of Grace*. Waco, TX: Baylor University Press, 2012.

———. *The Spirit Poured Out on All Flesh: Pentecostalism and the Possibility of Global Theology*. Grand Rapids: Baker Academic, 2005.

———. *Spirit-Word-Community: Theological Hermeneutics in Trinitarian Perspective*. New Critical Thinking in Religion, Theology and Biblical Studies Series. Aldershot, UK: Ashgate, 2002.

———. *Theology and Down Syndrome: Reimagining Disability in Late Modernity*. Waco, TX: Baylor University Press, 2007.

———. "Tibetan Buddhism Going Global? A Case Study of a Contemporary Buddhist Encounter with Science." *Journal of Global Buddhism* 9 (2008) 1–26.

———. "Tongues of Fire in the Pentecostal Imagination: The Truth of Glossolalia in Light of R. C. Neville's Theory of Religious Symbolism." *Journal of Pentecostal Theology* 12 (April 1998) 39–65.

———. "'Tongues', Theology, and the Social Sciences: A Pentecostal-Theological Reading of Geertz's Interpretive Theory of Religion." *Cyberjournal for Pentecostal/Charismatic Research* 1 (1997). http://pctii.org/cyberj/cyber1.html.

———. "Trinh Thuan and the Intersection of Science and Buddhism: A Review Essay." *Zygon: Journal of Religion and Science* 42, no. 3 (September 2007) 677–84.

———. "Whither Systematic Theology? A Systematician Chimes in on a Scandalous Conversation." *Pneuma: The Journal of the Society for Pentecostal Studies* 20, no. 1 (1998) 85–93.

———. *Who Is the Holy Spirit?: A Walk with the Apostles*. Brewster, MA: Paraclete, 2011.

Yong, Amos, and Peter Heltzel. "Robert Cummings Neville and Theology's Global Future." In *Theology in Global Context: Essays in Honor of Robert Cummings Neville,* edited by Amos Yong and Peter Heltzel, 29–42. London: T & T Clark, 2004.

Yong, Amos, with Jonathan A. Anderson. *Renewing Christian Theology: Systematics for a Global Christianity*. Waco, TX: Baylor University Press, 2014.

Yong, Amos, and Barbara Brown Zikmund, eds. *Remembering Jamestown: Hard Questions about Christian Mission*. Maryknoll, NY: Orbis, 2010.

Yong, Amos, and Peter Heltzel, eds. *Theology in Global Context: Essays in Honor of Robert Cummings Neville*. New York: T & T Clark, 2004.

Yukawa, Hideki. *Creativity and Intuition: A Physicist Looks at East and West*. Tokyo: Kodansha, 1973.

Zablocki, Abraham Mark. "The Global Mandala: The Transnational Transformation of Tibetan Buddhism." PhD diss., Cornell University, 2005.

Zajonc, Arthur. "Reflections on 'Investigating the Mind,' One Year Later." In *The Dalai Lama at MIT,* edited by Anne Harrington and Arthur Zajonc, 219–44. Cambridge, MA: Harvard University Press, 2006.

Zajonc, Arthur, ed. *The New Physics and Cosmology: Dialogues with the Dalai Lama*. Oxford: Oxford University Press, 2004.

Index